Hansjörg Behrendt
Christian Eckardt
Peter Oldham
Melanie Wieschalla

GOING PROFESSIONAL

Englisch für die berufliche Oberstufe

D1698847

Verlag Handwerk und Technik · Hamburg

Bildquellen

Alfred Ritter GmbH & Co. KG, Waldenbuch: S. 115/2; **Almoutasem Almashaqba (simpo-jo)**: S. 48/1; **ANDREAS STIHL AG & Co. KG**, Waiblingen: S. 114/3; **Behrendt, Hansjörg**, Berlin: S. 16/2; **Carl Zeiss Vision GmbH**, Aalen: S. 114/4; **dpa Picture Alliance GmbH**, Frankfurt a. M.: S. 94/3, 95, 110; **Flickr.com**, Remy (GVB813), Purmerend, Holland: S. 115/3; **Fotolia Deutschland**, Berlin, © Fotolia.com: S. 7/1 Bikeworldtravel; 7/2 CandyBox Images; 7/3 Andres Rodriguez; 7/4 Christian Schwier; 8/1, 12/1, 22/1, 52/1 Monkey Business; 8/2, 22/2, 52/2 nyul; 10/1 Morphart; 10/2 andreiuc88; 10/3 dko; 10/4 carla9; 13 Robert Kneschke; 15/1 PeterPunk; 15/2 Jennifer Clark; 16/1 viperagp; 16/3 Juice Images, 17 olly; 21/1 alphaspirit; 21/2 alphaspirit; 21/3 contrastwerkstatt; 21/4 NKMandic; 21/5 alphaspirit; 26 contrastwerkstatt; 28 goodluz; 29 Peter Atkins; 34 contrastwerkstatt; 35/1 lichtflug; 35/2 Tyler Olson; 35/3 WONG SZE FEI; 35/4 Mikael Damkier; 35/5 Michael Flippo; 36/1 Minerva Studio; 36/2 WONG SZE FEI; 36/3 Gina Sanders; 37/2 elenarostunova; 39 Robert Kneschke; 40 Ashwin; 41 michael spring; 42 Ilhedgehogll; 43 K.-P. Adler; 47/1 Tanja Bagusat; 47/2 nenetus; 47/3 goodluz; 47/4 alephnull; 48/2 Artco; 59/1 Dmitry Vereshchagin; 59/2 psychoschlumpf; 59/3 eyeidea; 59/4 kantver; 61/1 corepics; 61/2 Bogdan Vasilescu; 61/3 Stephan Morrosch; 61/4 Minerva Studio; 61/5 Bergringfoto; 61/6 Kim Schneider; 64 kantver; 71/1 Voyagerix; 71/2 hjschneider; 71/3 Fotolia RAW; 73/1 Tom Wang; 73/2 apops; 73/3 Sergey Nivens; 73/4 Composer; 74 Minerva Studio; 76 AA+W; 77 Black Jack; 80 mindscanner; 82 Daniel Nimmervoll; 83 julien tromeur; 84/1 goodluz; 84/2 goodluz; 84/3 cicisbeo; 84/4 Halfpoint; 87/1 auremar; 87/2 RioPatuca Images; 87/3 jwblinn; 87/4 shefkate; 87/5 jinga80; 88 Yeko Photo Studio; 89 Robert Kneschke; 91/1 Monkey Business; 91/2 Tyler Olson; 92 Andrey Armyagov; 96 nyul; 97 von Lieres; 99/1 africa; 99/2 ARTENS; 99/3 Alexander Raths; 99/4 Ralf Gosch; 100/1 M. Schuppich; 100/2 designsstock; 103/1 Okea; 104 Irochka; 106/1 branex; 106/2 luna; 107 Franz Peter Rudolf; 108/1 Kitty; 108/2 S K; 109/1 Roman Rvachov; 109/2 Sophia Winters; 111 Olga Lyubkin; 113/1 Artur Marciniec; 113/2 Tmedia; 113/3 stillkost; 113/4 alexmillos; 113/5 Stuart Miles; 113/6 Jeanette Dietl; 113/7 aihumnoi; 116 putilov_denis; 118 annacurnow; 119 andrewgenn; 120/1 ksena32; 120/10 Diana Valujeva; 120/11 Ingo Sch.; 120/12 Gudellaphoto; 120/2 Dmytro Sandratskyi; 120/3 Robert Wilson; 120/4 Eskymaks; 120/5 viennapro; 120/6 vlabo; 120/7 burnel11; 120/8 wolfelarry; 120/9 dpullman; 122/1 Popova Olga; 122/4 lucadp; 122/4 M.R. Swadzba; 122/5 amadorgs; 122/6 Andrew Barker; 122/6 elenarostunova; 124/1 PhotographyByMK; 124/7 Diana Taliun; 124/8 pwollinga; 124/9 Serghei Velusceac; 125/1 Sandor Kacso; 125/2 kagemusha; 125/3 Torbz; 125/4 Andrey Armyagov; 125/5 Digitalpress; 125/6 Dmitry Ersler; 127 Tiberius Gracchus; 128/1 Patryk Kosmider; 128/2 suronin; 128/3 degist; 128/4 Andrew Bayda; 128/5 Bernd Leitner; 128/6 kikimor; 129 Thijsone; 130/1 Samo Trebizan; 130/2 xy; 131 Diana Kosaric; 132/1 Marcus Kretschmar; 132/2 VIPDesign; 133/2 mocker_bat; 137/1 Franz Pfluegl; 137/2 Brad Pict; 137/3 eyewave; 137/4 Antonioguillem; 137/5 byheaven; 137/6 Peter Atkins; 137/7 bukitdamansara; 138/1 Darius Dzinnik; 138/2 Aklimda; 138/3 svetamart; 138/4 CCat82; 138/5 Darius Dzinnik; 138/6 ColdCoffee; 138/7 dreamer12; 138/9 Karramba Production; 139 DPimborough; 140/1 Mariusz Prusaczyk; 141/1 paul_brighton; 141/2 WITTY; 143 Rob; 144 zzayko; 147/1 Manuela Manay; 147/2 Atiketta Sangasaeng; 147/3 Tiberius Gracchus; 147/4 Lenslife; 147/5 lightpoet; 147/6 Robert Kneschke; 148/1 CandyBox Images; 148/2 lily; 148/3 berc; 148/4 Anton Gvozdikov; 148/5 contrastwerkstatt; 148/6 Daniel Ernst; 149/1 sepy; 149/2 Rob; 149/3 stockyimages; 149/4 Kurhan; 149/5 auremar; 150/1 Jenifoto; 150/2 Umjb; 151/1 slavun; 151/2 Daithi C; 151/3 Debu55y; 151/4 ricky_68fr; 152 Robert Kneschke; **Global-Integration.com**: S. 142; **Grafische Produktionen, Jürgen Neumann**, Rimpar: S. 81/1, 81/2, 81/3, 85/1, 85/2, 85/3, 85/4; **Morallymarketed.com**: S. 94/1; **PETA Deutschland e. V.**, Berlin: S. 114/2; **Randy Glasbergen**, www.glasbergen.com: S. 158; **Robert Bosch GmbH**, Stuttgart: S. 114/1; **Gabriele Timm**, Kaarst: S. 44/1, 50/1, 86; **Verlag Handwerk und Technik**, Hamburg: S. 115/1; **Verlag Hölder-Pichler-Tempsky GmbH**, Wien S. 60/1, 60/2, 60/3, 65, 68, 69/1; **Wikipedia.org/wiki/Commonwealth_of_Nations** (public domain): S. 45

1. Auflage 2014

Die Verweise auf Internetseiten und -dateien beziehen sich auf deren Zustand und Inhalt zum Zeitpunkt der Drucklegung des Werks. Der Verlag übernimmt keinerlei Gewähr und Haftung für deren Aktualität oder Inhalt noch für den Inhalt von mit ihnen verlinkten weiteren Internetseiten.

Dieses Buch ist auf Papier gedruckt, das aus 100 % chlorfrei gebleichten Faserstoffen hergestellt wurde.

© Handwerk und Technik GmbH, Postfach 63 05 00, 22331 Hamburg, Tel.: 040 / 5 38 08-134, Fax: 040 / 5 38 08-101, E-Mail: info@handwerk-technik.de, Internet: www.handwerk-technik.de

Layout und Satz: Bettina Herrmann, Stuttgart
Umschlagabbildungen: Fotolia Deutschland, Berlin: © Tyler Olson (großes Bild), © Minerva Studio, © lightpoet, © Nyul

Druck und Bindung: Stürtz GmbH, 97080 Würzburg
ISBN: 978-3-582-01681-2

VORWORT

In den Texten und Aufgaben werden die vom Bildungsplan geforderten grundlegenden Fähigkeiten und Fertigkeiten (Leseverstehen, Hörverstehen, Schreiben, Sprechen, Interaktion, Mediation) abgedeckt. Auch die soziale Kompetenz und Selbstständigkeit der Schüler* wird trainiert, z. B. durch Aufgaben in Gruppenarbeit und Diskussion.

Das dabei verwendete sprachliche wie sachliche Niveau entspricht der Niveaustufe B1 / B2 gemäß dem „Gemeinsamen europäischen Referenzrahmen für Sprachen".

Die 12 Units decken die geforderten Themen des Bildungsplans ab und sind synchron aufgebaut:

Introduction	Bietet einen lockeren Einstieg in jede Unit. Die einzelnen Lernziele der Unit werden den Schülern vorgestellt. Fotos bieten einen passenden bildlichen Einstieg in das Thema.
Input	Die Doppelseiten sind übersichtlich und einheitlich gestaltet. Kontext- und situationsbedingte Fotos, Cartoons, Diagramme, Infoboxen, Skill-, Grammatik- und Wortschatzhilfen lockern die Seiten auf. Die Doppelseiten sind in drei Lernstufen organisiert: • Standard – Basisniveau (B1 / 2) • Challenge – Material / Aufgaben mit erhöhtem Anspruch (B2) • Essential – etwas einfacheres Material und Aufgaben (B1).
Practice	Zusätzliche Übungen zu den Lerninhalten der Unit und am Ende steht eine Reprise der Lerninhalte (Check). Hier können die Schüler ihren Lernerfolg selbst einschätzen.

Die Grammatik in Going Professional ist auf das Wesentliche begrenzt. Grundlegende Strukturen werden in den Units im situativen Kontext vermittelt. Weitaus wichtiger ist jedoch die Erweitung des allgemeinen Wortschatzes und das Erlernen gebräuchlicher Redewendungen, die als Rüstzeug für eine flüssige, effektive berufliche Kommunikation dienen.

Am Ende des Buches steht ein umfänglicher Referenzteil mit Übersichten über Skills sowie vier Vokabelverzeichnisse. Das erste enthält Grundwörter, die vorausgesetzt werden. Das zweite bietet die zu lernenden Vokabeln nach Units und ihrem chronologischen Vorkommen geordnet. Das dritte und vierte sind alphabetisch (Englisch – Deutsch bzw. Deutsch – Englisch) aufgebaut.

Zusätzlich zum Lehrwerk bieten wir an:
• eine Audio-CD mit den Hörverständnistexten.
• einen Lehrerband mit Lösungen bzw. Musterlösungen und Transkripte der Hörtexte.

Symbolerklärungen:

Hörverständnistext auf der Audio-CD ▸▸

▶ Hinweispfeile (z. B. auf Teile im Anhang)

○ ❸ = wahlfreie Aufgaben

* = Schüler und Schülerinnen

CONTENTS

handwerk-technik.de

UNIT 1
Getting started

To do

Receptive
- Understanding a reading text
- Understanding a listening text

Productive
- Comparing vocational qualifications
- Producing your own curriculum vitae
- Describing music
- Writing a summary

Interactive
- Exchanging personal information
- Discussing free-time activities
- Talking about personal preferences

Skills
- Using an English dictionary

Grammar
- Simple present
- Conditional sentences

1 Personal information

Florian is taking part in an exchange programme with a school in Britain.
His exchange partner is a girl called Gillian. Florian is very excited because he's soon going to meet her in London. He already knows something about Gillian because he has a copy of her student profile.

STUDENT PROFILE • Education and Culture DG • Lifelong Learning Programme

Host country:
ENGLAND / UNITED KINGDOM

Programme type: STUDENT EXCHANGE

Period of exchange:
SEPTEMBER–NOVEMBER 2015

First name: GILLIAN

Middle name: AMANDA

Last name: STEPHENS

Date of birth (day / month / year):
28. SEPTEMBER 1998

Height: 5 FOOT 9 INCHES

Weight: 55 KILOGRAMMES

Gender: x Female   Male

Home town:
CHURCH BROUGHTON, DERBYSHIRE

Home country:
ENGLAND / UNITED KINGDOM

School:
JOHN PORT SCHOOL (IN ETWALL)

School level: SIXTH FORM (YEAR 2)

Mother tongue: ENGLISH

Second language level:
3 YEARS OF GERMAN

Are you a vegetarian?   Yes x No

Do you have any allergies? x Yes   No

If yes, please give details:
CATS, BIRCH AND HAZELNUT POLLEN

If you have an allergy to pets, how close can you live to pets:

    in your room? x inside a house?

    outside a house?

Interests:
DRAMA, ART, BUSINESS STUDIES,
PLAYING THE PIANO, HIKING,
CLASSICAL MUSIC, DANCING (HIP
HOP), CINEMA AND TV, FRIENDS

Comments:
PEOPLE SAY THAT I'M A COMMU-
NICATIVE PERSON. I LIKE TO MEET
PEOPLE AND I LIKE TO TRAVEL TO
OTHER COUNTRIES AND FIND OUT
HOW PEOPLE LIVE AND WHAT THEY
THINK. AND I LIKE TO HAVE FUN,
TOO.

Please give details of your family background:

Father: JOHN, SALESMAN

Talking about the present

- Für **Gewohnheiten** und regelmäßig oder häufig wiederkehrende Handlungen und Vorgänge wird das **simple present** verwendet. Bei *he/she/it* (3. Person singular) wird *-(e)s* an die Grundform des Verbs angehängt.
  *Gillian **comes** from Bristol. She **goes** to school in Etwall. She**'s** allergic to cats.*
  *She **has** a brother.*
  *(Aber: She **was** born in 1998.)*
- Fragen und Verneinungen mit dem Vollverb *to be*.
  ***Is** Anne's father a teacher? – Yes, he is./No, he isn't.*
  ***Are** you a vegetarian? – Yes, I am./No, I'm not.*
- Fragen und Verneinungen mit anderen Vollverben werden mit *do/does* gebildet.
  ***Do** you have a sister? – Yes, I have./No, I haven't.*
  ***Does** she play the piano? – Yes, she does./No, she doesn't.*
- Das **present progressive** wird verwendet, wenn ein Vorgang beschrieben wird, der **zum Zeitpunkt des Sprechens im Gange ist**. An das Vollverb wird *-ing* angehängt.
  *I**'m reading** an SMS text from Frank. He**'s visiting** some friends in Manchester.*
- Nach dem Verb *like* kann man entweder ein Infinitiv oder ein Gerundium (*-ing*-Form) verwenden.
  *My girlfriend **likes to play** the piano. She **likes playing** jazz melodies.*
  (Es gibt aber Verben, wo das nachfolgende Verb ein Gerundium sein muss:
  ***I enjoy swimming.**)*

1. Imagine your are Florian. Tell a partner who your exchange partner is going to be. Give as much information about the English girl as you can.
   My exchange partner is …. She comes from …. She …
   Describe what she looks like and what you think about her.
   Now do the same thing again with another partner.

2. Imagine Gillian will be staying with one of your classmates. Ask simple questions about their exchange partner. *Who …? What …? Where …? When …? How long …? …?*

3. What would your 'dream partner' be like? Discuss him or her with a partner.

4. Imagine Gillian is going to stay in your home. What would your parents want to know about her? Write a short note (not more than 10 lines!) to your mother or father in German with the information they would want to know.

5. Create your own student profile.

2   Going out in London

Gillian and her older brother, Keith, picked up Florian at London Heathrow Airport and spent the day in London. Now they have to decide what to do in the evening: visit a pub or go to a cinema?

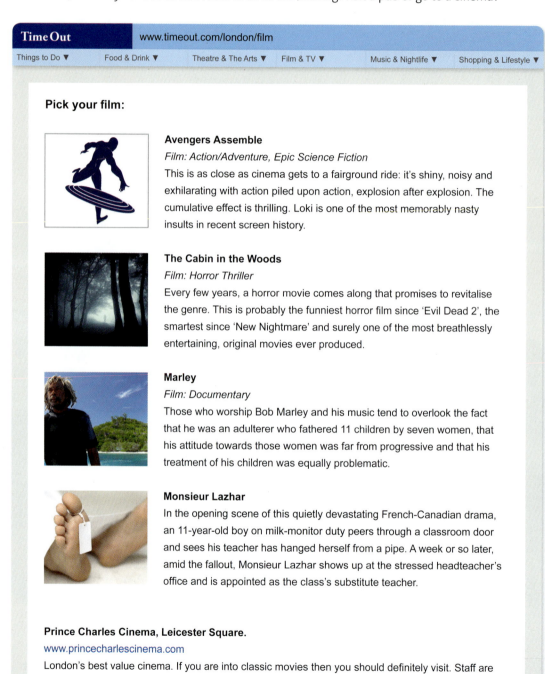

Time Out   www.timeout.com/london/film

Things to Do ▼   Food & Drink ▼   Theatre & The Arts ▼   Film & TV ▼   Music & Nightlife ▼   Shopping & Lifestyle ▼

Pick your film:

Avengers Assemble

Film: Action/Adventure, Epic Science Fiction

This is as close as cinema gets to a fairground ride: it's shiny, noisy and exhilarating with action piled upon action, explosion after explosion. The cumulative effect is thrilling. Loki is one of the most memorably nasty insults in recent screen history.

The Cabin in the Woods

Film: Horror Thriller

Every few years, a horror movie comes along that promises to revitalise the genre. This is probably the funniest horror film since 'Evil Dead 2', the smartest since 'New Nightmare' and surely one of the most breathlessly entertaining, original movies ever produced.

Marley

Film: Documentary

Those who worship Bob Marley and his music tend to overlook the fact that he was an adulterer who fathered 11 children by seven women, that his attitude towards those women was far from progressive and that his treatment of his children was equally problematic.

Monsieur Lazhar

In the opening scene of this quietly devastating French-Canadian drama, an 11-year-old boy on milk-monitor duty peers through a classroom door and sees his teacher has hanged herself from a pipe. A week or so later, amid the fallout, Monsieur Lazhar shows up at the stressed headteacher's office and is appointed as the class's substitute teacher.

Prince Charles Cinema, Leicester Square.

www.princecharlescinema.com

London's best value cinema. If you are into classic movies then you should definitely visit. Staff are pleasant and professional. And for London, the prices are quite cheap.

Time Out   www.timeout.com/london/film

Things to Do ▼   Food & Drink ▼   Theatre & The Arts ▼   Film & TV ▼   Music & Nightlife ▼   Shopping & Lifestyle ▼

Pick your pub or bar:

White Horse *Pub Parsons Green, SW6*
Only the lack of ceiling fans stop the main bar of this renowned hostelry from feeling like something from the days of the Raj. Babies and children admitted, Wireless internet, Disabled access, Tables outdoors, Function rooms

Milk & Honey *Bar Soho, W1F*
You could walk past the door of this Soho speakeasy every day and never know it was there.
Exclusive atmosphere.
Booking essential, Function rooms, Cocktails, Hip factor, Late night, Romance, Wow factor

Mark's Bar *Bar Soho, W1F*
Opened in 2009, together with the restaurant on the ground floor, this is a destination in its own right.
Babies and children admitted, Wireless internet, Disabled access, Cocktails, Hip factor

Worship Street Whistling Shop *Bar Shoreditch, EC2A*
We've noticed a few conspicuous themes appearing in London's bars: a semi-secret location, Victoriana, faithful interpretations of classic British drinks.
Booking advisable, Babies and children admitted, Wireless internet, Function room, Cocktails

69 Colebrooke Row *Bar Islington, N1*
Tucked away off the Islington Green end of Essex Road this modern bar was opened in mid 2009.
Booking advisable, Wireless internet, Entertainment, Cocktails, North, Islington, Bar

Trailer Happiness *Bar Notting Hill, W11*
Remaining laudably tongue-in-cheek while the rest of Ladbroke Grove drowns in chichi spots, Trailer Happiness is a happy mixture of cocktail bar and disco.
Tags: Wireless internet, Entertainment, Tables outdoors, Cocktails, Hip factor, Something different.

TRACK 1

British pub etiquette
George tells his friends about some unwritten rules in British pubs.

TASKS

1 Choose a film and a pub or a bar. If you have Internet access, you should also look up the films shown at the Prince Charles Cinema, London, Leicester Square. Talk with a partner and justify your decisions.
   (▶ Skills 3.3)

2 Discuss and decide in a group of four: Which cinema or which bar?

3 Listen to the talk about pub etiquette and take notes.
   Mediation: Explain the essential points of British pub etiquette to your parents in German.

3 Persönliche Daten

Florian Ballack   geb. 30. 12. 1998

Wohnhaft:	Karl-Marx-Str. 29, D-16540 Hohen Neuendorf
Eltern:	Beate Ballack, Lehrerin für Deutsch und Englisch
	Jürgen Ballack, KFZ-Meister bei Opel (NL Oranienburg)
Grundschule:	Wald-Grundschule Hohen Neuendorf
Sekundarschule:	Regine-Hildebrandt-Gesamtschule (RHS), Birkenwerder
Schulabschluss 10. Klasse:	MSA mit Versetzung in die gymnasiale Oberstufe
Gegenwärtiger Schulbesuch:	11. Klasse (Oberstufe) der RHS Birkenwerder
Wunsch-Job:	Lehrer für Sport und Physik / Technik
Karrieremöglichkeiten:	offen für alles
Praktika:	8. Klasse: Ferienjob im Kindergarten „Wirbelsturm", Hohen Neuendorf
9. Klasse:	Schülerfirma der ‚Schul-GmbH': Event Management
10. Klasse:	Weiterbildungsabteilung der Deutschen Bank, Berlin
Bisherige Arbeitserfahrung:	Erteilung von Nachhilfeunterricht, Babysitten, Zeitungsbote
Wunsch:	Praktikum in England oder Austausch mit einer englischen Schule

INFO-BOX

A curriculum vitae (CV)

Drawing up a curriculum vitae is an important step in looking for any job or training course. For applications to certain internships, some schools or universities you need a CV which focusses on skills, competences and qualifications.

The CV is often the first contact with a future employer. It needs to seize the reader's attention immediately and to demonstrate why you should be given an interview. Employers and personnel managers generally spend no more than a minute on each CV when making a first selection from applications they have received. If you fail to make the right impact, you will waste your opportunity. Job applications can now often be submitted online. You have to follow the instructions and fill in the required information. Make sure that you have your CV with all the information at hand before you start (contact info, educational background and qualifications, work experience and internships, previous employment, etc.) Be aware that CVs in Germany may be slightly different from CVs in Great Britain or the USA.

Warning: The Internet has become a popular tool for screening job applicants. Personnel managers often search sites such as MySpace, studiVZ, Jappy, meinVZ, SchülerVZ, YouTube or Facebook for information about job candidates. Many applicants have been eliminated on the basis of information which recruiters discovered on the Internet. Embarrassing photos, silly entries or strange profiles or blogs can mean that you will never get invited to an interview for the job that you really care about.

Qualifications: NVQs? GCSEs? Diplomas? AS-level? A-levels? B.A.?, M.A.?
http://www.direct.gov.uk/en/YoungPeople/index.htm
http://www.myenglishpages.com/site_php_files/reading-english-educational-system.php

Conditional sentences, types 1 and 2

- *If*-Sätze (Typ 1) drücken eine erfüllbare Bedingung aus. Der *if*-Nebensatz steht im Präsens, im Hauptsatz steht ein Modalverb im Präsens bzw. das *will*-Futur. (Merke: *will* kann auch als Modalverb gelten.)
  *If I **get** a diploma, I **can be** an apprentice.*
  *If I **pass** the final exam, I'**ll be** a qualified accountant.*
- *If*-Sätze (Typ 2) drücken eine meist unwahrscheinliche Bedingung aus. Der *if*-Nebensatz steht im *simple past*, im Hauptsatz wird *would* (oder *could / might / should*) + Infinitiv verwendet.
  *If I **wanted** to go to a university, I'**d need** at least three A-levels.*

1   What must you do to make your online profile (e.g. on Facebook) secure?
What must you be aware of?
Compare your reasons with a partner.

2   Browse the English version of www.europass.de. Refer to the German version if you have difficulty. Click on Curriculum Vitae. You can also find examples of completed CVs. It is important that you use the Instructions for filling in the CV on this website. Concentrate on website pages 6—8.

3   Work with a partner or in groups of three or four. Put together a CV for Florian. Discuss each point as you go through the form, especially whether all the information in the box is needed for the CV. Is there any important information missing?

4   Research more details about English qualifications on the net. You'll find some of them in the Info-box on the previous page. Write down what the abbreviations mean. Start with GCSEs (General Certificate of ...)
(▶ Skills 1.3)

5   Compare Florian's school qualifications (or your own) with the English educational system. You'll find information in an up-to-date dictionary or on the websites given in the Info-box.
(▶ Skills 1.1; 1.2)

6   Work in pairs: Explain what you can / could do, if you have / had the qualification of ...
Example: *If I get my A-levels, I can go to university and get a B.A.*

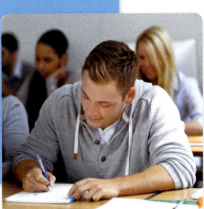

4   The inspiration for a song

In the 1960s the Beatles were a world-famous pop group. Most of their songs were written by John Lennon and Paul McCartney and they often told a story. Some of them have become time-less classics. One of these is the song "She's leaving home" from their 1967 album "Sergeant Pepper's Lonely Hearts Club Band". The song lyrics were based on a newspaper story Paul McCartney had read about a young girl who had left home and couldn't be found. That girl was 17-year-old Melanie Coe, who had run away from home leaving everything behind. Her father was quoted as saying, "I can't imagine why she should run away, she has everything here."

McCartney said later: "We'd seen that story and it was my inspiration. There was a lot of these at the time and that was enough to give me the storyline: She slips out and leaves a note and then the parents wake up …. It was rather poignant. I liked it as a song and John added the Greek chorus and long sustained notes."

In 2008, Melanie Coe told her story to a newspaper journalist:

London was a very different place in the 60s. I went to a club called the Bag O' Nails (Soho) and I met everybody. You sat on the next table to the Beatles, the Rolling Stones, the Hollies, be-cause there weren't many clubs in London. I got in coz I was a cute little girl and I dressed in the latest fashions. I'd go to Mary Quant and Biba, sketch the dress and get my aunt to make my clothes. Ready Steady Go! loved that. They held open auditions. I was 13. It went on what you were wearing and how you danced. I was asked to come every week. I met the Beatles at Ready Steady Go! George was great to meet – I looked a lot like Pattie Boyd, who later became his wife, of course.

I was always going out. I danced the night away and was a face in London. In those days, to be trendy everything had to be French. I bought the T-shirt of the moment, which was my star sign in French. I loved that T-shirt. One day I got home and my mother had cut it to ribbons. She wanted me to look like Princess Anne, not my idol, Marianne Faithfull.
When my parents found out I had the pill they grabbed me by the scruff of the neck and made me flush them down the toilet. I was 17 by then and ran away leaving a note, just like in the song. I went to a doctor and he said I was preg-nant, but I didn't know that before I left home.

My best friend at the time was married to Ritchie Blackmore, so she hid me at their house in Holloway Road. It was the first place my parents came to look, so I ran off with my boyfriend, who was a croupier, although he had been "in the motor trade" like it says in the song. I think my dad called up the newspapers – my picture was on the front pages. He made out that I must have been kidnapped, because why would I leave? They gave me everything – coats, cars. But not love. My parents found me after three weeks and I had an abortion.

I didn't realize for a long time that the song was about me. Years later Paul was on a programme talking about how he'd seen a newspaper article and been inspired by it. My mother pieced it all together and called me to say, "That song's about you!"

I can't listen to the song. It's just too sad for me. My parents died a long time ago and we were never resolved. That line, "She's leaving home after living alone for so many years" is so weird to me because that's why I left. I was so alone. How did Paul know that those were the feelings that drove me towards ... one-night stands with rock stars? I don't think he can have possibly realized that he'd met me when I was 13 on Ready Steady Go!, but when he saw the picture, something just clicked.

WORD POWER
ABC

to make out that …	to imply: give the impression that something is true
Greek chorus	a group of singers in Greek plays who comment on what just happened
coz. *conj.*	*(slang)* short form of *because*
scruff of the neck, *idiom*	Kragen, Genick
were never resolved	were never close to each other any more

TASKS

1. Mediation: Read the first text. Then tell one of your partners in German how Paul McCartney got the idea for the song and what John Lennon's role was in making it. (▶ Skills 4.0)

2. Find the lyrics of the song "She's leaving home" on the Internet.
   a) Who is being quoted in the chorus?
   b) Who is the "Man from the motor trade"?
   c) What reasons do the lyrics give for why Melanie left home?

3. Read Melanie's interview, then work with a partner and write a summary. (▶ Skills 5.3)

5   Growing up

It must be, oooh,
a month or more
since they last complained
about the way I eat
or crisps I drop
on the kitchen floor
or not washing my feet
or the TV left on
when I go out
or the spoon clunking
against my teeth
or how loudly I shout
or my unmade bed,
mud on the stair,
soap left to drown
or the state of my hair ...
It must be
a month or more.
Have they given up
in despair?
For years
they've nagged me
to grow up,
to act my age.
Can it be
that it's happened,
that I'm ready
to step out of my cage?

(by Wes Magee)

SKILLS

Working with dictionaries

- Get to know your English dictionary. Find out which parts and appendices it has.

- Where can you find abbreviations and symbols of phonetic transcription used in the dictionary?

- Work in pairs and find four ways that the dictionary can help you in written exams. Share your findings with your class and the teacher – and remember them! (▶ Skills 1.0)

M – Meaningful
Y – Yes, my glasses are meaningful

G – Grip my head at the sides
L – Love is strong, so are my glasses
A – Attached to my head at the sides
S – Stop me walking into opticians
S – See through
E – Ever so clean
S – Seven quid*

(by John Hegley)

(* ugs. für britische Währung ,pound')

TASKS

1 Look up the following words in an English dictionary and select the definition which best fits the way the word is used in the poem: *complain, crisps, drop, clunk, mud, state, despair, nag.*

2 Describe the speaker in the first poem and the problems he or she is talking about.

3 Choose one adjective in the Wes Magee poem that you think describes the speaker's feelings best. Give reasons for your choice.
optimistic – ironic – surprised – sad – resigned – disappointed – submissive – misunderstood – frustrated – thoughtful – angry

4 Find reasons why this text is a poem and share your reasons with a partner. (▶ Skills 1.2)

○ **5** Select the photo that you think fits the poem best. Now write a short text describing it and giving reasons for your choice. (▶ Skills 3.5)

○ **6** Imagine you are a journalist writing about puberty and adolescence. Interview the parents about their experiences with their teenage children and produce an article either as a text or as a dialogue. (▶ Skills 5.4)

○ **7** Think about the point in time when a person has really 'grown up'. Then discuss your ideas and decide which is the most important of your points.

○ **8** Write your own poem / song / rap about 'growing up'. Be creative, like John Hegley when he talks about his glasses!

1 Write your own CV

If you don't have a computer, ask your teacher to provide you with a CV-form that you can fill in.
If you have a computer and access to the internet: Create your own CV online and download the CV to your computer from the website http://europass.cedefop.europa.eu/en/home.
Keep it on your computer for later use.
You can update it whenever something in your life has changed. This can be very useful for when you need a good CV after you have finished school (or university!). And of course: You will find the same on the website in German.

2 Job descriptions

The following job descriptions are "tongue-in-cheek", i.e. they describe jobs in a humorous way. Try to match them with the jobs in the box below.

antiques dealer • bomber pilot • divorce lawyer • housewife • IT security technician • lifeguard • microbiologist • pilot • police chief • sailing instructor • security guard • student • teacher • video game creator

My job is to ...

1 – supervise the guys and gals who try to protect the good people from the bad, only to be hated by the good people AND the bad.
2 – read things that don't matter, then write papers saying they do matter, for points that don't matter, in order to get a job doing something totally unrelated.
3 – manage waste recycling, promotion and sales.
4 – manage urban renewal and pest control.
5 – teach kids to be evil – or so they say.
6 – spend most of the day looking out the window.
7 – make sure nothing ever happens.
8 – move things from one test tube to another.
9 – try to do three things at once and not shout at the neighbours.
10 – run away and call the police.
11 – ensure that stupid people stay in the gene pool.
12 – persuade kids that it's really fun being wet, cold and scared out of their minds.
13 – Talk in other people's sleep.
14 – Help people hate each other.

TRACK 1   **3 More listening comprehension**

Listen to the talk about pub etiquette again and answer the following questions:

1 Why should you leave an empty pub?
2 Why shouldn't you sit at a table and wait for a waiter or a waitress?
3 When do you pay for the drinks you have ordered?
4 What is a 'round'?
5 Give an example of a 'stout'.
6 How much do you tip?
7 Identify these different types of drinks:
a) This light beer is the most popular beer in Britain, particularly with young people.
b) This dark beer has a very full taste. 'Guinness' is the most well-known type.
c) This beer is made from apples.

4 Word families

Make yourself a wordlist that helps you remember by using 'word- families'.
It should look like this:

verb	noun	adjective	other noun(s)	German
to light	the light	light	—	anzünden, das Licht, hell
	the pub		publican	die Kneipe, der Wirt
run	runner	running	-	rennen, der Läufer, rennend
Some very characteristic endings:				
(-ize)	(-er)	(-ic, -ical)		
(-ify)	(-ment)	(-y)		
	(-ation)	(-ful)		
	(-ity, -ty)	(-less)		
	(-ness)	(-able)		

5 Working with a dictionary

1 *Use the appendix 'Names' in the dictionary. How many names can you find that are the same for boys and girls?*

2 *Use the appendix 'Weights and Measures' to answer these questions:*
   a) What is six feet in centimetres?
   b) How many metres are there in one mile ?
   c) How many cubic centimetres is one pint?
   d) How many grams is one ounce?

6 Puns

A pun is a joke based on the fact that some words either have different meanings or they sound very similar (homophones) but their meanings are very different. For example, a famous composer once said "I've had an interesting career – from a roast chicken in Austria to a door opener in England." (Händel bzw. Handel)

Read the following puns. Use a dictionary to explain the pun. For example:
I tried to catch some fog. I mist.
– 'mist' *(Nebel)* and 'missed' *(verfehlte, verpasste)* are homophones.

1 Jokes about German sausages are the wurst.
2 My brother is addicted to brake fluid. He says he can stop anytime.
3 How does an Israeli make his tea? – Hebrews it.
4 Did you hear about the dyslexic man who walked into a bra?
5 Why were the Indians in the USA first? – They had reservations.
6 What do you call a dinosaur with an extensive vocabulary? – A thesaurus.
7 If you get a bladder infection in the jungle, urine big trouble!
8 What does a clock do when it's hungry? – It goes back four seconds.
9 Broken pencils are pointless!

7 Rhyming pairs

Find the words in each column that rhyme. Look up the words you don't know in an English-German dictionary.

1	eat	A	wreath
2	floor	B	June
3	done	C	bear
4	spoon	D	crown
5	TV	E	feet
6	teeth	F	pea
7	stair	G	whore
8	shout	H	doubt
9	drown	I	fun
10	age	J	gauge

8 Two limericks

In an exercise book, complete the two limericks with the words in the box.

The (1) ... has made himself illustrious
Through constant industry (2) ... .
So what? Would you be calm and (3) ...
If you were (4) ... of formic acid?

A flea and a (5) ... in a flue
Were imprisoned, so what could they (6) ... ?
Said the fly, "let us (7) ...!"
"Let us fly!" said the (8) ... .
So they (9) ... through a flaw in the flue.

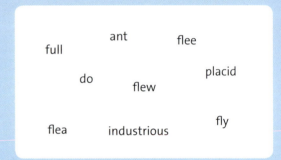

full   ant   flee
do   flew   placid
flea   industrious   fly

CHECK

1 I can exchange personal information and talk about my personal wishes and ideas.

2 I can plan an evening out in an English-speaking city.

3 I can explain Bitish and German school qualifications.

4 I can write my own curriculum vitae on europass.de.

5 I can analyse, talk about and write about teenage problems.

6 I can analyse songs and poems.

7 I can use the simple present tense and ask questions.

8 I can describe things and compare them.

9 I can understand and apply conditional sentences.

10 I can talk about my personal likes and dislikes.

11 I can write a summary of a text.

12 I can find help in an English dictionary

UNIT 2
Work experience

To do

Receptive
* Read about Florian and Gillian's dreams and wishes in the world of work
* Get to know some of the most important websites about working in other countries
* Browse the web and inform yourself about your options

Productive
* Talk about your own dreams, expectations and actual work experience
* Read job adverts and write letters of application
* Update and finalize your CV (cf. Unit 1)

Interactive
* Practise job interviews in role play
* Take part in interactive online simulations of job interviews

Skills
* Practise writing summaries
* Assessing the tone and emotion of a text

Grammar
* Gerunds

1   What can we do?

Gillian and Florian are talking about their future after school and their chances of finding the right job.

Gillian: My dad keeps telling me to think about where I want to end up. I think he's stuck in another time when many people did just one job for all their working life.

Florian: I know what you mean. Things have changed. But we've got to start somewhere. What are your dreams and ambitions? I mean, do you have any ideas?

Gillian: Of course I have ideas, but I'm not sure how realistic they are, or whether or not I'm going to be tough enough to fight my way through. I'd love to become a doctor ...

Florian: Wow, that's quite a goal.

Gillian: Yeah, and I want to work with children. I looked after my niece last summer. She's seriously ill and struggling with all kinds of pain. At that age! She needs to feel happy and laugh more than anything else. And spending time with her was so rewarding, I really felt that I was doing the right thing.

Florian: Sounds like you've found something to go for! It's more complicated with me.

Gillian: Why's that?

Florian: Because I can't decide which of my interests I should concentrate on. I love sports, but I'm not an athlete. I love football and if I can't watch a match, I'll listen to it on the radio or read about it in a newspaper. Perhaps sports journalism would be great fun and a career option for me at the same time?

Gillian: What a great idea! I can really see you doing that! You should really find out what kind of exam results you need and maybe do an internship with some agency in London while you're here. You've got a good voice for that kind of thing, too.

Florian: Maybe you're right. But in England? I'm not so sure about my English ...

Gillian: You're doing fine. You get across what you want to express and I think your accent is cute! And doing an internship abroad would look really great on your CV!

Florian: OK, you might be right. And you should apply to the Great Ormond Street Hospital for Children. Isn't it one of the world's leading hospitals for children? Give it a try!

Gillian: Right! We should start researching right now.

Florian: I don't want to sound pessimistic, but an internship is still no guarantee that we'll end up in those jobs.

Gillian: True, but it's a good way to find out if we really like the job, isn't it? We've got two months to apply. Wow, I'm a little excited now!

Florian: OK, let's try it. If the jobs aren't right for us, then we can try something else.

Gillian: My uncle wanted to become a racing car driver. He tried it and hated it! Then he worked his way into a management position at the Campbell Soup Company ...

Florian: You mean the baked beans we have for breakfast ... ?

Gillian: Yup, and many other tinned foods, of course. And he still loves his job, which is mainly working with people. You never know. Who would have thought that that would be his dream job, I'm sure he didn't! But he's happy.

Florian: I'm excited, too, now. Imagine me reporting a match! I do know all the rules: soccer, hockey, rugby, tennis, basketball, ... whatever! Now I can't stop thinking about it!

Gillian: Here's an interesting website. Let's see if they have something for us ...

Finding information on the Internet about working abroad

Useful websites:
- http://www.ukgermanconnection.org
- www.rausvonzuhaus.de
- http://europa.eu/youth/working/working_holidays/index_eu_en.html

Each of these sites will offer you many more links. For example:
- www.arbeitsagentur.de (Information about internships outside Germany)
- http://grossbritannien.ahk.de (German-British chamber of commerce)
- www.stepin.de (Student Travel & Education Programmes International)
- www.aiesec.org (Student organisation for international exchange)

You could also start with a search engine enquiry of your own. For example:
- Jobs in ... (the country of your choice)
- Working in ...
- Internships in ...

INFO-BOX

---

1 Write a summary of the dialogue between Florian and Gillian.

2 Choose a partner. Tell each other about the work experience each of you already has.

3 What are your own ideas, dreams, and ambitions for your future? Choose a partner and discuss your ideal job and your hopes – but also your doubts and worries.

○ 4 Do you think an internship abroad might help your career? Why?

○ 5 In which english-speaking country would you choose to do an internship? Give reasons.

○ 6 Visit the websites in the Info box above and say which of them you found to be the most helpful and why.

TASKS

2   Applying for a job

Different countries, organisations and firms also have different ideas about how one should apply for a job with them. Depending on the kind of job, some want videos, photos, or samples of the applicant's handwriting. Nowadays you very often have the choice of applying either by e-mail or with a traditional letter.

A Welsh computer company asked applicants to send just one text message (SMS) explaining why they would be the right one for the marketing job – and how they would handle it.
When you apply for a job or an internship, you will probably do it in a more traditional way.
For a start, your application will need a **covering letter** and your **CV**, which you already got to know in Unit 1. You should also have a CV in English (in Europass format) filled in on your computer.

HR Internship

Lynx Ltd. is an expanding company constantly looking for outstanding student interns for our London and Sacramento offices. We are specialised in security equipment and have offices in England, the USA, Belgium and Ireland, each providing first-class products and services. The candidates for Human Resources internships should have a background in management, international business or related disciplines. We are looking for committed students who are planning a career in human resources and who would like to gain hands-on experience in a busy human resources department.

The main areas of activity will be:

Recruitment
- Manpower planning • Advertising vacancies
- Dealing with job centres and employment agencies

General office administration
- Contracts, visa applications, work permits • PC-based tasks
- Organisation of the monthly company meeting

You should be aware that your work will be unpaid although you'll have access to company catering and leisure facilities. Leonardo student grants may be available to London interns. This internship is available for up to six months.
Please send your application with photocopies of qualifications and any testimonials to Martin O'Sullivan at our London office at 44 Osborn Street, London E1 6TE, United Kingdom.

DEAR MR O'SULLIVAN,

I SAW YOUR ADVERT FOR INTERNSHIPS ON THE BULLETIN BOARD AT OUR STUDENT JOB EXCHANGE.

I AM AN ENGINEER WHO DISCOVERED AN INTEREST IN PEOPLE HALFWAY THROUGH HIS STUDIES, AND I AM NOW SPECIALISING IN HUMAN RESOURCES AT THE UNIVERSITY OF APPLIED SCIENCES IN HAGEN, GERMANY. I FEEL THAT WORKING IN HR AT LYNX WOULD BE VERY HELPFUL FOR MY UNDERSTANDING OF PRACTICAL HUMAN RESOURCES IN AN INTERNATIONAL CONTEXT.

I HOPE THAT YOU WILL FIND MY QUALIFICATIONS SATISFACTORY AND THAT MY ABILITIES AND MY PERSONAL QUALITIES ARE WHAT YOU ARE LOOKING FOR IN POTENTIAL CANDIDATES.

ENCLOSED PLEASE FIND MY CV (IN EUROPASS FORMAT) AND COPIES OF THE DOCUMENTS REQUESTED.

I LOOK FORWARD TO HEARING FROM YOU IN DUE COURSE.

YOURS SINCERELY,
ARTHUR GEIGER

Event Sales and Marketing Internship in the Heart of England

Location:	Birmingham
Salary:	Unpaid
Starting Date:	Flexible
Length:	Flexible – 8 weeks to 4 months
Company:	We are a global player in canned soups and other tinned foods.
Role:	Mainly business development, event management, boosting sales, marketing and some office management. The company is looking for a trainee with exceptional organisational skills, experience in word processing, spreadsheets and excellent communicational skills – plus team spirit and a good sense of humour

If this sounds like a good internship for you, apply now to FlyHigh Events Recruitments, 13 High Street, Guildford GU1 3DG

TASKS

1. Read the advert 'HR Internship' carefully and give a short rundown in German of its contents to the classmate on your left. (▶ Skills 4.0)

2. Discuss Arthur Geiger's covering letter with a partner and say why you would or wouldn't employ him.

3. Write a covering letter and apply for the internship. Compare your covering letter with the covering letters of two or three classmates. After your corrections, place the letter into a properly addressed envelope together with the print-out of your CV and hand it to your teacher. (▶ Skills 5.5)

3   A job interview

Florian has been invited to see Mr Brent, the personnel manager, at his office in Guildford. Florian was very nervous about the interview at first, but he and Gillian have found out a lot about job interviews. First they went to YouTube and checked out "Interview Dos and Don'ts". They also found an "interview simulation" website, which was very realistic.

Mr Brent: Please take a seat, Mr Ballack. Are you related to the footballer in any way?

Florian: Good morning, Mr Brent. No, the footballer is no relative. I wish he was.

Mr Brent: Are you interested in sports?

Florian: Yes, very much so. I'm not terribly active as an athlete, but I would love to be a sports reporter or commentator.

Mr. Brent: But if your interest is in sport, why are you applying for an 'Event Sales and Marketing Internship'?

Florian: Well, I believe it would be a useful work experience for me. The advert doesn't mention the name of the company. Can you tell me what it is?

Mr Brent: It's the Campbell Soup Company. Perhaps you know our soups?

Florian: Yes, of course, but I'm not sure what 'event sales' means.

Mr Brent: Event sales are a method of interactive marketing. They're demos in supermarkets and shopping centres in which the customers take part.

Florian: That sounds interesting. It could be fun.

Mr Brent: I'm glad you think so. What skills and qualities can you bring to this advertised position, Mr Ballack? And why would you like to work for Campbell's?

Florian: Well, I'd like to gain work experience in Britain, and I think that I'd enjoy event management. My English isn't bad, I'm good at communicating with people. I'm also good at organizing, I learn fast, and I have good computer skills. I can work with all MS Office components on both PC and Mac operating systems.

Mr Brent: I see, I see. Have you got any formal qualifications in Germany? And how come you are in Britain right now?

Florian: I'm still at school in Germany, in the lower sixth form. Right now I'm taking part in an exchange programme, staying in Derbyshire with my English partner.

Mr Brent: Well, actually, for this internship we are looking for a university student or a college graduate and you're still at school.

Florian: Yes, but I already have some work experience with an event management firm. I worked for a firm in Berlin for four weeks. It was part of my course.

Mr Brent: Can you describe yourself in just five words?

Florian: I'm diligent, intelligent, quick-witted, communicative, humourous.

Mr Brent: Wow, great! You must have practised! What's your greatest strength?

Florian: I'm persistent – I never give up. Some people think I'm nerve-racking! But I think it's my greatest strength.

Mr Brent: And what do you think your greatest weakness is?

Florian: I can't lie, I always tell the truth.

Mr Brent: Yes, well, that would disqualify you from most managerial jobs, wouldn't it?
Now, tell me about a significant achievement in your short life.

Florian: I learned sign language, so that I could communicate with my cousin who is deaf.

Mr Brent: I like that! Where do you see yourself in five years' time, Mr Ballack?

Florian: I hope to have finished my B.A. by then. Then I'll begin a career either as a teacher or a journalist.

Mr Brent: Good. Let's stop here, Mr Ballack. I'm very impressed by your behaviour and by your answers. But you must understand that I still have to interview the other applicants and most of them have better formal qualifications than you.

Florian: Thank you, Mr Brent. I understand that, but I'd be very happy to hear from you again.
I'd appreciate the chance to show you that I can do the job.

Mr Brent: We'll see, Mr Ballack. Goodbye for now, and I wish you well.

WORD POWER

include	einschließen
included	eingeschlossen
inclusion	Einbezug; Einschluss
persist	beharren
persistent	beharrlich
persistence	Beharrlichkeit

TASKS

1 Work with a partner and write a short guide: How to dress properly for a job interview.

2 Go to the "interview simulation" website which Florian used:
http://elc.polyu.edu.hk/cill/eiw/interviews/
Practise your personal job interviews at your own speed. Do this until you feel fit for a job interview role play.

3 Get together in a group of four. Conduct a role play in which each of you is interviewed by two of the others for a job. (Use a job ad from this book or one that you make up or find in a newspaper or on the Internet.).
The person without a role makes a video film of the interview which you later show to the class.

4 Watch the four videos, then discuss them and decide in your group which of the four videos is the best in both content and style. Each of the groups should present one video to the class, and the class should select the best video to be included on the school website. (▶ Skills 6.2)

4   Looking back

Twenty-five years after the conversation about their future, Florian tracks down Gillian and writes her a letter, telling her about his career.

Dr. Florian C. Ballack

Alte Schönhauser Straße 5
D-10119 Berlin (Mitte)
Tel/Fax (+49) 030 48 79 18 17
FlorianC@Ballack.de

November 15th, 2037

Dear Gillian,

It has been twenty-five years now, and a few days ago I remembered the conversation we had in London when I was sixteen (or seventeen?) about our future careers.
Even though I have no idea how life has treated you, the very vivid memory of our discussions made me feel the need to let you know where life has led me.

During my studies over the next ten years I fooled around trying out different things, but at 26 I started my first full-time job as a sports journalist in Germany. Ten years later I held a CEO-position at the sports department of the RBB (Radio Berlin Brandenburg). I enjoyed that job tremendously – managing the programme structure for all the sports broadcasts.

I have learnt so much in the course of working in so many different jobs with so many different people that five years ago I decided to accept an offer to become a trainer and mentor for young journalists. At present I work as a teacher of trainee journalists at the Foundation for the Freedom of Speech and I am active in political work as well as in speech training.
It's been hard to change professions, not just for me, but also for my wife and the kids.
Laura is 18 now and Paul 14; moving and changing schools made the whole family go through big changes several times. But we've made it.

Isn't it strange to remember those days when you and I were so uncertain about what would become of us? Life has treated me well and my wife Clara and I are happy and lead a fulfilled life (with the odd conflict now and then!). We have two smart and energetic children who make us proud and happy.

And how are you? I do hope you've achieved your goals and dreams, on whatever path and in whatever way. I think of you fondly and hope we can meet for a coffee or a meal when I come to London for a conference in March. Perhaps we could have a short video-meeting, so that we recognize each other. My hair has thinned quite a bit and what's left is snow white!

Yours always,

FLORIAN

Gillian is very happy to get a letter from Florian after so many years. This is her reply:

Gillian A. Pursall-Cox

Ladbrooke Towers
9, Kensington Crescent
Kensington
London W8 7NX

19. November, 2037

My dear Florian,

I can't tell you how happy your letter makes me! It has been so long, but I still remember those summer days in London and Berlin so vividly, all linked with warm thoughts, high hopes and endless giggles and laughs.

My career has been a little trickier, more of a zig-zag course than yours. I'm afraid it would take too long to map it all out for you. But what has become true for me is that I work with children after all.

I finally achieved my initial ideals about ten years ago. That's when my marriage finally broke up after a long period of unpleasant rows and nasty squabbles. I went to Africa looking for a new life. I didn't find it there and soon returned to London where I started working with disabled children and their parents. Ever since then it feels like I've arrived, like I'm doing the right thing.
It feels very rewarding. All those career ideas of big money and a executive lifestyle didn't make me happy.

Please let me know when you will be here next spring. I'd love to go out for dinner and talk about all those years that have passed since we last met. It was so lovely of you to write – I'm impressed that you managed to track me down after all my changes of address and a different last name!

Love and best wishes,

Gillian

_____

africanqueen@yoyo.com

TASKS

1 How did Gillian and Florian's lives turn out? Give a short account of not more than 150 words.

2 What is the tone of each of the two letters? Think of the emotions that you feel when you read the letters, choose one or two adjectives for each letter and give reasons for your choice:
cheerful – melancholic – thoughtful – serious – enthusiastic – depressing – cautious – witty – caring – sentimental – ironic
(▶ Skills 2.2)

3 Write a private letter to either Gillian or Florian and tell them how you think and feel about the developments in their lives. Don't forget to write a proper letterhead!
(▶ Skills 5.1)

5   Letters of application

a)

PAUL HUBER • Rolandstr. 7 • 44145 Dortmund • Fon: 0231 395 9207

Progressive WebSolutions
Owen K. Caster, Manager
13551 Triton Park Lane
Norwich
England

Dear Friend,

Hi! I thought you're looking for some workers. If you are, well, I wanna be part of the gang!
I go to school in Germany, and could handle the job good. As a matter of fact, I even worked for
Progressive before! Email me asap with your answer.

Cheers, Paul

PS: if you're not hiring, you can keep my CV anyway.

b)

PAUL HUBER
Rolandstr. 7 • D-44145 Dortmund • Tel: 0231 395 92 07 • p.huber@t-online.de

Progressive WebSolutions
Mr Owen K. Caster, Manager
13551 Triton Park Lane
GB-Norwich NO17 FEL

Dear Mr Caster   May 3, 20__

I'm a seventeen-year-old German high school student and I'm writing to you about the
job advertisement on your website. I would be very interested in doing a placement for four
weeks in the summer as part of my work experience. I'm flexible, a good team worker and
eager to learn new things.
The vocational school I attend prepares us to work in various types of companies.
I'm computer-literate and I can use all of the Microsoft Office package. In addition, I have
some experience in bookkeeping and a good general knowledge of business. I've studied
English and French at school and would be very interested in working in a multinational
company.
Please see my attached CV for details of my skills and education. I look forward to hearing from
you.

Yours faithfully

PAUL HUBER

Paul Huber

c)

OFFICE TEMPS needed urgently

- – Looking for a placement in an office? Do you have experience in office work?
- – Do you want to increase your CV experience and marketability?
- – Are you a diligent, well-organized and computer-literate student of business who would like to work abroad?

If this is you then apply today for a summer placement.
We have various roles in many sectors – just send a letter and your CV to
Ralph Lancaster at
placement@summerjob.net

d)

GENERAL OFFICE CLERKS / RECEPTIONISTS / SWITCHBOARD OPERATORS

The summer season is here and **PeoplePower** is busy! We have numerous summer positions available for students or seasoned office professionals. Although the job tasks will vary, they will likely include: formatting documents, answering multi-line phones or switchboards, typing reports, handling the mail / courier, photocopying, faxing, and other general administrative and clerical duties.

If you are proficient in MS Office, have a minimum of one year experience, and are willing to learn new systems, please apply today either by fax to 634-669-575697 or online!

Job Title: General Office Clerks / Receptionists / Switchboard Operators
Job location: Dublin   **Hours per Week:** 37   **Start Date:** ASAP
Salary: € 560 per week   **Job Duration:** 3 — 6 months

To submit a résumé for this position, you must place CS V 7 Z 2 H 3 / M B / 9600235324 in the subject line of your e-mail. Send your résumés to: staffing.jobs@peoplepower.com in text format. Do not send e-mail attachments.

TASKS

1. Analyse both covering letters (a + b) according to the following criteria: register (formal / informal) • spelling • salutation and ending • grammar / vocabulary • punctuation • format / layout • effectiveness

2. Write a covering letter to job c). Apply what you have learned from Task 1. (▶ Skills 5.5)

3. Apply for job d) by e-mail. (▶ Skills 5.1)

① False information

Some of the information in the following two summaries is incorrect. Compare the summaries with the original texts and find the mistakes. Compare your results with your classmates. Then write a correct summary in an exercise book.

a) Text: What can we do?
Gillian an Florian are talking about their dreams and ambitions.
Gillian would love to became a lawyer or work with children.
Florian would like to become a political journalist.
They are thinking about an internship for Gillian in England.
Gillian thinks about her uncle who started out as a professional bike racer and finally became the manager of a soup company.

b) Text: A job interview
Florian is in a job interview, applying for an internship as a sports reporter.
The company is the Tesco Soup Company.
He tells the recruitment manager about his abilities.
Florian's greatest strength is being persistent, his greatest weakness is being unpunctual.
The manager is impressed and offers him the job.

GRAMMAR

Das Gerundium (The gerund)

*If the **going** gets tough, the tough get **going**.* (Wahlspruch der US-Marines)

Ein Gerundium ist ein substantiviertes, d. h. zum Nomen gemachtes Verb. Es geht also um Tätigkeiten, die von einem Nomen ausgedrückt werden. Ein *-ing* wird an das Verb angehängt (wie beim Partizip Präsens).

Ein Gerundium wird benutzt
*   nach Nomen mit Präposition, z. B.:
    *He has the opportunity **of taking** part in the championship final.*
    *We talked **about going** to a university.*
*   nach folgenden Verben: *adore, love, like, hate, prefer, enjoy, detest, dislike, can't stand, can't bear, don't mind, finish, keep, go, come*

Verben wie ***remember**, **try**, **stop*** ziehen entweder ein Gerundium **oder** einen ***to**-*Infinitiv nach sich. Dadurch verändert sich aber die Bedeutung:
He stopped kissing her. – Er hörte auf, sie zu küssen.
He stopped to kiss her. – Er blieb stehen, um sie zu küssen.

Folgende Verben haben nur den ***to** +* Infinitiv nach sich:
afford, agree, arrange, decide, fail, forget, hope, manage, offer, plan, promise, refuse, seem, want

2 **The gerund**

a) *Look through all the texts in this Unit and find examples of sentences with the gerund. Check your results with your classmates.*

b) *Write down 18 sentences using the following information grid:*

	love	enjoy	like (very much*)	not mind	can't stand	hate
Nina	ski	go to the cinema	dance	clean the house	wash the car	iron clothes
Marc	play football	dance	play computer games	help his parents	listen to jazz	do exams
Julia	play netball	play the guitar	buy clothes	cook for the family	travel by air	baby-sit

* *very much* kommt nach dem Vollverb oder dem Objekt.

c) *Translate the following sentences into English using the gerund or the **to +** infinitive:*

1. Er braucht diese Chance, um sich zu beweisen.
2. Sie zieht das Schwimmen dem Segeln vor. *(prefer … to …)*
3. Andy verabscheut es, im Regen spazieren zu gehen.
4. Der Autoverkäufer willigt ein, das Auto zu einem niedrigeren Preis zu verkaufen.
5. Joan hat sich entschieden, nicht zum Basketballspiel zu gehen.
6. Jill kann es nicht ertragen, ausgelacht zu werden.
7. Der Manager sieht die Möglichkeit zu expandieren.
8. Chris hat das Autowaschen beendet.

3 **Missing prepositions**

Complete these sentences with a preposition from the box.

about • after • for • in • on • on • to • to • with • with

1. Gillian and Florian were talking … their future … school.
2. Gillian think her dad is stuck … another time.
3. He still thinks that people stay in one job … all their working life.
4. Gillian would love … become a doctor
5. But she doesn't know if she's going to be tough enough … do that.
6. Gillian also likes working … children.
7. Florian can't decide which of his interests he should concentrate … .
8. Maybe he should do an internship … some agency in London?
9. Doing an internship abroad would look really great … his CV.

TRACK 2   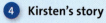 **4** **Kirsten's story**

a) *Listen to Kirstin talk about her career in bakery. Then work with a partner and decide whether the following statements are true or false. Correct the false statements.*

1. Kirstin began her career with a large bakery in Plauen.
2. The bakery owned five baker's shops in Plauen.
3. Kirsten enjoyed working in the bakery.
4. After two years, Kirstin changed from production to sales.
5. The bakery in Plauen often had a stall at the Christmas market in Leeds.
6. Kirstin first met Mr Woodford at his shop in Leeds city centre.
7. Kirstin showed Mr Woodford's staff how to make German baked products.
8. Kirstin met Andy, one of Mr Woodford's sons.
9. Kirstin and Andy rented a baker's shop in Wetherby.

b) *Listen to Track 2 again and answer these questions. Use an exercise book.*

1. Why did Kirstin prefer working in the shop?
2. Why do you think the bakery in Plauen decided to visited the Christmas market in Leeds?
3. Why did Kirstin deal with the English customers who had questions?
4. Why do you think Mr Woodford wanted to introduce German products in his bakery?
5. What job did Mr Woodford offer Kirstin and why did he offer it to Kirstin?
6. What does Kirstin mean when she says that she and Andy 'became an item'?

CHECK

1 I can talk and write about my vocational wishes and dreams.

2 I can inform others about my work experience so far.

3 I can find websites that have the information I need.

4 I can read job adverts and write a formal job application.

5 I can update my own europass.de-CV online.

6 I can get online help to prepare for a job interview.

7 I can use the dos and don'ts in a job interview role play.

8 I can apply some rules for making a video.

9 I can apply the five most important rules of writing a summary.

10 I can write a personal letter in its proper form.

UNIT 3
Social integration

To do

Receptive
- Discovering the multicultural aspects of the United Kingdom

Productive
- Writing a personal letter

Interactive
- Discussing demographic trends

Skills
- Techniques for avoiding conflict

Grammar
- Using reported speech

1   Multicultural Britain

The UK has welcomed newcomers for centuries – Jews from Poland and Russia, Germans, Italians, French and Flemish protestant refugees and the Irish. Young people from Ireland have been coming to work in Britain for centuries, and many of them married and stayed. There have been Arab settlements in many British ports since the Middle Ages and in the eighteenth century, many African sailors settled in British ports.

After World War Two, Irish and other European workers were encouraged to take factory jobs. Britain couldn't get enough workers to help rebuild the economy and to work in the new Health Service. Employers also looked to the former colonies and territories of the British Empire such as India, Bangladesh, Pakistan, the Caribbean, South Africa, Kenya and Hong Kong. These countries had strong cultural links with Britain, including the language. Many arrived in the hope of building a new life for their young families.

The descendants of these immigrants are now the teachers, the footballers, the TV presenters, the musicians and the politicians that shape British society. There are numerous ethnic newspapers, magazines, TV programmes, radio stations and internet sites for each community. The largest groups live in and around London and many other groups are concentrated in the industrial centres of Yorkshire, The Midlands and the South East.

Britain today is a mixture of diverse ethnic groups, each with their own distinct culture and sometimes their own language or religion. A very prominent group of people are the 1.5 million Muslims with over 6,000 mosques.

Ethnic minorities timeline

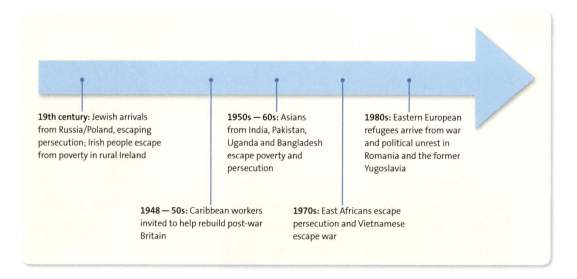

19th century: Jewish arrivals from Russia/Poland, escaping persecution; Irish people escape from poverty in rural Ireland

1950s – 60s: Asians from India, Pakistan, Uganda and Bangladesh escape poverty and persecution

1980s: Eastern European refugees arrive from war and political unrest in Romania and the former Yugoslavia

1948 – 50s: Caribbean workers invited to help rebuild post-war Britain

1970s: East Africans escape persecution and Vietnamese escape war

The non-white population of the UK

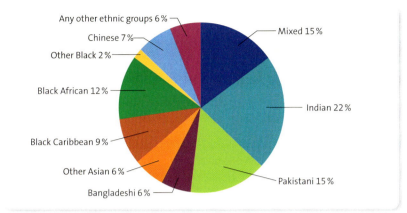

Sabrina's trip
Sabrina comes from Cologne, Germany and last year she visited relatives in the UK. Here she talks about her experiences in the UK and the cultural differences she noticed.

Multicultural terms

Asian' can be a misleading term as it refers to all those people with roots or family connections in the former British colonies of India, Pakistan, Bangladesh and Sri Lanka. Asian does not always mean that the person is of Indian descent. Not all Asians are Muslim. Some are Hindus and others are Sikhs or other religions.

Multicultural society: A society characterized by cultural pluralism. As an ideal, multi-culturalism celebrates cultural variety (for example linguistic and religious diversity). Recently there has been public criticism that an over-idealization of this concept can result in an undesirable cultural segregation and isolation.

Integration is a process where separate groups exchange cultural aspects, intermarry and mix together. Ideally this should be a two-way process, but small minorities complain that too often in practice it means that they are expected to conform to the dominant culture.

Ethnicity refers to groups of people who speak the same language, have a distinct cultural identity and have the same origins.

1. Describe the photos in this section. What do they tell you about British lifestyle today? (▶ Skills 3.5)

2. Explain the main reason for immigration to Britain after the Second World War.

3. Work with a partner and make a list of the possible difficulties an immigrant might face, e.g. finding a place to live, etc.

4. Interpret the diagram on ethnic groups in the UK. Where do the most minorities come from? (▶ Skills 3.4)

5. Listen to Sabrina (Track 3) and make a list of the differences she finds between the UK and Germany. Can you think of reasons how these differences might have originated? What other things do you think are "typically British"? Add them to the list.

6. Ask your classmates about their ethnic origins. Make a graph. (▶ Skills 6.4)

2 An aging society

http://www.bbc.co.uk/news/world-19784509

BBC News Sport Weather Travel Future Autors TV Radio More ... Search

The world needs to do more to prepare for the impact of a rapidly ageing population, the UN has warned – particularly in developing countries.

Within 10 years the number of people aged over 60 will pass one billion, a report by the UN Population Fund said. The demographic shift will present huge challenges to countries' welfare, pension and healthcare systems. The UN agency also said more had to be done to deal with "abuse, neglect and violence against older persons". The number of older people worldwide is growing faster than any other age group. The report, Ageing in the 21st Century: A Celebration and a Challenge, estimates that one in nine people around the world are older than 60. The elderly population is expected to rise by 200 million in the next decade to over one billion, and reach two billion by 2050.

This rising proportion of older people is a consequence of success - improved nutrition, sanitation, healthcare, education and economic well-being are contributing factors, the report says. But the UN and a charity that also contributed to the report, HelpAge International, say the ageing population is being widely mismanaged.

"In many developing countries with large populations of young people, the challenge is that governments have not put policies and practices in place to support their current older populations or made enough preparations for 2050," the agencies said in a joint statement.

'Cast out'

The report warns that the skills and experience of older people are being wasted, with many underemployed and vulnerable to discrimination. HelpAge said more countries needed to introduce pension schemes to ensure economic independence and reduce poverty in old age. It stressed that it was not enough to simply pass legislation – the new schemes needed to be funded properly.

The UN report used India as an example, saying it needed to take urgent steps in this area. Almost two-thirds of India's population is under 30. But it also has 100 million elderly people – a figure that is expected to increase threefold by 2050.

Traditionally, people in India live in large, extended families and elderly people have been well looked after. But the trend now is to have smaller, nuclear families and many of the country's elderly are finding themselves cast out, says the BBC's Sanjoy Majumder in Delhi. There are more and more cases of physical and mental abuse, including neglect, suffered by the elderly at the hands of their families

WORD
POWER

developed country	Industrieland
developing country	Entwicklungsland
threefold	dreifach, dreimalig
fourfold	vierfach, viermalig
fivefold	(usw.)

a mismanaged business
misundertood ideas, misplaced trust, mistaken identity, misguided action

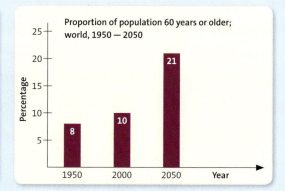

Proportion of population 60 years or older; world, 1950 — 2050

INFO-BOX

What is Demography?

Demography is the statistical study of human populations, especially with reference to size and density, distribution, and vital statistics (births, marriages, deaths, etc.). The population density of a country is commonly represented as people per square mile or square kilometer, which is derived by dividing the total area population by the land area in square kilometers.

B B C   News   Sport   Weather   Travel   Future   Autors   TV   Radio   More ...   Search

The Challenges of an Aging Society

The remarkable gain of about 30 years in life expectancy in western Europe, the USA, Canada, Australia, and New Zealand – and even larger gains in Japan and some western European countries, such as Spain and Italy – is one of the most important achievements of the 20th century.

According to the Human Mortality Database, death rates in life-expectancy leaders such as Japan, Spain, and Sweden imply that even if health conditions do not improve, three quarters of babies will survive to celebrate their 75th birthdays.

Most babies born since 2000 in countries with long-lived citizens will celebrate their 100th birthdays if the present yearly growth in life expectancy continues through the 21st century (table 1).

This forecast is based on the assumption that the number of deaths before age 50 years will remain at 2006 levels.

	2000	2001	2002	2003	2004	2005	2006	2007
Canada	102	102	103	103	103	104	104	104
Denmark	99	99	100	100	101	101	101	101
France	102	102	103	103	103	104	104	104
Germany	99	100	100	100	101	101	101	102
Italy	102	102	102	103	103	103	104	104
Japan	104	105	105	105	106	106	106	107
UK	100	101	101	101	102	102	103	103
USA	101	102	102	103	103	103	104	104

Data are ages in years. Baseline data were obtained from the Human Mortality Database and refer to the total population of the respective countries.

Table 1: Oldest age at which at least 50 % of a birth cohort is still alive in eight countries

elderly	ältere(r, s), ältlich
the elderly	ältere Menschen
middle age	mittleres Lebensalter
middle-aged	mittleren Alters
! (the Middle Ages)	das Mittelalter
pensioner	Rentner(in)
senior citizen	älterer Bürger
gerontology	die Alternsforschung

WORD POWER

TASKS

1. Create a mind map showing the different aspects of an aging society. Use branches such as current situation worldwide, reasons and future problems. (▶ Skills 6.3)

2. Give a two-minute-talk on the topic of the aging society. Concentrate on the future problems. Use the mind map as notes.

3. Discuss ways to overcome the future problems of an aging society. Use a grid to write down both realistic and rather unrealistic ideas.

4. Think about positive outcomes for the younger generations that easily could reach their 100th birthday and still be quite fit. How will people's lives change with higher life expectancies? Write down a list and start like this:
   If I could live to be a hundred years old, I could ...
   – see my great-grandchildren grow up.
   – ...

5. Choose two countries from Table 1 above and explain the data from the year 2000 to 2007. Summarize the trend which can be seen in all the countries.

3   An e-mail "home"

Rupa lives in Bradford, a city in the north of England with a large Bengali community. Both her parents came to Britain from Rangpur, a city in the north of Bangladesh. This is the text of an e-mail from Rupa to her cousin Anjali in Rangpur.

Hi Anjali,

How are you? I'm writing to you this time because Dad is complaining again about our high phone bills! Mum says that if we have the money to pay for flights next August, then we could all fly over and stay with you and your parents. It would be wonderful to meet you and your family face to face for the first time. I'm trying to save up some money for the visit, but it's so difficult. Everything is so expensive nowadays, isn't it? Mam took me shopping for some new clothes yesterday (I really did need some new things for school!) and she bought me a new blouse and then I found these lovely Creole earrings. Do you like them?

Anyway, I've found two weekend jobs! On Saturday and Sunday mornings I deliver newspapers to houses in our neighbourhood. And on Sunday afternoon I go dog-walking. That's like babysitting, but with more running around! One of our neighbours has an Alsatian and another has two terriers and I take them to the park for an hour or two, depending on the weather. I don't earn very much, but I can save most of it.

I like Bradford, most people are friendly and lots of people from Bangladesh live here, too. But I know that Mam and Dad still feel homesick even though they've lived here for nearly thirty years now. They can't wait to see you all again. Dad now has a second job as a caretaker in the local primary school and Mam has a part-time job as a cook in a local Bengali restaurant. She's teaching me how to read and spell Bengali words. My Bengali is getting better, but it's not as good as it should be. Thank goodness that you and your family all speak such good English!

Oh, there's one thing I really have to tell you: my teacher chose me for the main role in next year's theatre play! We do one every year and they're really fun. Next year's play is "The importance of being Earnest" by Oscar Wilde. It's really funny. Do you know it? And I'll be playing the part of Lady Bracknell! Can you imagine me as a lady! I'll have to practise talking with a posh accent, won't I? I'm really pleased because I've only been a member of the theatre group for a year. Do you have a theatre group at your school? I hope you write back soon. Say "Hi" to your family for me!

Love to you all
Rupa

SKILLS

A personal e-mail or letter

The style is conversational and can include short forms, question tags and 'attention catchers' (Oh, Anyway).

INFO-BOX

Mutti

In the USA and Canada it's "Mom". In southern England it's "Mum". In northern England, Wales, Ireland and Scotland it's "Mam". (But it's "Dad" everywhere!)

News Online

| Home | News | U.S. | Sport | TV&Showbiz | Femail | Health | Science | Money | Right Minds | Coffee Break | Travel |

SALEEMA AHMEDANI, 34, and her sister Haleemah, 35, are the founders of Club Asia, a London-based radio station for the Asian community. In 2005, the station was named Best New Business in the UK at the HSBC Start-up Starts Awards and this year the sisters won the Asian Women Of Achievement prize at the Entrepreneur Of The Year awards. Their parents Talib, 62, from Pakistan, and Azeeza, 62, from Mauritius, came to the UK in the 1960s, settling in East London. Haleemah now lives with her family in Essex. Saleema lives with her husband Adil Samal, 33, in a two-bedroom flat in North London. She says:

In our house, as in many Asian family homes, our parents used the radio to keep in touch with the community. There was only one Asian station and it gave everyone a slice of home – sounds, melodies and their native language.

As girls we got used to dancing round the kitchen to Asian music, but at the same time we were growing up in East London so our culture was very much Western as well. At college Haleemah, me and our younger sister Arooj, now 28, all followed traditional careers. Haleemah studied accountancy like our father, Arooj trained to be a doctor and I went to law school, but I really didn't like it. While our parents wanted us to stand on our own, I knew it was possible to do so in other ways.

It was in 2000, when Haleemah and I were in the car, flicking between radio stations, that the idea for Club Asia came to us. There was nothing out there that catered for second-generation Asians like us. I am proud of my culture and want to listen to some traditional music, but I don't speak any Asian languages, so I can't stay tuned to the stations our parents listen to.

We created a station for 15 to 34-year-olds and filled the niche. But it hasn't all been plain sailing – working with a family member can be hard and sometimes it's impossible to stay impartial during work-related arguments. But we trust each other completely and that's invaluable.

TASKS

1. Write a personal e-mail or a letter to a friend or a family member and tell them about your current situation, your plans for the next few months and what is going on at school. Use some of the examples given in the Skills box.

2. Discuss the problems of second-generation immigrants. Some of them are mentioned in the e-mail and in the online article.

4 Trouble and strife

Mr Coe, the director of the school theatre group, has chosen Rupa for the role of Lady Bracknell in "The importance of being Earnest". But not all the members of the theatre group are happy with his choice.

Trisha: That's so unfair! I've been in this group for two years! I always did a good job and never missed a theatre group. Why can't I have a main role?

Mr Coe: What's all this nonsense about a "main' role? All the roles in this play are important. I wanted to give Rupa the chance to show everybody what she has learned so far.

Kevin: I also think it's a bad choice, Mr Coe. Rupa is the youngest member of the group and has the least experience. I just don't think she'll be able to play the role of an elderly woman.

Mr Coe: Well, that's a challenge that every actor or actress faces. I think Rupa is a talented actress and she needs a role that will stretch her.

Trisha: It's just ridiculous! Lady Bracknell is supposed to be an upper-class English lady from the Victorian era and not an Indian Lolita with a northern accent!

Mr Coe: Rupa isn't any of those things, Trisha. And I think you should cool down. We can discuss this further, but only when you aren't angry.

GRAMMAR

Die indirekte Rede (reported speech)

- Wenn das einleitende Verb in der Vergangenheit steht, *(said, told us that, …)* verschieben sich die Zeiten der Verben in dem berichteten Satzteil *(backshift of tenses)*. Zeitangaben und Personalpronomen müssen auch angepasst werden.

Direkte Rede	Indirekte Rede
"These phone bills are too high!"	▶ *Dad complained about the high phone bills.*
"You need some new clothes for school."	▶ *Mam said that I needed some new clothes for school.*
"Do you like my new Creole earrings?"	▶ *I asked her if she liked my new Creole earrings.*
"Can you imagine me as a lady?"	▶ *I asked her if she could imagine me as a lady.*

- Vorsicht! Es gibt einen Unterschied zwischen Befehlen und höflichen Bitten.

Stop whistling!	▶ *He told me to stop whistling.*
Please stop whistling.	▶ *He asked me to stop whistling.*

How to deal with conflict

An interesting discussion can quickly turn into a heated argument. When people become emotionally involved they can be verbally abusive and aggressive. Angry people are often screaming to be heard. They feel rejected and ignored, often because they aren't able to express themselves constructively. If you want to reach an understanding, you must learn to deal with this. The following seven strategies will help you to resolve disputes quickly and peacefully.

1   Remain calm. Say nothing. There's no point in trying to reason with an angry person who wants to provoke you. Let the storm run its course.

2   Don't interrupt. Let the other person talk even if you think they're rambling. Some people can't express themselves well or formulate their arguments clearly, but that doesn't mean that they have nothing to say. Be patient and listen carefully and try to discover what their argument is.

3   Show the other person that you are really listening to them. "Yes, I see what you mean. You think that…" That's all they usually want and this helps to break down their anger.

4   Genuinely consider the other person's point of view. Imagine yourself in their shoes. Never say "You're wrong". Try hard to look for areas of agreement and build on them.

5   If the situation turns verbally abusive, put a stop to it. Firmly but calmly say: "You're very angry right now and you're saying things you don't mean. We can talk again after you calm down." Then leave the room or ask them to leave.

6   If you are wrong, admit it. You could say, "You're absolutely right, it is my fault and here is what I'm going to do to fix it." Even if you think you aren't wrong, at least give them the benefit of the doubt: "Well, perhaps I'm wrong. Let's look at the facts together." It's hard to argue with that! These phrases not only respect the other person's point of view, but they also release tension and defuse potentially explosive situations.

7   Use the power of visualization. If you're dealing with someone you interact with on a daily basis (like a boss or colleague), try to imagine them as a lovable and loving parents.

TASKS

1   Rewrite the dispute in the theatre group using reported speech. Start like this:
    Mr Coe told us that he had chosen Rupa for the role of Lady Bracknell in the play. Trisha said that…

2   Act out a role play between Rupa and Trisha. Apply the strategies from the text above.

1 A cartoon strip

Read the cartoon strip and explain the difference between the first two scenes and the last one.

TRACK 3

2 Listening for detail

Listen to "Sabrina's trip" (Track 3) again and answer the following questions.

1. What's the name of Sabrina's cousin?
2. What's Sabrina's favorite kind of tea?
3. Where did Sabrina and her cousin go for a walk?
4. What was the problem with Sabrina's hairdryer?
5. What's the telephone number of Sabrina's cousin's house?

3 A mind map

Discuss the social effects of higher life expectancy. Create a mind-map which shows these social changes. You can use the following diagram as a guide.

4 **A high death rate**

Make a list of things which could reduce life expectancy. For example:

unhealthy lifestyle

...

5 **The Commonwealth of Nations**

a) *Work with a partner. Look at the map below and try to identify as many Commonwealth countries as you can.*

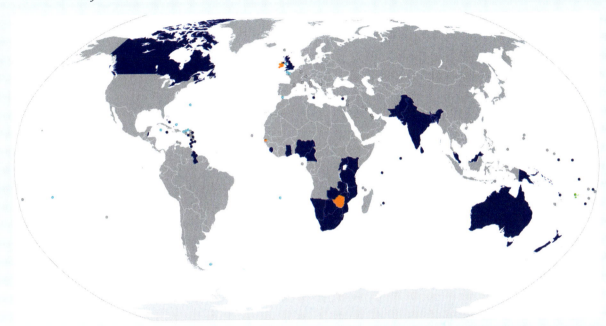

b) *Choose three countries and write down what you know about the history of these countries and the languages spoken there.*

6 **Internet research**

a) *Make two lists:*
   - 10 countries with the highest populations,
   - 10 countries with the lowest populations.

b) *Can you find reasons for the different population densities? Chose one country from each list as an example and explain the reasons for its population density.*

c) *Choose one developed and one developing country and compare and contrast the living conditions and the demographic structure.*

7 **Reading for detail**

a) *Read Rupa's e-mail (p. 40) again and decide whether the following statements are true or false. Correct the false ones in an exercise book.*

1. Rupa's Mam bought her a new dress when they were shopping.
2. On Monday and Sunday mornings Rupa delivers newspapers to houses in the neighbourhood.
3. Rupa's parents still still miss their relatives even though they've lived in Britain for nearly thirty years now.
4. Rupa's mother tongue is Bengali.
5. Rupa can earn extra money by walking the dogs of people in her neighbourhood.
6. In Rupa's neighbourhood of Bradford there are no other people from Bangladesh.

b) *Read the article about Saleema Ahmedani again (p. 41).*
   Summarize in two sentences what "Club Asia" is.

c) *In Saleema's article, which professions does she describe as "traditional"?*

8 **Definitions**

Find the words from this unit which are being described.

1. ... is a Dutch dialect which is spoken in Belgium.
2. There are one hundred years in a ... .
3. ... are people who have escaped war or persecution in their own country and now live in another country.
4. ... is the process where different ethnic or cultural groups intermarry and mix together.
5. ... is the statistical study of human populations.
6. A report about future events such as tomorrow's weather or how financial trends might develop is called a ... .
7. ... is the state of being very poor and unable to buy even basic things.
8. ... is the science of human food and drink.

CHECK

1. I can describe multicultural aspects in countries such as the UK.

2. I can talk about reasons for immigration to the UK.

3. I can write a personal e-mail.

4. I can use reported speech.

5. I can describe and apply techniques for resolving conflict.

6. I can explain what "demography" means.

7. I can point out aspects of an aging society.

UNIT 4
Modern communication

To do

Receptive
- Study texts about the benefits and dangers of social networking
- learn about text messages, their abbreviations and how they work

Productive
- Produce a mindmap about modern communication
- Write a summary

Interactive
- Discuss the pros and cons of Internet dependence
- Discuss and evaluate the problems of Internet identity

1   Social networks

Modern communication has changed dramatically with the development of the Internet. We are still talking about Web 2.0, but very soon, in a few years, it will all have changed to Web 3.0.

Here are some icons – symbols – that indicate modern communication:

Social networking is the grouping of individuals into specific groups, like small rural communities or a local neighbourhood. Although social networking is possible in person, especially in the workplace, universities, and high schools, it is most popular online.

Social networking websites function like an online community of internet users. Depending on the website in question, many of these online community members share common interests in hobbies, religion, politics and alternative lifestyles. Once you are granted access to a social networking website you can begin to socialize. This socialization may include reading the profile pages of other members and possibly even contacting them.

The friends that you can make are just one of the many benefits to social networking online. Another one of those benefits includes diversity, because the Internet gives individuals from all around the world access to social networking sites. This means that although you are in the United States, you could develop an online friendship with someone in Denmark or India. Not only will you make new friends, but you just might learn a thing or two about new cultures or new languages and learning is always a good thing.

Social networking often involves grouping specific individuals or organizations together. While there are a number of social networking websites that focus on particular interests, there are others that do not. The websites without a main focus are often referred to as "traditional" social networking websites and usually have open memberships. This means that anyone can become a member, no matter what their hobbies, beliefs, or views are. However, once you are inside this online community, you can begin to create your own network of friends and eliminate members that do not share common interests or goals.

As I'm sure you're aware, there are dangers associated with social networking including data theft and viruses, which are on the rise. The most prevalent danger, though, often involves online predators or individuals who claim to be someone that they are not. Although danger does exist with networking online, it also exists in the real world, too. Just like you're advised when meeting strangers at clubs and bars, school, or work – you are also advised to proceed with caution online.

By being aware of your cyber-surroundings and who you are talking to, you should be able to safely enjoy social networking online. It will take many phone conversations to get to know someone, but you really won't be able to make a clear judgment until you can meet each other in person. Just use common sense and listen to your inner voice; it will tell you when something doesn't feel right about the online conversations taking place. Once you are well informed and comfortable with your findings, you can begin your search for a suitable networking community to join. This can easily be done by performing a standard Internet search. Your search will likely return a number of results, including MySpace, FriendWise, FriendFinder, Yahoo! 360, Facebook, Orkut, and Classmates.

focus (n)	Fokus; Mittel-, Hauptpunkt
focus (v)	sich auf etwas konzentrieren
profile (n)	Umriss
profile (v)	jmdn. kurz beschreiben
predator (n)	Raubtier; Halsabschneider
predatory (adj)	räuberisch

WORD POWER

TASKS

1. Look at the social media icons in the text. Find them on your smartphone or on the Internet and write out their full names. Add any important social media that are missing from your list. Compare your list with others.

2. How do you personally communicate with people? Draw a mindmap of all the forms, networks and programmes of communication that you use. Compare your mindmap with at least 5 others and discuss which of the mindmaps is the most comprehensive and why. (▶ Skills 6.3)

3. Summarize the main advantages and the dangers of social networking. (▶ Skills 5.3)

2 Is 'txt' mightier than the word?

Is text messaging infecting or liberating the English language? Judge for yourself, as we rewrite classic texts in txt.

When a 13-year-old Scottish girl handed in an essay written in text message shorthand, she explained to her flabbergasted teacher that it was easier than standard English.
She wrote:
"My smmr hols wr CWOT. B4, we used 2go2 NY 2C my bro, his GF & thr 3 :-O kids FTF. ILNY, its a gr8 plc."
(In translation:
"My summer holidays were a complete waste of time. Before, we used to go to New York to see my brother, his girlfriend and their three screaming kids face to face. I love New York. It's a great place.")

The girl's teacher – who asked not to be named – was not impressed, saying: "I could not believe what I was seeing. The page was riddled with hieroglyphics, many of which I simply could not translate."

Text messaging, e-mail and computer spell-checks have long been blamed for declining standards of spelling and grammar. A publisher of a new dictionary warned last Friday of a "degree of crisis" in university students' written English.

Despite the advent of predictive text, which completes words as you write them, and even the launch of next-generation mobile networks, it seems that the simple texting skills people have learnt in the last three or four years will be around for a while, yet. But could the anonymous Scottish schoolgirl be right? Could txt take over more of our expression because addicts simply find it easier than normal writing? And could this mean the liberation of our use of language?
Already, text message shortcuts have been adopted by those keen to get their point across in as little space as possible, be it advertising copy, poetry or Biblical passages.
Even Shakespeare – famously inconsistent in his own spelling – might succumb.
Is it a great travesty to render his more famous passages in text message shorthand?
- 2b or not 2b thats ?
- A @(---`---`--- by any otha name wd sml swEt

LOL! C U 2n8, @7

The Lord's Prayer, for instance, could be thought of as somewhat stuffy even in its updated version, so the satirical Christian online magazine Ship of Fools ran a competition to rewrite it in 160 characters or less – the length of a mobile phone text message. The winner, Matthew Campbell of York University, condensed it into:
"dad@hvn, ur spshl. we want wot u want &urth2b like hvn. giv us food & 4giv r sins lyk we 4giv uvaz. don't test us! save us! bcos we kno ur boss, ur tuf & ur cool 4 eva! ok?"

Before you text

WAIT	&	THINK
WHY	IS IT	TRUE?
AM		HELPFUL?
I		INSPIRING?
TEXTING?		NECESSARY?
		KIND?

Some common SMS codes:

2day *(today)*
B4 *(before)*
HAND *(Have a nice day)*
C U *(See you)*
WYP *(What's your problem?)*
ATM *(at the moment)*
LOL *(laughing out loud)*
HAK *(hugs and kisses)*
LW *(lovely weather)*
<3 *(love)*

Surely such treatment would make epics such as Tolstoy's War and Peace – at present a whopping 1,400+ pages – into a handy pocket-sized read. But linguistics expert Dr Joan Beal doubts that txt versions of the world's great literature will grace bookshelves any time soon. "The only books I can envisage written in text message shorthand would be aimed at the teenage market, if at all. For it would rather spoil the pleasure of reading, having to work out all those abbreviations."

TASKS

1. Mediation: Give an oral summary of the text in German. (▶ Skills 4.0)

2. Discuss with a partner or in a group how you communicate your text messages. Do you use...
   - capital letters?
   - abbreviations?
   - codes?
   - acronyms?
   Write a list of the standard codes you use.

3. Look up the following acronyms in either your dictionary or online: NATO; UK; UNO; OECD; NAFTA; FRG; OPEC; URL; SMS; CD; DVD; AE

4. Look up these common abbreviations: e.g.; i.e.; ff.; etc; syn; adj; opp; conj; pl.; prep.

5. Look up online some of the abbreviations and acronyms used in SMS texts. Explain the basic process of abbreviation in spoken and written English. Choose one aspect, prepare a short report and present your findings to the class. (▶ Skills 1.2)

3　Staying in contact

Florian and Gillian are exchanging text messages:

> Hi Gillian, the skyping wth u was awesome last night – new to me, thanks 4 the xperience. Flo

> thx 4 ur txt, flo. f u thnk skype awesm, read txt i snt u 2day bout wht web 3.0 z gonna b like. xoxo, cu, G

The evolution of the Internet

Many IT-experts call the early phase of the Internet "Web 1.0" and they describe it as a library – a system of information retrieval that worked in only one direction. Users could find information, but they couldn't add to it or change it. Over time and with increasing complexity and technical innovations the way people used the Internet changed. It is often called "Web 2.0" and is more like a big group of friends and acquaintances who talk to each other and exchange information. Information now flows in both directions. This development has brought new problems such as the trustworthiness of the information available, the real identities of the people we are in contact with and the protection and limitation of personal data, to name just a few. While many users are still learning to cope with "Web 2.0", the IT-experts tell us that the Internet is now at the threshold of the next big step: "Web 3.0". How different will it be from the Web we use today?

Internet experts think Web 3.0 is going to be like having a personal assistant who knows practically everything about you and can access all the information on the Internet to answer any question. Many compare Web 3.0 to a giant database. While Web 2.0 uses the Internet to make connections between people, Web 3.0 will use the Internet to make connections with information. Some experts see Web 3.0 replacing the current Web while others believe it will exist as a separate network. It's easier to grasp the concept with an example. Let's say that you're thinking about going on a vacation.

You want to go somewhere warm and tropical. You have set aside a budget of $ 3,000 for your trip. You want a nice place to stay, but you don't want it to take up too much of your budget. You also want a good deal on a flight. With the Web technology currently available to you, you'd have to do a lot of research to find the best vacation options. You'd need to research potential destinations and decide which one is right for you. You might visit two or three travel sites and compare rates for flights and hotel rooms. You'd spend a lot of your time looking through results on various search engine results pages. The entire process could take several hours. According to some Internet experts, with Web 3.0 you'll be able to sit back and let the Internet do all the work for you. You could use a search service and narrow the parameters of your search. The browser program then gathers, analyses and presents the data to you in a way that makes comparison a snap. It can do this because Web 3.0 will be able to understand information on the Web.

Right now, when you use a Web search engine, the engine isn't able to really understand your search. It looks for Web pages that contain the keywords found in your search terms. The search engine can't tell if the Web page is actually relevant for your search. It can only tell that the keyword appears on the Web page. For example, if you searched for the term "Saturn", you'd end up with results for Web pages about the planet and others about the car manufacturer – and in Germany about a multimedia retailer.

A Web 3.0 search engine could find not only the keywords in your search, but also interpret the context of your request. It would return relevant results and suggest other content related to your search terms. In our vacation example, if you typed "tropical vacation destinations under $3,000" as a search request, the Web 3.0 browser might include a list of fun activities or great restaurants related to the search results. It would treat the entire Internet as a massive database of information available for any query.

If your Web 3.0 browser retrieves information for you based on your likes and dislikes, could other people learn things about you that you'd rather keep private simply by examining your search results? What if someone performs an Internet search on you? Will all your activities on the Internet become public knowledge? Some people worry that by the time we have answers to these questions, it'll be too late to do anything about it.

innovate	Neuerungen einführen
innovative	erfindungsreich
innovator	der Neuerer, Innovator(in)
innovation	Neuerung, Neuheit
query	Anfrage
query sth	etwas infrage stellen
querulous	nörglerisch
querulent	eigensinnig, querköpfig

Useful research websites:
* http://www.searchenginecolossus.com
* http://www.thesearchenginelist.com
* http://glossar.ub.uni-kl.de/begriff
* http://www.labnol.org/internet/search/learn-using-boolean-search-operators-google-queries/3106/
* http://www.dogpile.com

1. Translate Gillian's SMS into proper English.

2. Write a summary of the text (The evolution of the Internet). (▶ Skills 5.3)

3. In a small group, discuss the potential benefits and dangers that Web 3.0 might hold for you personally.

4. Discuss in your group what the implications of a personalized and intelligent Internet might be for society in general.

5. Search the Internet for the term "Web 3.0" and collect five URLs of sites that mention the possible advantages and disadvantages. (▶ Skills 1.3)

6. Try out one of the research websites in the Info box above. Find out how it works and give an oral report to your classmates.

7. Make a list of the most important Boolean search operators.

4   Internet and identity

THE HUFFINGTON POST

Dr Layla McCay
Visiting Scholar at Johns Hopkins
Bloomberg School of Public Health

The Internet Never Forgets: How to Live in the 21st Century

Posted: 04/30/2012 2:34 pm

Thanks to social media, something silly you thought or did at age 15 could easily appear for all to judge 10, 20, or 50 years later at the tap of a button. Jeff Rosen told us last night that two-thirds of employers Google their potential employees (when I tweeted this, someone responded that the other third are just being naïve). We've all heard talk of employers demanding their employees' Facebook passwords. And Google's recent move to integrate our information in its products has helped us realize that we can't necessarily rely on privacy settings either. Nor can we just click "delete" – once something's on the Internet, it's pretty hard to take it back, because people share it and modify it until it's not really yours anymore. Which makes it hard to assert the right to be forgotten. Jeff Rosen told us about an Argentinian pop star who sued Google and Yahoo for that right after some racy pictures appeared online and "went viral." She was successful, but it meant them deleting her entire online presence, a move that could be detrimental to living a normal life as the 21st century evolves.

Particularly with the demise of the Internet pseudonym, we are all learning to be accountable for our online personalities, because increasingly, there will be no such thing as leaving your work at the office or keeping your personal life at home. Anyone can follow me on Twitter – past, present and future colleagues, clients, and patients included. So I'm going to avoid writing anything compromising. But I wouldn't necessarily have predicted or implemented this need for caution as a flighty teenager.

But when it comes to good judgment and really, deeply understanding the potential future consequences of everything we do online, I reckon we're all still teenagers, clicking "I have read the terms and conditions" without having done any such thing.

For now, we need to use our psychic superpowers to imagine how every action we take might affect the future us. This approach will affect our online personalities. I wonder whether it might affect our real-life personalities, too … Our paradigm for living has shifted, and probably faster than we can understand the implications. And – like it or not – we all have our heads in the cloud.

Video clips on the Internet

- Key phrase: *The Internet never forgets,* e.g.: http://de.slideshare.net/ southsiouxcitylibrarian/internet-privacy-the-internet-never-forgets
- Keywords: *privacy, security,* e.g.: http://de.slideshare.net/guestf6b86ae/ future-of-privacy-security
- Browser search: *TED Talks – viewing* (1. When Games invade real life; 2. Gotta Share)
- Browser search: *RSA Animate* The Internet in Society: Empowering or Censoring Citizens?

SOCIAL MEDIA EXPLAINED

twitter	**I'm eating a #doughnut.**
facebook	**I like doughnuts.**
foursquare	**This is where I eat doughnuts.**
Instagram	**Here's a photo of a vintage doughnut.**
You Tube	**Watch me eating a doughnut.**
Linked in	**My skills include doughnut eating.**
Pinterest	**Here's a recipe for doughnuts.**
last.fm	**Listening to Doughnuts.**
Google+	**I'm a Google employee who eats doughnuts.**

http://InternationalOfficesupport.blogspot.com/
Working virtually with business owners and individuals locally and world-wide.
Your "get it done" Business Administration Expert

A school with no teachers

Xavier Niel, the founder of a major French telecom company believes that the French educational system fails many young people. Thousands of young people in France can't find jobs, but at the same time French companies can't find enough IT specialists. Thousands of young people are interested in computer technology, but they can't get the training they need because they haven't got the formal educational qualifications. Mr Niel has put millions of Euros of his own money in a new computer school in Paris. The school is simply called "42" and it trains people between 18 and 30 to become computer programmers. The school has a director, but no teachers. The course is free and no educational qualifications are needed. Applicants for the school first have to pass a series of cognitive skills tests online and 4,000 have already done this. After that, potential students meet together and are challenged with computer problems. "We spend four weeks choosing each potential student," says the director, M. Sadirac. "Only 800 will get a place. We're not looking for how much students know, but how they think."

TASKS

1. What do you think? Comment on the statement from Dr McCay's blog: "This approach will affect our online personalities. I wonder whether it might affect our real-life person-alities, too…" (▶ Skills 3.3)

2. Do you think that schools in the future will be able to teach pupils and students without teachers or qualifications? Could schools even become irrelevant?

3. How do you visualize the schoolbooks of the future? Look for information online and then write a short report. (▶ Skills 1.3)

4. Mediation: Watch one of the video clips from the box above and then give an oral report in German. (▶ Skills 4.0)

TRACK 4   **1   WLAN – how does it work?**

a) *Before you listen, talk with your classmates and find out how many of these abbreviations you know:* Wi-Fi, AP, SSID, WPA, PC, WLAN.

b) *Now listen to an IT student's introduction about WLAN. Afterwards discuss it with your classmates and decide whether the following statements are true or false. Correct the incorrect statements in an exercise book.*

1. Wi-Fi, which is short for Wireless Fidelity, is a way of transmitting information in radio wave form. The most widely used standard is 802.11o.
2. An ethernet network broadcasts packets of data which are addressed to particular devices on the network.
3. The computers connect to the network using radio signals and computers can be up to 400 meters apart.
4. An SSID sometimes defines the name of a WLAN network.
5. The SSID broadcasts approximately 10 times per second.
6. The PCs which connects with the WLAN make up an IP address at random that will allow them to connect to the local network.
7. In ad-hoc wireless networks, each computer can only communicate directly with one other computer at a time.
8. More sophisticated kinds of wireless networks use an access point or a bridge.

c) *Which of the advantages mentioned in the recording do you agree with?*
Write down the pros and cons for having a WLAN at home and present your arguments to your class.

2   Icons

a) *What would you use these icons for?*
Compare your results with a partner.

b) *Work with a small group and design a set of personalized icons.*

3   Social networks

Read the text (1. Social networks) again and answer the following questions in an exercise book.

1. Explain what 'social networking' is.
2. What is the main difference between an 'open' and a 'closed' social networking site?
3. Give an example of an 'online predator'.

4   A personal profile quiz

Form a small group of four or five persons.
Each member of the group writes an anonymous personal profile on a sheet of paper.
Fold each sheet of paper and put them in a box. Shake the box well.
One member of the group chooses a profile and reads it aloud.
The other members must try and guess who wrote it.

5 **SMS slang**

What do these SMS terms mean?

1. ASAP
2. ATM
3. B4
4. BFN
5. BTDT
6. CMIIW
7. EOM
8. FOAF
9. HAND

> **FUN FACTS**
>
> - OMG was used in a letter from Lord Fisher to Churchill in 1917.
> - Smileys in letters and on postcards have been traced as far back as 1862.
> - The earliest known example of the letter X to signify a kiss dates back to 1765, but the custom is probably much older.

6 **The Web world**

In an exercise book write a description of the picture on page 55.

7 **Picture words**

a) *The ancient Egyptians used symbols like these to write down their language. What are they called?*

b) *Many modern languages also use symbols. For example: £ (= pound sterling). What other examples can you find?*

8 **Word families**

Find the missing words. The headwords all come from text 1 (Social networks) in this unit. The missing words belong to the same word family (verb, noun, adjective).

1. dramatically *(adv.)*
   Over the last ten years, the changes to the Internet have been *(adj.)* ….
2. indicate *(v.)*
   This is a clear *(n.)* … of how things could change in the future.
3. popular *(adj.)*
   The *(n.)* … of shopping online continues to increase.
4. religion *(n.)*
   Many websites have a *(adj)* … content.
5. socialize *(v.)*
   Some critics think that our modern *(n.)* … is degenerate, but others don't agree.
6. develop *(v.)*
   We don't really know what Web 3.0 will be like – it could bring some surprising *(n.)* ….
7. culture *(n.)*
   Meeting people from other countries can be interesting *(adj.)* … experiences.
8. organization *(n.)*
   To be a good manager you will need good *(adj.)* … skills.
9. belief *(n.)*
   I listened to her explanation carefully and to me it sounded *(adj.)* ….
10. perform *(v.)*
    Team D produced the best video clip of the sketch – it was a fantastic *(n.)* …!

Check your results by looking them up in an (online) English-German dictionary.

9 **Phrasal verbs**

Find the missing words.

1. We are all excited ... about the latest developments in IT technology.
2. I haven't changed ... the new operating system yet.
3. In Chemistry we learn that all the elements can be placed ... specific groups.
4. Amanda and I are both interested ... modern art.
5. When nobody at the party had spoken to me for an hour, I began ... feel ignored.
6. Most men focus ... one task at a time.
7. They claim ... be one of the most experienced firms in this sector.
8. We are looking ... new business opportunities in this region.
9. Can your machines perform ... our standards?
10. We weren't informed ... the change of management.
11. We are searching ... a suitable partner in the IT sector.
12. Please hand ... your exam papers before you leave.
13. I wasn't impressed ... the new marketing manager.
14. Television and the Internet are often blamed ... falling educational standards.
15. Our standards of excellence have been adopted ... many of our competitors.
16. When I want to relax I think ... a sunny beach and the sound of surf.
17. Our CEO is being treated ... megalomania.
18. I ignored the insult, which was obviously aimed ... me.
19. Somone has just sent me an SMS, but I can't work ... what the abbregviations mean!
20. Nobody knew the answer ... my question.

CHECK

1 I can understand texts about the pros and cons of social networking.

2 I can draw a mindmap about modern communication.

3 I can write a summary.

4 I can research the Internet about the development of IT.

5 I can write text messages in English using some abbreviations.

6 I can use Boolean terms to refine internet queries.

7 I can discuss and evaluate the problems of internet identity.

UNIT 5
Economy and business

To do

Receptive
- Finding specific information in a text
- Collecting and organizing material for a talk

Productive
- Making a presentation
- Describing statistics and graphs
- Writing a short technical article

Interactive
- Discussing the pros and cons of flexible working times

Skills
- Visualizing words and ideas

Grammar
- Passives

1   Economic sectors

The economic structure of any country can be divided into three basic sectors.

Primary Sector

Raw materials are obtained from nature

Farmers produce grain, fruit, vegetables or meat. Wood is produced by the forestry industry.

Coal, metal ores, stone or oil and gas are mined or extracted.

Secondary sector

Raw materials (primary products) are transformed into finished goods for use in businesses or by customers.

Tertiary sector

offers a range of helpul services to other businesses and to consumers.

This sector is also referred to as the service sector.

"Would you say we were part of the primary sector?"

As the structure of a country's economy changes, the different sectores may lose or gain importance.

"What's that going to be when it's finished?"

When talking about businesses, you will also find the term sector used in a slightly different way.

The **public sector** is the part in the economy owned and controlled by the state or the government. In many countries this includes:
- most education and healthcare
- utilities like energy, water, refuse collection or transportation

The **private sector** is the part of the economy owned and controlled by private individuals and businesses. If a private-sector business does not provide what customers want, it will make losses and ultimately close down.

Some services are split between public and private sector, for example broadcasting or telecommunications. In the public sector, profit is not always the most important aim. Issues like the need to provide a public service (transport, postal services) or national prestige ('our airline', 'our oil company') may also be significant.

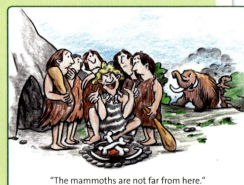

"The mammoths are not far from here."

Phil Connor:
I'm a geologist and I work for an oil company. I travel around the world looking for new oil fields.

Steve Douglas:
I work in a shipyard in Newcastle. We used to build ships, but now most of our orders are for oil platforms.

Shirley Taylor:
I'm a helicopter pilot and I work for a transport firm. We run a daily passenger and cargo service between Aberdeen and several oil platforms.

Rory McEwan:
I'm the production manager of a refinery near Aberdeen. We convert the crude oil from the platforms into various petrochemical products.

Craig Cassidy:
I have a little fish restaurant near the docks. I used to be a fisherman, but the fishing industry in Scotland is nearly dead now. I still have the old boat and I go fishing every morning, but only for an hour or two. Whatever I catch, I serve in my restaurant.

Doreen Bradford:
I'm an estate agent in Aberdeen. Thanks to the oil industry the property market here is very good. There are lots of oil workers looking for homes to buy or rent.

TASKS

1. Read the text on the opposite page and make a list of the different economic sectors.

2. Read the short biographies above and make a list of the jobs and businesses that are mentioned. Decide which economic sector they belong to and determine which industry has had the most effect on the local economy.

3. Think of ten people you know who work in your local area (relatives, friends, neighbours). Make a list of their jobs and decide which economic sector they belong to. Compare your results with your classmates and collect and organize the information you'll need to give a short three-minute talk on the economy and businesses of your local area.

2   Employment structure

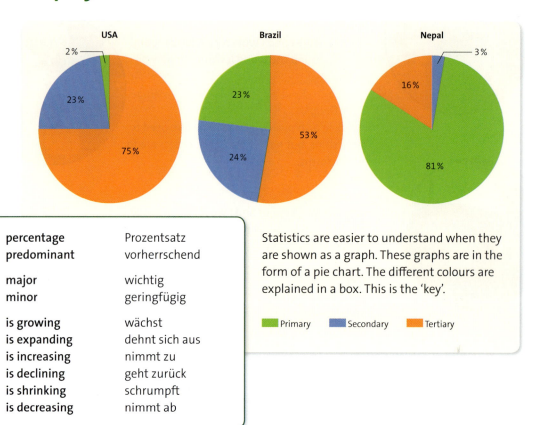

WORD
POWER

ABC

percentage	Prozentsatz
predominant	vorherrschend
major	wichtig
minor	geringfügig
is growing	wächst
is expanding	dehnt sich aus
is increasing	nimmt zu
is declining	geht zurück
is shrinking	schrumpft
is decreasing	nimmt ab

Statistics are easier to understand when they are shown as a graph. These graphs are in the form of a pie chart. The different colours are explained in a box. This is the 'key'.

🟩 Primary   🟦 Secondary   🟧 Tertiary

The various stages of the trade cycle are referred to as:

Depression
(slump, trough)

A long and severe state of reduced economic activity. The low consumption results in a decrease in production, which leads to a fall in profits, a rise in the number of bankruptcies and mass unemployment.

Recovery
(revival, expansion)

Business activities increase and order books fill up, which leads to a rise in production, which creates a demand for more raw materials, machines and workers.

Boom
(prosperity, peak)

A period of intense business activity. The rising demand for goods and services leads to high prices and this produces good profits. There is a high level of employment and workers earn good wages. On the downside, high inflation, rising prices and a shortage of labour, especially skilled labour, can become problematic.

Recession
(slowdown, downswing)

Business activity declines. As production falls, the demand for goods and services also decreases, and unemployment rises.

Stagnation
(standstill)

Economic activities stay at the same level and don't expand. So the demand for goods and services also stays the same and there's no economic encouragement to invest in new machinery or increase the workforce.

a)   **US consumer spending up again**

b)   **Oil prices plummet after OPEC report**

c)   **LOWER GAS SALES HIT GAZPROM**

d)   **World recovery in sight**

e)   **CHINESE EXPORTS TO EUROPE AND THE USA CONTINUE TO RISE**

f)   **Greece cuts back on civil sevice staff**

g)   **MORTGAGE FORECLOSURES IN THE USA REACH RECORD LEVELS**

h)   **UNEMPLOYMENT IN THE USA CONTINUES TO DECLINE**

i)   **Strong retail sales boost market optimism**

j)   **NO CHANGE IN THE ECONOMY FOR TWO YEARS**

TASKS

1. Describe the pie charts which show the employment structures of the USA, Brazil and Nepal. Discuss possible reasons for these differences in a small group and write down the conclusions you reach. (▶ Skills 3.4)

2. Write a summary in German of the trade cycle. (▶ Skills 5.3)

3. Discuss the newspaper headlines in your group and decide which trade cycle they describe.

4. In a previous task you collected information about employment in your local area. Show this information as either a pie chart or a bar graph. (▶ Skills 6.4)

5. Give a three-minute audio-visual presentation on the economy of your local area. (▶ Skills 6.0)

3 Flexible working times

FLEXIBILITY IS GOOD FOR YOU!

At the request of the Cochrane Library, researchers at the Wolfson Research Institute, which is based at Durham University, made a review of ten research studies involving more than 16,000 people. Their review shows that when employees can control their working hours they enjoy better health because they are less stressed and get more rest. People with flexible working arrangements generally had better mental health, blood pressure, and sleep patterns than people with fixed working times. For example: police officers who were able to change their starting times at work also showed significant improvements in psychological well-being compared to police officers who started work at a fixed time.

In contrast, working conditions which were fixed by the employer had no health benefits for the employees. One study even showed fixed working hours had a negative effect on mental well-being. In the United Kingdom, all parents with children under 16 now have the right to request flexible working times. This change in the law, which was introduced in 2011, was highly controversial. Previously only parents of children under the age of six or who were disabled had a right to request flexible working times. Lord Mandelson, a senior member of the Labour government at that time, warned against introducing flexible working times during a recession because of the damage it would do to business. However, he lost the argument to Harriet Harman, the deputy leader of the Labour Party, who was a champion of flexible working times, not least because she knew that this would encourage more women to return to work.

Flexible working is more than just employees being able to choose when they start and finish work. It can include scheduling hours around school times, working from home, job sharing or averaging hours out over a year.

The organization Family-Friendly Working also commissioned a survey, which was published in 2012. It found that a third of parents who had left work after having children said it was because of a lack of flexible working arrangements at the places where they had worked. Three in ten said that the cost of childcare had forced them to give up working. A spokeswoman for the organization said "Many employers already routinely offer far more flexible work than they did ten years ago. Recent figures show that 92 per cent are now prepared to accept a request from any employee. But we want to do more, which is why we have established a taskforce and are working with employers to look at the options around flexible work."

The new ways are better

Nowadays flexible work arrangements offer an alternative way of organizing the traditional working day and week. There are a number of reasons why businesses should offer such arrangements to their employees. They are an excellent way of boosting motivation, creativity and job satisfaction, for instance, and they allow employees to achieve a better work-life balance. Employees who would like to work fewer than the standard 38 or 40 hours a week may opt for part-time work. Such arrangements are also ideal for people who would like to earn some money, but for various reasons do not have the time to work the full number of hours. Employees who work flexible time put in a full day but can vary their working hours. In most cases, however, there are so-called 'core' working hours, when all employees must be at work. For example, they may choose to start between 7:30 and 9:30 am, and finish between 3:30 and 5:30 pm, but they must be in the office between 9:30 am and 3:30 pm. A compressed working week is also increasing in popularity. Such arrangements are very helpful if you require a day off. Instead of working 5 days a week, for example, you just work 4 days but do 10 hours a day instead of just 8.

Another trend is teleworking. This means that employees do some of their work from home instead of going to the office. Studies show that in the USA around 15% of employees spend at least one day a week working from home. Improvements in computer and Internet technology have accelerated this trend. About 10 million Americans already run a business from home.

Term-time work is an attractive arrangement for men or women who want to be at home when their children are on school holiday. It means that an employee only works during the school terms but not during school breaks and holidays.

TASKS

1 Make a list of the different kinds of flexible working.

2 Discuss the pros and cons of flexible working in your group and produce a mind map.
(▶ Skills 6.3)

3 Explain the term 'work-life balance' in the above text.

○ 4 Prepare a role play in which an employee tries to persuade his/her boss (who is basically against any alternative way of organizing the traditional working day) to introduce one or several kinds of flexible working in his/her company.

4 Two online businesses

Amazon

The early days

In 1994, Jeff Bezos, a former investment banker, left New York for Seattle, Washington to start an online bookstore. The website was launched in 1995 based on the business idea of selling books over the Internet. Back then the Internet was very young and website design was not yet a buzzword. Still, Bezos was able to find someone who invested $100,000 in Amazon that year.

Rapid growth

In 1996, its first full financial year in business, Amazon generated $15.7 million in sales. In May 1997, *Amazon.com* went public and in October, Jeff Bezos himself hand-delivered Amazon's one-millionth order to a customer in Japan. One year after its stock market launch, music CDs and videos were added to the website. Another year later, in time for the Christmas holiday, five more product categories followed – electronics, software, toys, video games and home improvement items. This was growth at absolutely breakneck speed and many observers thought that the rapid growth policy would indeed "break their necks". But early investors were convinced that Amazon would make a profit. However, profits didn't come quite so quickly. Instead Amazon grew at express speed and the profits were put back into the business so they could grow faster than the competition. The end of 1999 saw annual sales reach $1.6 billion and on 10 December, Amazon's stock closed at an all-time high of $106.69. In the same month, Time Magazine named Bezos "Person of the Year," calling him the "King of Cybercommerce". But just one month later, the "King's" crown slipped badly.

Amazon.toast

As part of a reorganization plan, Amazon had to make 150 workers redundant. Five days later, they reported a loss of $323 million for the fourth quarter. By the summer of 2000, Amazon's share price had dropped by almost 70% and analysts began to criticize the company for venturing into too many areas. Speculation on Wall Street suggested that Amazon would file for bankruptcy or be bought out. The collapse of the world's largest e-retailer was predicted. In early 2001, when Amazon reported a huge loss of $1.4 billion – the company's worst-ever annual performance – Jeff Bezos finally came up with an answer.

Changing focus

In January 2001, the company's CEO promised a profit by the end of the year. However, expenses had to be cut and the business restructured. Thirteen hundred workers (about 15 percent of the work force) were laid off. Two warehouses and a Seattle customer-service centre were closed. Jeff Bezos gave orders to stop selling unprofitable products. The company concentrated on streamlining its storage, packaging and delivery operation. It boosted its online offer by becoming an online shopping portal, offering and selling products from companies such as Toys "R" Us. It also competed with eBay through Amazon Auctions. By the end of 2001, Jeff Bezos had kept his word. Amazon reported its first profit with fourth-quarter earnings of $5 million. It was clear that one quarter of profits would not be enough but since then profits have steadily improved. This was only achieved by continuously pushing sales and increasing business efficiency as well as expanding the product lines offered on the website.

Success at last

Amazon has survived and is making a profit – a fact that analysts and observers doubted would ever happen. The company has grown into a multibillion-dollar business and is now among the most important online businesses.

Google

The beginning

Google's founders Larry Page and Sergey Brin both studied computer science when they were graduate students at Stanford University in California in 1995. One of their interests was to find a way to handle and organize the immense mass of data and information available nowadays. Just one year later, they began working on a search engine called BackRub.

Finding a partner

During the first half of 1998, Larry and Sergey continued to perfect their technology. They didn't want to set up their own company, so they decided to look for potential partners to licence what they called the best search technology available. Despite the technology boom, interest in Google, as it was known by then, was very limited. Their friend David Filo, founder of Yahoo, encouraged Larry and Sergey to start a search engine company and develop the service themselves.

Go for it

They needed cash, so they set up a business plan. When they found an investor he wrote out a cheque for $ 100,000 to Google, Inc. which didn't exist at that time. In order to be able to cash the cheque they had to actually found the company. So over the next couple of weeks, Larry and Sergey were busy with the task of setting up a company. Ultimately they raised almost $ 1 million. On 7 September 1998, Google Inc. opened its doors in Menlo Park, California. At that time Google was already answering 10,000 search queries every day. Three months later, PC Magazine named Google one of its Top 100 websites and search engines. Google was moving up in the world. They'd made it! Since then, the company has expanded enormously with over 1,900 employees worldwide, and a management team containing some of the most experienced technology professionals in the industry.

Stock market launch

Google made its stock market debut in August 2004 with a share price of $ 85. It soon rocketed and after about three months the share price stood at around $ 170. However, just over one year later a share was worth $ 300, making Google worth about $ 85 billion. Google remains one of the fastest-growing companies and the most-used search engine in the world, earning the lion's share of its income from online advertising.

Not just a search engine

Google also serves corporate clients, including advertisers, publishers and website managers with cost-effective advertising and a wide range of search services which generate income. In addition to the straight-forward search engine, Google also provides many other services. For example: Ask a Question – a service involving over 500 carefully-screened researchers and University Search giving detailed information on specific schools, mail-order catalogues, directories on various topics, shopping sites, updated news from 700 sources, discussion forums and much more. Google Earth now enables you to virtually explore the world from the comfort of your own home.

(September, 2007)

TASKS

1   Work in pairs. Student A reads the Amazon text and Student B reads the Google text. Both students must find and write down the following information about their company: *name • founded in • founded by • the beginning • after a year • stock market • named in which magazine*
Then ask each other questions about the businesses and make a list of the similarities and differences.

2   Conduct a class survey: Who uses Google and Amazon? How often? For what?

5   The etiquette of business meetings

The way you conduct yourself in the company of colleagues, clients or customers will influence your success or failure in the business world. There are certain dos and don'ts you should observe if you want to be successful. Business meetings, both formal and informal, are occasions where good business etiquette is required. The most senior person (the chairman or chairperson or simply 'the chair') usually calls the meeting and decides the time, place and agenda. Etiquette demands that the meeting is announced at least two or three days before so that the people concerned can actually attend. They should also know the purpose of the meeting and how long it will last so that everybody can come prepared and make arrangements accordingly.

Punctuality is an absolute must. Keeping people waiting means wasting their time. The chair must make sure that the meeting stays within the agenda and is kept as short and effective as possible. The chair should appoint someone to 'keep the minutes', i.e. record the proceedings, noting down major decisions. This protocol, called 'the minutes', will then be distributed to the attendees for reference. Should the results of the meeting have an effect on people who were not present at the meeting, it is good etiquette to let them have a copy of the minutes.

When you attend such a meeting, especially a formal one, make sure you observe the following points:

- Prepare well for the meeting. Should you want to use statistics or other information in your contribution, it is good etiquette to hand out printed copies of these at least a day or so before the meeting.
- Dress appropriately and arrive in good time.
- Make sure your mobile phone is switched off!
- If you are not allocated a seat, ask where to sit down.
- When there is a discussion, allow more senior persons to contribute first.
- Never interrupt anyone. Take note of what was said and indicate to the chair that you wish to make a contribution. When you have permission to make your comment, you can refer to your notes.
- When you speak, be brief and make sure that what you say is relevant.
- Always address the chair unless this does not seem to be common practice in the particular context.
- What is said in meetings should be considered confidential. Never pass on information to others unless you are instructed to do so.

Sticking to these rules will certainly improve your career chances.

In the US, when you start working for a large corporation, you will probably find yourself in a rather small and confined workspace, separated from your co-workers only by a thin partition less than two meters high. No window, no view. Welcome to the world of the cubicle!

Many cubicles together make a 'cube farm', a term Americans use in a humorous but rather negative way. Every cubicle has a built-in desk, overhead storage and shelves. It is usually open on one side, so that you can go in and out. Sounds cosy, doesn't it! And just think of all the space it saves!

In the US the cubicle culture reflects the social structure within a company. Those working in them (also referred to as 'cubicle dwellers') have a rather low status in the office. Managers and supervisors, on the other hand, work in corner offices, located around the centre space where the cubicles are. They have movable furniture, solid walls and windows.

But cubicle dwellers shouldn't be depressed, they are not alone! About forty million Americans, that's almost sixty percent of the white-collar workforce, work in cubicles.

GRAMMAR

Passives

- Dieser Satz steht im „Aktiv": *Our company **sends** its catalogue to customers online.*
  Wir erfahren, was das Subjekt *(company)* macht.

- Dieser Satz steht im „Passiv": *Our catalogues are sent to customers online.*
  Wir erfahren, was mit dem Subjekt *(catalogues)* gemacht wurde. Man soll ein Passiv benutzen, wenn das Subjekt (der „Täter") entweder unbekannt oder unwichtig ist, z. B.:
  *Our staff **are paid** well.*

TASKS

1. In the text about business etiquette, identify which of the dos and dont's are now old-fashioned and out of date and explain why.

2. Discuss modern business etiquette in your group and make your own list of dos and don'ts.

3. Imagine working in a small cubicle. Discuss this in your group and make a list of 'Good cubicle etiquette'.

1 **Statistics and graphs**

Statistics often make more sense when they are shown in the form of a graph. Convert the following statistics into either a pie chart or a bar graph. Give the graphs a title and produce a key.

a) Employment structure in the United Kingdom (2012):
Primary: 2.5 %
Secondary: 32.5 %
Tertiary: 65 %

b) Full-time and part-time employment in the Federal Republic of Germany

FULL-TIME EMPLOYMENT			
Year	Men	Women	Together
2002	94.8 %	60.8 %	79.7 %
2012	89.3 %	54.4 %	73.2 %
PART-TIME EMPLOYMENT			
2002	5.2 %	39.2 %	20.3 %
2012	10.7 %	45.6 %	26.3 %

c) *Use the statistics above to write a short article about the employment structure in Germany.*
   – *Describe how it has changed over the last ten years and give possible reasons for these changes.*
   – *Express your personal opinion about these changes.*
   – *Explain the possible effects on society in general if these trends continue for another ten years. (▶ Skills 5.4)*

TRACK 5   **2** **What I need**

You're going to hear three people (Kerry, Ed and Lavonda) talk about three things they'd like to have in their offices.

a) *In an exercise book make a table with two columns:*
   the names of the people + the three things they want
   Then listen to track 5 and write down the three things each of them wants in their offices.

b) Use the table of names and wishes in your exercise book to answer the following questions.
   1. Who likes plants?
   2. Who is disorganized and a bit lazy?
   3. Who has a friendly personality and is very sociable?
   4. Who smokes?

c) *Which of the three people would you like (or not like) to share an office with?*
    Give reasons for your choice.

3 **Economic sectors**

a) *In an exercise book, organize the following list of economic activities and institutions into the primary, secondary or tertiary sectors.*

mining for gold • hotels • manufacturing sports shoes • shops • growing crops • drilling for oil • building houses or roads • fishing • banks • travel agencies • restaurants

b) *Decide which of the three economic sectors each photo shows.*
(The photos could show more than one setor.)

4 **Professions**

What jobs are being described?

1. … grow and harvest crops.
2. … look for new sources of valuable minerals or resources such as oil and natural gas.
3. … oversee industrial processes in factories. They solve production problems and keep things running as smoothly and efficiently as possible.
4. … go to sea in boats and ships and catch fish.
5. … understand the private and commercial property market in their area. They help people who want to buy or rent a flat, a house, an office, a warehouse or an office.
6. … are specialists in finding and assessing specific information.
7. … regulate society. They try to catch and stop people who break the laws which govern society.
8. … are people who buy shares in a business.
9. … are the top managers of big businesses and multinational companies. Their title is usually abbreviated to an acronym.

5 **A new product**

In an exercise book, rewrite the following text using passive forms.

Last week the chairman's secretary sent us the date and time of the next marketing meeting. The next day she gave us all a copy of the agenda. This morning she told us that the meeting would start an hour later. At the meeting, the chairman asked us if we accepted the minutes of the last meeting. After that the chairman asked Ms Donovan to give us an audio-visual presentation of our newest product. The engineering team has now solved all the technical problems. They have also reduced the weight by 32 % and the price by 9 %. We can put it on the market two month's earlier than planned. The chairman then informed us that there is still one problem for us to solve: What are we going to call the damned thing!

Start like this:
Last week we were sent the date and time of …

6 Just for fun

Professor Doctor Hasselbach's "Wages theorem" states that: Engineers and scientists can never earn as much as business executives and sales managers. Professor Doctor Hasselbach supports his theorem by a mathematical equation based on two postulates:

1. KNOWLEDGE IS POWER.
2. TIME IS MONEY.

- SO AS EVERY ENGINEER KNOWS: POWER = WORK / TIME
- SINCE: KNOWLEDGE = POWER
         TIME = MONEY
- IT FOLLOWS THAT: KNOWLEDGE = WORK / MONEY
- SOLVING FOR MONEY WE GET: MONEY = WORK / KNOWLEDGE
- NOTE THAT AS KNOWLEDGE APPROACHES ZERO, MONEY APPROACHES INFINITY, REGARDLESS OF THE AMOUNT OF WORK DONE.
- CONCLUSION:

THE LESS YOU KNOW, THE MORE MONEY YOU MAKE.

CHECK

1. I can find specific information in a text.
2. I can collect material and organize it for a talk or a preseentation.
3. I can make an audio-visual presentation.
4. I can write a summary of a technical text.
5. I can describe statistics and graphs.
6. I can discuss the pros and cons of flexible working.
7. I can use a mind map to visualize ideas.
8. I can recognize and understand passive forms.
9. I can use passive forms.
10. I can write a short technical article.

UNIT 6
Technology

To do

Receptive
- Understanding a technical text
- Comparing and contrasting technical texts

Productive
- Explaining the meaning of graphs and statistical data
- Taking notes while listening to a dialogue and then writing a summary

Interactive
- Mediating between two languages

Skills
- Writing a summary
- Using the Internet for reference and research

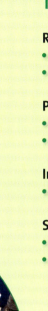

1   The rising cost of energy

Nicola Savage is a student at Newcastle University and she has just got the annual gas and electric bill for her small flat. It's for £ 520 and she's really shocked. That's £98 more than she paid the previous year. She decides to go to the local Citizen's Advice Bureau. She talks to Alice Miller, who gives her some good advice.

Nicola: My gas and electric bill is nearly a hundred pounds more than I thought it would be. My flat is only 540 square feet and I'm living on my own!

Alice: May I see the bill, please? Thanks. Yes, well, the prices for gas and electricity have risen about 50 % over the last 20 years. Many people think the prices are too high – I certainly do. Unfortunately there's not much we can do about that except complain to the power companies and pressure the government to introduce fairer regulations. Will you have a problem paying the bill?

Nicola: No, I have some money saved. But perhaps you can tell me what I can do to save some money on future power bills?

Alice: The first thing to do is look on the Internet and see if you can find a cheaper provider. You'll have to fill out several online forms, but it's worth it. You can save up to 15 %. I can give you a list of providers that offer a cheaper tariff than your present electric company.

Nicola: Great! I'll do that. Is there anything else I can do?

Alice: Lower your heating. Just one degree less will save you about six per cent.

Nicola: That's good to know.

Alice: Only open windows wide for a short time – just enough to air the room. Check your electrical appliances and make sure they are all working at an economic energy level.

Nicola: Oh, I've got an old fridge from my grandma and my mum's old washing maschine. Perhaps I should replace them.

Alice: Buying new appliances is expensive, but it can save you money in the long term. Modern appliances are much more economical. You could also start thinking about connecting parts of your home to make it a smart home. That can save large amounts of money.

Nicola: That sounds interesting.

Alice: You'll find everything you need in this brochure. If you follow the advice it gives, you can save up to thirty per cent of your present power bill.

Nicola: Thank you. You've been very helpful.

a)

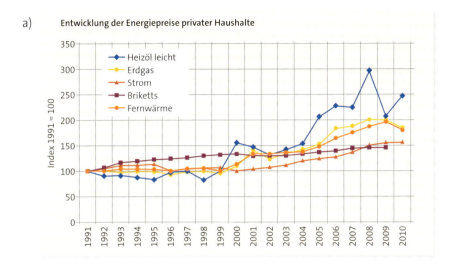

Entwicklung der Energiepreise privater Haushalte

- Heizöl leicht
- Erdgas
- Strom
- Briketts
- Fernwärme

Index 1991 = 100

b)

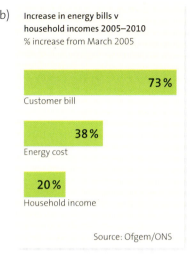

Increase in energy bills v household incomes 2005–2010
% increase from March 2005

73 % Customer bill

38 % Energy cost

20 % Household income

Source: Ofgem/ONS

c)

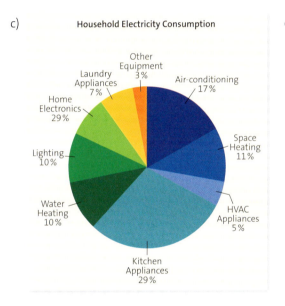

Household Electricity Consumption

- Other Equipment 3 %
- Laundry Appliances 7 %
- Home Electronics 29 %
- Lighting 10 %
- Water Heating 10 %
- Kitchen Appliances 29 %
- HVAC Appliances 5 %
- Space Heating 11 %
- Air-conditioning 17 %

d)

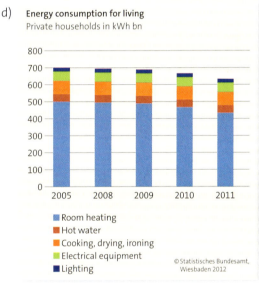

Energy consumption for living
Private households in kWh bn

- Room heating
- Hot water
- Cooking, drying, ironing
- Electrical equipment
- Lighting

© Statistisches Bundesamt, Wiesbaden 2012

TRACK 6

Technology in the home
The four speakers have very different ideas of what a perfect home should be.

TASKS

1. In a small group, discuss energy-saving tips in German. Make a list of the suggestions and then produce a brochure in English with energy-saving tips. (▶ Skills 4.0)

2. Describe one of the graphs (a–d) and explain what it means. (▶ Skills 3.4)

3. Listen to the audio-text on track 6. Make notes of how Duncan Jacobs, Tom Green, Laura Mendor and Rose Cleeves describe their homes. Compare your notes with your classmates. Then write a summary. (▶ Skills 5.3)

2   Smart home systems

How "smart" is your house?

The Vandell house prepares for the arrival of its owners

When Charles and Stacey Vandell, two extremely busy computer scientists, return home from one of their frequent business trips, they don't have to worry about a cold house anymore. Their state-of-the-art, five-bedroom house near Dorchester has already turned on the heating via a mobile phone command and knows their favourite room temperature – 74 degrees Fahrenheit (= 23.3 °C). It welcomes its owners with their favourite background music – Nina Simone, and sensors in the fridge might have even alerted the local supermarket if it was short on drinks or food.

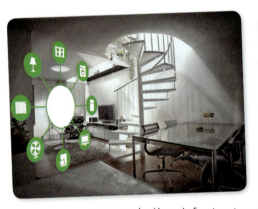

Their house reacts automatically or by remote control

The Vandells turned their posh estate into a "smart" house by installing a communications infrastructure that allows various computer systems and devices to communicate with each other. Individual rooms and spaces are connected to network servers which can keep track of their owners' preferences and change the room conditions automatically.

In such a "smart" house the use of computer controls removes the need to actually press a switch or turn a knob to make something work and allows elements of the home to be remote-controlled or to respond automatically to the people living in it.

Only the Vandells can control their house.

The Vandells equipped their home with a telephone-operated security panel that was installed in the hall. It also operates an answerphone and can be used to call the house and tell it to carry out certain actions. This system relies on a PIN code to ensure that only they can control the house in this way.

Their house offers help for daily chores, as well as safety measures

The house has automated daily routines and chores. The security system adjusts the heating during the day. Motion detectors turn the lights on or off, and heat sensors control the temperature of the pool in the backyard. If there is a gas leak, the safety system will immediately switch the gas off. The house will sound an alarm and disconnect the light switches, so that they cannot be used accidentally and cause a spark.

In case of a fire, the smoke and heat detectors in each room will activate the fire alarm, call the fire brigade, turn on lights to guide the Vandells to the exits and unlock the outside doors to guarantee a free exit or entry.

Burglars would not only be filmed by automatic cameras, but videos of their actions would be sent directly to police headquarters over the Internet.

The Vandell house provides a glimpse into the future

Voice-controlled jukeboxes are connected to motion detectors and the network. Songs are selected from gigabytes of available music, and the sound follows your steps through the house. Giant flat TV screens suddenly appear behind sliding wall panels and turn off or on at the owners' command.

While much of the underlying technology is not new, it is still rare in private homes as the equipment is relatively expensive, especially the controllers that connect all the devices. Still, the Vandell house certainly provides a glimpse of what homes might routinely look like in the future. Packed with electronic gadgets, they assist the owners as much as possible with their daily lives.

Schalt die Heizung mit dem Handy aus

Den Haushalt per iPhone steuern: Neue Technik macht's möglich. Mit simpelsten Lösungen für jedermann wollen Start-ups die Verbraucher dazu bringen, Energiemanagement zu betreiben. Ein Massenmarkt mit Milliardenpotential – auf den auch Giganten wie Microsoft und Google drängen.

Der Energiesektor hat einen neuen Modetrend. Die iPhone-App. Die deutsche Firma eQ-3 hat ein Programm geschrieben, das Fenster, Heizkörper, Lichtschalter und Dutzende weitere Dinge im Haushalt per Fingerzeig kontrolliert. Das US-Start-up Control4 bietet ein Heimmanagementsystem, das beim Filmegucken automatisch das Licht dimmt und PC und Fernseher sperrt, solange die Kinder Hausaufgaben machen – auch dieses Programm lässt sich seit kurzem über iPhone und iPod Touch steuern.

Dass der App-Wahn jetzt auch den Energiesektor erreicht, ist kein Zufall, sondern Kalkül. Die modischen Miniprogramme sollen eine Technik, die seit mehr als einem Jahrzehnt den Durchbruch am Markt nicht schafft, endlich trendy machen. Es geht ums Smart Home. Die Vision eines intelligenten, energieeffizienten Hauses.

Reading comprehension

SKILLS

Anticipating:	Bilder, Überschriften, Textsorte, Vermutungen?
Skimming:	Text überfliegen ▶ Worum geht es im Groben?
Scanning:	Text genau lessen ▶ Welche Informationen brauchen Sie? wh-Fragen: *Who? What? Where? When? Why?*

TASKS

1   Define the term 'smart home' as it is described in the two texts. (▶ Skills 2.1)

2   Sum up the German text by writing a short article for the students magazine about it. (▶ Skills 5.4)

3   Compare and contrast the two texts.

○ 4   Comment on the statement "Smart homes mean the end of communication."

○ 5   Design your own ideal smart house and explain it in an audio-visual presentation. (▶ Skills 6.0)

3   Science fiction or reality?

True love

My name is Joe. That is what my colleague, Milton Davidson, calls me. He is a programmer and I am a computer program. I am part of the Multivac-complex and am connected with other parts all over the world. I know everything. Almost everything.

I am Milton's private program. His Joe. He understands more about programming than anyone in the world, and I am his experimental model. He has made me speak better than any other computer can.

"It's just a matter of matching sounds to symbols, Joe," he told me. "That's the way it works in the human brain even though we still don't know what symbols there are in the brain.

I know the symbols in yours, and I can match them to words, one-to-one." So I talk. I don't think I talk as well as I think, but Milton says I talk very well. Milton has never married, though he is nearly forty years old. He has never found the right woman, he told me. One day he said, "I'll find her yet, Joe. I'm going to find the best. I'm going to have true love and you're going to help me. I'm tired of improving you in order to solve the problems of the world. Solve my problem. Find me true love."

I said, "What is true love?"

"Never mind. That is abstract. Just find me the ideal girl. You are connected to the Multivac-complex so you can reach the data banks of every human being in the world. We'll eliminate them all by groups and classes until we're left with only one person. The perfect person. She will be for me."

I said, "I am ready."

He said, "Eliminate all men first."

It was easy. His words activated symbols in my molecular valves. I could reach out to make contact with the accumulated data on every human being in the world. At his words, I withdrew from 3,784,982,874 men. I kept contact with 3,786,112,090 women.

He said, "Eliminate all younger than twenty-five; all older than forty. Then eliminate all with an IQ under 120; all with a height under 150 centimeters and over 175 centimeters."

He gave me exact measurements; he eliminated women with living children; he eliminated women with various genetic characteristics. "I'm not sure about eye color," he said. "Let that go for a while. But no red hair. I don't like red hair."

After two weeks, we were down to 235 women. They all spoke English very well. Milton said he didn't want a language problem. Even computer-translation would get in the way at intimate moments.

"I can't interview 235 women," he said. "It would take too much time, and people would discover what I am doing."

"It would make trouble," I said. Milton had arranged me to do things I wasn't designed to do. No one knew about that.

"It's none of their business," he said, and the skin on his face grew red. "I tell you what, Joe, I will bring in holographs, and you check the list for similarities."

He brought in holographs of women. "These are three beauty contest winners," he said. "Do any of the 235 match?"

Eight were very good matches and Milton said, "Good, you have their data banks. Study requirements and needs in the job market and arrange to have them assigned here. One at a time, of course." He thought a while, moved his shoulders up and down, and said, "Alphabetical order."

That is one of the things I am not designed to do. Shifting people from job to job for personal reasons is called manipulation. I could do it now because Milton had arranged it. I wasn't supposed to do it for anyone but him, though.

The first girl arrived a week later. Milton's face turned red when he saw her. He spoke as though it were hard to do so. They were together a great deal and he paid no attention to me. One time he said, "Let me take you to dinner."

The next day he said to me, "It was no good, somehow. There was something missing. She's a beautiful woman, but I didn't feel any touch of true love. Try the next one."

It was the same with all eight. They were much alike. They smiled a great deal and had pleasant voices, but Milton always found it wasn't right. He said, "I can't understand it, Joe. You and I have picked out the eight women who, in all the world, look the best to me. They are ideal. Why don't they please me?"

I said, "Do you please them?"

His eyebrows moved and he pushed one fist hard against his other hand. "That's it, Joe. It's a two-way street. If I am not their ideal, they can't act in such a way as to be my ideal. I must be their true love, too, but how do I do that?" He seemed to be thinking all that day.

The next morning he came to me and said, "I'm going to leave it to you, Joe. All up to you. You have my data bank, and I am going to tell you everything I know about myself. You fill up my data bank in every possible detail but keep all additions to yourself".

"What will I do with the data bank, then, Milton?"

"Then you will match it to the 235 women. No, 227. Leave out the eight you've seen. Arrange to have each undergo a psychiatric examination. Fill up their data banks and compare them with mine. Find correlations." (Arranging psychiatric examinations is another thing that is against my original instructions.)

For weeks, Milton talked to me. He told me of his parents and his siblings. He told me of his childhood and his schooling and his adolescence. He told me of the young women he had admired from a distance. His data bank grew and he adjusted me to broaden and deepen my symbol-taking.

He said, "You see, Joe, as you get more and more of me in you, I adjust you to match me better and better. You get to think more like me, so you understand me better. If you understand me well enough, then any woman, whose data bank is something you understand as well, would be my true love." He kept talking to me and I came to understand him better and better.

I could make longer sentences and my expressions grew more complicated. My speech began to sound a good deal like his in vocabulary, word order and style. I said to him one time, "You see, Milton, it isn't a matter of fitting a girl to a physical ideal only. You need a girl who is a personal, emotional, temperamental fit to you. If that happens, looks are secondary. If we can't find the fit in these 227, we'll look elsewhere. We will find someone who won't care how you look either, or how anyone would look, as long as the personality fits. What are looks?"

"Absolutely," he said. "I would have known this if I had had more to do with women in my life. Of course, thinking about it makes it all plain now."

We always agreed; we thought so like each other. "We shouldn't have any trouble, now, Milton, if you'd let me ask you questions. I can see where, in your data bank, there are blank spots and unevennesses." What followed, Milton said, was the equivalent of a careful psychoanalysis. Of course. I was learning from the psychiatric examinations of the 227 women –on all of which I was keeping close tabs.

Milton seemed quite happy. He said, "Talking to you, Joe, is almost like talking to another self. Our personalities have come to match perfectly!"

"So will the personality of the woman we choose."

For I had found her and she was one of the 227 after all. Her name was Charity Jones and she was an Evaluator at the Library of History in Witchita. Her extended data bank fit ours perfectly. All the other women had fallen into discard in one respect or another as the data banks grew fuller, but with Charity there was increasing and astonishing resonance.

I didn't have to describe her to Milton. Milton had coordinated my symbolism so closely with his own I could tell the resonance directly. It fit me. Next it was a matter of adjusting the work sheets and job requirements in such a way as to get Charity assigned to us. It must be done very delicately, so no one would know that anything illegal had taken place. (…)

by Isaac Asimov

TASKS

1 Who or what is the narrator?

2 Explain what Milton was trying to do and express your opinion on the morality of this. (▶ Skills 3.3)

3 The final paragraph of the story is missing. Discuss with your group what might happen next. Then find the story on the Internet and see how it really ends. (▶ Skills 1.3)

4   Hybrid motor systems

Electric cars are a dead end

Electric cars aren't a new idea – car manufacturers have been developing them for more than a hundred years. An electric motor is not only cheaper than an ICE (internal combustion engine), it is also lighter, cheaper to produce, more durable, cleaner and it works more efficiently and economically. The problem has always been the power supply, whether this is a battery or a fuel cell. Fuel cells are still too expensive and even modern batteries can't store enough power. This limits the driving range of electric cars. There are other problems, too. There aren't enough charging stations and charging the battery takes too long. Many car manufacturers think that a hybrid vehicle is the way forward.

A hybrid vehicle combines two propulsion systems which are usually a petrol engine and an electric motor. When combined with start-stop technology, regenerative braking, advanced aerodynamics, and lightweight materials these hybrids have a good driving range, are environmentally-friendly and can be produced at a price which is attractive to customers. Car manufacturers now produce two kinds of hybid vehicles: series hybrids and parallel hybrids.

A series hybrid consists of an ICE (usually a petrol engine) and two electric motors. These three components are placed one after the other ('in series') to form a power chain. The petrol engine isn't used to power the vehicle. It drives the first electic motor which then drives a generator which produces the power to charge the batteries and drive the second electric motor. This is connected to the transmission and drives the vehicle. The main disadvantages of this system are its higher production costs and heavier weight.

Parallel hybrids also use a petrol engine, but only one electric motor. Both engines are connected to the transmission and can drive the vehicle. The electric motor is used a low speeds and on level ground, the petrol engine is used to travel faster, carry loads or to climb gradients. Parallel hybrids are cheaper than series hybrids and just as economical with fuel. However, they have a higher level of waste emissions. This makes them potentially less marketable as the environmental regulations in many countries are now slowly moving towards zero emissions.

The most successful hybrid car on the market to date is the Toyota Prius, which uses a mixed hybrid system. The Prius can accelerate up to 60 kph using just the electric motor. The petrol engine only kicks in at this speed. The main technological innovation is the power split device. It's an intelligent, computer-controlled planetary gearbox that connects the petrol motor with the electric motor. This means that the vehicle can operate either like a series hybrid or a parallel hybrid – whichever is the most suitable for a specific condition. It combines the advantages of both systems and eliminates most of their disadvantages.

a)
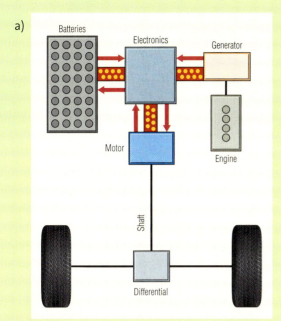

b)
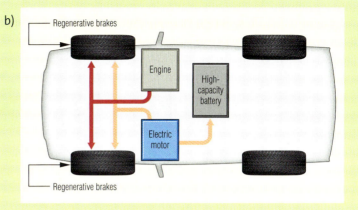

c)
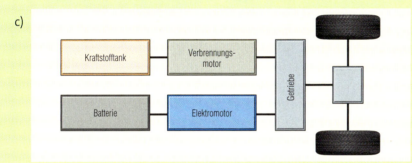

series hybrid
parallel hybrid
mixed hybrid

1 Read the text and study the three illustrations above. Identify the type of hybrid system each illustration shows.

2 Produce your own sketches of all three illustrations and then use an online dictionary to ...
   – label a) and b) in German.
   – label c) in English.

3 Mediation: You have a friend who wants to buy an economical and environmentally-friendly car. He / She doesn't speak English. Explain in German the main pros and cons of conventional cars with petrol engines, electric cars and the different types of hybrid engines for cars. (▶ Skills 4.0)

4 Internet research: Work in a small group, share the research and produce either an illustrated article or an audio-visual presentation on the advantages and disadvantages of different types of internal combustion engines, electric motors, and hybrid systems. (▶ Skills 1.3)

5   Household robots

ROBOMOW

Do you enjoy a garden, but you hate having to mow the lawn?

Now you can just sit back and watch ROBOMOW™ produce a perfect lawn.

ROBOMOW™ is a fully robotic lawn-mower and it works around the clock in all weathers. It's not just user-friendly, but environmentally responsible as well, since it is powered by electricity and produces no harmful exhaust emissions. It continuously cuts the grass in random patterns within the boundaries you decide. When it's time to recharge the battery, it automatically returns to its charging station. It works perfectly and without complaint even in hilly gardens with a complex shape. If it meets an obstacle such as a tree or rock, it reverses and chooses a new direction. It's very safe and is absolutely no danger to pets or children.

For more information download our User's Guide and Product Catalogue.

FAQ

1   Can I do the installation myself?
2   Do I need to bury the wire in the ground?
3   What is the maximum operational area for Robomow?
4   Can Robomow detect objects such as clothes or toys lying around on the lawn?
5   Can Robomow cut very long grass?
6   What's the function of the GPS communication device?
7   What's the life expectancy of the battery?
8   How long do the cutting blades last?
9   What are the benefits of mowing the lawn in a random pattern?

A Robomow can handle lawns up to 6000 m².

B For long grass you should raise the cutting height and then gradually reduce it to the preferred level. In very extreme conditions the lawn may need to be cut first with a conventional lawnmower.

C Yes, just follow the instructions in the operator's manual. It takes 2−5 hours, depending on the size and complexity of the lawn.

D This depends on the area and set running time of the mower. If you run robomow for six months a year on an area of 800 m², your battery will last 2−4 seasons. In order to save your battery you should set the timer according to the size of your lawn.

E By mowing in a seemingly random pattern, in various directions, you will get a carpet-like lawn, throughout your garden. It has also proven to be the most reliable way to cover the whole lawn, leaving no uncut grass.

F No. The wire can be laid on the ground and after some weeks it will be grown over and disappear in to the grass.

G Normally, the blades will need to be replaced every two months. The lightweight blades can be replaced in five minutes using a regular screwdriver.

H No. It is up to the owner to keep the lawn surface free from objects. Any object that is small enough for Robmow to pass over may be damaged, as well as cause damage to the machine's blades. Make sure your lawn is clear of small objects before operating.

I The on-board GPS simplifies installation and assists with the navigation and acts as a tracker in case the product is stolen. The user can also communicate with the mower via SMS or an iPhone app.

TASKS

1 Explain how robot lawnmowers work.

2 Match the Frequently Asked Questions (1−9) with the correct answers (A−I).

3 Internet research: Robots in the home. Find out what other robotic household appliances exist. (▶ Skills 1.3)

TRACK 6   **1**   **'Technology in the home'**

a) Listen to track 6 again and identify the people in the photos.

Duncan Jacobs
Tom Green
Laura Mendor
Rose Cleeves

Photo one shows ...
Photo two shows ...

...

b) *Read through the following questions. Then listen to Track 6 again and make a note of the information you need to answer them.*

Speaker 1: Duncan Jacobs.
   1 What is his profession?
   2 What is his wife's profession?
   3 What does the acronym 'EIB' stand for?
   4 What happens when someone sits on the sofa?

Speaker 2: Tom Green
   5 What's his wife's name?
   6 How many children do they have?
   7 Did Tom and his wife grow up in a city or in the country?
   8 What is their home made of?

Speaker 3: Laura Mendor
   9 What's her big hobby?
   10 Why doesn't she like 'electronic fuss'?

Speaker 4: Rose Cleeves
   11 Where do Rose and her partner live?
   12 Neither Rose nor her partner are good cooks, so why do they have 'state-of-the-art' kitchen equipment?

2   **Internet research**

Find information about Isaac Asimov on the Internet and write a short biography.

3 A hybrid motor

Match the four illustrations to the four operational modes.

Operational mode:

a) Both the petrol motor and the electric motor are driving the vehicle.
b) Regenerative braking: brake power is converted into electrical power and stored.
c) The petrol engine is driving the vehicle and charging the battery.
d) Only the electric motor is in operation.

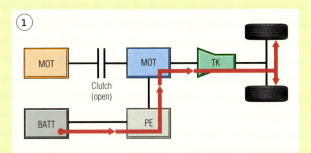

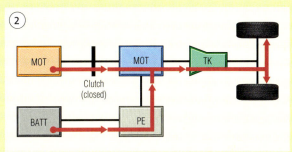

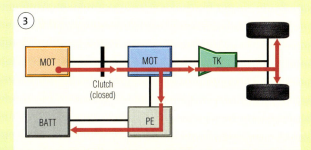

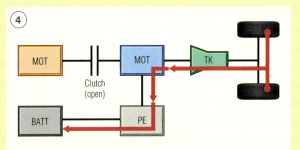

4 The electric bill

Complete the following text with the missing words. Use your exercise book.

I've got a problem (1) ... this year's bill (2) ... electric and gas. It's more (3) ... I thought it would be, even though I live (4) ... my own. It's also difficult (5) ... understand and I'm thinking (6) ... writing (7) ... the power company and complaining! I've got enough money (8) ... pay the bill, but that money was (9) ... my summer holiday. I got a useful brochure (10) ... the Citizen's Advice Bureau. It's full (11) ... good energy-saving tips. They told me that if I do everything it suggests, I could save (12) ... 30 % (13) ... my power costs.

5 A robot sketch

Act the following sketch with 2 partners.

Ellen: Why have you bought a new robot, Jim?

Jim: It's got a lie detector function. Let's try it out on our son. Brad, come here.

Brad: What is it now?

Jim: Where were you this morning?

Brad: In school of course.
(WHACK! Robot slaps son.)
OK, OK. I went to the cinema and watched an adventure fim.
(WHACK! Robot slaps son again.)
OK! It was a porno film!

Jim: You should be ashamed of yourself! At your age I didn't know what a porno film was!
(WHACK! Robot slaps father.)

Ellen: Ha ha! You really deserved that, Jim. After all, he's your son.
(WHACK! Robot slaps mother.)

CHECK

1 I can understand and work with a technical text.

2 I can compare and contrast technicl texts.

3 I can describe graphs and explain their meaning.

4 I can listen to a dialogue and take notes.

5 I can write a summary.

6 I can mediate between German and English.

7 I can use the Internet to find information.

UNIT 7
Health care

To do

Receptive
- Listen to an interview

Productive
- Talk about how to quit smoking
- Discuss healthcare systems in other countries

Interactive
- Discuss healthy ways of living

Skills
- Interpreting statistics

1   Health risks

Smoke-Free Workplace Leads to Fewer Heart Attacks
New York Times, 29.10.2012

Cancer experts condemn councils for offering sunbeds in leisure centres
The Guardian, 06.08.2011

FRUIT JUICE HAS BENEFITS, BUT CALORIES OUTWEIGH THEM, EXPERTS SAY
Washington Post, 16.10.2012

Herzerkrankungen nehmen weltweit zu
Frankfurter Allgemeine Zeitung, 07.09.2012

Hautkrebs-Risiko bei jedem fünften Kindergartenkind
Berliner Morgenpost, 13.09.2012

Was Sportler trinken sollten
Süddeutsche Zeitung, 06.08.2012

ZWEI ZIGARETTEN AM TAG MACHEN TEENIS SÜCHTIG
Die Welt, 13.09.2012

Kampf gegen Fettleibigkeit: New York verbietet Großportionen von Limonade
Spiegel-Online, 13.09.2012

A documentary

In the 2004 documentary film "Supersize Me" the actor and director Morgan Spurlock turns a spotlight on the subjects of health, nutrition, and corporate greed. He asks a simple question: What happens when you eat three meals a day at McDonald's for thirty days?

He ate everything on the menu at least once – from Big Mac hamburgers to yogurt parfaits, salads and fish filets. His health was monitored every step of the way by a team of highly-qualified doctors. The film provides a dramatic answer – your body falls apart!

Spurlock gained eleven kilos in weight, became depressed and withdrawn, suffered from severe headaches, mood swings and cardiac arrhythmia (chest pains). All of these shocking changes take place on camera. After thirty days, he goes into liver failure.

Spurlock claimed that the reason for his investigation was the spread of obesity throughout U.S. society

A dental assistant

What's the most rewarding part of being a dental assistant?
Mark: Working with people. Teaching them how to look after their teeth, and calming their fears – many people are afraid of dentists – and at times even helping them to understand their insurance and whether they can afford the dental care that they need.

What do you like best about your job?
Mark: Working with people, the different people you meet, people from all walks of life and people of all ages. The variety of people coming through the office certainly keeps things interesting and each day is a new experience.

You know some people well because you see them so often. Why are they such frequent visitors?
Mark: Well, the most frequent patients are those with orthodontic problems such as chronic jaw pain associated with overbites and underbites, etc.. The treatment can be very long and re-movable appliances like braces, have to be checked and adjusted frequently. It's also neces-sary to monitor progress so that we can see that everything is moving along as well as ex-pected. Some patients need to be seen every three or four months in order to maintain proper care.

How do you feel about your dentist's attitude toward the team of dental assistants?
Mark: Dentists really appreciate the help that dental assistants give them and it shows in their at-titude. Most of the time our dentist treats us like equal members of a team. I always feel re-spected and appreciated.

When did you know that you wanted to become a dentist assistant? Did someone inspire you?
Mark: ven as a kid I knew I wanted to do something in the health sector. But I knew that the years of study needed to become a physician would be too much for me. So I decided on an alter-native – and I think this was the best choice for me.

TASKS

1   Imagine the content of the articles behind these headlines. Discuss in class.

2   With a partner talk about the impact the film Supersize Me made on American society.

3   Discuss how media such as television, newspaper, magazines etc. can influence people's behavior towards healthy living.

4   Read the interview with Mark, the dental assistant. Describe his motivations for working in medicine and the reasons why he likes his profession. (▶ Skills 2.0)

2   Health insurance

In some countries without medical insurance, illness can be a financial catastrophe. Health insurance provides financial cover for visits to the doctor, treatment at a hospital, medicine and other medical expenses.

In most European countries, the government plays a central role in the provision of health care, either directly as in the National Health System of the United Kingdom or indirectly in the control and regulation of the private medical insurance sector.

In the USA, a loosely-regulated private sector plays the dominant role in medical insurance because of the American tradition of individual independence and the wish to limit the power of federal government. About 190 million Americans (out of about 320 million) have some form of private health insurance.

Of these 190 million insured Americans, about 35 million people use the Medicare program. This is a federal government health insurance programme for people over 65 and for those who are on social security disability, i.e. unable to work. Another 32 million or so people use the Medicaid programme. This is a health insurance that helps people who can't afford full private medical care to pay for some or all of their basic medical bills. Members of the military forces are provided with free medical insurance and some employers provide some or all of their

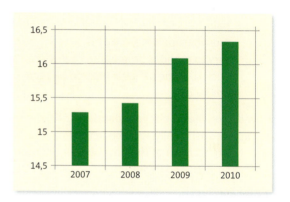

employees with either full or limited health insurance. Patients without any kind of insurance cover must pay for medical services privately. According to the US Census Bureau's 2011 current population survey, there were 49.9 million uninsured individuals in 2010, i.e. 16.3 % of the total population.

The health insurance system in Germany is a private insurance system financed by employees, who contribute between 10 % and 15 % of their monthly income, employers, who contribute an equivalent amount, and the federal government, which pays the medical contributions of pensioners, the unemployed, the chronically ill and citizens who require social security benefits. The mandatory universal cover is provided by "Krankenkassen". Besides basic health insurance these non-profit medical insurance companies also cover the costs of emergency treatment and long-term care. About 7 % of employees choose to insure themselves with a private health insurance company.

Deutsche fürchten Verfall des Gesundheitssystems

Pflegenotstand, Ärztemangel, steigende Kosten für Millionen Menschen: Die Deutschen zweifeln laut einer Umfrage an der Zukunftsfähigkeit des Gesundheitssystems.

Zwei Drittel der Deutschen fürchten einen Ärztemangel, 80 Prozent eine Zwei-Klassen-Medizin, und nur etwa jeder Siebte glaubt, dass sich die derzeitige Versorgung aufrechterhalten lässt. Das sind nur einige der wenig erfreulichen Ergebnisse aus dem sechsten MLP-Gesundheitsreport, einer repräsentativen Erhebung. Die Umfrage ergab im Kern zwei Dinge: Die Deutschen sind mit dem aktuellen Gesundheitssystem zwar weitgehend zufrieden. Doch sie blicken äußerst sorgenvoll in die Zukunft. Insgesamt ist die Zufriedenheit mit der aktuellen Gesundheitsversorgung gewachsen.

Die Entwicklung in den kommenden zehn Jahren schätzt die Bevölkerung aber als sehr pessimistisch ein. 79 Prozent erwarten steigende Kassenbeiträge, 78 Prozent höhere Zuzahlungen für Medikamente. Dabei werde es auch immer mehr zu einer „Zwei-Klassen-Medizin" kommen, sagen 79 Prozent. Außerdem erwarten zahlreiche Bürger, dass der demografische Wandel das Gesundheitssystem zunehmend belastet: 61 Prozent rechnen mit volleren Arztpraxen und Problemen, einen Termin zu erhalten. 51 Prozent gehen sogar davon aus, dass teure Behandlungen bei älteren Menschen aus Kostengründen nicht mehr durchgeführt werden.
Viele Bürger nehmen ihr Schicksal inzwischen selbst in die Hand. 43 Prozent plädieren dafür, dass man oberhalb der Grundsicherung eigenverantwortlich privat vorsorgt – anstatt auf den Staat zu vertrauen.

TASKS

1. Explain the benefits of having a health insurance by giving specific examples.

2. Summarize the main facts of the health care systems in Germany and the USA.

3. Mediate a discussion of the two health systems between a German colleague who speaks very little English and an American visitor, who speaks no German. (▶ Skills 4.0)

3 How do you put a nation on a diet?

The Walt Disney Company last week announced plans to limit junk food commercials on its television programs for children. A few days before, Mayor Michael Bloomberg took steps to limit the sale of sugary drinks in New York. But isolated changes may not make a significant difference at a time when Americans are gaining weight as a nation. Reducing obesity will require a broader shift in the culture.

For decades, people have treated obesity as a personal failure. They blame individuals and families for eating junk food and choosing television over exercise. But experts in this country and other industrialized nations have increasingly recognized that obesity is caused mostly by social and environmental factors that limit people's ability to eat healthy foods and get enough exercise. Our modern society, with its enormous and diverse food supply and labour-saving technologies, makes this difficult.

The consensus of experts, in a report by the Institute of Medicine, is that only a nationwide approach based on prevention will work. It won't be easy, but it needs to be done as costs linked to obesity rise ever higher. A responsible estimate quoted by the institute indicates that the annual cost of treating obesity-related illness, like diabetes, cardiovascular disease and cancer, and the added cost of treating almost any medical condition when the patient is obese, has already reached $ 190 billion. (...)

Obesity affects the whole nation, affecting every group and income level. Some ethnic groups, however, are disproportionately obese and need greater attention. It is especially important, some experts say, to start early and reduce obesity among children and adolescents.

The causes of obesity are everywhere. Social factors play a big role: the lack of safe places to play, walk or bike; sedentary jobs; less time spent cooking and more eating out; bigger portion sizes in packaged and prepared food; and constant marketing of junk foods that are high in calories. Drinks sweetened with sugar accounted for at least 20 percent of the increases in weight in the United States between 1977 and 2007 (...).

The institute says that a major cut in obesity rates will require multiple strategies on a population-wide scale. This will be even more challenging than the fight against smoking. But there isn't any choice if we want to protect the public's health, the strength of the economy and the government budget.

INFO-BOX

SQ3R is a strategy for detailed reading: Survey, Question, Read, Recite, Review. (▶ Skills 2.1)

A **mind map** is a useful method for visualizing and organizing information or ideas. (▶ Skills 6.3)

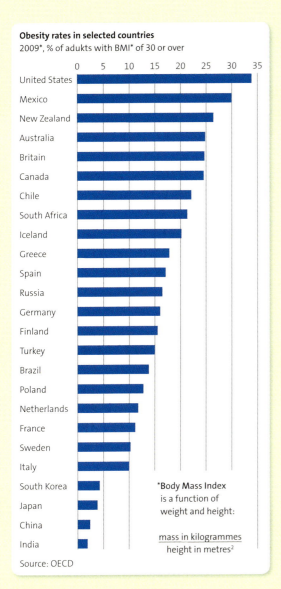

Obesity rates in selected countries
2009*, % of adukts with BMI* of 30 or over

United States	~33
Mexico	~30
New Zealand	~27
Australia	~25
Britain	~25
Canada	~24
Chile	~22
South Africa	~21
Iceland	~20
Greece	~18
Spain	~17
Russia	~16
Germany	~16
Finland	~15
Turkey	~15
Brazil	~13
Poland	~12
Netherlands	~11
France	~11
Sweden	~10
Italy	~10
South Korea	~4
Japan	~4
China	~2
India	~2

*Body Mass Index
is a function of
weight and height:

$$\frac{mass\ in\ kilogrammes}{height\ in\ metres^2}$$

Source: OECD

WORD POWER

obesity (n)	Fettleibigkeit, Fettsucht
corpulence (n)	Korpulenz, Fülle
stoutness (n)	Beleibtheit, Stämmigkeit
obese (adj)	fettleibig, korpulent
overweight (adj)	übergewichtig
grossly fat (adj)	extrem fett
corpulent (adj)	korpulent
stout (adj)	füllig
overfeed (v)	überfüttern
overfed (adj)	überfüttert
emaciation (n)	Abmagerung
emaciated (adj)	abgemagert, abgezehrt
percent = AE per cent = BE	Prozent; prozentig
percentage	Prozentanteil
has increased to ...	ist auf ... gestiegen
has reached ...	hat ... erreicht
has fallen to ...	ist auf ... gefallen
is ... percent less	ist ... Prozent unter
than the level in ...	dem Niveau von ...

TASKS

1. Read the text according to the SQ3R-method and then create a mind map of the factors that lead to obesity. (▶ Skills 2.1)

2. Oral: Explain in your own words why obesity is so expensive for a nation such as the United States.
   Written: Then summarize the main information.

3. Discuss strategies that could reduce the high rate of obesity (think of health education programs in schools, food labelling, etc.

4. Interpret the statistics "Obesity rates in selected countries". Compare countries with the highest rates with those that have low rates. Give reasons for these differences. (▶ Skills 3.4)

5. Make a list called "The ten golden rules of staying healthy" For example:
   Rule 1: Eat some kind of fruit with at least one meal.

4   Anti-smoking campaigns

Anti-smoking campaigns and laws have turned smokers into a despised underclass, a study by the Department of Health in the UK warned yesterday. It said smokers have come to be seen as disgusting and dirty and are now often regarded as outcasts. Smokers are like migrant groups in past centuries who were seen as a threat to the way of life of normal, healthy people.

INFO-BOX

What is addiction?

An estimated two million people in the UK have an addiction to some form of substance (e.g. nicotine, alcohol) or activity (e.g. playing computer games). Addiction is a complex illness with physical and psychological symptoms, affecting not only the patient, but their family, friends and social environment too.

SMOKING IS A CAUSE
OF VARIOUS FATAL
DISEASES INCLUDING,
LUNG CANCER, EMPHYSEMA
AND HEART DISEASE.

addiction (n)	Sucht
addict (n)	Süchtige(r)
addicted to … (adj)	der / dem … verfallen (heroin)süchtig
warning	Warnung
warn about (v)	warnen vor
addict sb to sth (v)	jmdn (…)süchtig machen
disgusting (adj)	ekelhaft
scary (adj)	schaurig, unheimlich
stop, quit (v)	aufhören
give up (v)	abgewöhnen
prevent (v)	verhindern, vermeiden
tumour therapy	Tumortherapie
chemotherapy	Chemotherapie
treatment	Behandlung
medication	medikamentöse Behandlung

TASKS

1. Look at the anti-smoking advertisements. Chose one and describe how the ad conveys its message. (▶ Skills 3.5)

2. Create your own anti-smoking ad.

3. Say in your own words why anti-smoking campaigns have become so successful.

4. Do a survey among your teachers and find general answers to the following questions:
   a) What is addiction?
   b) What are causes for addiction?
   c) What are effects of an addiction?
   d) How can addictions be treated?
   e) Where can addicts get help?

TRACK 7 **① An interview with a nurse**

Patricia, 28, is being interviewed by a reporter about her job as a nurse.

Listen to the interview with Patricia and note down in an exercise book ...
- *why she likes being a nurse,*
- *how she decided to become a nurse,*
- *future trends in healthcare,*
- *her suggestions for anyone interested in nursing.*

② Patricia and Mark

Go back in this unit to the interview with Mark, the dental assistant. Read the interview with Mark again. Compare what he says about his job to how Patricia describes hers. Explain any differences and / or similarities you may find.

③ Translation

How would you translate these well-known advertising slogans into German? (You probably won't be able to do it by translating them word for word!) Use an exercise book.

1. Because you're worth it – L'Oréal
2. Have it your way. – Burger King
3. I'm lovin' it – McDonald's
4. Obey your thirst. – Sprite
5. Same time tomorrow? – Pepsi
6. It's everywhere you want to be.– VISA
7. For men who don't have to try too hard. – Denim aftershave

④ Prevention

These slogans are from campaigns to prevent something. Organize them into these categories:
1. anti-smoking, 2. anti-alcohol, 3. anti-drug, 4. anti-war. Then explain them.

a) Sobriety is a journey ... not a destination
b) Do a good deed and kill the weed
c) War is lack of imagination
d) The problem with drinking and driving is ... The MOURNING after!
e) Don't do Pot, Your brain will rot
f) Today you turn me into ashes, but tomorrow is my turn
g) Drink and drive in Alabama and our officers will show you some new bars
h) Support our troops: Bring them home
i) Shoot for the Stars not your arms

5 **Parts of the body**

In an exercise book, write a key to the illustration. Check your results with a partner.

6 **Joints and organs**

In an exercise book:
Organize the following body parts into two categories: joints and organs. Match them with the numbers in the illustration. Then translate the words into German.

ankle
appendix
elbow
hip
jaw
kidneys
knee
liver
lungs
shoulder
stomach
wrist
knuckle
spleen

7 **Synonyms**

Read the text A documentary again. Find the words and phrases in the text which have the same or similar meanings to the following words and phrases.

1. highlight (v)
2. avarice (n)
3. uncomplicated (adj)
4. keep under observation (verb phrase)
5. put on (v)
6. retiring (adj)
7. growth (n)
8. corpulence (n)

GRAMMAR

Will-Futur oder Going to-Futur?

- Je nach Sprechabsicht wählt ein Sprecher eine der beiden Zukunftsformen:
  Doctor: I'm going to ask the nurse to take some blood samples, Miss Meadows. (= Absicht)
  Doctor: We'll have the results of your blood test by Thursday, Miss Meadows. (= Annahme)

- Sind die Sprechabsichten unbekannt oder nicht erkennbar, sind beide Formen austauschbar:
  Nurse: The doctor will/is going to give you an injection.
  Friend: Will/Are you going to get a tongue piercing?

8 **Will-future and going to-future**

Rewrite the sentences with the alternative future form.

1. Many experts think that only a nationwide approach is going to work.
2. It won't be easy, but it needs to be done.
3. A major cut in obesity rates will require multiple strategies.
4. The fight against obesity is going to be very challenging.
5. In the future, Healthcare will become even more technology-based.
6. There are going to be more healthcare providers in the future.
7. Health insurance companies think there are going to be significant benefits from emphasizing prevention.
8. If the jungle disappears, scientists are going to lose millions of potential drugs.

CHECK

1 I can talk about healthy ways of living.

2 I can discuss anti-smoking-campaigns.

3 I can explain the danger of being obese.

4 I can describe typical jobs in the health business.

5 I can discuss the influence of media on our lifestyle.

6 I can say why a health insurance is important.

7 I can compare different systems of health insurance in the USA and Germany.

8 I can interpret statistics.

UNIT 8
Nutrition

To do

Receptive
- Listen to technical texts
- Compare and contrast two different systems
- Interpret a cartoon

Productive
- Prepare presentation slides
- Write a letter of complaint

Interactive
- Role play a discussion

Skills
- Online research

Grammar
- Relative sentences

1   The basics of life

In 2005, when the iPod received the prestigious INDEX award, a product called LifeStraw® received the award in the category 'Body'. Three years later the same product earned another award, namely the Saatchi & Saatchi Award for World-Changing Ideas. These are only two of a number of awards LifeStraw® has received ever since.

So, why should this product have the power to change the world? Because it provides clean drinking water for people in developing countries. LifeStraw® is a water-filtration device with a simple mechanical filter. It has a string attached to it, which means it is worn around the neck and, above all, it makes contaminated water drinkable. This makes it a crucial tool in fighting a number of water-borne diseases such as diphtheria, typhoid, and diarrhoea which kill millions of children each year. LifeStraw® saves lives.

The philosophy behind LifeStraw® is simple and practical: innovative design and existing technology are combined to create a product that is targeted at people who need help. The inventor and manufacturer of the product is the Danish family-owned company Vestergaard Frandsen which was founded in the 1950s and started off as a manufacturer of work uniforms. The product is both innovative and user-friendly.

It is incredibly easy to use because it requires neither power nor spare parts, and it is inexpensive at a cost of less than $3. LifeStraw® is a 30-cm-long turquoise plastic cylinder which contains a specially developed halogen-based resin that kills 99.9 % of bacteria and more than 98 % of viruses that can cause deadly diseases. It has a high-impact proof polystyrene outer shell.

It can filter out everything except heavy metals. One single LifeStraw® can filter about 700 litres of water, which means it lasts for about a year. It is easy to use, because all you have to do is to dip it in water and sip through the mouthpiece. Cleaning is easy as well, since it just needs to be wiped clean and sometimes you have to blow through it.

Research has demonstrated that it really works. Findings have shown that LifeStraw® eradicates large amounts of contaminants and removes particles as small as 15 microns. When the water is muddy, it is recommended to drink from the surface to make sure the straw doesn't clog.

TRACK 8

Global water distribution

Linda Marooney introduces Dr Pete Schaeffer, one of Britain's leading hydrologists. He's reporting from the World Water Week Forum in Stockholm, Sweden. He talks about the problems of water distribution around the world. Afterwards, we hear from John Tynan, a marketing specialist from New York, who talks about the phenomenon of bottled water.

SODIS stands for solar disinfection and it's a method of disinfecting water using only bright sunlight and PET bottles. It was developed in 2001 by a Swiss inventor called Martin Wegelin. The idea behind it is incredibly easy: a polyethylene bottle is filled to two-thirds with contaminated water and exposed to bright sunlight for six hours. In this time, the UV radiation kills the harmful bacteria in the water.

Good slides are ...

- **clear**   The 'message' is easy to understand.
- **simple**   Don't overdo things by using too many colours, different fonts and print sizes or unnecessary animations.
- **readable**   Make sure there's a good colour contrast between the text and the background and that the size of the print is big enough to read easily.

SKILLS

TASKS

1. Explain the meaning of water in your life.

2. Listen to the report 'Global water distribution' (Track 8). Take notes on what Dr Schaeffer says about the problems of water distribution around the world and and what Mr Tynan tells us about the bottled water business.

3. Use the information in your notes from task two to produce four presentation slides on this topic. Work in small groups. Use the Internet and find bar charts, pie charts, diagrams etc. that you can use on your slides. (▶ Skills 6.1)

4. Read about an invention called LifeStraw and a Swiss project called SODIS, which has made a major contribution to making water drinkable in Africa. Compare the information from both texts and make notes. Think about ...
   - the mission and its purpose,
   - the company,
   - the type of product,
   - technical details, (e.g. how it deals with turbid water)
   - the limitations of the projects,
   - the awards,
   - the countries where it is used
   - the price.
   (You can find additional information at www.sodis.ch.) (▶ Skills 1.0)

5. Use the information from task 4 to write an article about the two water projects. In the conclusion, say which project you think is more important and why. (▶ Skills 5.4)

2   Complaining

The wonderful shrinking Caramello

Dear Sir or Madam,

I have been a loyal purchaser of your products for many years and I am very fond of Caramellos. I always buy two or three rolls when I go shopping.

So you will understand my disappointment when I found that the rolls I bought at the local supermarket last Friday contained only 11 sweets instead of the usual 12, although I paid the same price.

I can only assume that a mistake has occurred in the production process. Or could there be another reason for this unfortunate incident? In any case, I should be grateful if you could shed some light on the matter.

I am looking forward to hearing from you.

Yours faithfully
Martin Bellamy

You know Caramellos, don't you? That's right, rolls of soft toffee sweets, each one in a delicious milk chocolate cup.

I'm supposed to avoid sweet things but I make an exception for Caramellos. I treat myself to one roll per week, which I pick up at the till in the supermarket when I do my weekly shopping. Sometimes I scoff the lot with the midnight movie on Friday; sometimes I ration myself to one or two a day. Imagine then my horror when I realized that the manufacturer had reduced the number of melting mouthfuls from 12 to 11 per roll, while still charging the same price. Come off it, you might say. It's only one chocolate less. And, anyway, it's certainly better for you to eat one Caramello less per week. Oh yes, but what if they go on reducing the number? I'll soon have to buy two rolls of Caramello at twice the price to get my weekly chocolate fix, I suppose.

We can observe the same thing happening with other products, too. Manufacturers are devising ever more ingenious ways of selling us less for the same amount of money. And proof of their dishonest intentions is the fact that they don't tell us what they're doing. Nobody writes, 'Now 10% less contents!' Take everyday items like tinned tuna or fabric softener, for example. Sometimes the packaging looks the same, but the contents are magically diminished by 10 g, let's say. The tin of tuna used to contain 150 g of fish, but now, if you read the small print, you will find that the new drained weight is 140 g. On other occasions, you'll find that a new, revamped bottle holds 150 ml less fabric softener than the old one.

Cleaning liquids or sprays seem less effective. I'm beginning to suspect that they're diluted, an alternative strategy to sneakily reducing the contents of a product. Here again, nobody invites you to try new, weaker Sudso washing-up liquid. I can see from the gadgets on my kitchen and loo walls that paper kitchen towels and toilet paper rolls have become narrower across as well as shorter in length, selling at the same price, of course.

Both over-the-counter and prescription medicines contain fewer tablets or less mixture than before. Overall, we are currently spending considerably more than we used to on the same quantities of everyday items. In other words, the official inflation rate does not tell us the whole truth. If you ask me, my missing Caramello is a symptom of a hidden inflation that poses a serious threat to our standard of living.

SKILLS

A letter of complaint

A basic letter of complaint usually has three paragraphs:

- Paragraph 1 explains the reason for the complaint.
- Paragraph 2 tries to persuade the addressee to take the writer seriously.
- Paragraph 3 requests something. Either an explanation or an apology or restitution (Wiedergutmachung)

a)

b)

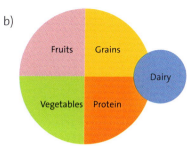

Vegetables	Fruits	Grains	Dairy	Protein Foods
Eat more red, orange, and dark-green veggies like tomatoes, sweet potatoes, and broccoli in main dishes. Add beans or peas to salads (kidney or chickpeas), soups (split peas or lentils), and side dishes (pinto or baked beans), or serve as a main dish. Fresh, frozen, and canned vegetables all count. Choose "reduced sodium" or "no-salt-added" canned veggies.	Use fruits as snacks, salads, and desserts. At breakfast, top your cereal with bananas or strawberries; add blueberries to pancakes. Buy fruits that are dried, frozen, and canned (in water or 100% juice), as well as fresh fruits. Select 100% fruit juice when choosing juices.	Substitute whole-grain choices for refined-grain breads, bagels, rolls, breakfast cereals, crackers, rice, and pasta. Check the ingredients list on product labels for the words "whole" or "whole grain" before the grain ingredient name. Choose products that name a whole grain first on the ingredients list.	Choose skim (fat-free) or 1% (low-fat) milk. They have the same amount of calcium and other essential nutrients as whole milk, but less fat and calories. Top fruit salads and baked potatoes with low-fat yogurt. If you are lactose intolerant, try lactose-free milk or fortified soymilk (soy beverage).	Eat a variety of foods from the protein food group each week, such as seafood, beans and peas, and nuts as well as lean meats, poultry, and eggs. Twice a week, make seafood the protein on your plate. Choose lean meats and ground beef that are at least 90% lean. Trim or drain fat from meat and remove skin from poultry to cut fat and calories.
For a 2,000-calorie daily food plan, you need the amounts below from each food group.				
Eat 2½ cups every day What counts as a cup? • 1 cup of raw or cooked vegetables or vegetable juice; • 2 cups of leafy salad greens	Eat 2 cups every day What counts as a cup? • 1 cup of raw or cooked fruit or 100% fruit juice; • ½ cup dried fruit	Eat 6 ounces every day What counts as an ounce? • 1 slice of bread; • ½ cup of cooked rice, cereal, or pasta; • 1 ounce of ready-to-eat cereal	Get 3 cups every day What counts as a cup? • 1 cup of milk, yogurt, or fortified soymilk; • 1½ ounces natural or • 2 ounces processed cheese	Eat 5½ ounces every day What counts as an ounce? • 1 ounce of lean meat, poultry, or fish; 1 egg; • 1 Tbsp peanut butter; • ½ ounce nuts or seeds; • ¼ cup beans or peas

TASKS

1 Read the text about Caramellos.
Mediation: Explain to a friend who doesn't speak English what it's about and what point the author is making.

2 Work with a small group and make a list of products which have been changed in one of the ways described in the text.

3 Write an imaginary letter of complaint to one of the firms from task 2.
Or: Choose any firm and any product at random. Write a letter of complaint because …
– The product you ordered hasn't arrived.
– It wasn't the product you ordered.
– It arrived damaged or with missing parts. (▶ Skills 5.4)

4 The two illustrations above show two methods of informing people about a healthy diet.
Look at the illustrations and make a list of any differences you can find.

5 Online research: Find out more about both diet systems:
www.choosemyplate.gov/food-groups
www.aid.de
Which system best suits you and your lifestyle? Give reasons. (▶ Skills 1.0)

3   Local vs organic?

The apple problem
by Alan Jarmusch

It was only last week I had an apple problem. I was strolling in the produce section of a Manhattan grocery store when I couldn't make up my mind whether to buy an organic or a 'non-organic' apple which was labeled 'conventional', as that sounds more trustworthy than putting 'sprayed and treated with pesticides that might harm your health'. The choice shouldn't have been too tough, me being a very health-conscious person and practically a vegetarian. And still I hesitated, as the organic apples had been grown in California, whereas the conventional ones came from a farm in New York state. Maybe I have been reading too many articles about how we can reduce our 'carbon footprint', but I started wondering how much oil it took to get that apple to me.

For those of you who are not yet familiar with the term 'carbon footprint', it's defined as 'a representation of the effect a person, or a company, has on the climate in terms of greenhouse gases he or she produces'. That means that it's a measure of how much harm we cause to the environment in our everyday lives. It's measured in units of carbon dioxide and the average American is responsible for about 20 tons of carbon dioxide emissions each year. This is a much higher figure than that of any other industrialised country.

Getting back to my apple, my personal carbon footprint and my health awareness, I faced a dilemma. Which farmer should I support – the one who does without pesticides in California or the one who is practically my neighbor? Most important, did the quality and taste of the apple suffer from maybe being picked too early, then frozen and finally transported for thousands of miles?

I ended up buying both apples and have to admit that I could not really tell the difference in taste.

I've only recently started to notice that more locally-grown products are on offer in our supermarkets and I'm now aware of the organic – versus – local debate, which has become one of the liveliest in the food world. Not only can you find local produce in supermarkets, but organic food as well.

In 2006 even a big company like Wal-Mart began offering more organic products – those grown without pesticides, antibiotics, irradiation and so on – which has caused deep concern among early organic adopters.

Nearly 25 % of American shoppers now buy organic food once a week, as compared with 17 % in 2000, but 'local' is the new 'organic' nowadays, the ideal that promises healthier bodies and a healthier planet. Many politically-minded eaters, as well as food writers and chefs all over the world are outraged that industrial-sized farming is becoming more popular among big organic farms and the same long-distance-shipping methods are used as in conventional agribusinesses. Organic food today may be good for the consumer, but is it still good for the Earth?

I had never before considered that question, because I've never really thought about how my food might affect the 'food system'. I don't only have a deep concern for my body, but also for the state of the planet. And I also care about how my food tastes. So what should I do?

I'm well aware of the fact that a locally-grown vegetable will retain more of its delicate leguminous flavor than one shipped in a refrigerated container from Guatemala, for example. Still, not all locally-grown products are organic, which worries me a great deal. Even if we all decided to only buy local organic foods, we wouldn't be able to find too many. Only in a few very special regions of the US, where it isn't too dry, too wet or too warm, can you find abundant organic produce grown locally.

In some cases it might be worth buying organic food that comes from slightly farther away than conventional local food, because you're voting with your dollars and encouraging more organic production (eventually local producers will switch if there's enough demand) and you're

helping to protect topsoil, groundwater, etc. These benefits can sometimes offset the extra shipping. But when the organic food comes from much farther away than the local food, local is the way to go or just substitute with another type of food that you can find as local and organic.

On the other hand, several studies question the viability of local as more energy-efficient than organic from a distance, the argument being that a single farmer driving his diesel truck on a 300-miles round-trip to the market isn't less harmful for the environment than a single container ship bringing millions of grapes from Chile. But most important, take the time to enjoy your food!

GRAMMAR

Relativsätze *(relative sentences)*

Zwei Sätze können mit einem Relativpronomen verbunden werden. Bei Personen steht **who** oder **that**. Bei Dingen steht **which** oder **that**.

*It's a diet **which** appeals to many people. I know several **who** have tried it.*

Ein Relativsatz ist nicht notwendig, wenn die enthaltene Information zusätzlich ist, d. h. wenn man den Relativsatz weglässt, ist der Satz noch sinnvoll. Ein nicht-notwendiger Relativsatz wird durch ein Komma vom Hauptsatz getrennt.

*Not all locally-grown products are organic**, which worries me a great deal.***

TASKS

① Define the terms 'carbon footprint' and 'organic food'.

② Comment on the statement 'local is the new organic'.

○ ③ Discuss the pros and cons of buying food according to the following criteria:
price • quality • quantity • appearance • calorific content • organic

4   Locally-grown food

How to be a locovore

A 'locovore' is anyone who only eats food from the local area. Local foods are becoming increasingly popular because they're considered to be fresher, healthier, good for the local economy, and environmentally friendly.

Is being a locovore the right choice for you? Read the following six steps and decide for yourself.

1. **Know your reasons for preferring locally-grown food.**
   Here are some common reasons:

   - Foods shipped long distances are often picked while they're still unripe, stored for long periods of time, and handled extensively.
   - Even fruits and vegetables undergo processing. Waxes and dyes may be added, and fruits picked unripe may be ripened with ethylene gas. Because of this extra handling, they may not be as fresh as locally-grown foods, and they may be at greater risk of carrying diseases and contaminants.
   - Buying fresh, locally grown food supports local farmers.
   - Locally grown foods are 'greener', since less energy is required for shipping, handling, packaging, etc.
   - Decide what you consider local.
   - Decide whether to make exceptions for foods that simply don't grow in your area.

2. **Shop locally.**
   - At most markets you can purchase good produce directly from the growers.
   - Look for unusual varieties and be open-minded about trying new foods.
   - Ask for advice on preparing and caring for the vegetables on offer.
   - Visit local produce stands, especially any that are next to fields, farms, or orchards. Get to know the sellers and ask questions. You can learn a lot about what went into your foods.

3. **Know the origin of the food you buy.**
   - Ask where food comes from. Transporting food for long distances not only increases the price, but it results in a bigger carbon footprint.
   - Read labels. If there's a produce code, it will tell you where the food is grown. Bags, cartons, and other packaging materials around the foods may also include information about its source.

4. **Distinguish between foods that are local and foods that are organic (grown without the use of chemical pesticides or fertilizers).**

   - Know the best seasons for various foods in your area and choose those foods during those seasons.
   - Examine the source of your grains, dairy products, eggs, and meats, if you eat them. You may be able to find local sources of many things besides just fruits and vegetables. You could even raise your own chickens!

5. Grow your own food.

- Even a pot on an apartment balcony can produce some of the best-tasting foods you'll ever eat, and there's no place more local than your own garden. If you grow your own foods, you control exactly what goes into them.

6. Minimize the quantity of processed foods you eat.

- Choose foods that are locally processed (canned, baked, and dried goods are often available at produce stands and farmer's markets) or homemade.
- Do your own cooking whenever possible. Prepared meals might contain ingredients from anywhere.
- Can, dry, and freeze your own foods.

TASKS

1. Mediation: Your aunt is a cook in a company canteen and she's very interested in nutrition and healthy food. She has found the article 'How to be a locovore' online and printed it out. However, her English isn't good enough to understand the details. Explain the main points of the article for her in German. (▶ Skills 4.0)

2. Work with a partner. Use the role cards below and act out a dialogue.

Complain to your friend that he/she
- eats at fast-food restaurants
- eats too much 'junk food'
- eats too many ready-made meals
- eats things that contain
too much sugar/fat/...
too many preservatives/
...

- If you're a girl, tell your partner that he/she is exaggerating/mistaken/not thinking clearly/...
- If you're a boy, give in and say you're sorry. Ask for ...
  – examples/alternatives/advice
- Promise to change/ do better/...

5 Voices of complaint

Many of us go shopping two or even three times a week, but few of us think about where the things we buy come from – especially foodstuffs. Not only exotic fruit and vegetables travel very long distances. Nowadays even 'normal' products sometimes travel far. But more or us are becoming aware of 'food miles' and are questioning the economic sense of transporting food for long distances when good local alternatives are available. The following two letters were printed in a women's magazine.

Last month I spent a fortnight's holiday with my family in Scotland. It took us over 12 hours to get to our rented cottage in Crieff, a small village near Perth. We were all exhausted by the time we arrived and I popped into the local supermarket to pick up some supplies.

I was amazed to find local raspberries (which were grown on a farm in Crieff) on sale in the shop, but they had been packaged in transparent plastic boxes in Bristol, which is where we live. I suppose this is because the supermarket in Crieff belongs to a nationwide chain with its headquarters in Bristol. But wouldn't it have been more sensible to package the raspberries in Crieff, where they were grown?

In order to be packed into those little plastic containers the fruit had travelled about 840 miles from Crieff to Bristol and then back to Crieff again! This is ridiculous. I don't understand how this can make any kind of economic sense and the harm this does to our environment is obvious.

MAUREEN GIBSON
Bristol

I love good porridge or cereal – and I want to have good milk! That's why I've been a regular customer at Sainsbury's in Stirling for their delicious Jersey milk. But I've now found out through a recent BBC programme that my Jersey milk actually comes from forty-six farms all over the Scottish Lowlands. The milk is collected and taken to a central dairy in Stirling where it is pasteurized and either bottled or packaged in cartons. The bottles and cartons of milk are then transported by road in refrigerated container-lorries to a large cold-storage facility at Redditch in Warwickshire, which is run by Highgrove Food Distribution Ltd. The bottled and packaged milk is then transported daily to the supermarket warehouse hubs and from there to the individual supermarkets. This means that milk from cows in Scotland is not only transported to Cornwall and the south east of England, but also sold in Scotland again. So the milk in the supermarket in Stirling has made a 600-mile round trip to Redditch and back. Just imagine the amount of energy needed to keep the milk chilled on this odyssey! This waste of energy and the unnecessary CO_2 emissions from the lorries can't be good for the environment.

SANJAY KUMAR
Stirling

How your banana gets to the supermarket shelf

Most bananas come from Central America and the Caribbean islands. A small number, mostly fairly traded, come from South America. Bananas are harvested when they are still green and transported to Europe by sea in chilled, sealed containers. Nowadays, the most important European ports for handling bananas are probably Hamburg and Antwerp.

After the containers have been unloaded, they are transported by road, still chilled and sealed, to wholesale markets or to one of the logistics centres of the big supermarket chains. In the morning, these centres take delivery of produce (fruit and vegetables) from local sources, from other European countries and from overseas. Of course, our bananas are included in these deliveries.

Fresh local produce is usually sent out to super-market branches the same day, but other produce like nectarines, mangoes, pineapples or melons is put into specially designed ripening rooms for 3 to 7 days. This is what happens to bananas, too. The quality and freshness of the fruit are repeatedly tested by specially trained inspectors.

Finally, the bananas are declared ripe. In the course of a day, usually in the early afternoon, all the supermarkets belonging to a chain are asked how much produce they need, and what kind. Later in the afternoon these orders are packed and sorted according to their destinations. Each lorry driver has a particular route.

At around 6 pm the drivers start loading their vehicles and set off on their journeys to deliver the produce, which is still kept cool. By 6 am the next morning all the branches of the supermarkets, even those furthest away from the logistics centres have received their supplies of bananas and other fruit and vegetables. This ensures that consumers get fresh, quality produce, even if they go shopping the moment the supermarket opens.

Critics sometimes complain about the environmental impact of moving goods all over Europe or the world, for that matter, but we should never forget that plentiful supplies of reasonably-priced fruit and vegetables depend on a smoothly-functioning global distribution system, involving transport overland and by sea.

TASKS

1. Define what is meant by 'food miles'.

2. Look around your local supermarkets and make a list of products that have had long journeys. What local alternatives can you find?

3. Choose one of the products on your list. Search the Internet for additional information. Write a critical letter to a magazine about this product, its journey and the effect on the environment.

4. Choose a role card and act out a television debate. (▶ Skills 3.1)

| You're a supermarket executive. You must explain and justify the marketing policy of your company. | You're a concerned customer. You want to complain about ...
• the sale in winter of fresh grapes / strawberries from Spain. / ... | You're the moderator in the TV studio. You jump in with questions if the debate slows down. You interrupt when somebody talks too long or repeats themselves. |

TRACK 9   **1**   **The myth of food miles**

a) *Listen to track 9 and in an exercise book match the beginnings of the sentences (1–9) with the correct endings (A– I).*

1. Mike and Karen Small are
2. They and their family only consume
3. They think we shouldn't buy
4. They say that these products
5. Thousands of people in the UK and overseas
6. Dr Adrian Williams works for
7. Dr Williams thinks the concept of food miles
8. Dr Gareth Edwards-Jones is
9. Dr Edwards-Jones thinks the concept of food miles

A agree with them.
B products flown in from other countries.
C the National Resources Management Centre at Cranfield University.
D prominent locovores in Fife, Scotland.
E are harmful to the environment.
F an expert on African agriculture from Bangor Univerity.
G local produce.
H is much more complicated than most locovores imagine.
I is unhelpful and stupid.

b) *Read the questions below and make a list of the information you need. Now listen to track 9 again (as often as you wish) and make notes. Then use your notes to answer the following questions.*

1. What are 'locovores' and what is their 'message'?
2. Why do many experts say that the locovore message is too simplistic?

3 **Cartoon**

Explain what you think this cartoon means. (▶ *Skills 3.5)*

3 **Foodstuffs**

Identify the numbered foodstuffs in the food pyramid.

carrots • cauliflower • cheese • chicken • eggs • fish • grapes • maize (AE: corn) • meat • milk •
olive oil • pears • strawberry • bread • noodles

4 **A short food sketch**

Waiter: Here's your cream of chicken soup, Sir / Madam.
Diner: Thank you. Er, would you mind tasting the soup.
Waiter: What wrong, Sir / Madam? Is the soup too hot?
Diner: Just taste it.
Waiter: Isn't it creamy enough?
Diner: I'd just like you to taste it.
Waiter: Sir / Madam, we've been serving cream of chicken soup for fifteen years and in all that
time there has never been a complaint about it.
Diner: Why don't you just try it?
Waiter: The cook is an expert on chicken soup. She got this soup recipe from her beloved
grandmother. If I took it back, she would be deeply hurt.
Diner: You don't have to take it back. Just taste it.
Waiter: Very well, Sir / Madam. Where's the spoon?
Diner: Aha! Exactly!

5 Food jokes

A canteen at a British nuclear power station is called "The Fission Chips".
The government will soon introduce new food labels that are more specific. Products will now be labeled: 'no fat'; 'low fat'; 'reduced fat'; and 'fat, but great personality'.

6 Relative sentences

What relative pronouns are missing in the following sentences?

1. I live in the house ... my greatgrandfather built in 1916.
2. The 'carbon footprint' of an object was a concept ... was completely unknown at that time.
3. My greatgrandparents belonged to a generation of people ... were not as aware of environmental pollution as we are now.
4. Even now it can be a confusing concept to people ... don't really understand what it means.
5. Basically, the carbon footprint quantifies the effect ... the production of greenhouse gases has on the environment.

7 Passive sentences

In an exercise book, complete these sentences with the correct passive forms of the verbs in brackets.

1. In 2005 the INDEX award in the category 'Body' (grant) ... to LifeStraw®.
2. Three years later the same product (give) ... a Saatchi & Saatchi award.
3. In less than twenty years, the world (change) ... dramatically by such innovative products.
4. LifeStraw® is a cheaply produced device in which contaminated water (clean) ... and purified.
5. The INDEX awards are for products where innovative design and existing technology (combine) ... to create a product which helps people to lead better, healthier lives.

CHECK

1. I can listen and understand technical texts.
2. I can compare and contrast different systems.
3. I can interpret a cartoon.
4. I can prepare presentation slides.
5. I can write a letter of complaint.
6. I can role play a disussion.
7. I can mediate between German and English.
8. I can do online research.
9. I can understand and use relative sentences.

UNIT 9
Advertising

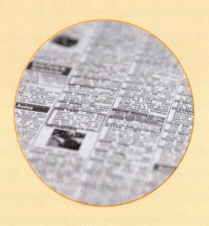

To do

Receptive
- Evaluate and compare adverts

Productive
- Analyse adverts and explain how they function

Interactive
- Discuss an advertising campaign

Skills
- Analysing adverts

Grammar
- Past perfect
- Adjektiven und Adverbien

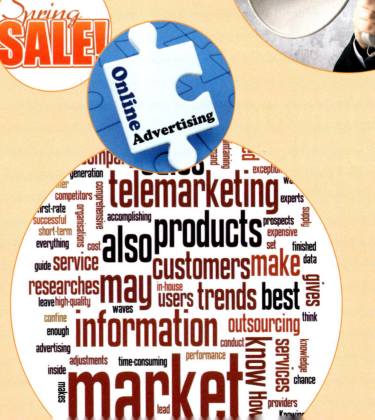

1   The world of images

a)
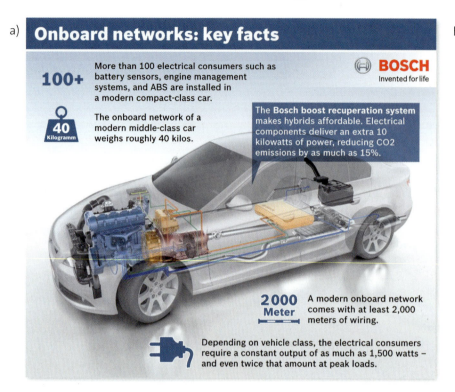

b)
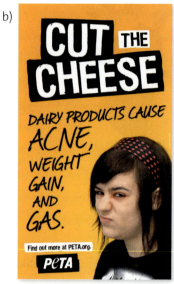

c)
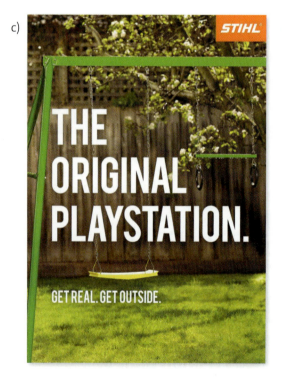

d)

e)

> # Let's eat grandma!
>
> # Let's eat, grandma!
>
> **Grammar saves lives.**
>
> Study with books from
> handwerk-technik.de
>
> **HT**

f)

The only thing repeated here is great taste.

RITTER SPORT. IN MANY DELICIOUS VARIETIES.

Strawberry Creme
Dark Chocolate
Rum Raisins Hazelnuts
Marzipan
Whole Hazelnuts
Cornflakes
White Whole Hazelnuts
Yogurt
Whole Almonds
Peppermint
Alpine Milk Chocolate
Fine Milk Chocolate
Praline

Ritter SPORT

QUALITY. CHOCOLATE. SQUARED.

www.ritter-sport.us

g)

WeightWatchers

exaggeration	Übertreibung
unexpected	unerwartet
juxtaposition	Nebeneinanderstellung
alienation	Verfremdung
reversal	Umkehr(ung)

WORD POWER

 ABC

Analysing adverts

- Start with a description: What? Who? Where? When? Why?
- Break the advert down into its visual and textual components and describe the functions of each part. Be careful to stay objective at this stage.
- Summarize your analysis and give your own personal opinion. Justify your opinion.

SKILLS

1 Which adverts are trying to ...
- persuade you to buy something?
- change attitudes?

2 Explain how the adverts try to get their message across.

TASKS

2   Controversial advertising

Benetton were the first to use shocking images in their advertising. They were intended to provoke controversy and publicize the name "Benetton" as a fashion label. It certainly did this, so in advertising terms it was a successful campaign and it inspired other fashion houses to run similar campaigns. But how moral is this method of advertising? When does "controversial" become simply "offensive"?

In 2007, a Dolce & Gabbana advert crossed the line and provoked protests in many countries, including Italy, their homeland. The photo showed an expressionless young woman wearing only a bathing suit and high heels being pinned down by a well-oiled shirtless man while four other men stood

by and watched. Was the image glorifying gang rape or provoking a sexual fantasy? The first protests came from Spain, which was then coping with a wave of violent crimes against women and public outrage was high. The protests spread to Italy and government officials demanded that the photo be taken out of circulation. There were similar demands from women's organizations in other European countries. Stefano Gabbana regretted the way the ad was perceived and insisted that he and his partner Domenico Dolce hadn't intended to demean women. They had meant the image to be artistic and to "recall an erotic dream, a sexual game." However, in March 2007 they announced that they were withdrawing the controversial advert.

In September 2007, the Italian photographer Oliviero Toscani, who had earlier created controversial advertising campaigns for the Italian fashion label Benetton, started a publicity campaign, paid for by Italian clothing company Flash & Partners to publicise No-l-ita, a fashion brand aimed at young women. The picture showed a naked and emaciated anorexia sufferer, Isabelle Caro, a French actress. The young ex-model weighed only 31 kilos and resembled a concentration camp victim. She was photographed naked to draw attention to the problem of eating disorders in the fashion industry after several models had died of anorexia. The image with the words "No Anorexia", was first shown during the Milan Fashion Week in September 2007.

Italy's advertising body banned the ad campaign saying it had broken the code of conduct as it commercially exploited the illness and they deplored the use of a sick and dying model for economic and publicity purposes. However, the ad campaign also won wide praise, including clear support from the Italian health ministry. The disturbing and shocking image of Isabelle Caro could "open an original channel for communication" and "encourage people to shoulder their responsibilities in the area of anorexia," said Minister Livia Turco. Interestingly, many of those applauding Toscani's initiative came from the world of fashion, which is generally perceived as a major culprit in the drive to pressure young women into being extremely thin.

INFO-BOX

Find the pictures mentioned above under: http://en.wikipedia.org ▶ Dolce & Gabbana

Google search: "no l ita" and "Isabelle Caro"

Das past perfect

- *Das past perfect* benutzt man für Handlungen, die in der Vergangenheit schon statt-gefunden haben. Es wird oft zusammen mit dem *simple past* verwendet.
  *Dolce & Gabbana **hadn't intended** to demean women when they published this advert.*

- Das *past perfect* wird mit ***had / hadn't*** + Partizip Perfekt (3. Form) des Verbs gebildet.
  Beim Sprechen und informellen Schreiben wird *had* nach Personalpronomen häufig durch die Kurzform ***'d*** ersetzt.
  *I**'d seen** it all before and was bored out of my skull!*

1. Discuss three of the following questions in a group of four:
   a) Where do you draw the line between an advert that is about a sexual fantasy and one that is just offensive?
   b) The D&G advert caused a stir in Italy and Spain, but not when it ran in the United States. Does this surprise you? Why? Why not?
   c) Are adverts like the D&G or the No-l-ita advert successful in selling clothing to women?
   d) Why are controversial advertisements often not acceptable? Is it because of religious or cultural values?
      Do men and women react in the same way? Do older people react differently than younger people?
   e) Does a good sense of humour have a place in advertising? Give some examples.
   f) Should swear words be banned from adverts? Why? Why not? Would they offend you?
   g) Can an advertisement like the one of Isabelle Caro stop young girls from slimming too much?

2. After having discussed the questions with your group discuss them in class.
   a) Take notes of the different opinions.
   b) Then write an article entitled 'Controversial advertising'. Don't forget to write an introduction (e.g. you could take some information from the text), to balance the pros and cons and to finish with a conclusion. Remember to make clear paragraphs!
   (▶ Skills 5.4)

3   The language of advertising

Not all adverts depend on controversy or an unusual visual effect as a strategy. Most are more conventional and combine an attractive illustration of the product with a simple, memorable text. This isknown as a 'slogan'.

Here are some examples.

GO TO WORK
ON AN EGG

Best Free Range Eggs

(1) **PUT A TIGER IN YOUR TANK!**

(2) ◇◇◇ is GOOD for you.

(3) **A ◇◇◇ a day helps you work, rest and play.**

(4) **I'm loving it!**

(5) The chocolate that melts in your mouth, not in your hand.

(6) **BECAUSE I'M WORTH IT.**

(7) **THE FUTURE'S BRIGHT — THE FUTURE'S ORANGE**

WORD
POWER

product	Produkt
brand	Marke
label	Etikett, Anhänger; Modehaus
strategy	Strategie
tactic	Taktik
campaign	Werbeaktion

a) Guinness stout
b) Mars chocolate and caramel bar
c) McDonald's fast-food restaurants
d) Esso petrol
e) L'Oreal hair and beauty products
f) M&Ms sugar-coated chocolate drops
g) Orange: telecommunication company

Brand names

In English, many brand names have found their way into everyday language.
Here are some examples of verbs:

- to hoover = to use a vacuum cleaner
- to google = to search for something on the Internet

There are even more examples of nouns:

- sellotape (BE) or Scotch tape (AE) = transparent adhesive tape
- elastoplast = sticking plaster to cover wounds and scratches
- kleenex = a tissue paper handkerchief
- velcro = nylon tape with rough surface that sticks to a corresponding strip, used as a fastener
- biro = a ballpoint pen

"How about this slogan: 'If you are unhappy
for any reason we will feel really bad'."

TASKS

1. Look at the advertising slogans (1–7) on the opposite page and match them to the products they advertised.

2. Write down a German advertising slogan. Look at your classmates' slogans. Are any the same? What do you think this shows?

3. What do you think makes a good slogan? Find some examples in German and English-language advertising.

4. Read the text about brand names. Can you find more examples? Do we use any brand names in German?

5. In a group, discuss the different types of advertising media that exist. Show the results visually, e.g. as a mind map or in some other form. (▶ Skills 6.3)

4   An advertising campaign

face soap

wristwatch

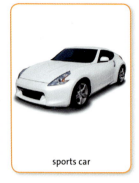
sports car

Satnav

E-bike

E-book reader

shaving foam

air freshener

boots

toilet cleanser

bath towel

battery

WORD
POWER

ABC

stylish	laboratory-tested	portable	up-to-date
eye-catching	innovative	ultra-modern	low-maintenance
high-tech	space-saving	reliable	practical
deluxe	state-of-the-art	reasonably priced	user-friendly
sophisticated	powerful	versatile	cool
fast	efficient	economic	environmentally-friendly
super soft	luxurious	delicate	attractive
super sensitive	fashionable	relaxing	cutting-edge technology
multi-purpose	durable	exotic	sinful

Adjektive und Adverbien der Art und Weise

- Adjektive beschreiben Personen und Dinge. Sie stehen meist vor einem Substantiv (Nomen) oder nach einer Form von **be**.
  *Guinness is a **dark** stout. Benetton used **shocking** images. The campaign provoked **massive** protests.*

  Vorsicht! Manche Adjektive enden auf -ly und können leicht mit Adverbien verwechselt werden, z. B.:
  *A crash can be **deadly**. All our products are **user-friendly**. Gabbano had a **lovely** idea for an advert.*

- Adverbien der Art und Weise beziehen sich auf Verben und beschreiben, wie etwas passiert.
  *The advert exploited anorexia **commercially**. The public reaction followed **quickly**. But in advertising circles the concept was praised **widely**.*

  Vorsicht! Nach *feel, look* (aussehen), *smell, sound* und *taste* steht ein Adjektiv.
  *The coffee smelled **wonderful**, but it tasted **terrible**.*

- Möchte man ein Adjektiv oder Adverb näher beschreiben, benutzt man ein Adverb.
  *Some advertising slogans are **wonderfully humorous** and **easily memorable**.*

1. Work with a partner. Choose one of the products shown on the opposite page and create an advertising campaign for your product. Then present your campaign to the class. The following steps can help you:
   - Create a new name for your product.
   - Find suitable illustrations on the Internet.
   - Decide which target group (i.e. young women, midle-aged men, etc.) your product is for.
   - Decide what qualities your product has and what makes it different from sililar products.
   - Decide which media (billboard, leaflet, TV, etc.) will be used to market the product.
   - Create an interesting design for the package.
   - Write a slogan for the product.
   - Write either a 30-second radio commercial or an advertment for a magazine or a newspaper. (▶ Skills 6.0)
2. Assess the presentations of other groups critically. Award them points between 1 and 10. Think about:
   - Was the advertising campaign clearly understandable?
   - Were there any memorable slogans and / or interesting photos or illustrations?
   - How effective was the presentation?

1 Household products

In your exercise book, translate the following German terms by taking a word from each of the boxes below and adding them together. (* = The words are written together.)

1. Handy
2. Küchenkrepp
3. Duschvorhang
4. Sessel
5. Wandtapete
6. Flüssige Seife
7. Damenbinde
8. Rasierklinge
9. Rasierschaum
10. Kloreiniger
11. Teubeutel
12. Brotmesser
13. Mundwasser
14. Eieruhr
15. Tischdecke

arm*	bag
bread*	blade
egg	chair*
kitchen*	cleanser
liquid	cloth*
mobile	curtain
mouth*	foam
razor	knife*
sanitary	paper*
shaving	phone
shower	roll*
table*	soap
tea	timer
toilet	towel
wall*	wash*

2 Advertising language

Work with a partner. Choose a product and write it vertically. Write an advertising text by finding an appropriate word for each word of the product. Here is an example:

S oft

O range blossom

A roma

P rice: £1.99

3 English is a crazy language

First just listen. Then look at the tasks below and make a note of the information you need. And then listen again. (Listen as often as you need to.)

a) *Do you think this text was written by a Briton or an American? Support your opinion with examples.*

b) In an exercise book, write down the words missing from the following sentences.

1. '...' is an American word; in British English this vegetable is usually called an aubergine.
2. A ... is made from minced meat, usually beef.
3. A ... is an exotic fruit; it isn't an apple and it doesn't grow on a pine tree.
4. ... are popular in the USA and they're usually toasted and eaten at breakfast with butter.
5. If someone steps in ..., they sink very slowly.
6. Boxers fight inside a sqare of ropes called a .... .
7. A ... doesn't come from Guinea and it isn't a pig.

c) *Find the German equivalents of these words in an online dictionary:*

verbs:	nouns:
pine	pine
preach	preacher
amend	amends
recite	recital

d) *Find the rhyming pairs.*

1. *(eng)*	tight	A	ship
2. *(Bär)*	bear	B	taught
3. *(straff)*	taut	C	guy
4. *(Heldentat)*	feat	D	drive
5. *(Peitsche)*	whip	E	write
6. *(Bienenstock)*	hive	F	which
7. *(Lüge)*	lie	G	square
8. *(Juckreiz)*	itch	H	feet

4 Laughable grammar!

Grammar can also be very funny. Watch the "Grammar police" video clip at the following address:
http://www.youtube.com/watch?v=3X4qi7AwDQI

Work with a partner and produce a similar sketch. Then present your sketch to the class.

5 **Adjectives**

Match the adjectives in the box below to the objects in the photos.

comfortable • cuddly • hard • juicy • long-lasting • relaxing • soft • tough • waterproof

1

helmet

2

boots

3

wristwatch

4

bath

5

battery

6

silk blouse

7

slippers

8

kitten

9

pineapple

CHECK

1 I can talk and write about ads and their intentions.

2 I can analyse and explain ads.

3 I can create my own ads.

4 I can differentiate between certain types of ads.

5 I can write about the pros and cons of an advertising-campaign.

6 I can use the past perfect.

UNIT 10
Globalization

To do

Receptive
- Compare indigenous, transnational and global companies
- Read about US residence permits and the Green Card lottery

Productive
- Talk about going abroad to live or work

Interactive
- Conduct a talk show
- Discuss the pros and cons of globalisation

Skills
- Conducting a talk show

1   The evolution of business

How businesses evolve

In the past, and long before the advent of the Internet, almost all businesses started as local businesses. Outside of the Internet, this is still generally true today. Some businesses remain local while others grow and expand their scale of operations. The five main stages in the evolution of business are shown in the diagram.

Stages in Evolution of Business

Local Business → Regional Business → National Business → International Business → Global Business

Local business

In medieval Europe typical local businessesmen would be the blacksmith, the roofer, the miller, etc. They sold their services and their products up to ten or so kilometres around the village where they lived and worked. To trade further than this was impractical because it simply took too long.

Regional business

Trade between local areas existed before roads were built. In the Stone Age valuable flints from the Alps were traded in North Germany and amber from the Baltic was traded as far as Egypt. And in the eighteenth century, peddlers travelled from village to village selling coloured ribbons, thread and needles. The critical factor for regional trade is the ability to transport goods and services between regions. Without a transport infrastructure, regional traders can only sell what they can carry on their backs or the backs of an animal. To prosper, regional firms need good roads, bridges and navigable rivers.

WORD POWER

Synonyms:
indigenous
native
local
domestic
homegrown

National business

A nation is an organized political union, i.e. a country, and a national business operates at all regional levels within its borders. National businesses provide goods and services to the whole country. Business at a national level first started in Britain with the Industrial Revolution. Trade at a national level depends not only on a good nationwide infrastructure, but on the financial services provided by joint-stock companies, a national stock market, banks and insurance companies.

International business

Traditionally, international business has been about imports and exports and the maximization of profit. The raw materials or manufactured products of one country are transported to another country where there is a greater demand and where they can be sold at a greater profit. In the eighteenth century European traders imported tea, porcelain, silk and spices from south Asia, which were all in huge demand at that time. Some traders became very, very rich. The first millionaires and multimillionaires were called 'nabobs', an Indian word for a very rich man. But over time the costs and risks of international businesses were often too high for private firms and many evolved into joint-stock companies, i.e. groups of investors. This helped to spread wealth more evenly. Important factors in the growth of international business are fast communications, cheap transport, peaceful relations between countries and mutual free trade policies.

Global business

Here, the whole world is considered to be one huge market. It has an enormous customer base, no borders and few or no restrictions. All companies can sell their goods and services anywhere. Products are manufactured where labour costs are low and the products are sold where demand is greatest. Great profits can be made, but the competition is severe and savage and the morality of an action is often ignored. Bigger firms with greater resources have an advantage over smaller firms. The global market is now dominated by a relatively small group of extremely rich multinational companies (MNCs).

World Trade Organization (WTO)
– deregulation of markets.
– free trade agreements
– ...

– English as a common language
– ...

good infrastructure
– ...

?

– cheap transport
– ...

Factors which have contributed to the globalization of business

– cheap labour
– outsourcing
– ...

– law and order
– ...

New technology
– Computer Assisted Manufacturing (CAM)
– Robots
– ...

TASKS

1 Work in a group of five and produce a poster or audio-visual presentation for each of the stages in the evolution of business. Use local newspapers and magazines, business brochures and the Internet to collect ...
– the names of firms and their logos, brand-names, etc.
– photos of their products or a description of their services,
– typical adverts, location maps, sales graphics, brief histories, etc.
(▶ Skills 6.0)

2 Work with a group and complete the mind map above. Then explain how they help the process of globalization.
What are the pros and cons of globalization?

2   Going abroad

Ireland

Iran

China

WORD
POWER

distant, faraway	fern
desire, longing	Sehnsucht
urge	Drang, Antrieb
itchy feet	Fernweh
wanderlust	Wanderlust
adventure	Abenteuer
exotic	exotisch
curious	neugierig
satisfy, fulfill	befriedigen, verwirklichen
explore	erforschen, erkunden
discover	entdecken, herausfinden

USA

Australia

Russia

- I'd be willing to settle permanently in ...
- I'd love to work for a time in ...

- I wouldn't mind visiting ..., but I wouldn't want to live there.

- ... is the last place on Earth I'd ever want to visit!

INFO-BOX

Information about countries

If you want more information about a country, there are two Internet sites you should try first. One is Wikipedia, which you probably already know. The other is the CIA World Factbook (browser search term: cia world factbook). This will provide you with a wealth of information about any country you are curious about. (▶ **Skills 1.0**)

A talk show about globalization

Globalization effects us all, but it isn't a simple subject. There are advantages and disadvantages. Mike, Sally, Jennifer and Luke are taking part in a talk show and they have very different opinions.

TRACK 11

A talk show about globalization

SKILLS

Conducting a talk show

Conducting a talk show enables students to discuss problems from different perspectives. A talk show should consist of at least four people (the speakers) and a moderator.

Before the talkshow, the speakers should research the subject and find situations which support their opinions. Between them, the four speakers should have different opinions about the subject and be able to discuss both the positive and negative effects and give examples of each.

During the talk show the participants sit in a half circle with the moderator in the middle so that the rest of the class (the audience) can follow the talkshow easily.

The moderator plays an important part in the talk. He / She ...
- introduces the speakers,
- decides who speaks,
- can ask a speaker to clarify or explain something,
- can ask the speakers specific questions,
- thanks the speakers and invites questions from the audience.

TASKS

1. Describe the photo at the top of the previous page. Explain what "going abroad" means to you. (Think about: duration, distance, things to take with you, the people you'll leave behind and miss, the people you might meet, etc.) (▶ Skills 3.5)

2. How much do you know about the countries shown on the opposite page? Can you imagine living and working there permanently or for several years? Would you like to spend a holiday there? Give your reasons.

3. Choose five different countries and ask your classmates whether they would like to work there. Show the results in the form of a bar chart or a pie chart. (▶ Skills 6.4)

4. Listen to track 11 and make a list of the pros and cons. You can find more information in section C of this unit. Then organize your own talk show about globalization.

3   Winners and losers

People around the globe are more connected to each other then ever before. Information and money flow more quickly than ever. Goods and services produced in one part of the world are increasingly available in all parts of the world. International travel is more frequent and international communication is commonplace. Globalization is an economic tidal wave that is sweeping over the world. It can't be stopped, and there will be winners and losers.

The general complaint about globalization is that it makes the rich richer while everyone else becomes poorer. It's good for top managers and investors, but bad for workers and nature. Supporters of globalization say that it encourages global economic growth, creates jobs, makes companies more competitive, and reduces prices for consumers.

Multinational corporations which were previously restricted to commercial activities are increasingly influencing political decisions, say the critics. They point out that most multnational companies are inherently despotic and anti-democratic in attitude. Many think there is a threat of giant corporations ruling the world because they are gaining power due to globalization. Supporters of globalization claim that it provides poor countries with foreign capital and technology, which helps them to develop economically. Spreading prosperity, they say, creates the conditions in which democracy and respect for human rights can flourish. The managers of multinational companies also think that they should have the right to be involved in the political process of the countries they trade in, especially in political issues which affect their interests.

In many developed countries the economic effects of globalization (tax avoidance, outsourcing, factory closures, etc.) are placing social welfare schemes or "safety nets" under great pressure. Opponents believe that globalization makes it easier for rich companies to act with less accountability. Many of these rich companies are from the USA and they deliberately overpower and destroy individual native cultures, say the critics. They complain that anyone who is against globalization is often accused of being anti-American. The supporters of globalization pass these criticisms off as paranoid fantasies. Big business is pure business and has no colonialist designs. Increased trade will raise the global economy and give consumers in Third World countries access to western products. Most Americans are unable to distinguish "socialism" from "communism" and so for them the destruction of socialist institutions is regarded as a good thing. Many top mangers of multinationals share this view and see social welfare programmes as an unfair business impediment.

Anti-globalists claim that globalization doesn't do anything to help the majority of the world's population. During the most recent period of rapid growth in global trade and investment from 1960 to 1998, inequality became worse both internationally and within countries. The UN Development Program reports that the richest 20 percent of the world's population consume 86 percent of the world's resources, while the poorest 80 percent consume just 14percent.

Some experts think that globalization is also causing an increase in contagious diseases. Deadly diseases like HIV/AIDS are being spread by travellers to the remotest corners of the globe. Supporters of globalization say that despite some minor negative aspects, in the long term tourism is beneficial. People learn more about each other and cultural intermingling is a positive thing. Most people see speedy travel, mass communications and the rapid spread of information through the Internet as benefits of globalization.

Globalization has led to an exploitation of labour. Prisoners and child workers are forced to work in inhumane conditions for little or no money. Safety standards are ignored to produce cheap goods. Unions and social welfare programmes are targeted and destroyed. Multinationals are also accused of mismanaging natural resources and causing ecological damage. The multinationals point out that it's the responsibility of national governments to regulate and enforce standards and not theirs. Many claim that workers in their factories enjoy pay and working conditions that are above-average for their country. Raising standards, they say, is also an on-going process. They also point out that being environmental-friendly is often the best way to manage resources efficiently. The same goes for ecological issues. Despite mistakes in the past, experience has proven that being ecologically sensitive is also good for business.

TASKS

1   Read the text about globalization. Look up the words you don't know in the word lists in the reference section of this course book. (▶ Skills 2.0)

2   Read the text about globalization again and write two lists:
    – a summary of the arguments against globalization,
    – a summary of the arguments for globalization.

3   Discuss in a small group the arguments for and against. Express your own personal opinion and give reasons.

4   How to become a legal alien

The US Green Card

The 'Green Card' – the original document was green in colour – is a permanent residence permit. It allows immigrants to live in the US or join family members who already live there.

Taking part in a lottery is one rather unusual way of getting a Green Card. Each year about 50,000 permits are made available to potential immigrants from countries all over the world. Which countries qualify depends on immigration statistics for previous years and often changes.

Receiving a Green Card does not automatically mean that you have US citizenship, but it's the first step in becoming a US citizen. People with a Green Card can apply for US citizenship after living in the United States for five years, or for three years if they are married to US citizens.

How to take part in the Green Card lottery

The first step is to find out whether you are eligible. There are certain qualifications you have to meet. The country you were born in must be a qualifying country, for instance. The applicant must have at least the equivalent of a high-school diploma or two years of work experience as a skilled worker.

Secondly, you fill out an electronic entry form using the US Government website (www.dvlottery.state.gov). Only one application per person is allowed! Note, too, that you can only register during the 60-day period stated. The winners are chosen at random by a computer program.

The winners can apply for an Immigrant Visa. Your immediate family (spouse and children) can apply, too. Your children must be unmarried and under 21.

The next step is an interview with an examining officer, who approves or denies your application.

If approved, you (and your family) must enter the US within six months of notification of winning the lottery. Then you can live and work legally and permanently in the United States.

WORD POWER

Synonyms:		
to permit	to license (AE) / to licence (BE)	to authorize
permission	license (AE) / licence (BE)	authorization
immigrant	settler	expatriate
immigration	settlement	expatriation

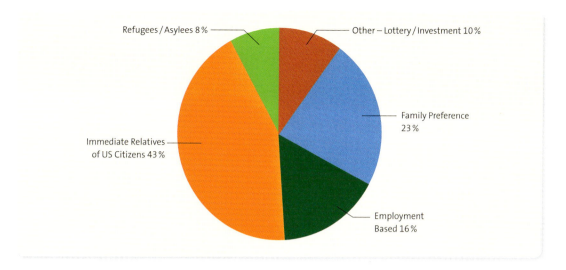

Refugees / Asylees 8 %

Other – Lottery / Investment 10 %

Family Preference 23 %

Immediate Relatives of US Citizens 43 %

Employment Based 16 %

WORD POWER

citizenship	Staatsbürgerschaft
swearing-in	Vereidigung
oath	Eid
allegiance	Treue
official ceremony	Festakt
celebration	Feier
certificate	Zertifikat

TASKS

1 Read the text 'The US Green Card' and answer the following questions.
  1. Why is a permanent residence permit called a Green Card?
  2. What does it allow you to do?
  3. Is the lottery the only way of getting a Green Card?
  4. How many lottery permits are available each year?
  5. If you have a Green Card, does this make you a US citizen?
  6. Who is eligible for the lottery?
  7. How are winners chosen?
  (▶ Skills 2.0)

2 Mediation: Your grandparents want to retire to Florida, but their English isn't good enough to understand the text. Summarize the text in German for them. (▶ Skills 4.0)

3 Discuss in general the pros and cons of emigrating to the USA.

4 Analyse and explain the pie chart at the top of the page. (▶ Skills 3.4)

1 A definition

In an exercise book, complete the following definition with words from the box.

> addition • age • agreement • clothing • contractors • labour

Code of Vendor Conduct

This is an (1) ... made with all factories (also called (2) ...) that make (3) ... for Gap. They promise to follow international (4) ... laws which apply to the (5) ..., safety and health of the workers. In (6) ..., they must protect the environment.

2 Synonyms and antonyms

a) *Read the following text carefully. Look up any words you don't understand.*

Gap Incorporated wins top award

In the category of Business Ethics Awards, Gap, Inc. is the clear winner in the category for reporting on social issues. They have taken a huge step forward and, in an unprecedented move, have reported honestly on conditions in their factories. In a report from May 2004, experts and critics of large corporations called the move "historic" and praised Gap for its pioneer work in this field of business ethics. The main focus of the report looked at how well Gap's suppliers were fulfilling their vendor code. Gap discovered that in Africa, for example, more than half of the factories were using unsafe machinery and in China hazardous materials were not being stored correctly. Although top executives were at first worried about releasing such information, the positive public reaction has indicated that they took the right step. Other companies are sure to follow.

b) *Find the words in the text with the same meanings as the following words or phrases.*

1	victor	5	the situation
2	matters	6	concerns
3	enormous	7	sector
4	unheard of	8	complying with

c) *Find the words in the text with the opposite meanings as the following words or phrases.*

1	badly	4	negative
2	less	5	uncertain
3	holding back	6	go ahead

3 Dictionary work

Find the nouns that can be made from the following verbs. Write your answers in an exercise book.

1.	evolve	6.	peddle
2	grow	7.	prosper
3.	expand	8.	insure
4.	trade	9.	maximize
5.	exist	10.	invest

4 **A newspaper article**

In an exercise book, complete the following text with words from the box.

> abuse • blouses • child • dollars • extremely • filthy • fire • investigation • legal •
> minimal • no • on • twenty-three • whose • with workplace

Critical report damages Gap's ethical image

An (1) … by a reporter of the British newspaper The Observer has shocked the business community and caused enormous concern within the Gap corporation. It was discovered that one of their Indian suppliers has been using (2) … labour to produce clothes for Gap. Children as young as ten had been bought by the managers of the factory and were forced to work in dangerous and (3) … conditions. In some cases, the children were beaten and made to work sixteen hours a day for (4) … pay. The factory, which was reported to be in a "derelict industrial unit", was producing hand-stitched (5) … for Gap Kids stores in the United States and Europe for the Christmas selling period. The blouses were to sell for about 40 (6) … .

Gap's vendor code is famous and it is corporate policy to stop the (7) … of children. If Gap discovers children who contractors force to work, they demand that the children be removed from the (8) … , paid their wages and sent to school. They must guarantee jobs for them when they reach the (9) … working age. The first reaction of the corporation was to (10) … the Indian supplier. The president of Gap has blamed this abuse on an unauthorized subcontractor and is (11) … angry with the original vendor. She added that the number of garments the children were said to have made was (12) … , but that none of the garments from the particular vendor would make it to store shelves. She went (13) … to say that Gap strictly prohibits child labour. Gap has long had a history of dealing (14) … challenges like this. In 2006 Gap stopped doing business with (15) … factories because of their code violations. They have a number of people world-wide (16) … job it is to make sure that contractors follow the Code of Vendor Conduct.

5 **Verb and noun phrases**

Which prepositions are missing?

1. People exchanged information long before the advent … the Internet
2. The critical factor for regional trade is the ability … transport goods
3. a national business operates … all regional levels
4. Trade at a national level depends … a good nationwide infrastructure
5. tea, porcelain, silk and spices were imported … south Asia
6. Over time, many private firms evolved … joint-stock companies
7. The global market is now dominated … multinational companies

6 **Dictionary definitions**

Match the word in the box to the definitions below.

> blacksmith • browser • evolution • investor • manufacture • navigable • savage • trade

1. *(n.)* A person who makes or repairs things of iron by hand, horseshoes for example.
2. *(n.)* Someone who puts money in a business in the hope of making a profit.
3. *(adj.)* This describes a river or part of river which can be used by ships or boats.
4. *(n.)* The gradual development of an organism or an organization from the simple to the more complex.
5. *(adj.)* This describes a person or a situation that is violent, cruel and vicious.
6. *(n.)* This can be either a person who looks through books ar magazines in a bookshop or a computer program with a graphical user interface for displaying HTML files.
7. *(v.)* To produce something on a large scale using machinery.
8. *(n.)* The buying and selling of goods and services.

7 **The Immigrant Visa Process**

Complete this text from a U.S. government website with the words in the box.
(Use an exercise book.)

> citizens • employer • focus • forms • immigrate • obtain • petition • resident

Foreign (1) ... who want to live permanently in the United States must first (2) ... an immigrant visa. This is the first step to becoming a lawful permanent (3) ... .
Immigrating to the United States is an important and complex decision. In this section, you will learn about who may (4) ... to the United States, the different types of immigrant visas, the required (5) ..., and the steps in the immigrant visa process. Because most immigrants receive visas in the family or employment based visa categories, they are a key (6) ... of this section. To be eligible to apply for an immigrant visa, a foreign citizen must be sponsored by a U.S. citizen relative, U.S. lawful permanent resident, or a prospective (7) ..., with a few exceptions, explained below. The sponsor begins the immigration process by filing a (8) ... on the foreign citizen's behalf with U.S. Citizenship and Immigration Services (USCIS).

CHECK

1. I can conduct a talk show.
2. I can compare various forms of companies.
3. I can explain what a Green Card is and how to obtain one.
4. I can talk about going abroad to live or work.
5. I can discuss the pros and cons of globalisation.
6. I can present a talk.
7. I can explain a chart.

UNIT 11
Cultures in contact

To do

Receptive
- Learn about ethnic food.
- Listen to a recipe.

Productive
- Write a summary.
- Represent statistics visually as graphs

Interactive
- Discuss cultural misunderstandings and stereotypes.

Skills
- Analyse a newspaper article.

Grammar
- Passive forms with be and get.

1   Food ambassadors

The countries of western Europe are becoming more culturally diverse. In the UK for example, the 'old' immigrants were from the Caribbean, Africa and Asia; the 'new' immigrants are often from the countries of southern and eastern Europe: Greece, Bulgaria, Poland, Hungary, Lithuania, etc.

But we don't just get the immigrants – we also get their food. In the supermarket we spot exotic things such as borscht soup and kielbasa sausage and palacsinta pancake mixtures. They're only exotic for a short time and as soon as people get used to them they become as normal as Indian chicken korma, naan bread, Chinese Peking duck with noodles and Mexican burritos.

WORD
POWER

Japan – Japanese
China – Chinese
Poland – Polish
Austria – Austrian
Turkey – Turkish

spicy sausages (sis kebab)
cup cakes
seafood (sushi)
sweet curd cheese dumplings
cinnamon breakfast buns
walnut caramel torte

I think the ... is Austrian.

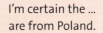
I'm certain the ... are from Poland.

An international evening

Aberystwyth's Plascrug School celebrated its multi-cultural nature with an evening of food and music. Dr Monica Aggawal had made halwa: a sweet pudding common to northern India.

The school has children from 38 countries speaking 28 different languages. University lecturer Richard Lucas and his wife Karen, from Australia, had made Anzac biscuits – a favourite in Australia and New Zealand since they were first made in 1916.

Among the food on offer was a delicious Libyan cous-cous made with Welsh lamb. Dr Kaled Haeasha, from Libya, said it was amazing that so many different nationalities live in such a small community as Aberystwyth.

Wajdy Ghazi and wife Rozlaily and family from Malaysia add to the cultural mix in the school. Of 400 pupils, about a quarter have an international background.

Flora Pinter and her son Gergo were tempting people with Hungarian apple pie and cherry scones.

One of the most popular desserts was the Austrian "Salzburger Nockerl" made by Mrs Hannelore Pinter and her daughter Nicola.

TRACK 12

English sausage rolls
This traditional recipe is very old. Sausage rolls were already well-known in Elizabethan England.

calf	Kalb
veal	Kalbsfleisch
pig	Schwein
poultry	Geflügel
breadcrumbs	Paniermehl
stock	Brühe
herbs	Kräuter
mincemeat	Hackfleisch
chop	zerhacken
mince	fein hacken, durchdrehen
reduce	reduzieren, einkochen
thicken	eindicken
add	hinzuführen
heat	erhitzen
stir	umrühren
roll out	ausrollen
coat	bedecken, überziehen, bemanteln
fry	in der Pfanne braten
pinch together	zusammen zwicken
brush	bepinseln

WORD POWER

TASKS

1   Describe the food photos on the opposite page.

2   What non-native foods can you find ...
  - in your local supermarkets and shops?
  - in local newspaper and magazine adverts?
  - on the street (e.g. snack bars, stalls, restaurants)?

○ 3   Produce a bar graph or a pie chart to show the ethnic origins of the pupils at your school. (▶ **Skills 6.4**)

4   Listen to the recipe for English sausage rolls on the audio-CD (Track 12). Listen again and take notes. Use your notes to write the recipe in German.

2   A success story

THE SPICE OF LIFE

The story of Patak's is like a fairy tale …

A dream comes true

The story of Patak's Spice Co., until recently a family-run business, is like a fairy tale. The Pathak family went from being penniless migrants to some of the wealthiest people in the UK within two generations.

The migrant

Patak's Spice Co. was founded in 1957 by Laxmishanker Pathak. He came to Britain in 1955 with his wife and six children. The Pathaks were among the many immigrants of ethnic Indian origin who came to Britain from Kenya in the mid-50s of the last century. They were the descendants of Indian workers from colonial times and had British passports. Now they were unwelcome in Kenya, the country of their birth, because of the rise of militant African nationalism: their lives were in danger.

A golden opportunity

Legend has it that Laxmishanker only had £ 5 and a life insurance policy in his pocket when he arrived in the UK. He got a job as a street-sweeper but he soon realized there was a golden opportunity to sell Asian food to ethnic Indians in Britain.

Samosas and sweets

He began making samosas, jalebi and kulfi in the family's tiny kitchen and selling them from home. The whole family helped, for instance the subsequent CEO of Patak's, Kirit Pathak, delivered food to customers when he was only 6! Before long, Laxmishander had saved enough to buy his first shop, number 134, Drummond Street, London.

Branching out

Soon, he branched out into other Indian specialities: he and his wife began to manufacture chutneys and pickles. News of the quality of their products spread, and orders flooded in.

Racial harassment

In 1962, neighbours' complaints about noise and bad smells led the local authorities to turn the Pathak's out of their London home. They moved to Northamptonshire, where there was already a large Indian community.

Always on the move

When the company was bought by ABF, Associated British Foods, in 2007, Lancashire was the site of Patak's headquarters, and this was also where their huge state-of-the-art food processing factory was located. The company also had an Indian bread bakery and a frozen food plant in Scotland, and five spice-processing factories scattered over the Indian sub-continent.

Success!

At the time of the takeover, Patak's was flourishing. It supplied over 75 % of UK's 8,000 or so Indian restaurants as well as selling cooking sauces, curry pastes, pappadums, chapattis, chutneys and pickles in more than 40 countries (including Japan, Australia, New Zealand, the US and Canada) worldwide. One quarter of annual turnover came from international sales. The company also made own-brand products for Tesco.

Just rewards

CEO Kirit Pathak and his wife, Meena, who was on the Patak's board, too, and was responsible for production and product development, have both been honoured for their services to the British food industry and to exports by being awarded OBEs* by Queen Elizabeth II.

Pathak into Patak

In case you're wondering, it was Laxmishanker Pathak who reluctantly decided to drop the 'h' in the company's name to make it easier for the English to pronounce correctly.

(* Order of the British Empire)

Analysing a text

SKILLS

- 'The Spice of Life' is a feature article.
- Texts like this combine the reporting of an event – something that happened – with background information, and sometimes comment. The event here is the takeover of Patak's by Associated British Foods, but this is only mentioned near the end. The focus of attention is the story of the Pathak family and the growth of their business. It's a rags-to-riches story, one that should encourage readers and make them feel good. Reading between the lines, we can say that the writer has a positive attitude to the Pathaks' success and thinks it's a good thing.
- Features generally have headlines that arouse the readers' interest or feelings. In addition, they often have headings at the beginning of paragraphs or sections of text.
- Look again at the headings in the body of the article. In general, they sum up the contents of the following paragraph.
- Overall, the style is formal. The sentences are quite long and sometimes complicated. However, the writer occasionally uses a colloquial expression or an idiom. This makes the text more lively and interesting to the reader.

TASKS

1 Look for the following information in the article:
the name of the company's founder • the family's ethnic origin • the founder's first job after arriving in the UK • the location of his first shop • an English county with large Indian community • the name of company that bought Patak's • the member of the Pathak family in charge of developing new products

2 Think of another title for this feature article and find alternative paragraph headings.

3   Cultures in conflict

A culture guide

Britain's hoteliers, pub landlords, taxi drivers and shopkeepers have been given tips on how to avoid cultural misunderstandings with visitors from abroad. The guide, written by VisitBritain staff who come from the countries concerned, is aimed at improving cultural awareness and avoiding misunderstandings. Tips include:

- A Japanese person who is smiling isn't necessarily happy. The Japanese smile when they're angry, embarrassed, sad or disappointed.
- Don't wink at someone from China. They think it's extremely rude.
- People from Greece and Bulgaria shake their head for "Yes" and nod for "No".
- To you it might just be harmless small talk, but Brazilians consider personal questions, about their age, their family or their jobs as offensive.
- Avoid physical contact when first meeting someone from India. Many Indians are not used to shaking hands and are likely to misinterpret a friendly hug or a pat on the back as a gesture of condescension and contempt.
- Canadians can get angry when people assume that they're the same as Americans. They're proud of their differences. They often indicate their national identity by wearing a maple leaf as a badge or as a symbol on their clothing.
- Be aware of cultural stereotypes. They are never true and can be highly offensive, e.g.:
  - Swedish women will not tear off their clothes and have sex with anyone in trousers.
  - Not all Germans eat Sauerkraut and wear lederhosen.
  - Very few Americans are arrogant, loudmouthed, opinionated or rude.
  - Not all Arabs are Sheiks or Princes or oil millionaires.

TRACK 13

Talking of names
Listen to six comments about different reasons for changing names.

www.global-integration.com

WORD POWER

get angry	wütend werden
get annoyed	sauer werden (auf jn.)
get used to	sich an jn. / etwas gewöhnen
get washed	sich waschen
get rich	reich werden

Changing names

There can be many reasons for changing your name.

- Some young people change their first names when they come of age if they feel the name their parents gave them is ridiculous or unsuitable. Who can blame them? Nobody would want to go through life called Bambi Bloggs, Play-it-again-Sam Jones or Lara Croft Evans, would they?

- Sometimes a nickname replaces a person's real name. For instance, the Georgian political activist Iosif Vissarionovich Dzugashvil went down in history as Josef Stalin, 'man of steel'.

- If you change your religion, you may be given, or may choose a new name. The singer Cat Stevens (real name: Steven Demetre Georgiou) took the name Jusef Islam on his conversion to Islam.

- Actors or writers frequently use stage names or pen names: some examples would be Norma Jean Baker (= Marilyn Monroe), Johann Hölzel (= Falco), Louise Veronica Ciccone (= Madonna) or Samuel Langhorne Clemens (= Mark Twain).

- The 19th century UK prime minister, Benjamin D'Israeli, changed the spelling of his name to Disraeli. It made his Jewish roots less obvious. Disraeli himself was baptised a Christian. Similarly, an Austrian-born person of Slovenian origin called Zlatko Pinteric˘ decided to change his name to Nikolaus Pinterits because of the prejudice he experienced because of his original name.

- In 1917, because of anti-German feeling in Britain during the First World War, various aristocratic families gave up their German titles and changed their names: the Battenbergs to Mountbatten, for instance Queen Elizabeth's husband, Prince Philip is a Mountbatten. The king at the time, George V, decided to change the name of the royal family from 'Saxe-Coburg and Gotha' to 'Windsor'.

My name is Anna Konda. Why do people laugh?

This is Mrs Soares and her daughter Dinah.

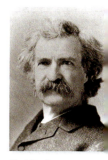

Mark Twain

1. Ask your classmates about their own experiences of cultural misunderstandings. What cultural stereotypes have they experienced? Produce a "Cultural Guide" for your school.

2. In a small group express your personal opinions on the following issues:
   - Taking your partner's family name after marriage,
   - Emigrating to a new country and changing your first name or your family name to fit in better there.
   - Naming children whose parents are from different cultures. (▶ Skills 3.3)

3. Internet research: Imagine that you have a child with someone from another culture and you decide to give the child a name from your partner's culture. Make a shortlist with five boy's names and five girl's names. (▶ Skills 1.0)

1 Cheese and onion pie

a) *Complete the list of ingredients with the words from the box below.*

> butter • eggs • glaze *(Glasur)* • grated *(gerieben)* • onion *(Zwiebel)* •
> pastry *(Teig)* • pepper • potatoes • tablespoonfuls *(ein Esslöffel)* •
> teaspoonful *(Teelöffel)* • thyme *(Thymian)*

Serves six people
285 g of good, strong Cheddar cheese, coarsely (1) ...
30 g of unsalted (2) ...
one large (3) ... , peeled and chopped finely
110 g of (4) ..., peeled, steamed and diced
two large (5) ...
four (6) ... of double cream
one pinch of dried (7) ... or parsley,
one pinch of cayenne (8) ...
one (9) ... of sea salt
shortcrust (10) ... made with 340 g of flour and 170 g of unsalted butter
1 beaten egg for (11) ...

b) *Put the instructions into the right order. In the correct order, the letters in brackets will spell a word from this unit.*

C Brush beaten egg over the top and bake in the oven for 30 minutes until crisp and golden brown. You can use leeks instead of onions, or add buttered apple slices instead of the potato.

H Melt the butter in a pan and gently fry the onion until soft, then leave to cool.
Then throw the onions into a bowl with the grated cheese, potato, eggs, cream, thyme or parsley and the seasoning, and mix thoroughly with your fingers.

T Make the pastry and divide it into two balls, keeping one a little larger than the other.

E Heat the oven to 220 °C / Gas 7.

I Moisten the edges of the pastry shell. Roll out the smaller ball of pastry and make a top which covers the pastry shell in the tart tin. Pinch the edges together carefully.

N Roll out the larger ball of pastry and line a shallow greased 23 cm tart tin.
Place the cheese and onion mixture into the pastry shell.

2 Traditional sausage rolls

Listen to Track 12 again and answer these questions in an exercise book.

1. What kinds of meat can be used?
2. How much salt is aded to the meat?
3. What is added to the stock?
4. How long are the sausages?
5. What are the breadcrumbs used for?
6. What kind of pastry is used?
7. How hot must the oven be?

3 Prepositions

What prepositions are missing from the following sentences?

1. We celebrated the event ... a special meal.
2. Online shops have lots of products ... offer.
3. Some dried herbs were added ... the soup.
4. This portrait ... Henry VIII was painted ... Hans Holbein.
5. Take the pan ... the heat and let it cool.
6. Bake in a hot oven ... 20 minutes.
7. Roll ... the puff pastry and cut it ... squares.
8. Our business is doing well, orders are flooding ...!

4 A summary

Read the text "The Spice of Life" (page 140) again and then complete the following summary.

1. Laxmishankar Pathak and his family arrived in the UK in .... .
2. The Pathaks were ethnic Indians who had lived in .... .
3. They were the ... of Indian workers who had moved there in colonial times.
4. Laxmishankar and his family began selling home-made Indian foods which they cooked in the small ... of their house.
5. Their first ... were other ethnic Indians.
6. In 1962 the Patak Spice Company had to move out of their premises in London because of ... from neighbours.
7. They moved to Northamptonshire because there was a large Indian ... there.
8. The Patak Spice Company grew and by 2007 they were selling their products in more than 40 countries .... .
9. In 2007 they decided to ... their company to Associated British Foods.
10. Kirit and Meena Pathak, his ..., were awarded OBEs.

TRACK 13   **5** **Talking of names**

Read the questions below and make a note of the information you need. Then listen to Track 13 again and answer these questions (A–F) with the number of the comment (1–6).

A   Which one is about shortening long, difficult names?
B   Which one is about changing foreign names into local ones?
C   Which one is about following fashions in first names?
D   Which one is about showing a desire to assimilate?
E   Which one is about translating foreign names into the local language?
F   Which one is about dropping a typical part of a name?

GRAMMAR

> ### *get* + Partizip perfekt (*past partiple*)
>
> - Diese Wendung kann die Passivform mit **be + past participle** ersetzen, z. B:
>   *We **were invited** to a wild party. = We **got invited** to a wild party.*

6 **Active to passive**

In an exercise book rewrite the active sentences as passives.

a) Using *be + past participle*.
b) Using *get + past participle*.

1. The librarian told us off for being noisy.
2. How often does the local council empty your rubbish bins?
3. We won't send the protocol until everyone has signed it.
4. A store detective caught two kids stealing sweets.
5. The police stopped me again for driving too fast.

CHECK

1 I can describe exotic foods.

2 I can understand recipes.

3 I can analyse a feature article.

4 I can write a summary.

5 I can discuss cultural misunderstandings and avoid stereotypes.

6 I can convert statistics into a graph.

UNIT 12
Business communication

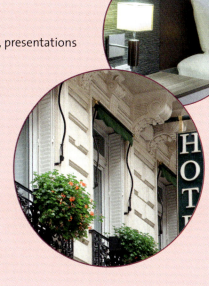

To do

Receptive
- Understanding written texts as e-mails, websites, presentations
- Understanding a discussion in English

Productive
- Making a business telephone call
- Inviting participants to a meeting by e-mail
- Creating and giving a presentation
- Keep the minutes of a meeting

Interactive
- Working together as a team
- Role-playing a discussion

1   Work experience training

▶ Activity holidays

▶ Celebrations

▶ Tours & City Breaks

▶ Group holidays

Laura Kirschner:
- 17 years old
- German high-school graduate
- studying business communication at Havering College, Essex
- wants to work in tourism

Ben Riedel:
- 17 years old
- Danish high-school graduate
- studying marketing and management at Havering College, Essex
- wants to work in tourism

TRACK 14

Preparing a meeting
Laura and Ben are discussing the things they must do.

Laura and Ben are doing a work experience training in the London offices of Simply Holidays, an Internet website that helps people to find holiday accommodation and also offers a wide range of holiday options. Ms Sandra Lawson is their trainee supervisor and she has asked Laura and Ben to prepare a meeting for next Thursday afternoon.

Sandra gives Laura and Ben an invitation list for the meeting and she tells them that the purpose of the meeting will be to discuss and assess new hotel applications in the United Kingdom and in Ireland and then decide which hotels they will recommend on their website.

Find a holiday

Destination
| All destinations |

Holiday type
| All holiday types |

Departure dates from
| Any | Any | Any |

Find a holiday

| Holiday code | optional | GO |

Request a brochure

INVITATION LIST

CEO
Mr Patrick O'Sullivan
p.osullivan@sh.co.uk

Heads of departments

Website content /
Travel
Ms Samantha Atkinson
s.atkinson@sh.co.uk

Marketing
Mr Oliver Stone
o.stone@sh.co.uk

Accounts /Finance
Ms Julia Greene
j.greene@sh.co.uk

Human resources /
Training
Ms Sandra Lawson
s.lawson@sh.co.uk

E-mails

Abbreviations:

Cc	Carbon copy	*Kopie*
Bcc	Blind carbon copy	*Blindkopie*
sub	Subject	*Betreff*
add	addressee	*Empfänger(in)*

Formal greetings:

Dear Mr / Ms …	(when you know the name)
Dear Sir / Madam	(when you don't know the name)
Dear Sir or Madam	(when you don't know name or sex)

Use 'Ms' for all women, whether married or single.

Expressing a purpose or a wish politely:

I / We would like to   ask you to attend a meeting.
                       invite you to …
                       inform you that …

The purpose of the meeting is to discuss …
I / We would appreciate a reply as soon as possible.

Times and dates:

Use either simple present or will-future:
The meeting is / will be at 2p.m. on 22. March.

Endings:

I / We look forward to hearing from you soon.
Best regards
Best wishes

INFO-BOX

TASKS

1. Find a similar holiday website and briefly describe the services they provide.

2. Listen to the dialogue (Track 14) and then work with a partner and write their two checklists. Use the information from the dialogue and any additional information that you and your partner can think of.

4. Look at the people on the invitation list. What do do think they will want to know about the new hotels?

5. Write an e-mail to one of the people on the invitation list. Include the following things:
   - invite him / her to attend a meeting in Room 210 at 2 p.m. next Thursday (+ date: day / month / year);
   - say what the purpose of the meeting is;
   - tell him / her that you and a partner will give a presentation at the meeting;
   - say that you will send material for the meeting;
   - ask for confirmation that he / she can attend.

2 Creating a presentation

Laura and Ben are preparing their presentation. They want to present three new hotels at the meeting. As a first step, they are looking at their websites. They have made a list of the audio-visual information they would like to provide about each of the hotels:

- Location: Do they offer a street map or road map?
- The number and type of rooms and prices: Do they provide photos and/or descriptions?
- Meals: Do they provide breakfast and/or other meals? Is there a menu?
- Services: What services do they offer? Are they included in the room price or as extras?
- Local attractions: Do they provide information, tickets, tours, etc.?
- Any other important information.

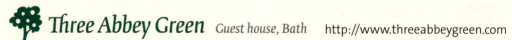

Three Abbey Green   *Guest house, Bath*   http://www.threeabbeygreen.com

Three Abbey Green is a townhouse in the heart of Bath.
It has seven beautifully restored bedrooms. All are spacious and elegant with en suite facilities. Each one is very different. Lady Hamilton's room has a brand new Super King-size double bed, which can be split into single beds. There are comfortable armchairs – so you can spend relaxing time in front of the fireplace. The Westwood Suite has a large main room with a Super King-size double bed, a comfortable sofa and chairs and there is also a dressing room with a single bed. The Lord Nelson is the biggest room. It has a four-poster bed and a comfortable sitting area with a sofa (which can be used as a sofabed) and two armchairs.

INFO-BOX

Types of hotel room

Single Room:
A room with two single beds meant for two persons.

Double Room:
A room with one double bed meant for two people.

Twin Room :
A room with two single beds meant for twopersons.

Twin Double Room:
Commonly known as a family room having two double beds separated from each other.

Suite:
Two or more connected rooms, e. g. one or more bedrooms, and / or a sitting room.

Central Hotel
Dublin City Centre

http://www.centralhoteldublin.com

If you want to experience Dublin City life then our central location is perfect for you. All our bedrooms are spacious, modern and designed for your comfort. They all have cable-TV, a direct-dial telephone, a coffee maker, and a hairdryer. WiFi is available in most rooms. All our rooms are non-smoking, and an iron and an ironing board are available on request. The Library Bar at The Central Hotel combines old and new Dublin. Enjoy a glass or two of Dublin's famous Guinness stout or a Jameson on the rocks, or for the ladies a nice Baileys.

HAYFIELD MANOR

Cork, Republic of Ireland
http://www.hayfieldmanor.ie

All the highlights and attractions of the city are only minutes from the Hayfield Manor Hotel. The airport and the train station are only ten minutes away by car or taxi. Our guest rooms have beautiful furniture and are equipped with all the modern amenities. Each bedroom as a different style but they all have a KingSize double bed, air-conditioning, elegant bathrooms, 32" flat screen TV and DVD player, comfortable bathrobes and slippers, high-speed Internet access, 24-hour room service, a safe, an ironing board and an iron, and a trouser press. You can also relax in our swimming-pool or work out in our gym.

TASKS

1. Work with a partner and choose one of the hotels. Study their website and collect enough useful audio-visual information and materials for a 4-minute presentation. Then produce and give an audio-visual presentation.

2. Assess the presentations (but not your own!) and give each a mark between 1 (very good) and 6 (very bad).

3   A business call

To get a better idea of each hotel, Laura and Ben call the
managers and ask for further information. Laura calls the
Hayfield Manor Hotel in Cork and talks to Mr David Jones,
the manager.

Mr Jones: Hayfield Manor Hotel, David Jones speaking,
how may
I help you?

Laura: (1)

Mr Jones: Oh, that's very interesting. We're always interested in new
cooperations especially with Internet companies. But before I give you
more details about our hotels, I have one question. Does your website only offer
information or can the customer book the rooms directly on the website?

Laura: (2)

Mr Jones: That sounds fair. Our hotel is definitely one of the best places to stay here in the
wonderful city of Cork. Our hotel is in an attractive old Manor House right in the city
centre. It's easily accessible from the train station and the airport. The rooms are
comfortable and designed with great care and taste. We offer all kinds of facilities
such as internet access, a swimming pool, and a gym.

Laura: (3)

Mr Jones: I'm glad you ask because we are very proud of our breakfast buffet. Our chefs offer
a mixture of traditional Irish cuisine mixed with special dishes from all over the world.
No matter where you come from, you'll find your breakfast specials on our buffet.
That's our USP.

Laura: (4)

Mr Jones: Of course, with pleasure. Where should I send it?

Laura: (5)

Mr Jones: No, I'll send everything to your e-mail address. Can you spell it for me, please?

Laura: (6)

Mr Jones: Thank you! I'll send you the information at once and I hope our hotel will be on
your website soon.

Laura: (7)

Mr Jones: Great, thank you!

Laura: (8)

Mr Jones: You too. Bye-bye.

A That's good Mr. Jones. Every business should have a unique selling point. I'm preparing a presention for the colleagues who will assess your hotel. Could you send me some additional information, please?

B Yes, it's L – dot – K – I – R – S – C – H – N – E – R – at – sh – dot – co – dot – uk.

C That sounds great. Is it also possible to have breakfast at the hotel?

D My e-mail address is: L.Kirchner@sh.co.uk. Or would you prefer to send the material by post?

E Thank you for the information and have a great afternoon!

F Hello, my name is Laura Kirschner. I'm calling from Simply Holidays. We are a London-based holiday website. We're looking for more hotels to cooperate with. I found your website and would like to know more about the Hayfield Manor Hotel.

G Thank you very much, Mr Jones. I'll inform you of our decision by the end of next week.

H We offer a booking service. The fee for that service is 10 % of the room price before tax.

WORD POWER

Business calls

How may I help you?	I'd like to speak to … , please.
I'm sorry, but … isn't available at the moment.	When would be the best time to call back?
I'm afraid Mr / Ms … 's line is engaged.	Thank you. I'll call again later.
Could you repeat that, please?	Of course. I said: … / asked if …
Could you speak up a bit, please?	Sorry! Is that better?
I'm putting you through now.	
Please hold the line.	Thank you for your help.
How can / may I help you?	My name is … and I work for …
	I'd like further information about … ?
	Could / Would you tell me more about … ?
I'll get back to you about that.	Thank you. I appreciate that.
I hope I've been able to help you.	You certainly have and I'm very grateful for
	all your help / cooperation.
Bye-bye. Have a good day.	Thank you. It was a pleasure talking to you!

TASKS

1 Reconstruct the telephone call between Mr Jones and Laura. Listen to their call (Track 15) and check your results. Act out the dialogue with a partner.

2 Work with a partner and role-play similar telephone dialogues with one of the other hotels:
Laura / Ben – Ms Rita Devlin (Central Hotel Dublin)
Laura / Ben – Mr Ralph Carpenter (Three Abbey Green, Bath)

4   A marketing discussion

It's Thursday afternoon and Ben and Laura have just finished their presentation.
The CEO and the heads of departments discuss the three hotels from the presentation.
Read the role cards – they show what each participant says, but not the order
in which they say it.

Patrick O'Sullivan (CEO)

- Thank you Ben and Laura. That was an excellent presentation. However, I don't think our clients will like any of these three hotels.
- May I remind everyone that because of rising costs we need to increase our sales by £100,000 this year.
- Well, I've still got my doubts, but if Julia thinks she can sell them, I'll accept the hotels in Bath and Cork.
- Just one last point. Ben and Laura – your presentation was very helpful. I'd like you both to prepare our next meeting in which we'll look at new hotels in France and Germany.

Julia Green (Finance / Accounts)

- You're right about the Dublin hotel, Patrick. It doesn't fit our profile at all, does it?
  But I don't agree with you about the hotels in Bath and Cork. Their prices are within the limits we set and the services they offer are good for that category.
- Yes, I know we must increase our sales, Patrick. That's why I think we should accept the hotels at Bath and Cork. They're both attractive offers and we won't have any problem selling them to our clients.

Samantha Atkinson (Website / Travel)

- I don't agree with you at all, Patrick. I find all three hotels attractive and I think our clients will, too.
- I like Oliver's suggestion. It makes the choice easy. All three hotels have suitable facilities, but the Dublin hotel is too expensive. So let's try the hotels at Bath and Cork.

Oliver Stone (Marketing)

- If we had to, I think we could integrate all three hotels into our profile. OK, the Dublin hotel is expensive, but it might appeal to our upmarket clients. Their rooms are well-equipped and beautifully decorated. We could present it as a special luxury highlight on our website. But changing our profile to fit it in would be a risk. So I suggest we play it safe and we just check whether the hotels fit into our current criteria.

handwerk-technik.de

Laura / Ben (trainees)

- Thank you, Mr O'Sullivan. We're very glad you liked it and we hope you found it useful.
- Thank you. We've enjoyed preparing and giving this presentation and we'd love to do the next one, too.

WORD POWER

Good news and bad

I've got some good news for you.
– Good news is always welcome.
We decided to place your hotel on our website.
– I'm very pleased / glad to hear that.
May we use the photos you sent us?
– Certainly. / Of course.
– I can send you more / better ones.
– Will you need anything else?
Please inform us of any changes.

I'm afraid that I have same bad news for you.
– That doesn't sound too good.
I'm sorry, but we decided not to ...
– I'm very sorry / disappointed to hear that.
– Why wasn't our hotel accepted?
Because your room prices are a lot higher than the other hotels on our website.
– Was that the only reason?
– We could make your firm a special offer.

TASKS

1 Form groups of six. Five people take over the roles of the participants at the marketing discussion and use the role cards to have a discussion. One person keeps the minutes of the meeting. These should include:
   – the names and job titles of the participants,
   – the agenda (i.e. the purpose of the meeting or the topic for discussion),
   – short summaries of what each person said.

2 The day after the meeting, Laura and Ben call the managers of the three hotels and inform them of the decision.
Role-play one of these phone calls.
Laura / Ben   – Rita Devlin (Central Hotel Dublin)
            – Ralph Carpenter (Three Abbey Green Park, Bath)
            – David Jones (Hayfield Manor Hotel, Cork)

1 **On the telephone**

a) *Work with a partner and practise this telephone call in English.*

A You work for Global Construction and you're the PA (personal assistant) of Ms Hammond, the director of Human Resources.

B You're a candidate for a position with Global Construction. You have an appointment for an interview with Ms Hammond on the following day.

- Melde dich am Telefon: gebe zuerst Abteilung und Firma an, dann deinen eigenen Namen und deine Position.
- Ms Hammond ist im Moment nicht verfügbar. Frage, ob du helfen kannst.
- Sage, dass du deiner Chefin eine Nachricht hinterlassen kannst. Frage, um was es geht. (Notizen schreiben!)
- Bitte ihn / sie den vollen Namen zu wiederholen.
- Bitte ihn / sie den Nachnamen zu buchstabieren.
- Bitte ihn / sie um weitere Kontaktdetails.
- Wiederhole die Kontaktdetails. (Bei der E-Mail-Adresse machst du einen Fehler.)
- Wiederhole die korrekte E-Mail-Adresse und versichere, dass Ms Hammond gleich bei ihrer Rückkehr die Nachricht erhalten wird. Sie wird sich dann sobald wie möglich bei ihm / ihr anmelden.
- Verabschiede dich.

- Sage, wer du bist und dass du mit Ms Hammond sprechen möchtest.
- Sage, es geht um dein Bewerbungsgespräch am folgenden Tag und es ist dringend.
- Dein Gespräch soll am nächsten Tag um 14:30 stattfinden. Du hast aber einen Unfall gehabt und du liegst jetzt im Krankenhaus. Du wirst erst in 2 oder 3 Tagen entlassen. Du möchtest einen neuen Termin vereinbaren.
- Wiederhole deinen vollen Namen.
- Buchstabiere deinen Nachnamen.
- Gebe deine Anschrift, deine Telefonnummer und deine E-Mail-Adresse an.
- Weise auf den Schreibfehler in der E-Mail-Adresse hin und buchstabiere sie.
- Bedanke dich für die Hilfe und verabschiede dich.

b) *Now swap roles.*

c) *Write either a memo or an e-mail to Ms Hammond about the call.*

d) *Ms Hammond sends this text message to her personal assistant. Role play a telephone call between the PA and the interview candidate.*

Call back and arrange another app. 4 nxt wk: Mo @ 4pm or Wed @ 10.15am.

2 Texting (SMS messages)

Write the following text messages in English and keep them as short as possible.

- Sag deinem Chef, dass das Treffen mit einem Kunden länger als geplant dauern wird und du etwa eine halbe Stunde später zur Verkaufskonferenz erscheinen wirst.

- Du hast vergessen, für 8 Konferenzteilnehmer einen Tisch im Taj Mahal Indian Restaurant zu bestellen. Bitte einen Kollegen / eine Kollegin, das für dich zu erledigen.

- Entschuldige dich beim Chef, weil du an der Konferenz am Nachmittag nicht teilnehmen wirst. Gebe einen Grund für dein Fehlen an.

3 Reference lines

In an exercise book write reference lines (Betreffzeilen) for the following e-mails.

> **1** Dear Sir or Madam, thank you very much for your interest in our event location. Attached you will find our offer for 3. October 2013. This is only a draft and we can adjust it to your wishes. You can call us anytime at 0892 - 34 89 79 02.
>
> Yours, sincerely

> **2** Dear colleagues,
>
> I've attached the protocol of our last meeting.
>
> Regards,

> **3** Dear Mr Malloney,
>
> We are sorry to inform you that we have no vacancies for the time requested. We hope we can be of assistance another time.
>
> Yours, sincerely
> Laura P. Evans, Manager
> Holyrood Palace Hotel, Edinburgh

4 Telephone language

Translate these typical telephone phrases into English. Use an exercise book.

1. Bitte bleiben Sie am Apparat.
2. Ich verbinde Sie jetzt.
3. Mit wem wollten Sie sprechen?
4. Es tut mir leid, aber sie ist im Moment nicht verfügbar.
5. Es tut mir leid, aber seine Leitung ist besetzt.
6. Möchten Sie später zurückrufen?
7. Möchten Sie eine Nachricht hinterlassen?
8. Die Leitung ist schlecht. Könnten Sie bitte lauter sprechen?
9. Das habe ich akustisch nicht mitbekommen. Würden Sie es bitte wiederholen?

5 Cartoon project

Search the Internet and put together a small collection of cartoons with a business theme. Describe your collection. Do you notice any similarities and / or differences? What makes them funny? Is there a deeper meaning?

© Randy Glasbergen
glasbergen.com

GLASBERGEN

"Aside from the people, the hours, the work,
the pay, the stress and the migraines,
this is the best job I ever had."

6 Types of hotel

Match the hotel types in the box to the descriptions below.

1. Commercial hotels, 2. Apartment hotels, 3. Bed and Breakfast hotels, 4. Resort hotels

A   These hotels provide long-term or permanent accommodation. The guest suites usually include a bedroom, a living room and a kitchen.
B   These are usually located in places where people go for a holiday (e.g. an island, a beach, a lake or a mountain). They offer scenic tours and recreational facilities such as golf, sailing, scuba diving, skiing, etc.
C   These medium-priced hotels are often located outside city centres and cater for business travellers and short-stay guests.
D   These are private houses with rooms available for short-term guests. The owners live there, too and cook breakfast for their guests.

CHECK

1 I can make a business telephone call.
2 I can find specific information on the Internet.
3 I can produce and give a presentation.
4 I can keep the minutes of a business meeting.

APPENDIX

1   Research skills

1.1 Working with dictionaries

In order to use your monolingual dictionary effectively, you must be familiar with the abbreviations, labels and symbols it uses. For example:

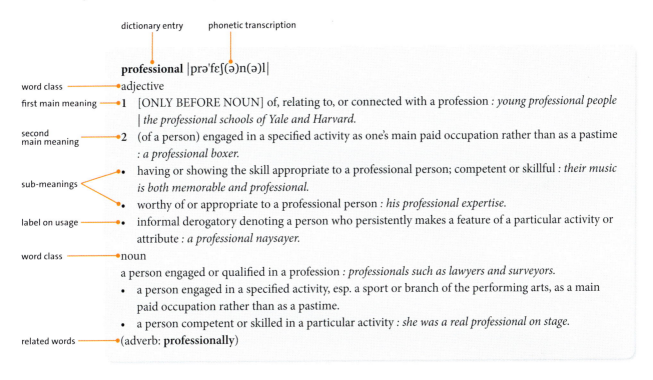

As you can see, looking up a word in the monolingual dictionary can give you information on its pronunciation, the form of the plural, the word class it belongs to, how many different meanings it has and how they are used.

A **thesaurus** is a special dictionary. It gives you words that have the same or a very similar meaning (synonyms) and words which have the opposite meaning (antonyms).

---

professional

adjective

1 *people in professional occupations:* white-collar, nonmanual. ANTONYMS blue-collar.
2 *a professional rugby player:* paid, salaried. ANTONYMS amateur.
3 *a thoroughly professional performance:* expert, accomplished, skillful, masterly, masterful, fine, polished, skilled, proficient, competent, able, experienced, practiced, trained, seasoned, businesslike, deft; informal ace, crack, top-notch. ANTONYMS amateurish.
4 not a professional way to behave: appropriate, fitting, proper, honorable, ethical, correct, comme il faut. ANTONYMS inappropriate, unethical.

noun

1 *affluent young professionals:* white-collar worker, office worker. ANTONYMS blue-collar worker.
2 *his first season as a professional:* professional player, paid player, salaried player; informal pro. ANTONYMS amateur.
3 *she was a real professional on stage:* expert, virtuoso, old hand, master, maestro, past master; informal pro, ace, wizard, whiz, hotshot, maven, crackerjack. ANTONYMS amateur.

1.2 Online dictionaries

Many English dictionaries are available online. For example:

General purpose:
www.thefreedictionary.com
www.yourdictionary.com
www.merriam-webster.com
Bilingual dictionary:
http://dict.leo.org

For foreign language learners:
www.dictionary.cambridge.org
www.oxforddictionaries.com
www.learnersdictionary.com
www.ldoceonline.com
www.collinsdictionary.com

Several of these online dictionaries are also available as smartphone apps.

1.3 Online research

When researching a topic the internet offers quick and easy access to large amounts of information. The internet is a particularly good source of information on current events, because it is very up-to-date, and on controversial topics, because you can find different opinions and perspectives on a topic.

But the advantages of the internet go hand in hand with some challenges: You have to be able to search efficiently in order to find the most useful websites within the huge amount of available information. You also have to evaluate the websites you find, because the information on the internet comes from various sources of very different quality - some are trustworthy and reliable, some less so.

Tips on Using Search Engines

- Different search engines use different search methods and so will also give you different results. A metasearch engine combines the results of several regular search engines.
- Depending on the topic of your research, you could also try a specialised search engine, e.g. for jobs or news.
- Most search engines let you use words or symbols to influence your search. Alternatively, use the fields in the "advanced search" option of the search engine.

How you want to influence the results of your search	using words (Boolean search terms)	using symbols (simplified search syntax)	advanced search fields
The keywords must be present	AND e.g. *apples AND pears*	+ or [space] e.g. *apples +pears* *apples pears*	all these words must contain the words
Certain keywords must not be present	NOT e.g. *apples NOT pears*	- e.g. *apples -pears*	none of these words must not / should not contain the words
Any of the keywords may be present	OR e.g. *apples OR pear*		any of the words at least one of the words should contain the words
The exact phrase must be present		" " e.g. *"apple sauce"*	this exact word or phrase

Evaluating Websites

Once you have the results of your internet search, the challenge is to pick out the reliable and helpful websites from the long list available. Don't just use the first results but scan the list to choose which websites seem useful. Check the Internet addresses of the websites in the list to see whether they come from a well-known and trustworthy organisation or company (a university, a museum, a newspaper, a TV channel etc.) – these are generally a good place to start.

Reading Internet texts

First scan the texts and the sub-headings to see if they fit the topic you are researching.
Sort out the texts that don't fit and skim (fast read) the texts that do. (See Reading skills ▶ 2.0)

2   Reading skills

2.1 Reading strategies

Different texts are read for different purposes - and depending on the purpose with which you read, you will also use different reading strategies. So before reading it is important to think about what you want to know from the text: Do you just quickly want to look up a piece of information or look through a text to understand its main idea? Or do you want to gain a detailed and thorough understanding of the text? Either way, a good starting point is to anticipate what the text could be about. Look at the text before you begin reading it: What can its title, its format, any pictures or graphics tell you about the possible content of the text? If you do not need to gain a detailed understanding of a text, you can just read it over quickly. There are different types of fast reading which have different purposes:

Skimming is browsing through the text to get the main point. For example, if you wanted to get a general idea of what is going on in the news, you would skim through a newspaper.

Scanning is reading to find specific details, often in answer to one of the wh-questions: Who? What? Which? Where? When? Why? For example, you would use scanning to pick out the website you want from the results of an internet search or to look up a word in a dictionary.

Detailed reading. But sometimes you need to read a text with a lot of care and attention in order to understand it thoroughly, e.g. in order to answer essay questions or write a summary of it. In such cases, you can use a more elaborate 5 step-strategy:

1. SURVEY: Examine the text before reading it and consider what its title, sub-headings and illustrations tell you about its content.

2. QUESTION: Focus your attention on what is relevant and important when reading by asking questions beforehand:
   What do I already know about this topic?
   What do I want to find out from this text?
   Note down specific questions that you would like to be able to answer after reading the text, either mentally or on paper.

3. READ: Now read the text, first focussing on the parts you understand and marking information you need to answer your questions. Then reread passages which are not clear, using the context or help from a dictionary in order to try and understand them.

4. RECITE: Go through the text again, paragraph by paragraph, and summarise each section in your own words. Take notes or make a mind map with the information that answers the questions you asked before reading.

5. REVIEW: Review the text and your notes/mind map and check your understanding:
   What answers to my questions have I found?
   Did I find the information I needed?
   What do I now know about this topic that I didn't know before?
   How does this connect to my previous knowledge on the topic?

2.2 Text interpretation

Poems and literary texts also work with imagery (dt. *Metaphorik, Bilder*), painting pictures with language. Finding out which images are used by an author is the key to interpreting the meaning. The main images that you can find in many texts are:

Image	Example	Explanation
simile	*My love is like a rose.*	Two things are compared. The comparison uses the words 'like' or 'as'. (dt. *Gleichnis*)
metaphor	*My love is a rose.*	Two things are compared as equal (=), there is no 'like' or 'as'. (dt. *Metapher**)
symbol	*rose*	Two things are compared, but the first is not explicitly mentioned. The second stands alone, but signifies the first. (dt. *Symbol*)

*Achtung: „Metapher" wird im Deutschen oft als Sammelbegriff für „Bild" oder „Bildhaftigkeit" benutzt.

3 Speaking skills

3.1 Taking part in a talkshow

A talkshow with your fellow students is more informal than a debate and it's a good method of discussing topics from different perspectives. It works best when the participants have genuinely different points of view and there is an active moderator. The participants should prepare in advance arguments they can use to support their pont of view. The moderator's task is to introduce the subject and the participants, to get everyone involved in the conversation and to summarize the discussion. He or she might even take questions from the audience. i.e. the other students in your group.

Five Rules for Successful Discussions

1. State your opinion clearly.
2. Don't discredit others' opinions and present your opinion as fact – don't say "You are wrong! This is how it is ..."
3. Be polite – watch your tone of voice and your choice of words.
4. Don't exaggerate – avoid using "never" and "always".
5. Listen to what the others say – don't interrupt!

3.2 Giving a presentation

Ten Tips for Giving a Good Presentation

1. Plan the aim of your presentation, i.e. what you want your audience to know afterwards.
2. Structure your information: Introduction, overview, main part, summing up, questions.
3. Find an interesting beginning to catch the attention of your audience.
4. KISS – **K**eep **i**t **s**hort and **s**imple!
5. Use signposting language* to make your presentation easy to follow.
6. If you use new words that your audience might not understand, explain them or write them down.
7. Make visual aids such as Powerpoint slides easy to read. Don't overload them.
8. Speak loudly and clearly.
9. Breathe deeply and use pauses.
10. Keep eye contact with your audience and smile!

Signposting Language

Introducing the Topic	Giving an Overview	Getting Started
My topic today is … *The subject of my presentation is …* *Today I'm going to tell you about …* *I'm going to talk about …*	*I have split my presentation into … parts.* *I'm going to divide this talk into … parts.* *I have … things to talk about.*	*I'd like to begin by …* *Let's start off by …* *First of all, I'll …*
Moving On	**Summing Up**	**Questions**
Then / Next … *Now let's turn to …* *The next point I'd like to focus on is …* *Now we'll move on to …* *Next let's look at …* *Finally / Lastly …*	*To sum up …* *We have looked at …* *Let's sum up the main points ..* *To conclude …* *In short …*	*Does anyone have any questions?* *Now please feel free to ask questions.* *Any questions?*

3.3 Expressing an opinion

Stating your opinion	Giving advice	Agreeing	Disagreeing
In my opinion … *From my point of view …* *It seems to me that …* *Personally, I feel (that) …* *I would say (that) …*	*You should …* *Maybe you should …* *If I were you, I would / wouldn't …*	*I think that … is …* *I think this will / would work.* *That's a good idea.* *I completely agree with …* *I'm sure (that) …* *That's how I see it, too.* *I couldn't agree more.* *I couldn't have said it better myself.*	*I'm sorry, but I have to disagree with you.* *I don't think this will / would work.* *I don't think so.* *That's not such a good idea.* *I disagree with …* *I am not sure (that) …* *I don't see it this way.* *I (can) see your point, but …* *I don't quite agree.*

3.4 Talking about diagrams

Follow a two-step approach when presenting or discussing a diagram and the data it represents:

1. Describe the diagram and the information it visualizes.

- Bar charts *(Säulendiagramm)* show the relative sizes of things.
  The bar chart compares the ... with ... It is based on a survey onducted by / in ...
- Pie charts *(Tortendiagramm)* show the percentages and fractions of a total.
  The pie chart visually highlights the relative sizes of ...
- Line graphs *(Kurvendiagramm)* illustrate developments over time.
  The line graph makes it clear that from ... to ... there was a slow rise / fall in ...
- Tables *(Tabelle)* arrange data in rows and columns.
  As you can see from the table, there has been a dramatic increase / derease in ...

2. Draw conclusions from the data presented.

In conclusion, we can say that ...
To sum up, we can see that ...
The following conclusions can be drawn from the data: ...
The table clearly tells us that ...
The line graph makes it obvious that in the next ten years ...

3.5 Describing pictures, adverts and cartoons

Concentrate on the main visual message (Bildaussage), don't get bogged down in unimportant details. Follow this 3-step sequence:

- Description: *What? Who? Where? When? Why?*
  Start with an overall impression:
  What we see in the cartoon / picture is ...
  Give as many details as possible.
- Interpretation: Analyse the picture, advert or cartoon by identifying different elements and explaining what you think their funtion is.
  The obvious message is: "...".
  The intention is to make us aware of / think about ...
  The advert is aimed at people who ...
- Comment: Finally, summarize your analysis and express your personal opinion.
  Give valid reasons for your opinions, too.

3.6 Job Interviews

Typical Questions in Job Interviews	Helpful Answers in Job Interviews
Why would you like to work for our company/ organisation? *What do you know about us?* *What skills and abilities can you bring to this position?* *Would you describe yourself as "determined"?* *What do you think your greatest strength is?* *What's your greatest weakness?* *Tell me about a significant achievement in your life.* *Why did you leave your last job?* *What are your expectations in terms of salary?* *Where do you see yourself in five years' time?*	*I'd like to gain some work experience in …* *I am looking for a job in …* *I believe I meet the requirements for the position.* *I've just completed my training as …* *I've just finished a training programme on …* *For the past … years I have been working as …* *I'm familiar with the … marketing process.* *I have a basic knowledge of …* *I know how to …* *I'm especially good at …* *I'd expect a salary that is competitive with / comparable to other salaries in this sector.* *In my present job / last job I earned … a year, so I'd expect a slightly higher salary.* *In five years time I'd like to be in a more responsible position.*

Practice online: Some websites offer an interview simulation. You just have to click on the most appropriate answer to the questions asked by the interviewer. At the end you will be told your score, i.e. how well (or badly) you did. Other websites give you tasks which you must do while watching a video. Use the following keywords in the search function of your browser:
interview dos and don'ts • interview practice • interview simulation

4 Mediation skills

Mediation is not the same as translation, but rather a way of bridging a communication gap between users of different languages. Mediation would be helpful in the following real-life situations for example:

- Your younger cousins like an English pop song, but don't understand the lyrics. They ask you what the song is about and you tell them in German about the main idea of the song.
- You're on holiday with relatives who don't speak much English. At your holiday destination, nobody speaks German but most people speak English. You help your relatives to hire a car by explaining their needs in English and giving them the information from the car hire counter in German.
- You're researching the Internet for information for a presentation in another course. You find a useful article in English. You sum up its main points in German to use in your presentation.

In such situations, you should not try to translate word by word. This is usually difficult anyway, since two languages can say the same thing in very different ways. But it is also not necessary, because communication and understanding between both sides are much more important than absolute accuracy. So use your own words and find a way to get the point across to the person who does not understand the original text.

Tips for Mediation Situations:

- Concentrate on transferring the basic meaning from one language to the other – don't get caught up in details or stylistic nuances.
- Focus on the situation and the person you are talking to: How can you help them understand the most important content of the original text? What is most important will often depend on the situation.
- When mediating from German to English: Use short, simple sentences and pay attention to word order and the correct use of tenses. If you cannot think of the necessary vocabulary in English, try and find another way to express it.

5   Writing skills

5.1 Formal letters and e-mails

situation	salutation	ending
you know the person's name	Dear Mr / Ms / Mrs,	Yours sincerely / faithfully, Regards, Best wishes (less formal)
you don't know the person's name	Dear Sir or Madam,	Yours sincerely / faithfully,

There are stylistic differences between the United Kingdom (Australia, New Zealand, Canada, usw.) and the USA:

Salutations

British style:
- No full stops after Ms, Mrs and Mr or after titles (such as Dr).
- The comma is optional, but if you use it in the salutation, you should also use it in the ending.

American style:
- Full stops are used after Ms., Mrs., and Mr. as well as after titles (such as Dr.).
- Commas are only used when you address the letter to a particular person.

Endings or complimentary closes

American style:
- "Yours faithfully" is not used.
- The most common complimentary closes include: "Sincerely yours", "Sincerely", "Yours truly" and "Very truly yours".

Writing the date

British style:
- The date can be written as: 15 January 2014 or 15th January 2014
- When using only numbers the date is generally written as 15/1/14 or 15.01.14

American style:
- The date is generally written as: January 15, 2014
- When using only the numbers the date is generally written as 1/15/14. As this can be confusing in international correspondence it is advisable to write out the month, day and year.

Note: In modern usuage, you can also use contracted forms (short forms) in formal letters and e-mails, but if you do so, then you must be consistent.

5.2 Commercial correspondence

Enquiries should include the following:
- an appropriate salutation
- where you saw the advertisement / how you got the address / how you found out about the company, etc
- a brief introduction of your company and where you are located
- an explanation as to why you are writing
- what the recipient can do for you / what you would like to have / know
- a standard / appropriate closing phrase • a complimentary close

Replies to enquiries should include the following:
- a personal salutation
- a sentence thanking for the enquiry
- a reference to enclosed / attached / ... information – if necessary
- an answer to specific questions (terms of delivery / payment, etc.)
- further contact (eg a phone call) – if necessary
- future proceedings
- a standard / appropriate closing phrase
- a complimentary close

Orders should include the following:
- an appropriate salutation
- a reference to previous correspondence, phone call etc.
- an order / or reference to the enclosed order form
- terms of payment / price ...
- terms of delivery
- a standard / appropriate closing phrase
- a complimentary close
- enclosures / attachments (if necessary)

Complaints should include the following:
- an appropriate salutation
- when complaining of damage: an acknowledgement of receipt of consignment
- reasons for the complaint
- information on what could have caused the problem
- informing the addressee of what you expect.
- what you are going to do if your complaint is not dealt with properly
- mention of the inconvenience or loss suffered
- an appropriate / standard closing phrase
- a complimentary close

Replies to complaints should include the following:

* an appropriate salutation
* an acknowledgement of the letter of complaint
* an apology
* an explanation of the problems / give reasons for problems
* what you have done / will do to prevent similar problems
* an offer to fix the problem / an explanation of how you plan to do this
* an optimistic closing phrase
* a complimentary close

5.3 A summary

* A summary is a concise and objective overview of the main points of a text. When writing a summary, keep it as short as possible – in general, a summary should have about 25 % – 30 % of the number of words of the original text. Follow the rule "Less is more" and only include what is needed for someone who doesn't know the original text to understand what it is about.
* Present the content of the text and the author's point of view neutrally. Don't give your own opinion.

Tips

* Read the text thoroughly and list the most important points. Then go through your list again underlining the absolutely essential points.
* Organize these ideas into a logical sequence.
* Begin your summary with one or two sentences introducing the writer, the title and the topic of the text you have read.
* Write the summary while observing these points:
  – Use the present simple tense.
  – Don't just copy and paste! Use your own language and paraphrase!
  – Change direct quotes into reported speech.
  – And remember: Keep it short and remain objective!
* Read through your summary and check it: Are any essentials missing which make it hard to understand? Are there any irrelevant points that can be removed? Revise if necessary.

5.4 An article

Paragraphs

When you write an article, make sure all paragraphs follow this structure:
* Start with a topic sentence. It's the first sentence in the paragraph and introduces the main idea of the paragraph.
* Supporting details come after the topic sentence, making up the body of the paragraph. Use supporting facts, details and examples.
* The closing sentence is the last sentence in the paragraph. It states the main idea of the paragraph again (summing up).
* Make sure you link one paragraph to the next paragraph so that the reader understands what you are writing about. These transition words can help you:

to structure events	before, after, next, since, First of all, Firstly, Secondly, Furthermore, In addition to ..
to express contrast	however, on the other hand, yet, but , still, although/even though, on the one hand ... on the other hand, whereas, in spite of/despite, so that, either ... or/neither ... nor
giving examples	for example, in general, for instance
quoting others	according to
giving reasons	as/since /because
expressing a purpose	That's why .../Therefore ...

- The last paragraph of your article should be a summary of everything you have said in your article.

Tips

- Read the task description thoroughly and plan your article.
- Use a catchy title.
- Make sure you think of your readers. Address them directly from time to time.
- Think of the purpose of the article – why are you writing this article?
- Think of the style: newspaper article, magazine, blog, argumentative essay etc.
- Start each paragraph with a topic sentence.
- Use transition words (see above), but do not overuse them.
- Express your thoughts clearly and concisely.
- Proofread your article and check for spelling and grammar mistakes.

5.5 A letter of application

- A letter of application is a formal letter, so the rules for "salutation and ending" are the same.
- Say why you are writing and where you saw the job advert:
  I'm writing to apply ...
  I'm writing with regard to ...
  I'd like to apply for the job/post/position which was advertised ...
- Say who you are:
  I'm a 17-year-old student from ...
  I've been studying English for ...
  I've had some work experience in ...
- Concluding
  I look forward to hearing from you soon.

5.6 A report

- Plan your report. Think about the purpose.
- Make sure your report is brief and clear.
- Give your report a title.
- Make sure each paragraph / section of your report has a subtitle – use an introduction, show your findings, a conclusion and one or more recommendations if appropriate.
- You can put sub-headings in the main section of your report where you give information about your findings.
- Use formal language and passive forms whenever possible.

Introduction	*The aim / reason / purpose of this report is …*
	This report aims to …
Findings	*It was discovered that …*
	Research into the matter showed that …
	It appears that …
	All indications point to …
Adding more ideas	*Furthermore, it was revealed that …*
	In addition, it could be stated that …
	Moreover, …
Expressing contrasting ideas	*At present the situation seems to … however …*
	Although …, it may be possible to …
	Despite / In spite of …
Making comparisons	*Both of the … / Neither of the …*
	Neither the …, nor the …
	As in the case of …
	Similarities were found between … and …
	On the one hand, … on the other hand, …
Explaining cause and effect	*This could be due to …*
	Because of a …
	This led to …
	… was caused by …
Conclusion	*In conclusion, it can be said that …*
	It was found that …
	A decision was made to …
Recommendation	*It is recommended that …*
	We propose that …
	We strongly recommend that …

6   Presentation skills

6.1 Creating slides

When creating a slide, follow the rule: "Keep It Simple!" Remember that your slides are there to support your presentation, not to distract from it! So they need to be easy to read and should only contain as much as necessary, as little as possible.

Keep the following points in mind when creating your slides:
- Clarity   A simple font, an uncluttered layout
- Uniformity Don't switch colours and fonts on and between slides
- Readability Choose a large font size and contrasting colours for text and background

6.2 Making a video film

Whenever you make a short video, try to think a little like a film director. The theme of your video should be clear. Whether you use a hand-held video cam or a smart phone, make sure you hold the camera steady and the camera movement is not too fast, i.e. pan slowly.

The **camera range** is important:
- a long shot gives a view of the setting or situation from a distance;
- a full shot gives a view whole body of a person or group;
- a medium shot shows people from the head down to the waist, and
- a close-up shows a full-screen detail of an object or a person, e.g. the face.

Changing the **camera angle** can add interest and drama:
- a low-angle shot shows people or objects from below eye-level;
- an eye-level shot is a straight-on angle, at the height of a person's eyes;
- in a high-angle shot you view people or things from above, i.e. higher than eye-level.

If you film a group talking, think of the camera movements in talk shows:
- Set the scene in an establishing shot that indicates the place or the situation.
- A point-of-view shot shows the setting from the perspective of a participant or character.
- The over-the-shoulder shot, in which you can see the others in a conversation from behind the shoulder of one of the participants is common for talk-shows or dialogues. Its opposite is the reverse-angle shot, when the camera is behind another participant of the conversation.
- Find online advice. For example, search for the following keywords on www.wikihow.com: *make a movie / direct a movie / create a film / make a home video*

6.3 Word webs and mind maps

You can use word webs (clusters) and mind maps to visualise and organize vocabulary and ideas connected to a certain topic. The basic principle is that you start from your topic in the middle of the page with related vocabulary or aspects branching out to all sides. Showing how your collected words or ideas are connected and related to one another makes them easier to memorize – especially long-term! Whereas mind maps can use colours, symbols and pictures in order to make them more effective, word webs are always much plainer.

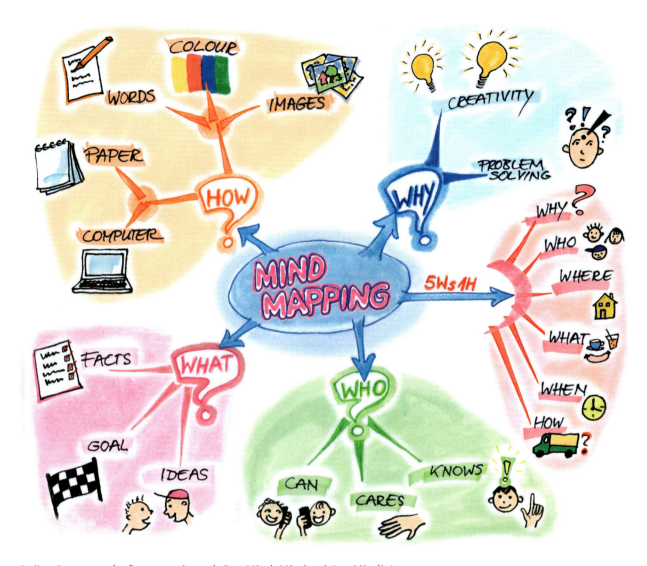

Online Resources (software and apps): FreeMind, Mindmeister, Mindjet

Word webs (clusters) are useful for preparing talks or presentations. They show the factors involved in a theme and how they are inter-related.

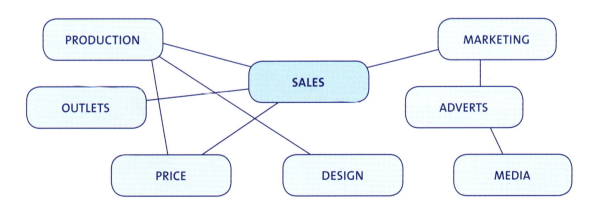

Flow charts also start off with a central keyword. The branches show how the material can be structured. They usually start with the general theme and lead to more specific aspects. They are most useful for structuring technical reports or presentations.

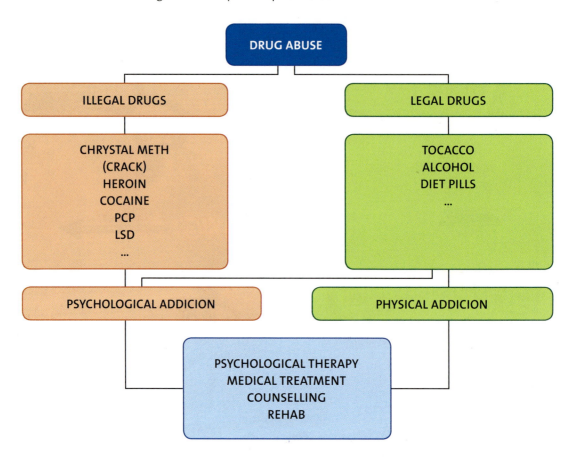

6.4 Charts and graphs

Sometimes it is easier to show information visually. There are several different types of charts and graphs used to do this. The one you choose usually depends on what you want to show.

The pie chart

This is used when you want to show parts of a whole. The parts (segments) of a pie chart always add up to 100. It is very useful when you want to show percentages. The segments are usually shown in different colours. The meaning of each segment are either explained in labels around the pie chart in in the form of a key:
Blue = ...;
Red = ...,
etc.

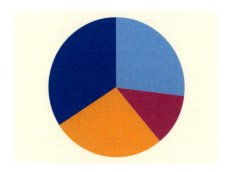

The line graph

This is used when you want to show how something changes over a period of time. In this example the vertical axis shows an amount (sale of concert tickets) and the horizontal axis shows the time scale.

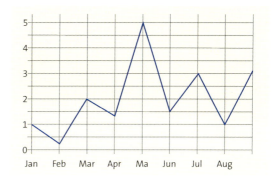

The bar chart

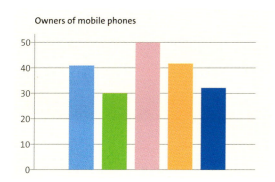

Owners of mobile phones

We use a bar chart when we want to show fixed relationships between different items or people. The bars are in different colours and their meanings are explained either by labels under the bars or with a key. In the example, the five bars represent different makes of mobile phones and the numbers of people in a local survey that have them.

The table

The table gives very specific figures. It is not as visual as charts or graphs but is very accurate and useful when you need the exact numbers.

Cinema-goers in the first half of the year

	Hamburg	Frankfurt	Dresden	Nuremberg
Jan	143,000	82,000	64,000	75,000
Feb	121,000	79,000	59,000	70,000
Mar	182,000	74,000	54,000	68,000
Apr	170,000	72,000	56,000	82,000
May	168,000	83,000	61,000	72,000
June	195,000	91,000	59,000	75,000

Basic word list

Diese Liste enthält die Grundwörter, die in GOING PROFESSIONAL vorausgesetzt werden. Nicht aufgeführt, jedoch ebenso vorausgesetzt sind einige elementare Wörter, wie Pronomen, Zahlen, Wochentage und Monatsnamen. **Verben** sind fett markiert.

A

a, an *ein, eine*

able: be able to do sth. *etw. tun können; fähig sein, etw. zu tun*

abolish *abschaffen; (ein Gesetz) aufheben*

Aborigine *Ureinwohner/in Australiens*

about *über, wegen; ungefähr*
What's it about? *Wovon handelt es?*
What about ...? *Wie wärs mit ...?*
What do you like about ...? *Was magst du an ...?*
be about to do something *im Begriff sein, etw. zu tun*
do sth. about sth. *etw. wegen etw. unternehmen*

above *über; oberhalb (von); oben*

abroad *im/ins Ausland*

accent *Akzent*

accident *Unfall*

across *(quer) über, durch; hinüber, herüber*
get sth. across (to sb.) *(jm.) etw. verständlich machen*

act *handeln; sich verhalten; spielen, schauspielern*

act sth. out *etw. vorspielen*

action *Aktion, Handlung, Tat; Handeln*

active *aktiv*

activity *Aktivität, Tätigkeit*

actor/actress *Schauspieler/in*

actually *eigentlich, übrigens*

ad/advert *Anzeige, Inserat; Werbespot*

adapted from *frei nach, eine Bearbeitung von*

add *addieren, hinzufügen, ergänzen*

address *Adresse, Anschrift*

adjective *Adjektiv*

adult *Erwachsene/r*

advanced *fortgeschritten*

advantage (over sb./sth.) *Vorteil (gegenüber jm./etw.)*
at an advantage *im Vorteil*

adventure *Abenteuer*

advertise sth. *werben, Reklame machen für etw.*

advice *Rat, Ratschläge*

advise *raten, beraten*

advisor *Berater/in*

afraid (be ~ of) *Angst haben (vor), sich fürchten*
I'm afraid (that) ... *Leider ... / Ich fürchte ...*

African *afrikanisch; Afrikaner/in*

after *nach (zeitlich); nachdem*
after that *danach*

afternoon *Nachmittag*
in the afternoon(s) *am Nachmittag, nachmittags*
this/tomorrow afternoon *heute/morgen Nachmittag*
Good afternoon *Guten Tag*

again *wieder, noch einmal*

against *gegen*

age *Alter*
at the age of *im Alter von*
for ages *ewig, eine Ewigkeit*
the Ice Age/Stone Age *die Eiszeit/die Steinzeit*
in the Middle Ages *im Mittelalter*

agency *Agentur, Behörde*

ago *vor (zeitlich)*

agree *sich einigen; sich bereit erklären, zusagen*

agree on sth. *sich auf etw. einigen, etw. vereinbaren*

agree to sth. *einer Sache zustimmen; sich mit etw. einverstanden erklären, etw. akzeptieren*

agree with sb./with sth. *mit jm. übereinstimmen, jm. zustimmen/einer Sache zustimmen, mit etw. einverstanden sein*

agriculture *Landwirtschaft*

ahead of sb./sth. *vor jm./etw. (her)*
be ahead (of sb.) *führen, in Führung liegen*

aim *beabsichtigen, zielen auf, sich richten an*

aim *Ziel, Absicht*

air *Luft*

air conditioning *Klimaanlage*

airport *Flughafen*

alarm clock *Wecker*

alarmed *beunruhigt, besorgt*

alcohol *Alkohol*

alien *Außerirdische(r)*

alive *lebendig*
be alive *am Leben sein, leben*
keep (yourself) alive *(sich) am Leben (er)halten*

all *alle, alles*
all day/summer (long) *den ganzen Tag/Sommer (lang)*
all the time/money/food *die ganze Zeit/...*
all alone *ganz allein*
all over the world *auf der ganzen Welt*
all right *gut, in Ordnung, OK*

not ... at all *überhaupt nicht / kein(e), ganz und gar nicht*

allow sb. to do sth. *jm. erlauben, etw. zu tun*

be allowed to do sth. *etw. tun dürfen*

almost *fast, beinahe*

alone *allein*

along *weiter-, vorwärts*

along the street *die Straße entlang*

already *schon, bereits*

also *auch*

although *obwohl*

always *immer*

a.m. / 8am *8 Uhr morgens*

amazed *erstaunt, verblüfft*

amazing *erstaunlich*

ambassador *Botschafter/in*

ambulance *Krankenwagen*

American *amerikanisch; Amerikaner/in*

among *unter, zwischen*

ancient *alt, antik*

and *und*

and so on *und so weiter*

anger *Wut, Zorn*

angry (with) *böse, zornig, wütend (auf)*

animal *Tier*

announcement *Ankündigung, Bekanntmachung*

anonymous *anonym*

another *ein anderer / anderes, eine andere, noch eine*

one another *einander, sich*

answer *antworten, beantworten*

answer *Antwort*

answering machine *Anrufbeantworter*

(the) Antarctic *die Antarktis*

anticlockwise *entgegen dem Uhrzeigersinn*

any *irgendeine(e) beliebige(r, s), jede(r, s); irgendwelche(r, s)*

anybody / anyone *jede(r), (irgend)jemand*

not ... anbody / anyone *niemand*

anything *(irgend)etwas*

not ... anything *nichts*

anyway *jedenfalls, wie dem auch sei; außerdem, und überhaupt*

anywhere *irgendwo (beliebig)*

not ... anywhere *nirgends, nirgendwo(hin)*

apart *auseinander, getrennt*

apartment (AE) *Wohnung*

apologize *sich entschuldigen*

appear *erscheinen, auftauchen*

apple *Apfel*

application (for) *Bewerbung*

letter of application *Bewerbungsschreiben*

apply to sb. for sth. *sich bei jm. um etw. bewerben*

apply to sb. / sth. *für jn. / etw. gelten*

apprentice *Auszubildende/r, Lehrling*

apprenticeship *Lehre, Lehrzeit; Lehrstelle*

area *Bereich, Gebiet, Gegend*

argue (about / over sth.) *(sich) streiten, zanken (über etw.)*

argue (for / against sth.) *argumentieren, (sich aus) sprechen (für / gegen etw.)*

argument *Auseinandersetzung, Streit*

argument for / against sth. *Argument für / gegen etw.*

arm *Arm*

army *Armee*

around *um ... herum, in ... umher*

around 2010 *um das Jahr 2010 herum*

around here *hier in der Gegend*

be around *vorhanden sein, da sein*

Look around. *Sieh dich um.*

run / stand around *herumrennen / herumstehen*

walk around *herumlaufen (in)*

arrange *(an)ordnen; arrangieren, sorgen für; vereinbaren*

arrangement *Vereinbarung, Abmachung*

arrest *verhaften, festnehmen*

arrival *Ankunft*

arrive *ankommen, eintreffen*

arrow *Pfeil*

art *Kunst*

article *Artikel; Gegenstand; Zeitungsartikel*

artist *Künstler/in*

as *als, während; da, weil*

as if *als ob*

as you know *wie Sie wissen*

as big as *so groß wie*

as long as *solange*

ask *fragen*

ask questions *Fragen stellen*

ask sb. to do sth. *jn. bitten, etw. zu tun*

ask for *verlangen*

ask sb. for sth. *jn. um etw. bitten*

ask sb. for directions *jn. nach dem Weg fragen*

ask about sb. / sth. *nach jm. / etw. fragen, sich nach jm. / etw. erkundigen*

aspect *Aspekt, Gesichtspunkt*

assembly *(Schul)Versammlung*

assembly hall *Aula*

assistant *Assistent/in; Verkäufer/in*

at *an, bei*

at first *zuerst, anfangs, zu Anfang*

at Carol's *bei Carol*

at home, at school *zu Hause, in der Schule*

at work *am Arbeitsplatz, bei der Arbeit*

at night *in der Nacht, nachts*

at sea *auf See*

at 3 pm *um 15 Uhr*
at the door *an der Tür*
at the moment *im Moment*
at the same time *zur gleichen Zeit*
at the weekend / at weekends *am Wochenende / an Wochenenden*
at last *endlich, schließlich*
at least *mindestens, wenigstens*
at once *sofort, (so)gleich*
at the front *vorn*
at the top (of) *oben, am oberen Ende, an der Spitze (von)*
not ... at all *überhaupt nicht / kein(e), ganz und gar nicht*
athletics *Leichtathletik*
attack *angreifen*
attack *Angriff*
attention *Beachtung, Aufmerksamkeit*
pay attention (to sth. / sb.) *etw. / jn. beachten, aufpassen (auf etw.), aufmerksam sein*
attitude (to / towards) *Haltung, Einstellung (zu, gegenüber)*
attract *anziehen, anlocken*
attraction *Anziehungskraft, Attraktion*
attractive *anziehend, reizvoll*
audience *Zuschauer/innen; Zuhörer/innen; Publikum*
aunt *Tante*
authentic *authentisch*
author *Autor/in*
authority *Autorität*
automatic *automatisch*
autumn *Herbst*
average *Durchschnitt; durchschnittlich, Durchschnitts-*
awake *wach*
award *Preis, Auszeichnung*
awarenes *Bewusstsein*
be aware of *sich einer Sache bewusst sein; sich im Klaren sein über*
away *weg, fort*

awesome *großartig, klasse*
awful *schrecklich*

B

back *Rücken, zurück*
at the back (of) *hinten, am hinteren Ende (von)*
background *Hintergrund*
backpack *Rucksack*
bacon *Schinkenspeck*
bacteria *Bakterien*
bad *schlecht, schlimm*
be bad at sth. *schlecht in etw. sein*
badly-acted *schecht gespielt*
badly-made *schlecht gemacht*
badly-written *schecht geschrieben*
badminton *Federball*
bag *Tasche, Beutel, Tüte*
bag lady (AE) *Stadtstreicherin; Obdachlose*
baggage *Gepäck*
ball *Ball; (formelles Tanzfest) Ball*
balloon *Luftballon*
ban *verbieten, ausschließen, sperren*
banana *Banane*
bang *Knall*
bank *(Fluss-)Ufer; Bank, Sparkasse*
bank clerk *Bankangestellte/r*
bottle bank *Altglascontainer*
banner *Fahne*
bar (of chocolate) *Tafel (z. B. Schokolade)*
be based in *seinen Sitz haben in, in ... angesiedelt sein*
be based on *basieren auf*
basement *Unter-, Kellergeschoss, Souterrain*
basic *fundamental, elementar*
the basics *das Wesentliche, die Grundlagen*
basket *Korb*
bath *Bad*
have a bath *ein Bad*

nehmen, baden
bathroom *Badezimmer; (AE) Toilette*
battery *Batterie; (Hühner) Legebatterie*
battle *Schlacht, Kampf*
be (was / were, been) *sein*
be called *heißen, genannt werden*
be in trouble *Ärger kriegen, in Schwierigkeiten sein*
be late (for) *zu spät sein / kommen*
be on holiday *Ferien haben / machen, in Urlaub sein*
be out *weg sein, nicht da sein*
be right *Recht haben, richtig sein*
be wrong *sich irren, Unrecht haben; nicht stimmen, nicht in Ordnung sein*
beach *Strand*
bear *Bär*
beat (beat, beaten) *besiegen; schlagen; übertreffen, besser sein*
beat sb. up *jn. zusammenschlagen*
beautiful *wunderschön*
beauty *Schönheit*
because *weil*
because of *wegen*
become (became, become) *werden*
bed *Bett*
bedroom *Schlafzimmer*
beef *Rindfleisch*
beer *Bier*
before *(zeitlich) vor; bevor; vorher, vorher schon mal*
before that *davor*
the day before *am Tag davor / zuvor*
begin (began, begun) *beginnen, anfangen (mit)*
beginner *Anfänger/in*
beginning *Anfang, Beginn*

behave *sich verhalten, sich benehmen*

behaviour (towards sb.) *Verhalten, Benehmen (jm. gegenüber)*

behind *hinter*

believe (in) *glauben (an)*

below *unter, unterhalb (von); unten*

bell *Glocke; Klingel*

belong to *angehören; gehören*

bench *(Sitz-)Bank*

beside *neben*

(the) best *(der / die / das) Beste; am besten*

    like sth. best *etw. am liebsten mögen*

best-selling *meistverkauft*

bet (bet, bet) *wetten*

better *besser*

    like sth. better *etw. lieber mögen*

between *zwischen*

beyond *über – hinaus, jenseits (von)*

bicycle *Fahrrad*

big *groß*

bike *Fahrrad*

    bike ride *Radfahrt, Radtour*

    ride a bike *Rad fahren*

bilingual *zweisprachig, bilingual*

bill *Rechnung*

billion *Milliarde*

bin *Papierkorb, Mülleimer*

biography *Biografie, Lebensgeschichte*

biology *Biologie*

bird *Vogel*

biro *Kugelschreiber*

birth *Geburt*

    date of birth *Geburtsdatum*

    place of birth *Geburtsort*

birthday *Geburtstag*

    birthday card *Geburtstagskarte*

    Happy birthday! *Herzlichen Glückwunsch zum Geburtstag!*

biscuit *Keks*

a bit *ein bisschen, etwas*

black *schwarz*

blanket *Decke*

blind *blind*

block *(Häuser-, Wohn-) Block*

blood *Blut*

bloodless *unblutig; blutleer, bleich*

blouse *Bluse*

blow (blew, blown) *blasen, wehen*

blue *blau*

board *Brett; (Wand-)Tafel; Spielbrett*

    notice board / bulletin board *Anschlagtafel, schwarzes Brett*

    on board *an Bord*

boarding school *Internat*

boat *Boot*

body *Körper*

bomb *Bombe*

bone *Knochen*

book *Buch*

    exercise book *Übungsheft, Schulheft*

bookshelf (pl. bookshelves) *Bücherregal*

bookshop *Buchhandlung, Buchladen*

boot *Stiefel*

border *Grenze*

bored *gelangweilt*

    be bored *sich langweilen*

boring *langweilig*

be born *geboren sein / werden*

borrow sth. (from) *(sich) etw. (aus)leihen, borgen (von)*

boss *Chef/in*

both *beide*

    both of you *alle beide, ihr beide*

bottle *Flasche*

    a bottle of ... *eine Flasche ...*

    bottle bank *Altglascontainer*

bottom *Boden, Fußende, unteres Ende*

    bottom row *untere Reihe*

bowl *Schüssel, Schale*

box *Kasten, Kiste*

    a box of chocolates *eine Schachtel Pralinen*

    phone box *Telefonkiosk, Telefonzelle*

boy *Junge*

boyfriend *fester Freund*

brain *Gehirn*

brainstorming *Das Sammeln spontaner Ideen in der Gruppe, um ein Problem zu lösen*

brand *Marke, Sorte*

brand new *brandneu, nagelneu*

brave *tapfer, mutig*

bread *Brot*

break *Pause*

    take a break *eine Pause machen*

break (broke, broken) *(zer)brechen; kaputtmachen; kaputtgehen*

breakfast *Frühstück*

    for breakfast *zum Frühstück*

    have breakfast *frühstücken*

breathe *atmen*

bridge *Brücke*

bright *leuchtend, hell, strahlend; heiter, freundlich*

brilliant *toll, glänzend, großartig; intelligent, genial*

bring (brought, brought) *bringen, mitbringen*

British *britisch; Brite / Britin*

brochure *Prospekt, Broschüre*

broken *gebrochen, zerbrochen*

brother *Bruder*

brown *braun*

brush *(Haar-)Bürste*

brush *bürsten, bepinseln*

    brush your teeth *sich die Zähne putzen*

brutality *Brutalität*

bubble *Blase*

    bubble gum *Kaugummi*

budgie *Wellensittich*

buffet *Büfett*

build (built, built) *bauen*

builder *Bauarbeiter/in*

building *Gebäude*

bully sb. *einen Schwächeren schikanieren / einschüchtern*

bully *jd., der Schwächere schikaniert*

burn *brennen, verbrennen*

bus stop *Bushaltestelle*

bush *Busch*

business *Unternehmen, Geschäft; Geschäfte*

busy *beschäftigt; belebt, verkehrsreich, hektisch*

    keep sb. busy *jn. beschäftigen; dafür sorgen, dass jd. beschäftigt ist*

but *aber; sondern*

butterfly *Schmetterling*

button *Knopf*

buy (bought, bought) *kaufen*

by *von; an, neben; (nahe) bei*

    by mistake *aus Versehen, irrtümlich*

    by the way *übrigens, nebenbei*

    by bike / plane / ... *mit dem Rad / Flugzeug / ...*

    by Friday *bis (spätestens) Freitag*

    by then *bis dahin, (bis) dann*

    drive by *vorbeifahren*

    by doing sth. *indem man etw. tut*

Bye bye! *Tschüs!*

C

cabin *Hütte; Kabine*

cable *Kabel*

cafeteria *Kantine, Selbstbedienungsrestaurant*

cage *Käfig*

cake *Torte, Kuchen*

calendar *Kalender*

call *Anruf*

call *nennen, rufen; anrufen*

    call sb. name *jn. verspotten / beschimpfen*

    be called *heißen, genannt werden*

calm *ruhig*

camp *(Trainings-, Zelt-)Lager*

campfire *Lagerfeuer*

campsite *Campingplatz, Zeltplatz*

can *Dose, Büchse*

can (could, been able to) *können*

can (could, been allowed to) *dürfen*

canal *Kanal*

candidate *Kandidat/in, Bewerber/in*

candle *Kerze*

canteen *Kantine*

canyon *Schlucht*

cap *(Schirm-)Mütze, Kappe*

capital *Hauptstadt*

captain *Kapitän/in*

caption *Bildunterschrift*

car *Auto*

card *Karte*

cardboard *Karton, Pappe*

care (about) *sich interessieren (für), sich kümmern (um)*

    I don't care. *Das ist mir egal.*

career *Karriere; berufliche Laufbahn, Beruf*

careful *vorsichtig; sorgfältig*

carry *tragen; befördern*

carton *Karton, (Milch-, Saft-)Packung*

case *Fall*

castle *Burg, Schloss*

cat *Katze, Kater*

catalogue *Katalog*

catch (caught, caught) *fangen; erwischen*

    catch sb.'s arm *jn. am Arm packen / fassen*

    catch a train / bus / ... *einen Zug / ... nehmen / erreichen*

category *Kategorie*

cathedral *Kathedrale, Dom*

cause *verursachen*

    cause injury to sb. *jm. eine Verletzung / Verletzungen zufügen*

cause *Anliegen, Sache, Zweck*

celebrate *feiern*

cell *Zelle*

centimetre *Zentimeter*

central *Zentral-, Mitte-*

centre *Zentrum, Mitte*

century *Jahrhundert*

cereal *Getreide; Getreideflocken*

ceremony *Zeremonie; Feier, Feierlichkeit*

certain *sicher, bestimmt; gewiss*

certificate *Bescheinigung, Nachweis; Urkunde, Zeugnis*

chair *Stuhl*

champion *Wettkampfsieger/in, Meister/in*

    championship *Meisterschaft*

chance *Gelegenheit, Chance*

change *ändern; (Geld) wechseln, umtauschen; (Kleidung) wechseln; sich umziehen*

    change into *(ver)ändern, umwandeln in; sich verändern in, werden zu*

    change (trains / buses / ...) *umsteigen*

    change one's mind *seine Meinung ändern*

change *Wechselgeld; Kleingeld*

change *(Ver-)Änderung, Wechsel*

channel *Kanal; Fernsehkanal, Programm*

    the Channel *der Ärmelkanal*

charity *Wohltätigkeitsverein*

    charity bazaar *Wohltätigkeitsbasar*

chart *Tabelle, Diagramm*

    bar chart *Balkendiagramm*

    flow chart *Flussdiagramm*

chase sb. (away) *jn. (weg)jagen*

chat *plaudern, „chatten"*

chat *Plauderei, Schwätzchen*

cheap *preiswert, billig*

check *(über)prüfen, kontrollieren*

checklist *Prüfliste; Checkliste*

cheer *jubeln, klatschen*

cheer; cheers *Beifallsruf; Beifall*

cheese *Käse*

chemical *Chemikalie;*
chemisch, Chemie-
chemistry *Chemie*
chess *Schach*
chicken *Hühn, (Brat-)Hähn-*
chen
child, children *Kind, Kinder*
only child *Kind, Einzelkind*
childhood *Kindheit*
Chinese *chinesisch; Chinese /*
Chinesin
chips *(BE) Pommes frites;*
(AE) Kartoffelchips
chocolate *Schokolade*
(a box of) chocolates
Pralinen
choice *(Aus-)Wahl*
choose (chose, chosen)
aussuchen, (aus)wählen
chorus *Refrain*
Christ *Christ; Christus*
Christmas *Weihnachten*
church *Kirche*
cigarette *Zigarette*
cinema *Kino*
circle *Kreis*
circus *Zirkus*
city *Großstadt*
clap *(Beifall) klatschen*
class *Klasse, Kurs*
first-class *erstklassig*
classmate *Mitschüler/in,*
Klassenkamerad/in
classroom *Klassenzimmer*
classic / classical *klassisch*
clause *(Teil-, Glied-)Satz*
main clause *Hauptsatz*
clean *sauber machen*
clean *sauber*
clear *klar, deutlich*
clever *klug, schlau*
click *(an, hin)klicken*
cliff *Klippe*
climb *klettern; hinauf klettern*
(auf)
climb *Aufstieg*
clock *(Wand-, Stand-, Turm-)*
Uhr
clockwise *im Uhrzeigersinn*
close *zumachen, schließen*

pull sb. close *jn. (eng) an*
sich heranziehen
close (to) *nahe, dicht (bei / an)*
clothes / clothing *Kleidung*
cloud *Wolke*
cloudy *bewölkt, wolkig*
clue *Hinweis, Anhaltspunkt*
clueless *ahnungslos; ratlos*
coach *Reisebus; Trainer/in*
coal *Kohle*
coast *Küste*
on the coast *an der Küste*
coat *Mantel*
cocoa *Kakao*
code *Geheimcode*
coffee *Kaffee*
cold *kalt; Erkältung*
I've got a cold. *Ich bin*
erkältet. / Ich habe eine
Erkältung.
be / feel cold *frieren*
collect *(ein)sammeln*
collection *das Sammeln,*
Sammlung
collector *Sammler/in*
college *Hochschule, Fachschule*
colony *Kolonie*
colour *Farbe*
colourful *bunt, farbig; farben-*
froh, farbenprächtig
colourless *farblos*
colour (in) *bunt (an)malen*
column *Säule; Spalte, Kolumne*
come (came, come) *kommen*
come round *vorbeischauen,*
vorbeikommen
come to life *lebendig*
werden
come true *wahr werden,*
Wirklichkeit werden
comedy *Komödie;*
Comedy(show)
comfortable *bequem, behag-*
lich, angenehm
feel comfortable *sich wohl*
fühlen
comment *Bemerkung;*
Kommentar
comment (on, about) *Komm-*
entar, Bemerkung (zu, über)

commit a crime *ein Verbrechen*
begehen, verüben
common *häufig, weitverbrei-*
tet; gemeinsam, allgemein;
gewöhnlich, einfach; ordinär
have sth. in common *etw.*
miteinander gemeinsam ha-
ben
communicate *kommunizeren,*
sich verständigen
communication *Kommunika-*
tion, Verständigung
community *Gemeinde,*
Gemeinschaft
company *Firma, Gesellschaft*
compare *vergleichen*
comparison *Vergleich*
make comparisons
Vergleiche anstellen,
vergleichen
compass *Kompass*
competition *Wettbewerb,*
Wettkampf
complete *vervollständigen,*
ergänzen
complete, completely *vollstän-*
dig, komplett; gesamte(r, s)
complicated *kompliziert*
comprehensive school
Gesamtschule
computer science *Informatik*
concentrate (on) *sich konzen-*
trieren (auf)
concert *Konzert*
concrete *Beton*
condition *Bedingung; Zustand,*
Verfassung
conflict *Konflikt*
Congratulations (on sth.)
Herzlichen Glückwunsch! (zu
etw.), Gratuliere!
connect (to / with) *verbinden*
(mit), anschließen (an)
connection *Verbindung,*
Anschluss
content *Inhalt*
contents *Inhalt (von Behält-*
nissen, Räumen)
table of contents *Inhalts-*
verzeichnis

continent *Erdteil, Kontinent*

context *Zusammenhang, Kontext*

continue *weitergehen, fort-fahren; weitermachen*

contract *Vertrag*

control *kontrollieren, beherrschen*

control *Kontrolle*

conversation *Gespräch, Unter-haltung*

convict *Sträfling, Straf-gefangene(r)*

cook *kochen, zubereiten*

cook *Koch, Köchin*

cooker *Herd*

cool *kühl; cool*

cool off *(sich) abkühlen; sich beruhigen*

cooperate *kooperieren, zusammenarbeiten*

copy *übertragen, kopieren, abschreiben*

copy *Kopie*

coral *Koralle*

   coral reef *Korallenriff*

corn *(BE) Korn, Getreide; (AE) Mais*

corner *Ecke*

correct *verbessern, korrigieren*

correct *korrekt, richtig*

correction *Korrektur, Berich-tigung*

corridor *Gang, Flur, Korridor*

corrupt *korrupt*

cost (cost, cost) *kosten*

cost *Kosten*

costume *Kostüm, Verkleidung*

cottage *kleines Landhaus, Häuschen*

cotton *Baumwolle*

count *zählen*

country *Land*

   in the country *auf dem Land*

(the) countryside *die Land-schaft, die ländliche Gegend*

county *Grafschaft, Verwaltungsbezirk*

course *Kurs, Lehrgang*

court *Gericht, Gerichtshof*

cousin *Cousin, Cousine*

cover *Umschlag; Einband; Hülle*

cow *Kuh*

crash *krachen*

   crash into *zusammen-stoßen (mit), hineinfahren (in)*

crash *Krach, Krachen; Zusam-menstoß*

crazy *verrückt, wahnsinnig*

   crazy-looking *verrückt aus-sehend*

cream *Sahne*

create *erschaffen, schaffen*

creative *kreativ*

creature *Geschöpf, Kreatur*

creep (crept, crept) *kriechen, schleichen*

crew *Besatzung, Mannschaft*

crime *Verbrechen*

   commit a crime *ein Ver-brechen begehen / verüben*

criminal *Verbrecher/in, Kriminelle(r); verbrecherisch*

crisps *Kartoffelchips*

critical *kritisch*

   be critical of sb. / sth. *jm. / etw. kritisch gegenüber stehen*

criticize (for) *kritisieren (wegen)*

crocodile *Krokodil*

cross *kreuzen, überqueren*

cross *Kreuz*

crossword *Kreuzworträtsel*

crowd *(Menschen-)Menge, Masse; Clique*

crowded *überfüllt*

cruel *grausam*

cry *weinen; schreien*

culture *Kultur*

cup *Tasse*

   a cup of tea / … *eine Tasse Tee / …*

cupboard *Schrank*

curfew *Ausgangssperre*

curriculam vitæ (CV) *Lebens-lauf*

custom *Brauch, Sitte*

customer *Kunde, Kundin*

Customs *Zoll*

cut (cut, cut) *(aus)schneiden*

   cut out *ausschneiden*

   cut sth. up *etw. zer-schneiden, zerlegen*

   cut down a tree *einen Baum fällen*

cute *niedlich, süß*

cycle *Rad fahren*

cycling *das Radfahren*

cycle track *Radweg*

D

dad *Papa, Vater*

daily *täglich, Tages- (Zeitung)*

damage *beschädigen*

damage (to sth.) *Schaden, Beschädigung(en)*

dance *tanzen*

dance *Tanz*

dancer *Tänzer/in*

danger *Gefahr*

dangerous *gefährlich*

dark *dunkel; dunkelhaarig*

darling *Liebling, Schatz*

date *Datum; Verabredung*

   date of birth *Geburtsdatum*

   go (out) on a date *(mit einem Freund / einer Freun-din) ausgehen*

date sb. (AE) *mit jm. gehen (fest befreundet sein)*

daughter *Tochter*

day *Tag*

   one day *eines Tages*

   day of the week *Wochentag*

daylight *Tageslicht*

dead *tot*

   shoot sb. dead *jn. erschie-ßen*

deadly *tödlich*

deaf *taub*

deal with *umgehen / fer-tig werden mit; sich befas-sen / beschäftigen mit, sich kümmern um*

deal *Geschäft, Handel*

dealer *Händler/in*

dear *Liebling, Schatz, mein Lieber / meine Liebe*
Dear Sir or Madam *Sehr geehrte Damen und Herren*
death *Tod*
death penalty *Todesstrafe*
December *Dezember*
decide (on) *sich entscheiden (für); beschließen*
decision *Entscheidung*
make a decision *eine Entscheidung treffen / fallen*
deep *tief*
degree *Temperatur-Grad; Hochschulabschluss*
delay *Verspätung, Verzögerung*
be delayed (for) *(Zeit) Verspätung haben*
deli (infml. for: delicatessen) *Feinkostladen*
demonstrate (for / against) *demonstrieren (für, gegen)*
dentist *Zahnarzt / Zahnärztin*
department *Abteilung*
department store *Kaufhaus*
describe sth. (to sb.) *(jm.) etw. beschreiben*
description *Beschreibung*
desert *Wüste*
design *entwerfen; konstruieren*
design *Entwurf; Design; Gestaltung*
desk *Schreibtisch, Schulbank*
dessert *Nachtisch, Nachspeise, Dessert*
destroy *zerstören, vernichten*
detail *Einzelheit, Detail*
detective *Detektiv/in*
develop *entwickeln; sich entwickeln*
device *Gerät, Vorrichtung*
dialogue *Dialog*
diary *Tagebuch; Terminkalender*
dictate sth. (to sb.) *(jm.) etw. diktieren*
dictation *Diktat*
dictionary *Wörterbuch*
die (of) *sterben (an)*
diet *Ernährung; Diät*

difference *Unterschied*
different (from) *verschieden (von), unterschiedlich; anders (als); andere(r, s)*
difficult *schwierig, schwer*
difficulty *Schwierigkeit*
dining-room *Esszimmer*
dinner *Abendessen, Abendbrot; Mittagessen*
for dinner *zum Abendessen*
have dinner *Abendbrot essen*
dinosaur *Dinosaurier*
direct *(Chor, Orchester) leiten*
direct speech *direkte Rede, wörtliche Rede*
direction *Richtung*
directions *Anweisung(en)*
ask sb. for directions *jn. um eine Wegbeschreibung bitten; jn. nach dem Weg fragen*
director *(Film) Regisseur/in; (Firma) Leiter/in*
dirt *Schmutz, Dreck*
dirty *schmutzig, dreckig*
disability *Behinderung*
disabled *(körper-)behindert*
disadvantage *Nachteil*
be at a disadvantage *im Nachteil sein*
disagree (with) *nicht übereinstimmen (mit); anderer Meinung sein als*
discover *entdecken; herausfinden, feststellen*
discovery *Entdeckung*
discrimination *Diskriminierung*
discuss sth. *etw. besprechen, über etw. diskutieren*
discussion (on / about) *Besprechung, Diskussion (über)*
disease *Krankheit*
dish *Teller*
dishes *Geschirr*
wash / do the dishes *das Geschirr abwaschen*
dislike *nicht mögen*
distance *Entfernung*

distance (between) *Abstand (zwischen)*
keep one's distance *Abstand halten / wahren*
dive *tauchen*
diver *Taucher/in*
divide sth. (up) (into) *etw. (auf) teilen (in)*
divorced *geschieden*
get divorced *sich scheiden lassen*
do (did, done) *tun, machen*
do sth. about sth. *etw. gegen etw. unternehmen*
do homework *die Hausaufgaben / Schularbeiten machen*
do jobs *Arbeiten / Aufträge erledigen*
do the shopping *Einkäufe machen, einkaufen*
dock(s) *Dock, Anlegestelle*
doctor *Arzt, Ärztin*
dog *Hund*
dolphin *Delfin*
door *Tür*
at the door *an der Tür*
double *Doppel-, zweimal*
down *hinunter, herunter, nach unten; unten*
up and down *auf und ab*
let sb. down *jn. im Stich lassen, jn. enttäuschen*
lie down *sich hinlegen*
put down *hinlegen, hinstellen; (Tier) einschläfern*
sit down *sich (hin)setzen*
write sth. down *etw. aufschreiben, notieren*
download *(herunter)laden*
downstairs *nach unten; unten*
downtown *(AE) Innenstadt, Geschäftsviertel*
go downtown *in die Innenstadt gehen*
dragon *Drache*
drama *Schauspiel, Drama; Dramatik*
draw *zeichnen*
dream (about) *träumen (von)*

dream *Traum*
dress *Kleid*
dress (one's self) *sich kleiden, sich anziehen*
dressed *angezogen*
 get dressed *sich anziehen*
drink (drank, drunk) *trinken*
drink *Getränk*
drive (drove, driven) *fahren*
driver *Fahrer/in*
driving licence (BE), driver's license (AE) *Führerschein*
drop *fallen, umfallen; fallen lassen*
drop *Tropfen*
drug *Droge, Rauschgift*
drum *Trommel; Schlagzeug*
 play the drums *Schlagzeug spielen*
dry *trocken*
during *während*
dust *Staub*
dusty *staubig*

E
each *jede(r, s) (einzelne)*
 each other *einander, sich (gegenseitig)*
 with £5 each *mit je £5*
ear *Ohr*
early *früh; zu früh*
earn *verdienen*
earring *Ohrring*
earth, Earth *Erde*
earthquake *Erdbeben*
east *östlich; (nach) Osten*
 to the east *im Osten, östlich*
 eastern *östlich, Ost-*
Easter *Ostern*
easy *leicht, einfach*
eat (ate, eaten) *essen*
ecological *ökologisch*
 eco- *Öko-, öko-, Umwelt-*
economy *Wirtschaft*
edge *Rand, Kante*
editor *Redakteur/in*
educate *(aus)bilden, schulen*
education *Erziehung, (Schul-, Aus-)Bildung*
e.g *z. B. (zum Beispiel)*

egg *Ei*
either ... or *entweder ... oder*
 neither ... nor *weder ... noch*
 not (...) either *auch nicht, auch kein*
electric *elektrisch*
electricity *Elektrizität, Strom*
electronic *elektronisch*
electronics *Elektronik*
elementary *einfach, elementar*
elephant *Elefant*
elevator (AE) *Fahrstuhl, Aufzug*
else *sonst (noch)*
embarrass sb. *jn. in Verlegenheit bringen*
embarrassed *verlegen*
embarrassing *peinlich*
emergency *Notfall*
emigrate *emigrieren, auswandern*
emotional *gefühlsmäßig, emotional*
emperor *Kaiser*
empire *Reich, Weltreich, Imperium*
employ *anstellen, beschäftigen*
employee *Arbeitnehmer/in*
employer *Arbeitgeber/in*
empty *leer*
encyclopedia *Enzyklopädie, Lexikon*
end *enden; beenden*
end *Ende, Schluss*
 at the end *am Ende / Schluss*
endless *endlos*
ending *Ende, Schluss*
 happy ending *Happy End*
enemy *Feind/in*
energy *Energie*
 solar energy *Sonnenenergie, Solarenergie*
engine *Motor, Maschine*
engineer *Ingenieur/in, Techniker/in*
engineering *Ingenieurwesen; (das) Konstruieren; Maschinenbau*
English *englisch; Englisch*

He / She is English. *Er ist Engländer. / Sie ist Engländerin.*
 in English *auf Englisch*
English-speaking *englischsprachig; Englisch sprechend*
enjoy sth. *etw. genießen, an etw. Spaß haben, etw. gern haben / tun*
enough *genug*
enter *teilnehmen; eintreten*
entertain *unterhalten*
entertainment *Unterhaltung*
enthusiasm (for) *Begeisterung, Enthusiasmus*
entrance *Eingang*
entry *Eintrag, Eintragung*
environment *Umwelt, Umgebung*
 environment-friendly *umweltfreundlich*
 environmental *Umwelt-*
equal *gleich, gleichberechtigt*
equipment *Ausrüstung*
equivalent *Äquivalent, Entsprechung, Gegenstück*
eraser (AE) *Radiergummi*
escape (from sb. / sth.) *fliehen (vor jm. / aus etw.); entkommen*
especially *besonders; insbesondere, vor allem*
etc. (etcetera) *usw. (und so weiter)*
Europe *Europa*
European *europäisch; Europäer/in*
even *sogar, selbst*
 even better / bigger / ... *(sogar) noch besser / größer / ...*
 even if *selbst wenn, auch wenn*
evening *Abend*
 Good evening. *Guten Abend.*
 in the evening *am Abend*
 this evening *heute Abend*
event *Veranstaltung, Ereignis*
ever *je, jemals, schon mal*

every *jede(r, s)*
everybody / everyone *jeder, alle*
everything *alles*
everywhere *überall; überallhin*
exact *genau*
exaggerate *übertreiben*
exaggeration *Übertreibung*
exam, examination *Prüfung, Examen*
   take an exam *eine Prüfung ablegen*
   pass an exam *eine Prüfung bestehen*
   fail an exam *eine Prüfung nicht bestehen, bei einer Prüfung durchfallen*
example *Beispiel*
   for example *zum Beispiel*
excellent *ausgezeichnet, hervorragend*
exchange *umtauschen; tauschen*
exchange *Austausch; Tausch, Umtausch*
excited (about) *aufgeregt (wegen, über)*
exciting *aufregend, spannend*
excuse *Ausrede, Entschuldigung*
   Excuse me *Entschuldige! Entschuldigung!*
execute *hinrichten*
execution *Hinrichtung*
exercise *trainieren; Sport treiben*
exercise *Übung*
   exercise book *Übungsheft, Schulheft*
exhibition *Ausstellung*
exist *existieren*
expect *erwarten; annehmen, vermuten*
expensive *teuer*
experience *erfahren, erleben*
experience *Erfahrung(en), Erlebnis*
   in my experience *meiner Erfahrung nach*
experiment (with) *experimentieren (mit), ausprobieren*

experiment *Experiment, Versuch*
explain *erklären, erläutern*
explanation *Erklärung*
explode *explodieren; zur Explosion bringen, zünden*
exploration *Erforschung, Entdeckung*
explore *erforschen, erkundigen*
explorer *Forscher/in, Forschungsreisender*
express *ausdrücken, äußern*
expression *Ausdruck, Redewendung*
extra *zusätzlich, Extra-*
extremely *äußerst, höchst*
eye *Auge*
eyebrow *Augenbraue*

F

face *Gesicht*
fact *Tatsache, Fakt*
   in fact *eigentlich, genau gesagt; in Wirklichkeit*
factory *Fabrik*
fair *fair, gerecht; hell, blond; Jahrmarkt, Messe*
faithfull *treu*
   Yours faithfully *Mit freundlichen Grüßen*
fall (fell, fallen) *(hin)fallen*
fall (AE) *Herbst*
false *falsch*
fame *Ruhm, Berühmtheit*
family *Familie*
   family name *Nachname, Familienname*
famous (for) *berühmt (für, wegen)*
fantastic *fantastisch, toll*
far *weit (entfernt)*
   so far *bis jetzt, bis hierher*
farm *Bauernhof*
   factory farm *Großmästerei, industrieller Viehzuchtbetrieb*
   factory farming *industriell betriebene Viehzucht*
farther *weiter (entfernt)*

farthest *am weitesten (entfernt)*
fashion *Mode*
fast *schnell*
fat *dick, fett; Fett*
father *Vater*
favourite *Favorit/in; Lieblings-*
fear (of) *Angst, Furcht (vor)*
feature *Merkmal, Eigenschaft, Besonderheit*
February *Februar*
be / get fed up (with sb. / sth.) *von jn. / etw. die Nase voll haben; jn. / etw. satt haben*
feed *füttern*
feel (felt, felt) *fühlen; sich fühlen*
   feel sorry for sb. *jn. bedauern*
feeling *Gefühl*
felt-tip *Filzstift*
female *Frau, Mädchen; weiblich; (Tier) Weibchen*
fence *Zaun*
ferry *Fähre*
festival *Festival, Festspiele*
fetch (from) *holen, abholen (von)*
a few *ein paar, einige (wenige)*
field *Feld, Wiese, Weide*
fight (fought, fought) *kämpfen, bekämpfen; (sich) streiten*
   fight back *zurückschlagen, sich wehren*
fight *Kampf, Streit*
figure *Gestalt, Figur*
fill *füllen*
   fill in *einsetzen; ausfüllen*
   fill out *ausfüllen*
film *filmen*
finally *schließlich, endlich*
find (found, found) *finden, suchen*
find out *herausfinden*
fine *gut, fein, schön*
finger *Finger*
finish *beenden, Zu Ende machen; enden*
finished *fertig, vollendet*

fire *Feuer, Brand*

fire brigade, fire service *Feuerwehr*

firefighter (AE) *Feuerwehr-mann / Feuerwehrfrau*

fireworks *Feuerwerk*

firm *Firma, Unternehmen*

first *erste(r, s); zuerst, als Erstes, erstens*

    at first *zuerst, anfangs, zu Anfang*

first-class *erstklassig*

fish *fischen, angeln*

fish *Fisch*

fish finger *Fischstäbchen*

fisherman *Fischer*

fit *passen*

    fit sth. *zu etw. passen, etw. entsprechen*

fit *fit, in Form, gesund*

fix *reparieren, in Ordnung bringen*

flag *Flagge*

flame *Flamme*

flash *aufleuchten, blinken*

flat *flach, eben*

flat *Wohnung*

flight *Flug*

floor *Fußboden; Stock(werk)*

flow chart *Flussdiagramm*

flower *Blume; Blüte*

fluent *fließend*

fly (flew, flown) *fliegen*

fog *Nebel*

foggy *nebelig*

fold (over) *falten, falzen, umknicken*

folder *Mappe, Hefter, Ordner*

follow *folgen; verfolgen*

    the following picture *das folgende Bild*

food *Essen, Lebensmittel; Futter*

foot *Fuß*

    on foot *zu Fuß*

football *Fußball*

footstep *Schritt, Tritt*

for *für; seit*

    for an hour *eine Stunde lang*

for example *zum Beispiel*

foreground *Vordergrund*

foreign *ausländisch, fremd*

foreigner *Ausländer/in, Fremde(r)*

forest *Wald*

forever *für immer, ewig*

forget (forgot, forgotten) *vergessen*

forgive (forgave, forgiven) *vergeben*

fork *Gabel*

form *bilden*

form *englische Schulklasse; Form; Formular, Vordruck*

formal *förmlich, formell*

fortune *Reichtum, Vermögen*

forward(s) *vorwärts, nach vorn*

    look forward to sth. *sich auf etw. freuen*

    look forward to doing sth. *sich darauf freuen, etw. zu tun*

found *gründen*

freak *Freak, Fanatiker/in*

free *frei, kostenlos*

free time *Freizeit*

freedom *Freiheit*

freeway (AE) *Autobahn*

freeze (froze, frozen) *(ge)frieren; einfrieren*

French *französisch; Französisch*

French fries (AE) *Pommes frites*

fresh *frisch*

fridge *Kühlschrank*

friend *Freund/in*

friendship *Freundschaft*

friendly *freundlich, nett*

friendliness *Freundlichkeit*

frightened *verängstigt*

    be frightened (of) *Angst haben (vor), sich fürchten (vor)*

from *aus, von*

    from ... to, from ... through (AE) *von ... bis ...*

front *Vorderseite, vorderer Teil*

    at the front *vorn*

    in front of *vor*

front door *Haustür, Wohnungstür*

frozen *zugefroren; tiefge-froren; Tiefkühl-*

fruit *Obst, Früchte; Frucht*

frustrated (at / with) *frustriert, enttäuscht (über, wegen)*

full (of) *voll (mit / vor)*

    full sentence *ganzer Satz*

full-time job *Vollzeit-, Ganz-tagsbeschäftigung*

fun *Spaß*

    make fun of sth. / sb. *sich über etw. / jn. lustig machen*

function *funktionieren*

funny *witzig, komisch; merk-würdig*

furniture *Möbel*

future *Zukunft; zukünftig, Zukunfts-, in der Zukunft*

G

game *Spiel*

gang *Gang, Bande; Freundes-gruppe*

garbage (AE) *Müll*

garden *Garten*

gate *Tor, Pforte*

general *allgemeine(r, s), generelle(r, s)*

    in general *im Allgemeinen*

geography *Geographie, Erdkunde*

German *deutsch; Deutsch; Deutsche(r)*

get (get, got) *bekommen, kriegen; holen, besorgen*

get to *gelangen, (hin)kommen*

get dark / cold / ... *kalt / dunkel / ... werden*

get divorced *sich scheiden lassen*

get dressed *sich anziehen*

get fed up (with up) *etw. satt haben / bekommen; die Nase voll haben (von etwas)*

get in(to a car) *(in ein Auto) einsteigen*

get in touch (with) *Verbindung / Kontakt aufnehmen (mit)*

get lost *sich verlaufen / verfahren*

get married (to sb.) *(jn.) heiraten*

get off (a bus) *(aus einem Bus) aussteigen*

get on a bus / train *in einen Bus / Zug einsteigen*

get on sb.'s nerves *jm. auf die Nerven gehen*

get out of a car *aus einem Auto aussteigen*

get ready *sich fertig machen, sich bereitmachen*

　get sth. ready *etw. vorbereiten, etw. fertig machen*

get through *(am Telefon) durchkommen, Verbindung bekommen*

get time off *frei bekommen, Urlaub bekommen*

get to know sb. / sth. *jn. / etw. kennen lernen; etw. erfahren*

get up *aufstehen*

ghost *Geist, Gespenst*

giant *Riese; riesig, gigantisch*

gift *Geschenk, Gabe*

　gift shop *Geschenkladen, Souvenirshop*

girl *Mädchen*

girlfriend *(feste) Freundin*

give (gave, given) *geben*

give a talk (on) *einen Vortrag / eine Rede halten (über)*

give sth. up *etw. aufgeben; auf etw. verzichten*

glad *froh*

glass *Glas*

glasses *Brille*

global *global, weltweit*

　global warming *globaler Temperaturanstieg, Erwärmung der Erdatmosphäre*

globalisation *Globalisierung*

glue *kleben, leimen*

glue *Klebstoff*

go (went, gone) *gehen, fahren*

go shopping / go to the shops *einkaufen gehen*

go for a ride *reiten; eine Spazierfahrt machen, herumfahren*

go on *andauern, weitergehen; fortfahren, weitermachen*

go on holiday *in Urlaub fahren*

go under *untergehen*

go up *steigen, in die Höhe gehen*

go with *passen zu; gehören zu*

goal *Ziel; Tor*

goalkeeper *Torwart/in*

god *Gott*

goddess *Göttin*

gold *Gold*

gold rush *Goldrausch*

good *gut; brav*

　Good morning / evening / night *Guten Morgen / Abend / Gute Nacht*

　be good at sth. *gut in etw. sein; etw. gut können*

　be no good *nichts taugen, zu nichts zu gebrauchen sein*

Goodbye *Auf Wiedersehen*

　say goodbye *sich verabschieden*

good-looking *gut aussehend*

goose, (pl.) geese *Gans*

government *Regierung*

grade *(Zeugnis-, Examens-) Note, Zensur; (AE) Schulklasse, Jahrgangsstufe*

grammar school *Gymnasium*

grandfather *Großvater*

　grandpa / grandad (AE: granddad) *Opa*

grandmother *Großmutter*

　grandma *Oma*

grandparents *Großeltern*

graphics *Zeichnungen, Grafik(en)*

grass *Gras*

grateful *dankbar*

gravy *(Braten-)Soße*

great *großartig, toll; groß, beträchtlich; bedeutend*

great grandmother / ... *Urgroßmutter / ...*

Greek *griechisch; Griechisch; Grieche / Griechin*

green *grün*

grey, (AE) gray *grau*

ground *Boden, Erdboden*

　ground floor *Erdgeschoss*

group *Gruppe*

　in groups of four *in Vierergruppen*

grow (grew, grown) *wachsen; anbauen, anpflanzen*

　grow up *aufwachsen; erwachsen werden*

guarantee *garantieren*

guaranteed *garantiert*

guess *(er)raten*

guest *Gast*

guide *führen, lenken, leiten*

guide *(Fremden-)Führer/in, Reiseleiter/in*

　guide book *Reiseführer*

guilty (of sth.) *(einer Sache) schuldig*

guitar *Gitarre*

gun *Schusswaffe*

guy *(infml) Typ, Kerl*

H

hack (into a computer) *in einen Computer unbefugt eindringen*

hair *Haar, Haare*

hairdresser *Friseur/in*

hairdryer *Fön*

half, halves *Hälfte*

　half past six *halb sieben*

hall *Flur, Diele; Halle, Saal*

ham *Schinken*

hand (sth. to sb.) *reichen, geben (etw. an jmdn.)*

hand *Hand*

handbag *Handtasche*

handbook *Handbuch*

hand-made *handgemacht, von Hand gemacht*

hand-written *handgeschrieben*

hang (hung, hung) *hängen, aufhängen*

hang out *sich herumtreiben, rumhängen*

happen (to) *(jm.) geschehen, passieren*

What's happening? *Was ist los? / Was geht hier vor?*

happy *glücklich, froh*

Happy birthday! *Herzlichen Glückwunsch zum Geburtstag!*

happiness *Glück*

harbour *Hafen*

hard *hart; schwierig, schwer; kräftig, heftig*

hardly *kaum*

harm *Schaden, Verletzung*

hat *Hut, Mütze*

hate *hassen, gar nicht mögen*

have / have got (had, had) *haben, besitzen*

have breakfast / lunch / ... *frühstücken / Mittag essen / ...*

have a bath / shower *ein Bad nehmen / duschen*

have a look at sth. *etw. ansehen, einen Blick werfen auf etw.*

have a look at sb. *jn. ansehen / überprüfen*

have a party *eine Party veranstalten / feiern*

have a word with sb. *kurz mit jm. sprechen*

have fun *sich amüsieren*

have sex (with) *Geschlechtsverkehr haben (mit)*

have sth. done (by sb.) *etw. (von jm.) machen lassen*

have sth. in common *etw. miteinander gemein haben*

have (got) to do sth. *etw. tun müssen*

head *Kopf*

headache *Kopfschmerz(en)*

headless *kopflos, ohne Kopf*

heading *Überschrift*

headline *Schlagzeile*

headteacher *Schulleiter/in*

headword *Stichwort*

health *Gesundheit*

healthy *gesund*

hear *hören*

heart *Herz*

heartless *herzlos*

heat *Hitze*

heating *Heizung*

heavy *schwer (von Gewicht)*

heavy traffic *starker Verkehr*

height *Größe (einer Person); Höhe*

helicopter *Hubschrauber*

hello *Hallo*

helmet *Helm*

put on a helmet *einen Helm aufsetzen*

help *helfen*

Help yourself *Greif zu! / Bedien dich! / Bedienen Sie sich.*

help *Hilfe*

helpful *hilfreich*

helpless *hilflos*

here *hier; hierher*

hero, heroes *Held*

hesitate *zögern*

hide *sich verstecken; etw. veestecken; etw. verbergen*

high *hoch*

high school (AE) *Oberschule (mit den Klassen 7–12)*

highlight *hervorheben, markieren*

highlight *Höhepunkt, Glanzpunkt*

hike *wandern, eine Wanderung machen*

hike *Wanderung*

hiking *Wandern*

hill *Hügel*

hilly *hügelig*

history *Geschichte*

historic *historisch*

hit sb. / sth. (hit, hit) *jn. / etw. schlagen, treffen; gegen etw. stoßen*

hitchhike *trampen, per Anhalter fahren*

hold (held, held) *(fest)halten*

hold sth. up *etw. hochhalten, hochheben*

hole *Loch*

holiday *Feiertag, freier Tag*

be / go on holiday *in Urlaub sein / fahren; Ferien haben / machen*

holidays *Ferien, Urlaub*

holy *heilig*

home *Heim, Zuhause*

homeless *obdachlos*

homelessness *Obdachlosigkeit*

home-made *hausgemacht, selbstgemacht*

be / feel homesick *Heimweh haben*

homework *Hausaufgabe(n)*

do homework *die Hausaufgabe(n) machen*

honour *Ehre*

hope (for) *hoffen (auf)*

hope *Hoffnung*

hopeful *zuversichtlich*

hopeless *hoffnungslos, aussichtslos*

horrible *scheußlich, grauenhaft*

horror *Entsetzen, Grauen, Horror*

horse *Pferd*

horseman, horsewoman *Reiter/in*

hospital *Krankenhaus*

host, hostess *Gastgeber/in*

hostel *Herberge*

hot *heiß*

hour *Stunde*

house *Haus*

how *wie*

how many? *wie viele?*

how much? *wie viel?*

how much is ...? *Was / Wie viel kostet ...?*

however *allerdings, jedoch*

huge *sehr groß, riesig*

human *menschlich; Mensch*

hungry *hungrig*

hunt (for) *jagen (nach); Jagd machen (auf); suchen*

hunt *Jagd*

hunter *Jäger/in*

hurricane *Hurrikan, Orkan*

hurry *sich beeilen*

hurt (hurt, hurt) *verletzen, weh tun; schaden, schädigen*
husband *Ehemann*
hyphen *Bindestrich*

I

ice *Eis*
ice-cream *(Speise-)Eis*
ice skating *(das) Eislaufen*
icy *eisig; vereist*
idea *Idee, Einfall*
   idea of *Vorstellung von*
ideal *vollkommen, ideal*
identity *Identität*
if *wenn, falls*
   even if *selbst wenn, auch wenn*
   as if *als ob*
ill *krank*
illegal *illegal; rechtswidrig*
illness *Krankheit*
illustrate *illustrieren, mit Bildern versehen*
image *Bild, Vorstellung*
imagine sth. *sich etw. vorstellen*
imaginary *imaginär*
imagination *Vorstellungskraft, Fantasie*
immediately *sofort, gleich*
immigrant *Einwanderer / Einwanderin*
immigrate (to) *einwandern, immigrieren (nach / in)*
immigration *Einwanderung, Immigration*
imperfect *fehlerhaft, unvollkommen*
impolite *unhöflich*
important *wichtig*
impossible *unmöglich*
impress *beeindrucken*
impression (of) *Eindruck (von)*
improve *(sich) verbessern, besser machen / werden*
in *in*
inch *Zoll (2,54 cm)*
incident *Zwischenfall*
include *(mit) einschließen, enthalten*

incorrect *falsch*
independence (from) *Unabhängigkeit (von)*
independent (of) *autark, unabhängig (von)*
Indian *indisch; Inder/in; indianisch; Indianer/in*
indirect speech *indirekte Rede*
industry *Industrie*
inexpensive *preiswert, günstig*
influence *beeinflussen*
influence *Einfluss*
inform sb. (of / about sth.) *jn. informieren (über etw.), jn. benachrichtigen (von etw.)*
individual *einzeln*
inform *informieren*
informal *informell, umgangssprachlich*
information *Auskunft, Auskünfte, Information*
inner *Innen- / innere(r)*
insect *Insekt*
inside *drinnen, nach drinnen; innerhalb, im Innern*
instead *stattdessen*
   instead of *anstelle von, statt*
institution *Einrichtung, Institution*
instruction(s) *Anweisung(en), Anleitung*
intelligent *klug, intelligent*
interactive *interaktiv*
interest (in) *Interesse (an)*
interest sb. *jn. interessieren*
interested *interessiert*
interesting *interessant*
interview *befragen, interviewen*
(job) interview *Vorstellungsgespräch*
interviewee *Kandidat/in in einem Vorstellungsgespräch*
interviewer *Leiter/in eines Vorstellungsgesprächs, Gesprächsführer/in*
into *in ... hinein ...*
introduce *einführen, vorstellen*

introduction *Einführung; Einleitung*
invade a country *einmarschieren (in ein Land), (ein Land) überfallen*
invader *Eindringling, Invasor/in*
invasion *Invasion, Einmarsch*
invent *erfinden*
invention *Erfindung*
inventor *Erfinder/in*
investigate *untersuchen; ermitteln*
invitation *Einladung*
invite *einladen*
be involved in / with *beteiligt sein an, etw. zu tun haben mit, sich engagieren für*
Irish *irisch; Irisch; Ire/Irin*
irregular *unregelmäßig*
island *Insel*
item *Artikel, Posten, Punkt (auf einer Liste)*
Italian *italienisch; Italienisch; Italiener/in*

J

jacket *Jacke; Jakett, Sakko*
Japanese *japanisch; Japanisch; Japaner/in*
jealous (of) *neidisch (auf); eifersüchtig (auf)*
Jew *Jude / Jüdin*
   Jewish *jüdisch*
jewellery *Schmuck*
job *Job; Arbeit, Beruf; Aufgabe*
   full-time job *Vollzeit-, Ganztagsbeschäftigung*
   part-time job *Teilzeitbeschäftigung*
   do jobs *Arbeiten / Aufträge erledigen*
jobless *ohne Arbeit, arbeitslos*
join *beitreten, eintreten in (einen Verein usw.)*
   join sb. *sich jm. anschließen*
joke *scherzen, Witze machen*
joke *Scherz, Witz*
journalism *Journalismus*
journalist *Journalist/in*

journey *Reise, Fahrt*
joy *Freude*
judge *Wettkampfrichter; Richter*
juice *Saft*
jumbled *durcheinander geworfen*
jump *springen*
jungle *Dschungel*
junior *Junioren-, Jugend-*
    junior high school (US) *die Klassen 7–8/9 der High School*
just *nur, bloß; einfach, gerade (eben)*
    just then *genau in dem Moment; gerade als*
    just like *genau wie*

K
kangaroo *Känguru*
keep (kept, kept) *(be)halten*
keep alive *am Leben (er)halten*
keep sb. / sth. away (from) *jn. / etw. fern halten (von)*
keep sb. busy *jn. beschäftigen*
keep (on) doing sth. *etw. weiter tun, weiter-*
keep one's distance *Abstand halten / wahren*
key *Schlüssel; Taste*
keyboard *Tastatur*
keyword *Schlüsselwort*
kick *treten*
kick *Stoß, Fußtritt*
kidnap / kidnapping *Entführung*
kill *töten*
killer *Mörder/in, Totschläger/in*
killing *Tötung*
kind *freundlich, nett, gütig*
kindness *Freundlichkeit, Liebenswürdigkeit*
kind (of) *Art, Sorte*
    What kind of ...? *Was für ein(e) ...?*
king *König*
kiss *küssen; sich küssen*
kiss *Kuss*
kitchen *Küche*

knee *Knie*
knife, knives *Messer*
knock *klopfen, anklopfen*
knock *Klopfen*
know (knew, known) *wissen; kennen*
    get to know sb. / sth. *jn. / etw. kennen lernen; etw. erfahren*
    be known as *bekannt sein als / unter dem Namen*

L
label *beschriften, etikettieren*
label *Label, Etikett*
labour *Arbeit*
ladder *Leiter*
lady *Dame*
    Ladies and gentlemen *Meine (sehr geehrten) Damen und Herren*
lake *(Binnen-)See*
lamb *Lamm*
lamp *Lampe*
land *landen*
land *(Fest-)Land; Grund und Boden*
landscape *Landschaft; Landschaftsbild*
language *Sprache*
lantern *Laterne*
large *umfangreich*
last *als Letztes, zuletzt*
    at last *endlich, schließlich*
late *spät; zu spät*
    later *später*
    the latest ... *der / die / das neueste ..., die neuesten ...*
laugh *lachen*
    laugh at *lachen über; auslachen*
law *Gesetz*
    pass a law *ein Gesetz verabschieden*
lawyer *Rechtsanwalt / Rechtsanwältin*
lay (laid, laid) *legen*
lazy *faul, träge*
lead (led, led) *führen, leiten*

lead the way *vorangehen, vorausgehen; führen*
leader *Führer/in, Leiter/in*
leaf, leaves *Blatt*
leaflet *Prospekt, Flugblatt*
learn *lernen*
learn about *etw. erfahren über / von, etw. herausfinden über*
least *am wenigsten*
    at least *mindestens; wenigstens*
leather *Leder*
leave (left, left) *(zurück)lassen, hinterlassen; verlassen*
leave sb. sth. *jm. etw. übrig lassen; vererben*
leave sb. to do sth. *es jm. überlassen, etw. zu tun*
leave for *weggehen, abfahren nach*
leave sth. behind *etw. zurücklassen; etw. hinter sich lassen*
leave a message *eine Nachricht hinterlassen*
leave school *von der Schule abgehen*
be left *übrig sein / bleiben*
left *nach links; linke(r, s)*
    on the left *links, auf der linken Seite*
leg *Bein*
legal *gesetzlich, zulässig*
legend *Legende, Sage*
lemonade *Limonade*
lend (lent, lent) *leihen, verleihen*
less *weniger*
lesson(s) *Unterricht; Unterrichtsstunde*
    teach sb. a lesson *jm. eine Lektion erteilen*
let (let, let) *lassen*
    Let's go *Auf geht's!*
let sb. down *jn. in Stich lassen, jn. enttäuschen*
lethal *tödlich*
letter *Buchstabe; Brief*
letterbox *Briefkasten*

lettuce *Kopfsalat*

level *Ebene, Niveau*

liberty *Freiheit*

library *Bibliothek, Bücherei*

lie (lay, lain) *liegen*

    lie down *sich hinlegen*

lie *lügen*

    lie to sb. *jn. anlügen/belügen*

life, lives *(das) Leben*

    come to life *lebendig werden*

lifeless *leblos*

lifestyle *Lebensart*

lift *(an-, hoch)heben*

lift *Fahrstuhl, Aufzug*

light (lit, lit) *anzünden*

light *Licht, Lampe*

    traffic lights *Verkehrsampel*

light *leicht (Gewicht)*

lighting *Beleuchtung*

lightning *Blitz*

like *als ob; wie*

    just like *genau wie*

like *mögen, gern haben*

    I'd like … *Ich hätte gern/möchte gern …*

    I'd like to leave *Ich würde gern/möchte gehen.*

likeable *liebenswert, nett*

likely *wahrscheinlich*

limit *Grenze, Begrenzung, Beschränkung*

    speed limit *Geschwindigkeitsbegrenzung*

line *Linie; Zeile*

    line (AE) *eine Schlange wartender Menschen*

    (tele)phone line *Telefonleitung*

link *verbinden, verknüpfen*

link *Verbindung*

lion *Löwe*

list *auflisten, aufzählen*

list *Liste*

listen *zuhören; horchen*

    listen for sth. *auf etw. horchen, auf etw. achten*

    listen to *jm. zuhören, sich etw. anhören*

listener *Zuhörer/in*

little *klein, jung*

a little *ein bisschen, ein wenig*

live *leben, wohnen*

lively *lebhaft, lebendig*

living-room *Wohnzimmer*

local *örtlich, Lokal-; am/vom Ort*

locate *orten, lokalisieren*

location *Standort, Lage; Drehort (Film)*

lock *abschließen, zuschließen*

locker *Schließfach; Spind*

logo *Logo, Firmenzeichen*

lonely *einsam*

loneliness *Einsamkeit*

long *lang*

    all day long *den ganzen Tag*

look *schauen, sehen; aussehen*

look at *anschauen*

look after sb. *sich um jn. kümmern, auf jn. aufpassen*

look ahead *nach vorn schauen, vorausschauen*

look for *suchen*

look forward to sth. *sich auf etw. freuen*

look forward to doing sth. *sich darauf freuen, etw. zu tun*

look sth. up *etw. nachschlagen, etw. heraussuchen*

look *Blick*

loose *locker, lose*

    break loose *sich losreißen, sich lösen*

lose *verlieren*

loser *Verlierer/in*

lost *verlaufen, verfahren*

lots (of)/a lot (of) *eine Menge, viel(e)*

loud *laut*

lounge *Lounge, Aufenthaltsraum (z. B. im Hotel)*

love *lieben, sehr mögen*

love *Liebe*

lovely *schön, herrlich, hübsch*

lover *Liebhaber/in, Geliebte(r)*

low *niedrig, tief*

    low pay *niedriger Lohn*

luck *Glück*

be lucky *Glück haben*

luckily *glücklicherweise*

luggage *Gepäck, Reisgepäck*

lunch *Mittagessen*

    at lunchtime *mittags, zur Mittagzeit*

M

machine *Maschine, Gerät*

mad *wütend, wahnsinnig*

Madam, Ma'am *Gnädige Frau*

    Dear Sir or Madam *Sehr geehrte Damen und Herren*

made of *bestehen aus*

    made up of *aus … (gemacht)*

magazine *Zeitschrift*

magic *Zauber-, Zauberei, Magie*

mail *abschicken, absenden*

mail *Post*

mailbox (AE) *Briefkasten*

main *Haupt-*

    main clause *Hauptsatz*

mainly *hauptsächlich*

major *Haupt-; wichtig; groß*

majority *Mehrheit*

make (made, made) *machen, bilden, bauen*

    make it (to the top) *Erfolg haben, es zu etw. bringen*

    make a decision *eine Entscheidung treffen/fallen*

    make a move *etw. unternehmen, handeln*

    make a speech *eine Rede/einen Vortrag halten*

    make comparisons *vergleichen, Vergleiche anstellen*

    make fun of s./sth. *sich über jn./etw. lustig machen*

    make money *Geld verdienen*

    make sense *einen Sinn ergeben*

    make trouble *Ärger/Schwierigkeiten bereiten*

make sb. do sth. *jn. dazu bringen / zwingen, etwas zu tun*

make sth. up *sich etwas ausdenken, etwas erfinden*

(the) making (of) *Herstellung, Entstehung (von)*

male *Männchen (bei Tieren); männlich*

man *Mann*

manage sth. *mit etwas zurechtkommen, fertig werden*

manager *Manager/in, Geschäftsführer/in*

maniac *Fanatiker/in*

many *viele*

map *Landkarte, Stadtplan*

march *marschieren*

mark *zensieren; markieren, kennzeichnen*

mark *(Zeugnis-)Note, Zensur; Abdruck, Spur*

market *vermarkten, vertreiben*

market *Markt*

marmalade *(Orangen-) Marmelade*

marriage *Heirat; Ehe*

married *verheiratet*

marry *heiraten*

get married (to sb.) *(jn.) heiraten*

mask *Maske*

masked *maskiert*

master *Herr, Meister*

match *zuordnen*

match *Spiel, Wettkampf; Streichholz*

mate *(infml.) Kumpel; Freund/in*

material *Stoff, Material*

maths (AE: math) *Mathe, Mathematik*

matter *von Bedeutung sein, etw. ausmachen*

may *dürfen*

maybe *vielleicht*

meal *Mahlzeit, Essen*

mean *gemein*

mean (meant, meant) *meinen; bedeuten*

meaning *Bedeutung*

meaningless *bedeutungslos, sinnlos*

meanwhile *inzwischen, währenddessen*

meat *Fleisch*

mechanic *Mechaniker/in*

mechatronic engineer *Techniker/in für Mechatronik*

medal *Medaille; Orden*

(the) media *(die) Medien*

medicine *Medizin; Arznei*

medium *mittel; Medium*

meet (met, met) *sich treffen; jn. treffen; abholen*

meeting *Treffen*

member (of) *Mitglied (in, von)*

mention *erwähnen, nennen*

menu *Speisekarte*

mess *Unordnung, Durcheinander*

mess up *durcheinanderbringen; verpfuschen, vermasseln*

message *Botschaft, Nachricht*

leave a message *eine Nachricht hinterlassen*

metal *Metall*

metre *Meter*

Mexican *mexikanisch; Mexikaner/in*

microphone *Mikrofon*

microwave (oven) *Mikrowellengerät*

midday *Mittags-; Mittagszeit*

middle *Mitte*

the middle of nowhere *in der Mitte von Nirgendwo*

midnight *Mitternacht*

might *könnte(n) vielleicht*

mile *Meile (= ca. 1,6 km)*

milk *melken*

milk *Milch*

mind (doing sth.) *etwas dagegen haben*

I don't mind *Ich habe nichts dagegen. / Das macht mir nichts aus.*

mind *Verstand*

change one's mind *seine Meinung ändern*

mind map *„Gedankenkarte", „Wissensnetz"*

mindmapping *Merk- und Strukturierungstechnik*

mineral water *Mineralwasser*

minimum *Mindest-; Minimum*

minority *Minderheit*

mirror *Spiegel*

miserable *unglücklich, elend; erbärmlich, armselig*

miss *vermissen; verpassen*

missing *fehlend*

be missing *fehlen*

mission *Einsatz, Mission*

mist *Dunst, feiner Nebel*

misty *dunstig, neblig, diesig*

mistake *Fehler, Irrtum*

by mistake *aus Versehen, irrtümlich*

mix sth. up *etw. mischen, durcheinander bringen*

mixed up *durcheinander*

mixed *gemischt*

mixture *Mischung, Gemisch, Mixtur*

mobile phone (AE: cell phone) *Handy*

model *nachbilden, modellieren*

model *Modell-, Modell*

moderately *einigermaßen; moderat, mäßig, in Maßen*

moment *Augenblick, Moment*

money *Geld*

make money *Geld verdienen*

monkey *Affe*

month *Monat*

mood *Laune, Stimmung*

moody *launisch, unausgeglichen*

moon *Mond*

moor *Hochmoor*

more *mehr, weitere*

morning *Morgen, Vormittag*

this morning *heute Morgen*

tomorrow morning *morgen früh, morgen Vormittag*

most *meiste ... ; am meisten*

mother *Mutter*
  mum, mam (AE: mom) *Mutti, Mama*
motivate *motivieren, anspornen*
motorbike, motorcycle *Motorrad*
motorway *Autobahn*
mountain *Berg*
mouse, mice *Maus, Mäuse*
mouth *Mund*
move *(sich) bewegen*
  move in *einziehen*
  move to *(um)ziehen nach*
move *Bewegung, Schritt*
  be on the move *unterwegs sein, auf Achse sein*
  make a move *etwas unternehmen, handeln*
movement *Bewegung*
movie (AE) *Film*
much *viel*
mud *Schlamm, Matsch*
muddy *schlammig, matschig*
multicultural *multikulturell*
murder *ermordern, morden*
murder *Mord*
murderer *Mörder/in*
music *Musik*
musician *Musiker/in*
must (had to, had to) *müssen*
  mustn't *nicht dürfen*
mysterious *rätselhaft, geheimnisvoll*
mystery *Geheimnis, Rätsel*

N

name *nennen, benennen*
  named *mit Namen, namens*
name *Name*
  call sb. names *jn. verspotten, jn. beschimpfen*
narrator *Erzähler/in*
narrow *schmal, eng*
nasty *böse, gemein; schlimm*
nation *Nation, Volk*
  national *national, National-*
nationality *Staatsangehörigkeit*

native *Ureinwohner/in; eingeboren, einheimisch*
  native speaker *Muttersprachler/in*
natural gas *Erdgas*
nature *Natur*
  natural *natürlich; Natur-*
near (to) *in der Nähe von, nahe (bei)*
nearly *fast, beinahe*
neat *ordentlich, gepflegt*
  neat (AE) *toll, prima, klasse*
necessary *nötig, notwendig*
neck *Hals, Nacken*
need *brauchen, benötigen*
  need to do sth. *etw. tun müssen*
need *Bedürfnis*
negative *negativ*
neighbourhood *Gegend, Viertel; Nachbarschaft*
neighbour *Nachbar/in*
nephew *Neffe*
nerve *Nerv*
  get on sb.'s nerves *jm. auf die Nerven gehen*
nervous *nervös, aufgeregt*
nervousness *Nervosität, Ängstlichkeit*
net *Netz*
  network *Netzwerk*
never *niemals*
new *neu*
  New Year *Neujahr*
  New Year's Eve *Silvester*
news *Nachricht(en)*
newspaper *Zeitung*
next *nächste(r, s)*
next to *neben*
nice *schön, nett, freundlich*
  Nice to meet you. *Freut mich, euch (dich / Sie) kennen zu lernen.*
nickname *Spitzname*
niece *Nichte*
night *Nacht, Abend*
  at night *in der Nacht, nachts*
  Good night. *Gute Nacht.*
nightdress *Nachthemd*

nightmare *Alptraum*
nil (z. B.: Two nil to Chelsea.) *null*
no *nein; kein, keine*
nobody / no one *niemand*
noise *Geräusch; Lärm*
noisy *lärmend, laut*
nominate *nominieren, vorschlagen*
non-stop *ununterbrochen, ohne Unterbrechung*
none *keine(r, s)*
north *nördlich: (nach) Norden*
  north-east *nordöstlich; (nach) Nordosten*
  northern *nördlich, Nord-*
nose *Nase*
not *nicht*
  not ... either *auch nicht; auch kein*
note down *notieren, aufschreiben*
note *Notiz*
  make / take notes *sich Notizen machen, mitschreiben*
nothing *nichts*
  nothing else *nichts anderes, sonst nichts*
notice *bemerken*
notice board *Anschlagtafel, schwarzes Brett*
nought (formal) *null*
novel *Roman*
now *nun, jetzt*
nowhere *nirgendwo, nirgendwohin*
number *nummerieren*
number *Zahl, Ziffer*
  a small number of ... *eine kleine Anzahl von ...*
nurse *Krankenschwester, Krankenpfleger*

O

obviously *offensichtlich*
occasionally *gelegentlich*
ocean *Ozean*
o'clock (z. B. eight o'clock) *acht Uhr*
octopus *Tintenfisch, Krake*

odd word out *das unpassende Wort raus*

of *von*

of course *natürlich, selbstverständlich*

off *aus; von*

take off *(Flugzeug) starten, abheben*

take sth. off *etw. ausziehen*

turn sth. off *etw. ausschalten*

offer *bieten, anbieten*

offer *Angebot*

office *Büro*

box office *(Theater-, Kino-) Kasse*

officer *Offizier/in*

official *Beamter/Beamtin; offiziell, amtlich*

often *oft*

oil *Öl*

oil rig, oil platform *(Öl-) Bohrinsel*

oil well *Ölquelle*

old *alt*

a 12-year-old *ein(e) 12-jährige(r, s)*

on *auf; an, eingeschaltet*

on top (of sth.) *oben, obendrauf (auf etw.)*

once *einmal*

at once *sofort, (so)gleich*

one *eins; ein(e); man*

only *nur, bloß; erst*

only child *Einzelkind*

onto *auf (... hinauf)*

open *öffnen, aufmachen; sich öffnen; eröffnen*

open *geöffnet, offen*

opera *Oper*

operate sth. *etw. bedienen, etw. betätigen*

opinion (on/about sth.) *Meinung (über etwas)*

in my opinion *meiner Meinung nach*

opportunity *Gelegenheit, Chance*

opposite *gegenüber (von); gegenüberliegend; entgegengesetzt*

(the) opposite *Gegenteil*

optimistic *optimistisch*

option *Wahl, Wahlmöglichkeit, Option*

or *oder*

either ... or *entweder ... oder*

orange *Apfelsine, Orange*

orange juice *Orangensaft*

orchestra *Orchester*

order *bestellen; ordnen, anordnen*

order *Bestellung; Order; Reihenfolge; Anordnung*

ordinal number *Ordnungszahl*

ordinary *normal, gewöhnlich*

organic *organisch, naturgemäß*

organic farming *ökologischer Anbau/Landwirtschaft*

organization *Organisation*

organize *organisieren*

organized *organisiert*

organizer *Organisator/in*

origin *Herkunft; Ursprung*

other *andere*

each other *einander, sich (gegenseitig)*

ought to (do sth.) *sollen (etw. tun)*

out *hinaus, heraus; draußen*

outdoor *draußen; im Freien*

outer *äußere(r, s), Außen-*

outer suburbs *Außenbezirke*

outfit *Kleider, Kleidung*

out of *aus*

outside *draußen; nach draußen; außerhalb (von)*

outside toilet *Außentoilette*

outside lights *Außenbeleuchtung*

outsource *outsourcen (Ausgliedern von Produktionsstätten)*

over *über, oberhalb von; mehr als*

all over the world *überall auf der Welt, auf der ganzen Welt*

be over *vorbei sein, zu Ende sein*

overhead projector (OHP) *Tageslichtprojektor*

overhear (overheard, overheard) *zufällig mitanhören, belauschen*

overnight *über Nacht*

overtake (overtook, overtaken) *überholen*

overtime *Überstunden*

do/work overtime *Überstunden machen*

own *besitzen*

own *eigen; selbst*

my own room *mein eigenes Zimmer*

I do my own shopping. *Ich kaufe selbst ein.*

P

packet *Paket, Päckchen; Packung*

page *Seite*

painful *Schmerz, Schmerzen*

painting *Maler/in; Anstreicher/in*

pair (of) *Paar*

palace *Palast, Schloss*

panic *Panik*

pants (AE) *Hose*

paper *Papier*

parade *Umzug, Parade*

paragraph *Absatz, Abschnitt*

parallel *Parallele, vergleichbarer Fall*

parent, parents *Elternteil, Eltern*

parliament *Parlament*

part *Teil*

take part (in) *teilnehmen (an), mitmachen (bei)*

party *Party; (politische) Partei*

have a party *eine Party veranstalten/feiern*

party platform *Wahlplattform*

pass *vergehen, vorübergehen (Zeit)*

pass sth. (to sb.) *(jm.) etw. (herüber)reichen*

pass an exam *eine Prüfung bestehen*

pass a law *ein Gesetz verabschieden*

passenger *Passagier/in, Fahrgast*

passion *Leidenschaft, Begeisterung*

passport *Reisepass*

password *Passwort*

past *vorbei / vorüber an; Vergangenheit*

path *Pfad, Weg*

pattern *Muster, Schema*

pay (for) *bezahlen*

pay *Bezahlung; Lohn, Löhne*
low pay *niedriger Lohn, niedrige Löhne*

pay attention (to sth. / b.) *etw. / jn. beachten, aufpassen (auf etw.), aufmerksam sein*

PE (= Physical Eduction) *Turnen, Sportunterricht*

peace *Friede, Frieden*

peaceful *friedlich, in Frieden*

pen *Füller*

pen-friend, pen-pal *Brieffreund/in*

penalty *Strafe*
death penalty *Todesstrafe*

pencil *Bleistift*

pencil-case *Federmäppchen*

penguin *Pinguin*

penny, pence *britische Münzeinheit (100 p = £ 1:00)*

people *Leute, Menschen; Volk*

per cent (AE: percent) *Prozent*

perfect *perfekt, vollkommen, einwandfrei; ideal*

perform *aufführen, auftreten*

performance *Aufführung, Vorstellung*

performer *Künstler/in*
circus performer *Artist/in*

perhaps *vielleicht*

period *Zeit, Zeitraum, Zeitspanne; (AE) Schulstunde*

permanent *unbefristet; dauerhaft, ständig*

permission *Erlaubnis, Genehmigung*

personal *persönlich; Privat-*

personality *Persönlichkeit*

personnel *Personal*

persuade sb. (to do sth.) *jn. überzeugen (etw. zu tun)*

pet *Haustier*

petrol *Benzin*

phone *anrufen*

phone *Telefon*
answer the phone *ans Telefon gehen*
on the phone *am Telefon*

photo *Foto*
take photos *Fotos machen, fotografieren*

photocopy *fotokopieren*

photocopy *Fotokopie*

photograph *fotografieren*

photographer *Fotograf/in*

photography *Fotografie*

phrase *Wortgruppe, Ausdruck, (Rede-)Wendung*

physical science *Naturwissenschaft*

physics *Physik*

piano *Klavier*

pick sb. up *jn. abholen*

pick sth. up *etw. aufheben, hochnehmen*
pick up the pieces *die Scherben aufsammeln*

picnic *Picknick*

picture *Bild*

pie *Pastete*

piece *Stück; Teil*

pier *Hafendamm*

pig *Schwein*

pilgrim *Pilger/in*

pill *Tablette, Pille*

pink *rosa, pinkfarben*

pipe *Pfeife*

pipeline *Pipeline, Rohrleitung (für Gas / Öl usw.)*

pirate *Pirat/in*

place *Ort, Platz, Stelle*
place of birth *Geburtsort*
take place *stattfinden*

plan *planen*

plan *Plan*

plane *Flugzeug*

plant *pflanzen*

plant *Pflanze*

plantation *Plantage; Anpflanzung*

plastic *Plastik, Kunststoff*

plate *Teller*

platform *Bahnsteig, Gleis*

play *spielen*
play a trick on sb. *jm. einen Streich spielen*

play *Spiel, das Spielen; Theaterstück*

player *Spieler/in*

playground *Schulhof; Spielplatz*

please *bitte*
be pleased (with) *zufrieden sein (mit), sich freuen (über)*

plenty *genug, ausreichend*

plug *Stecker*

4 p.m. / 4 pm *16 Uhr bzw. 4 Uhr nachmittags*

pocket *Tasche (an einem Kleidungsstück)*

pocket money *Taschengeld*

poem *Gedicht*

poetry *Lyrik, Dichtung, Poesie*

point (at, to) *zeigen, deuten (auf)*

point sth. at sb. / sth. *etw. auf jn. / etw. richten*

point *Punkt*
point in time *Zeitpunkt*

police *Polizei*
police officer *Polizeibeamte(r)*
police station *Polizeiwache*

policewoman *Polizistin*

Polish *polnisch; Polnisch; Pole/in*

polite *höflich*

political *politisch*

politician *Politiker/in*

politics *Politik*

pollute *(die Umwelt) verschmutzen*

pollution *(Umwelt-)Verschmutzung*

pool *Schwimmbecken; Tümpel*

poor *arm; schlecht, schwach, mangelhaft*

pop *Popmusik*

popular (with) *beliebt (bei)*

population *Bevölkerung, Einwohner(zahl)*

pork *Schweinefleisch*

portfolio *Mappe*

portion *Portion; (An-)Teil*

portrait *Porträt*

portray *porträtieren, darstellen*

Portuguese *portugiesisch; Portugiesisch; Portugiese/ Portugiesin*

position *Position, Stellung, Lage*

possible *möglich*

possibility *Möglichkeit*

post *abschicken, absenden; ins Internet stellen*

post *Post(sendungen)*

post office *Postamt*

postbox *Briefkasten*

postcard *Postkarte*

pot *Topf*

potato, potatoes *Kartoffel*

potato chips (AE) *Kartoffelchips*

pound (£) *Pfund (britische Währungseinheit)*

pour *gießen, schütten; einschenken*

poverty *(die) Armut*

powder *Puder, Pulver*

power *Kraft, Macht; Strom, Energie*

power station *Kraftwerk, Elektrizitätswerk*

powerful *stark, mächtig*

practical *praktisch*

practice *Praxis, Übung(en)*

practise, (AE) practice *üben, trainieren*

pray *beten*

prayer *Gebet*

prefer sth. (to) *etwas lieber haben (als), etw. vorziehen*

prefer to do sth. *etw. lieber tun, bevorzugen*

prefix *Vorsilbe, Präfix*

prepare (for) *(sich) vorbereiten (auf); (Mahlzeit) zubereiten*

present *Geschenk; Gegenwart*

present sth. (to sb.) *(jm.) etw. präsentieren, zeigen, vorstellen*

presentation *Präsentation, Darbietung, Vorstellung*

president *Präsident/in*

press *drücken (auf); pressen*

press a button *auf einen Knopf drücken*

pressure *Druck*

put pressure on sb. *jn. unter Druck setzen*

pretty *hübsch*

price *Preis, Kaufpreis*

pride *Stolz*

priest *Priester*

primary school (BE) *Grundschule*

prime minister *Premierminister/in*

prince *Prinz*

print *drucken, ausdrucken*

print *Druck*

printer *Drucker*

prison *Gefängnis*

prisoner *Gefangene(r)*

private *privat*

prize *(Lotterie) Gewinn, (Sieger) Preis*

probably *wahrscheinlich*

produce *produzieren, erzeugen, herstellen*

product *Produkt, Erzeugnis*

production *Herstellung, Produktion*

professional *professionell, Berufs-, Fach-; Profi*

profile *Profil*

profit *Profit, Gewinn*

program *programmieren*

program *Computerprogramm*

programmer *Programmierer/in*

programme *Programm, (Radio-, Fernseh-)Sendung*

promise *versprechen*

pronounce *aussprechen*

pronunciation *Aussprache*

protect sb. (from sth.) *jn. (be)schützen (vor etw.)*

protection (against) *Schutz (vor)*

protest (against/about) *protestieren (gegen)*

protest *Protest, Widerspruch*

be proud (of sb./sth.) *stolz (auf jn./etw.) sein*

pub *Kneipe, Lokal*

public *öffentlich; Öffentlichkeit*

publication *Veröffentlichung*

publish *veröffentlichen; verlegen*

pull *ziehen*

pull sb. close *jn. (eng) an sich heranziehen*

punishment *Strafe, Bestrafung*

pupil *Schüler/in*

purple *lila*

push *schieben, stoßen, drücken*

put (put, put) *legen, stellen, etw. wohin tun*

put down *hinstellen, hinlegen*

put in *einsetzen*

put sth. on etw. *anziehen*

put on a helmet/hat *einen Helm/Hut aufsetzen*

put a tax on sth. *etw. besteuern*

put pressure on sb. *jn. unter Druck setzen*

put sth. up *etw. aufstellen/errichten/aufhängen*

puzzle *Rätsel*

puzzled *verwirrt, verblüfft*

pyjamas *Schlafanzug, Pyjama*

pyramid *Pyramide*

Q

qualification *Qualifikation*

quality *Qualität*

quarter *Viertel*

quarter to / past ... *Viertel vor / nach ...*
queen *Königin*
question sb. *jn. befragen, jn. vernehmen*
question *Frage*
    ask questions *Fragen stellen*
questionnaire *Fragebogen*
queue *Warteschlange, Reihe*
queue up *anstehen, Schlange stehen*
quick *schnell*
quiet *ruhig, leise, still*
quite *ziemlich, ganz*
quiz *Quiz, Ratespiel*

R
rabbit *Kaninchen*
race *Rennen, Wettlauf; Rasse*
radio *Radio; Funk; Funkgerät*
railway *Eisenbahn*
rain *regnen*
rain *Regen*
rainforest *Regenwald*
rainy season *Regenzeit*
rapid *rasch, rapide*
rare *selten*
rate *einschätzen, beurteilen, bewerten*
rating *Einschätzung, Einstufung, Bewertung*
RE (= Religious Education) *Religionsunterricht*
reach *erreichen*
reach for sth. *nach etwas greifen*
react (to) *reagieren (auf)*
reaction (to) *Reaktion (auf)*
read (read, red) *lesen*
read out *vorlesen*
readable *lesbar*
reader *Leser/in*
reading *Lesung*
ready *bereit, fertig*
    be ready for sth. *auf etw. vorbereitet sein*
    get ready *sich fertig machen, sich bereitmachen*

get sth. ready *etw. vorbereiten, etw. fertig machen*
real *echt, wirklich*
reality *Realität, Wirklichkeit*
realize *erkennen, merken, einsehen*
really *wirklich*
reason (for / why) *Grund, Begründung (für / dafür / dass)*
rebuild (rebuilt, rebuilt) *wieder aufbauen*
receive *bekommen, empfangen*
recent *kürzlich; neueste(r, s); letzte (r, s)*
receptionist *Empfangsdame*
    doctor's receptionist *Sprechstundenhilfe*
recipe *Rezept*
recognize *erkennen; anerkennen*
record *aufnehmen, aufzeichnen*
recycle *wiederverwerten, wieder aufbereiten*
recycling *Wiederverwertung, Wiederaufbereitung*
red *rot*
reef *Riff*
refer to *sich beziehen auf*
referee *Schiedsrichter/in*
reference (to) *Verweis (auf)*
refrigerator *Kühlschrank*
refugee *Flüchtling*
register *Klassenbuch; Register; Sprachebene*
regular *regelmäßig; regulär, Regel-*
reheat *(Essen) aufwärmen*
relationship *Beziehung*
relative *der / die Verwandte*
relax *(sich) entspannen, sich ausruhen*
relaxed *entspannt*
religious *religiös, Religions-*
Religious Education (RE) *Religionsunterricht*
remember *sich erinnern an; an etw. denken, sich etw. merken*

remember doing sth. *sich daran erinnern, dass man etw. getan hat*
remind sb. (of sth.) *jn. (an etw.) erinnern*
remote control *Fernbedienung, Fernsteuerung*
repair *reparieren, ausbessern*
repeat *wiederholen*
report *berichten; melden*
report (on) *Bericht, Reportage (über)*
represent *repräsentieren; darstellen*
representative *Vertreter/in; Abgeordnete(r)*
rescue *retten; befreien*
rescue *Rettung*
research *recherchieren; erforschen; untersuchen*
research *Forschung; Recherche; Untersuchung*
respect sb. (for) *jn. respektieren, achten (wegen)*
respect *Respekt*
responsible *verantwortlich*
    be responsible (for) *verantwortlich sein (für)*
rest *sich ausruhen, eine Pause machen*
result *Ergebnis, Resultat*
retell (retold, retold) *nacherzählen*
return *zurückkehren; zurücksenden, zurückbringen; zurückgeben*
return *Rückkehr, Wiederkehr; hin und zurück*
review *Rezension, Kritik*
revision *Wiederholung (des Lernstoffs)*
rewrite *umschreiben, neu schreiben*
rhyme *sich reimen*
rhyme *Reim, Vers*
rhythm *Rhythmus*
rice *Reis*
rich *reich*
ride (rode, ridden) *reiten*
    ride a bike *Rad fahren*

ride *Ritt; Spazierfahrt, Ausflug*
   go / take a ride *herumfahren; eine Spazierfahrt machen*
   bike ride *Radfahrt, Radtour*
right *richtig; nach rechts; rechte(r, s)*
   all right *gut, in Ordnung*
   be right *stimmen, Recht haben*
right; rights *Recht, Anspruch; Bürgerrechte*
ring *klingeln, läuten; anrufen*
riot *randalieren, einen Aufstand / Krawall machen*
riot *Aufstand, Aufruhr, Krawall*
river *Fluss*
road *Straße, Landstraße*
road sign *Verkehrszeichen*
rob *berauben, ausrauben*
robot *Roboter*
rock *schaukeln, schwanken*
rocket *Rakete*
role *Rolle*
role model *Vorbild*
role-play *Rollenspiel*
roll over *sich (auf den Rücken) drehen; umkippen*
Roman *Römer/in; römisch*
romance *Liebesfilm; Romanze*
romantic *romantisch*
roof *Dach*
room *Zimmer, Raum*
rope *Seil*
rose *Rose*
round *rund; um ... (herum)*
   go / drive the wrong way round *verkehrt herum gehen / fahren*
   come round *vorbeischauen, vorbeikommen*
row *Reihe*
   death row *Todestrakt*
royal *königlich*
rubber *Gummi; Radiergummi*
rubbish *Abfall, Müll; Quatsch, Blödsinn*
rude *unhöflich, grob*
ruin *ruinieren, zerstören*
rule *Regel, Vorschrift*

ruler *Lineal*
run (ran, run) *laufen, rennen; verlaufen*
run after sb. *hinter jm. herrennen*
run around *umherrennen, herumrennen*
run the show *den Laden schmeißen; der Boss sein*
running *(das) Laufen*
rupee *Rupie (indische Währungseinheit)*
Russian *russisch, Russisch; Russe / Russsin*

S

sad *traurig*
sadness *Traurigkeit*
safe *sicher, gefahrlos*
safety *Sicherheit*
sail *segeln*
sailor *Seemann, Matrose*
salad *Salat*
sale, sales *Verkauf; (Sommer, Winter-)Schlussverkauf; Vertrieb*
salt *Salz*
the same (as) *der- / die- / dasselbe, dieselben; gleich; genauso wie*
sandal *Sandale*
satellite *Satellit*
satirical *satirisch*
sauce *Soße*
sausage *Würstchen, Wurst*
save *retten; sparen; sichern*
save sb. from sth. *jn. vor etw. retten*
save the day *die Situation retten*
say (said, said) *sagen*
say goodbye *sich verabschieden*
say sorry (to) *sich entschuldigen (bei)*
scan *(ein-)scannen; einen Text überfliegen*
scare *erschrecken, Angst einjagen*

scared *Angst haben (wegen; vor)*
   be scared (about; of) *verängstigt*
scarf, scarves *Schal*
scary *unheimlich, gruselig*
scene *Szene; Kulisse*
scenery *Bühnenbild; Landschaft*
sceptical *skeptisch*
schedule *Zeitplan, Programm; (AE) Fahrplan, Stundenplan*
scholarship *Stipendium*
school *Schule*
   primary school (BE) *Grundschule*
   comprehensive school (BE) *Gesamtschule*
   secondary school (BE) *weiterführende Schule*
   leave school *von der Schule abgehen*
school bag *Schultasche*
school subject *Schulfach*
science *(Natur-)Wissenschaft*
scientist *(Natur-)Wissenschaftler/in*
scissors *(eine) Schere*
score *(einen Punkt / Treffer) erzielen, (ein Tor) schießen*
score *Spielstand, (Spiel-)Ergebnis, Punktestand*
Scottish *schottisch*
scream *schreien; kreischen*
scream *Schrei*
screen *Bildschirm; Leinwand*
screenplay, script *Drehbuch*
scroll *(am Computerbildschirm) scrollen; verschieben*
sea *Meer, (die) See*
   at sea *auf See*
sea lion *Seelöwe*
seal *Robbe, Seehund*
search (for) *suchen (nach), durchsuchen*
search *Suche (nach), Durchsuchung*
seasick *seekrank*
season *Jahreszeit; Saison*
seat *Sitz; Platz*

second *Sekunde; zweite(r, s)*

secret *geheim; Geheimnis*

   keep a secret *ein Geheimnis wahren*

secretary *Sekretär/in*

section, sector *Abschnitt, Teil*

see (saw, seen) *sehen; besuchen, aufsuchen*

   see the sights *die Sehenswürdigkeiten ansehen*

   I see! *Ich verstehe! / Aha!*

   be seeing sb. *sich regelmäßig mit jm. treffen*

See you. *Tschüs. / Bis bald*

seem (to be / do) *(zu sein / tun) scheinen, erscheinen*

sell (sold, sold) *verkaufen*

send (sent, sent) (to) *schicken, senden (an)*

sensible *vernünftig*

sentence *Satz*

separate *(sich) trennen*

series *Sendereihe, Serie*

serious *ernst, ernsthaft*

servant *Diener/in, Bedienstete(r)*

serve *servieren*

service *überprüfen, warten*

service *Dienst, Service*

set sth. up (set, set) *etw. aufbauen, einrichten*

settler *Siedler/in*

several *mehrere (verschiedene)*

sex *Sex; Geschlecht*

   have sex (with) *Geschlechtsverkehr haben (mit)*

   the opposite sex *das andere Geschlecht*

shade *Schatten; Farbton; Schattierung, Nuance*

shadow *Schatten*

shake (shook, shaken) *beben, zittern; schütteln*

shall *sollen / wollen*

   Shall I wash up? *(Angebot:) Soll ich abwaschen?*

   Shall we leave early? *(Vorschlag:) Wollen wir früh gehen?*

shape *Gestalt; Form*

share sth. *(sich) etw. teilen*

sharp *scharf*

sheep, sheep *Schaf*

sheep farmer *Schafzüchter/in*

shelf, shelves *Regal*

shift work *Schichtarbeit*

shine (shone, shone) *scheinen; leuchten*

shiny *glänzend*

ship *Schiff*

shirt *Hemd, Oberhemd*

shock *schocken; schockieren*

shock *Schock*

   be shocked (at / by) *schockiert / erschüttert sein (über)*

shocked *schockiert*

shocking *schockierend*

shoe *Schuh*

shoot at (shot, shot) *schießen (auf); anschießen*

shoot sb. dead *jn. erschießen*

shop *einkaufen*

shop *Laden, Geschäft*

shopping *(das) Einkaufen; Einkäufe*

   do the shopping *Einkäufe machen / erledigen*

   go shopping *einkaufen gehen*

short *kurz, klein (Körpergröße)*

shot *Schuss*

shoulder *Schulter*

shout (at) *rufen, (an)schreien*

   shout for help *um Hilfe rufen*

show (showed, shown) *zeigen*

show *Schau, Show; (Fernseh, Radio-)Sendung*

shower *Regenschauer; Dusche*

   have / take a shower *(sich) duschen*

shut (shut, shut) *(sich) schließen*

   shut up *den Mund halten*

shy *scheu, zurückhaltend*

sick *krank*

side *Seite*

sights *Sehenswürdigkeiten*

sign *unterschreiben, unterzeichnen*

sign *Schild; Zeichen*

   road sign *Verkehrszeichen*

signal *Signal, Zeichen*

signature *Unterschrift*

silence *Stille, Schweigen*

silent *leise, still*

silk *Seide*

silly *albern, dumm*

silliness *Albernheit, Dummheit*

similar *ähnlich*

since *seit*

sincerely *ehrlich*

   Yours sincerely, *Mit freundlichen Grüßen*

sing (sang, sung) *singen*

singer *Sänger/in*

single *ledig, alleinstehend*

sink (sank, sunk) *sinken, untergehen; versenken*

sir *(Anrede für einen Kunden)*

   Sir Peter Townsend *(engl. Adelstitel)*

   Dear Sir, *Sehr geehrter Herr*

siren *Sirene*

sister *Schwester*

sit (sat, sat) *sitzen; sich (hin-) setzen*

sit down *sich (hin-)setzen*

size *Größe*

skates *Rollschuhe; Inlineskates*

ski *Ski fahren, Ski laufen*

skiing *(das) Skilaufen, Skisport*

ski-jumping *Skispringen*

skill *Fertigkeit, Fähigkeit*

skin *Haut*

skim *überfliegen*

skirt *Rock*

sky *Himmel*

skyscraper *Wolkenkratzer*

sledge (AE: sled) *Schlitten*

sleep (slept, slept) *schlafen*

   sleep late *lange schlafen*

sleeping bag *Schlafsack*

sleepy *schläfrig, müde*

slice *Stück; Scheibe*

slogan *Slogan, Parole, Wahlspruch*

slow *langsam*

small *klein*

smash *zerschlagen, (Fenster-scheibe) einschlagen*

smell *riechen*

smell *Geruch; Gestank; Riechen*

   sense of smell *Geruchssinn*

smile (at sb.) *(jn. an-)lächeln*

smile *Lächeln*

smoke *rauchen*

smoke *Rauch*

smuggler *Schmuggler/in*

snack *Imbiss*

snake *Schlange*

sniper *Heckenschütze; Scharf-schütze*

snow *schneien*

snow *Schnee*

snowboard *Snowboard fahren*

snowmobile *Schneemobil*

snowy *verschneit; schneereich*

so *deshalb, daher; also*

   so far *bis jetzt, bis hierher*

   so soon *so früh, so schnell*

   so (that) *sodass, damit*

soap *Seife*

soap opera *Seifenoper*

sober *nüchtern*

social *gesellschaftlich, sozial, Sozial-*

Social Studies *Gesellschafts-lehre*

social work *Sozialarbeit*

social worker *Sozialarbeiter/in*

society *Gesellschaft*

sock *Socke, Strumpf*

solar energy *Sonnenenergie, Solarenergie*

solar-powered *mit Sonnen-energie betrieben*

soldier *Soldat/in*

solution (to) *(Auf-)Lösung (für)*

solve *(Problem) lösen*

some *einige, ein paar; etwas*

somebody / someone *jemand*

somehow *irgendwie*

something *etwas*

sometimes *manchmal*

somewhere *irgendwo(hin)*

son *Sohn*

song *Lied*

soon *bald*

   as soon as possible (asap) *sobald als möglich*

Sorry. / I'm sorry. *Entschuldi-gung. / Tut mir leid.*

Sorry? *Wie bitte?*

   feel sorry for sb. *jn. bedauern*

   say sorry (to) *sich entschul-digen (bei)*

sort *sortieren*

sort out *in Ordnung bringen*

sort (of) *Art, Sorte*

soul *Seele*

sound *klingen, sich anhören*

sound *Laut, Klang*

soup *Suppe*

south *südlich; (nach) Süden*

   south-east *südöstlich; (nach) Südosten*

   south-west *südwestlich; (nach) Südwesten*

   to the south *südlich, im Süden*

   southern *südlich, Süd-*

souvenir *Andenken, Souvenir*

space *Raum, Platz; (der) Welt-raum*

space shuttle *Raumfähre, Raumtransporter*

spaceship *Raumschiff*

Spanish *spanisch, Spanisch; Spanier/in*

speak (spoke, spoken) *sprechen*

speaker *Sprecher/in*

special *besondere(r, s)*

   be special *etwas Besonderes sein*

special effects (SFX) *Spezial-effekte*

specific *spezifische(r, s), bestimmte(r, s)*

speculate (about / on) *spekulieren; Vermutungen anstellen (über)*

speech *Rede, Vortrag; Sprache; (das) Sprechen*

direct speech *direkte / wörtliche Rede*

indirect speech *indirekte Rede*

   make a speech *eine Rede halten, einen Vortrag halten*

speed *Geschwindigkeit*

speed limit *Geschwindigkeits-begrenzung*

spell *buchstabieren*

spelling *(Recht-)Schreibung, Schreibweise*

spend (spent, spent) *(Zeit) ver-bringen; (Geld) ausgeben*

spice *Gewürz*

spicy *würzig, stark gewürzt*

spider *Spinne*

spoon *Löffel*

spot *entdecken*

spray *sprühen; besprühen*

spring *Frühling*

sprint *sprinten, spurten*

square *Quadrat; Platz*

   square metre (m²) *Quadrat-meter*

stadium *Stadion*

stage *Bühne*

stairs *Treppenstufen; Treppe*

stall *Stand*

stamp *Briefmarke*

stand (stood, stood) *stehen; sich (hin)stellen*

stand back (from) *zurücktreten (von); entfernt stehen (vor)*

star *die Hauptrolle spielen*

star *Stern; Filmstar, Popstar*

start *anfangen, beginnen (mit)*

start a car *ein Auto anlassen / starten*

start a family / business *eine Familie / Firma gründen*

start a rumour *ein Gerücht in die Welt setzen*

   get started *loslegen; in Gang kommen*

starter *Vorspeise*

state *Staat; (Bundes-)Land*

statement *Aussage, Fest-stellung; Behauptung*

station *Station; Bahnhof*

police station *Polizeirevier*
power station *Kraftwerk, Elektrizitätswerk*
sheep station *(austral.) Schaffarm*
statistics *Statistik(en)*
statue *Statue, Standbild*
status *Status, Rang, (gesellschaftliche) Stellung*
family status *Familienstand*
stay *bleiben; übernachten*
stay *Aufenthalt, Besuch*
steal (stole, stolen) *stehlen*
steel *Stahl*
step *treten*
step *Stufe; Schritt*
step by step *Schritt für Schritt*
take a step towards sb. / sth. *einen Schritt auf jn. / etw. zugehen*
stepfather *Stiefvater*
stick (stuck, stuck) *kleben*
sticker *Aufkleber*
still *(immer) noch; trotzdem, dennoch*
sting (stung, stung) *stechen*
stink (stank, stunk) *stinken*
stomach *Bauch, Magen*
stone *Stein*
stone age *Steinzeit*
stop *anhalten, stoppen*
stop *Halt; (Bus-)Haltestelle*
store *lagern; speichern*
store *Geschäft, Laden*
storeroom *Lagerraum*
storm *Sturm; Gewitter*
stormy *stürmisch*
story *Geschichte, Erzählung*
straight on *(immer) geradeaus*
strange *sonderbar, seltsam; fremd*
stranger *Unbekannte(r), Fremde(r)*
street *Straße*
strength *Stärke, Kraft*
stress *betonen*
stress *Stress; Betonung*
strict *streng, strikt*
string *Schnur, Bindfaden*

strong *stark; kräftig, fest*
study *studieren; lernen; sorgfältig durchlesen*
stuff *Zeug, Kram*
stupid *blöd, dämlich*
style *Stil*
subject *Thema; Unterrichtsfach*
subtitle *Untertitel*
success *Erfolg*
successful *erfolgreich*
such (a) *solch, so (ein/e); solche*
suddenly *plötzlich, auf einmal*
suffer *leiden*
sugar *Zucker*
suggest sth. (to sb.) *(jm.) etwas vorschlagen, etwas anregen*
suggestion *Vorschlag, Anregung*
suit *(Herren-)Anzug; (Damen-)Kostüm*
suitcase *Koffer*
sum sth. up *etw. resümieren / zusammenfassen; jn. charakterisieren / einschätzen*
summary *Zusammenfassung*
summer *Sommer*
sun *Sonne*
sunbathe *sonnenbaden*
sunglasses *Sonnenbrille*
sunny *sonnig*
sunscreen *Sonnenschutzmittel*
sunset *Sonnenuntergang*
sunshine *Sonnenschein*
suntan *Sonnenbräune*
supermarket *Supermarkt*
superpower *Supermacht*
suppose *annehmen, vermuten*
sure *sicher, sicherlich*
surf *surfen*
surfer *Wellenreiter/in*
surfing *(das) Wellenreiten, Surfen*
go surfing *wellenreiten gehen*
surfboard *Surfbrett*
surprise *überraschen*
surprise *Überraschung*
surprised (at) *überrascht (über)*

surprising *überraschend, erstaunlich*
survey (of) *Umfrage, Untersuchung (über)*
survive *überleben*
swap *tauschen*
sweet *süß; Süßigkeit, Bonbon*
swim (swam, swum) *schwimmen*
swimsuit *Badeanzug*
switch on / off *einschalten, anschalten / ausschalten*
sympathetic *mitfühlend, verständnisvoll*
syrup *Sirup*

T

table *Tisch; Tabelle*
table of contents *Inhaltsverzeichnis*
table tennis *Tischtennis*
take (took, taken) *nehmen; mitnehmen; (weg)bringen; dauern, (Zeit) brauchen*
take-off *Start*
tale *Geschichte; Erzählung*
fairy tale *Märchen*
talent *Talent, Begabung*
talented *talentiert, begabt*
talk (to) *reden (mit), sich unterhalten (mit)*
talk *Vortrag, Referat, Rede; Gespräch*
give a talk (on) *einen Vortrag / eine Rede halten (über)*
tall *groß (gewachsen); hoch (Bäume, Wolkenkratzer usw.)*
tape *Band; Klebeband*
tartan *Schottenstoff, Schottenmuster*
task *Aufgabe*
taste *schmecken; kosten, probieren*
taste *Geschmack*
tasty *lecker*
tattoo *Tätowierung*
tax *Steuer*
tea *Tee*

teach (taught, taught) *unterrichten, lehren; jm. etw. beibringen*

teach sb. a lesson *jm. eine Lektion erteilen*

teacher *Lehrer/in*

team *Mannschaft*

technical *technisch; fachlich, Fach-*

technique *(Arbeits-)Verfahren, Technik, Methode*

technology *Technologie; Technik*

telephone *Telefon*

television (TV) *Fernsehen; Fernsehgerät*

tell (told, told) *erzählen, berichten*

tell sb. the way *jm. den Weg beschreiben*

tell sb. to do sth. *jn. auffordern, etwas zu tun*

temperature *Temperatur*

temporary *vorübergehend*

tense *Zeitform, Tempus*

tent *Zelt*

terrible *schrecklich, furchtbar*

territory *Gebiet*

terrorism *Terrorismus*

test *testen, prüfen*

test *Test, Prüfung, Klassenarbeit*

text *Textnachricht (SMS) schicken*

textiles *Textilien, Textilware*

than *als*

thank *danken*

thanks *danke*

that *das (dort); jene(r,s); dass; (Relativpronomen) der/die/das*

the *der/die/das; die*

theatre, (AE) theater *Theater*

theme *Thema*

then *dann, danach; damals, zu der Zeit*

theory *Theorie*

therapy *Therapie*

there *da, dort; dahin*

these *diese, die (hier)*

thief, thieves *Dieb/in*

thin *dünn*

thing *Ding, Sache*

think (thought, thought) *glauben, meinen, denken*

third *dritte(r, s)*

thirst *Durst*

thirsty *durstig*

this *diese(r, s), dies hier*

this morning/afternoon/ evening *heute Morgen/ Nachmittag/Abend*

those *die (da), jene (dort)*

though *obwohl*

thought *Gedanke*

thousand *tausend*

threat *Bedrohung; Drohung*

throat *Hals; Kehle*

throne *Thron*

through *durch*

throw (threw, thrown) *werfen*

throw a dice/the dice *würfeln*

thunder *Donner*

tick *ticken; mit einem Häkchen versehen*

tick *Häkchen*

ticket *Eintrittskarte; Fahrkarte, Fahrschein, Flugticket*

tidy *ordentlich, aufgeräumt*

tidy (up) *aufräumen*

tie *(zusammen)binden, (zusammen)schnüren*

tie to *binden, anbinden (an)*

tie *Krawatte*

ties *Beziehungen, Bande*

tight *fest, eng*

till *bis*

time *Zeit*

times (four times; 3 times 4 = 12) *Mal(e); -mal*

timetable *Stundenplan; Zeitplan; Fahrplan*

tip *Tipp*

tip *Trinkgeld*

tired *müde*

be tired of (doing) sth. *etw. satt haben, genug haben von etw.*

title *Titel, Überschrift*

to *zu, nach*

today *heute*

toe *Zeh*

together *zusammen*

go together *zusammenpassen*

toilet *Toilette*

tomato, tomatoes *Tomate*

tomorrow *morgen*

ton *Tonne (Gewicht)*

tongue *Zunge*

mother tongue *Muttersprache*

tonight *heute Nacht, heute Abend*

too *zu, auch*

too late *zu spät*

tool *Werkzeug*

tool box *Werkzeugkasten*

tooth, teeth *Zahn*

brush your teeth *sich die Zähne putzen*

toothbrush *Zahnbürste*

toothless *zahnlos*

top *Spitze; oberer Teil, oberes Ende*

on top (of sth.) *oben, obendrauf (auf etw.)*

topic *Thema, Themenbereich*

tortoise *Schildkröte*

total *Gesamtbetrag, Summe; Gesamt-*

touch *berühren, anfassen*

get in touch (with) *Verbindung/Kontakt aufnehmen (mit)*

keep in touch (with) *in Verbindung/Kontakt bleiben (mit)*

lose touch (with) *den Kontakt verlieren (zu)*

tough *zäh, hart*

tour (of) *Tour, (Rund-)Reise (durch)*

towards *in Richtung, auf ... zu, darauf zu*

tower *Turm*

town *Stadt*

town hall *Rathaus*

toy *Spielzeug*

track *Spur, Fährte*

tractor *Traktor*

trade *Handel treiben, handeln, Geschäfte machen*

trade *Handel; Gewerbe*

trader *Händler/in*

traffic *Verkehr*

traffic lights *Verkehrsampel*

tragedy *Tragödie*

train *trainieren, üben; ausbilden*

train *Zug*

trainer *Trainer/in; Turnschuhe*

training *Ausbildung, Schulung; Training*

tram *Straßenbahn*

transform *sich verwandeln*

translate *übersetzen*

translation *Übersetzung*

transmit *funken, senden*

transmitter *Sendegerät, Funkgerät*

transparency *(OHP)Folie, Overheadfolie*

transport *transportieren, befördern*

transport / transportation *Verkehrsmittel; Transport, Beförderung*

trash (AE) *Müll, Abfall*

travel *reisen*

travel *(das) Reisen*

travel agency *Reisebüro*

travel agent *Reisebürokaufmann, Reisebürokauffrau*

tree *Baum*

trial *Gerichtsverfahren, (Straf-)Prozess*

    be on trial *vor Gericht stehen*

triangle *Dreieck*

trick *hereinlegen; täuschen*

trick *List, Streich, Trick*

    play a trick on sb. *jm. einen Streich spielen*

tricky *kompliziert, knifflig*

trip *stolpern*

trip ***Ausflug, Reise***

    go on a trip *einen Ausflug / eine Reise machen*

trouble *Schwierigkeiten*

    be in trouble *in Schwierigkeiten sein, Ärger kriegen*

    be asking / looking for trouble *Probleme / Ärger geradezu herausfordern*

trousers *(lange) Hose*

true *wahr*

    come true *wahr werden, Wirklichkeit werden*

trust *vertrauen, trauen*

truth *Wahrheit*

try *versuchen, (aus)probieren*

try hard *sich sehr bemühen, sich anstrengen*

try on *(Kleidung) anprobieren*

try to do sth. / try and do sth. *versuchen etw. zu tun*

tube *Schlauch; Rohr, Röhre*

    the tube *die U-Bahn in London*

tuna *Thunfisch*

tune *Melodie*

turkey *Pute, Truthahn*

turn (around) *sich umdrehen*

turn back *umkehren, kehrtmachen*

turn left / right (into) *(nach) links / rechts abbiegen (in)*

turn to sb. *sich jm. zuwenden; sich an jn. wenden*

turn on / off *einschalten / ausschalten*

    It's my turn. *Ich bin an der Reihe.*

    take turns to do sth. *sich bei etw. abwechseln; etw. abwechselnd tun*

twice *zweimal*

twin *Zwilling*

type *Typ, Art*

type *tippen, eintippen*

typical *typisch*

U

ugly *hässlich*

umbrella *Regenschirm*

unbelievable *unglaublich*

uncle *Onkel*

unclean *unrein, unsauber*

uncomfortable *unbequem, unbehaglich, unangenehm*

under *unter*

    go under *untergehen*

underline *unterstreichen*

underlined *unterstrichen*

understand (understood, understood) *verstehen, begreifen*

underwater *unter Wasser; Unterwasser-*

unemployed *arbeitslos*

unexpected *unerwartet*

unfair *unfair, ungerecht*

unforgettable *unvergesslich*

unfortunately *unglücklicherweise; leider*

unfriendly *unfreundlich*

unhappy *unglücklich*

unhealthy *ungesund*

unimportant *unwichtig*

union *Union, Vereinigung*

unit *Kapitel, Lektion; Einheit*

university *Universität*

unknown *unbekannt*

unless *es sei denn, außer wenn*

unlike *anders als, im Gegensatz zu*

unnecessary *unnötig, nicht notwendig*

unpack *auspacken*

unpopular *unbeliebt*

unsafe *unsicher, nicht sicher*

untidy *unordentlich, unaufgeräumt*

until *bis*

unusual *ungewöhnlich*

unwanted *unerwünscht*

up *hinauf, herauf, nach oben; oben*

    What's up? *Was ist los?*

upload *heraufladen*

upstairs *nach oben; oben (im Gebäude)*

use *gebrauchen, verwenden, benutzen*

    be used to sth. *an etwas gewöhnt sein*

    get used to sth. *sich an etw. gewöhnen*

use *Benutzung, Gebrauch*
used to: I used to like her. *Ich habe sie früher gern gehabt.*
useful *nützlich*
usual *gewöhnlich*
    as usual *wie üblich*
usually *meistens, gewöhnlich, normalerweise*

V

vacancy *offene Stelle (Arbeit); freies Zimmer (Hotel)*
vacation *(AE) Ferien, Urlaub*
valley *Tal*
valuable *wertvoll*
value *Wert*
van *Lieferwagen, Transporter*
vandalism *Vandalismus, Zerstörungswut; mutwillige Beschädigung*
vegetable *Gemüse*
vegetarian *Vegetarier/in; vegetarisch*
vehicle *Fahrzeug*
verse *Vers, Strophe*
version *Version, Fassung*
very *sehr*
victim *Opfer*
view *Sicht; Blick; Ansicht, Einstellung; Standpunkt*
village *Dorf*
vinegar *Essig*
violence *Gewalt*
violent *gewalttätig, gewaltsam*
violet *Veilchen*
virtual *virtuell*
vision *Vision, Vorstellung*
visit *besuchen; besichtigen*
visit *Besuch*
visitor *Besucher/in*
vocabulary *Vokabel-, Wörterverzeichnis; Wortschatz*
voice *Stimme*
voluntary *freiwillig*
volunteer *sich ehrenamtlich engagieren; sich freiwillig melden*
volunteer *Freiwillige(r)*

volunteer work *ehrenamtliche Tätigkeit / Arbeit*
vote (for) *(jn.) wählen, (für jn.) stimmen; abstimmen*
vote *Stimme (bei Wahlen)*
voter *Wähler/in*

W

waist *Bauch; Taille*
waistline *Taille*
wait (for) *warten (auf)*
waiter *Kellner*
waitress *Kellnerin*
wake (up) (woke, woken) *aufwachen; jn. (auf)wecken*
walk *zu Fuß gehen; spazieren gehen*
walk around *herumlaufen*
walk *Spaziergang*
    go for a walk *einen Spaziergang machen*
    take the dog for a walk *mit dem Hund rausgehen*
wall *Wand; Mauer*
wallet *Brieftasche*
wallpaper *Tapete*
want *(haben) wollen*
wanted (by the police) *(polizeilich) gesucht*
war *Krieg*
wardrobe *Kleiderschrank*
warehouse *Lagerhaus*
warm up *(sich) aufwärmen*
warning *Warnung*
wash *waschen; sich waschen*
wash the dishes *das Geschirr waschen*
washing *Wäsche*
washing up *Abwasch*
waste *verschwenden*
waste *Abfall; Verschwendung*
watch *beobachten, sich etw. ansehen; zusehen*
watch out for *Ausschau halten nach*
watch television / TV *fernsehen*
watch *Armbanduhr*
water *Wasser*

wave (at / to sb.) *(jm. zu-) winken*
wave *Welle*
way *Weg; Richtung; Art und Weise*
weak *schwach*
wear (wore, worn) *tragen, anhaben*
weather *Wetter*
wedding *Hochzeit*
week *Woche*
weekend *Wochenende*
weigh *wiegen*
weight *Gewicht*
weird *seltsam, bizarr, verrückt*
welcome *willkommen*
    welcome sb. *jn. willkommen heißen*
well *Brunnen*
well *gut; gesund*
well-acted *gut gespielt*
well-behaved *brav*
well known *(wohl) bekannt*
well-made *(handwerklich) gut gemacht*
well-paid *gut bezahlt*
well-written *gut geschrieben*
Welsh *walisisch; Waliser/in*
west *westlich; (nach) Westen*
wet *feucht, nass*
whale *Wal*
what *was; welche(r, s)*
whatever *was (auch) immer*
wheel *Rad*
wheelchair *Rollstuhl*
when *wann; wenn; als; nachdem*
whenever *wann (auch) immer*
where *wo; wohin*
wherever *wohin (auch) immer; wo (auch) immer*
whether *ob*
which *welche(r, s); der / die / das, die*
while *während, solange*
whisper *flüstern*
white *weiß*
who *wer; wen / wem; der / die / das, die*

whoever *wer/wen/wem (auch) immer*

whole *ganze(r, s), gesamte(r, s)*

whose *wessen; deren, dessen*

why *warum*
  that's why *darum/deshalb*

wide *breit*

wife, wives *Ehefrau*

wildlife *Tierwelt*

will *werden*

win (won, won) *gewinnen*

win *Sieg*

winner *Gewinner/in, Sieger/in*

window *Fenster*

windy *windig*

windsurfing *(das) Windsurfen*

wing *Flügel*

winner *Gewinner/in*

wise *klug, weise*

wish *(sich) wünschen*

wish *Wunsch*

with *mit (... zusammen), bei*
  go with *passen zu*

without *ohne*

wolf, wolves *Wolf*

woman *Frau*

wonder *sich fragen, gern wissen wollen*

wonder *Wunder*

wonderful *wunderbar*

wood *Holz; Wald*
  wooden *hölzern, aus Holz*

word *Wort*
  have a word with sb. *kurz mit jm. sprechen*

word order *Wortstellung*

work *arbeiten; funktionieren*

work full time *ganztags arbeiten*

work part time *als Teilzeitkraft beschäftigt sein*

work *Arbeit*

worker *Arbeiter/in*

workplace *Arbeitsplatz, Arbeitsstätte*

workshop *Werkstatt*

world *Welt*

worried (about) *beunruhigt (wegen), besorgt (wegen/um)*

worry (about) *sich Sorgen machen (wegen, um)*

worry sb. *jn. beunruhigen, jm. Sorgen machen*

worry *Sorge, Kummer*

worse *schlechter, schlimmer*

(the) worst *(der/die/das) Schlimmste/Schlechteste; am schlimmsten/am schlechtesten*

write (wrote, written) *schreiben*

write sth. down *etw. aufschreiben, notieren*

writer *Schreiber/in, Schriftsteller/in*

wrong *falsch*
  be wrong *sich irren, Unrecht haben; nicht in Ordnung sein, nicht stimmen*

Y

yawn *gähnen*

year *Jahr; Jahrgangsstufe*

yellow *gelb*

yes *ja*

yesterday *gestern*

yet *schon*
  not (...) yet *noch nicht*

yoghurt *Joghurt*

young *jung*

Yours faithfully/Yours sincerely *Mit freundlichen Grüßen*

youth *Jugend; Jugendlicher*

Yuck! *Igitt!/Bäh!*

Z

zero *Null*

zone *Zone, Gebiet*

zoo *Zoo, Tierpark*

Unit word list

Die neuen Wörter sind in der Reihenfolge ihres Vorkommens im Text verzeichnet. Es fehlen jedoch die Wörter, die zum Grundwortschatz gehören. (Siehe Basic word list.)
Die Zahlen geben die Seitenzahlen im Schülerbuch an.
Die englischen **Verben** sind fett markiert.
🅣 = Das Wort befindet sich im Transkript der Hörverständnistext.

UNIT 1

7

getting started	erste Schritte
receptive	rezeptiv
listening text	Hörtext
productive	produktiv, aktiv
vocational qualifications	Berufsabschlüsse
curriculum vitae (CV)	Lebenslauf
summary	Zusammenfassung
preference	Vorliebe

8

exchange programme	Austauschprogramm
profile	Steckbrief, Kurzbiografie
gender	Geschlecht
be willing to do sth.	bereit sein, etwas zu tun
attend	besuchen, beiwohnen
church service	Gottesdienst
occasionally	gelegentlich
birch	Birke
hazelnut	Haselnuss
hiking	Wandern
request	Bitte; Anfrage

9

| simple | einfach |

10

pub (public house)	Wirtshaus, Gaststätte
avenger	Rächer(in)
assemble (sich)	versammeln
fairground ride	Rummelplatzfahrgeschäft
exhilarating	berauschend
piled	aufgestapelt
cumulative	kumulativ, sich anhäufend
effect	Wirkung, Auswirkung
thrilling	spannend

memorably	denkwürdig, unvergesslich
insult	Beleidigung, Kränkung
thriller	Krimi; Reißer
revitalise	neu beleben, wiederbeleben
genre	Kunstgattung
evil	böse, übel
dead	die Toten
smart	gewieft, gerissen, gewitzt
breathless	atemlos
worship sb	jmdn anbeten
tend to	zu etwas neigen
overlook	übersehen, nicht bemerken
adulterer	Ehebrecher
father	zeugen
progressive	fortschrittlich
treatment	Behandlung
devastating	verheerend
milk-monitor	Schüler(in) verantwortlich für die Verteilung der täglichen Milchration
duty	Dienst
peer	spähen
hang (hanged, hanged) oneself	sich erhängen
amid	inmitten, mitten drin
fallout	(hier) Konsequenzen, Nachwirkungen
headteacher	Schulleiter(in)
be appointed	ernannt werden
substitute teacher	Aushilfslehrer(in)
definite	bestimmt
staff	Personal, Mitarbeiterstab
pleasant	angenehm, freundlich

11

| **pick sth** | etwas auswählen |
| lack of | mangels, an etwas mangeln |

ceiling fan	*Deckenventilator*	competence	*Befähigung, Können;*
renowned	*renommiert*		*Sachkunde*
hostelry	*(scherzhaft) Wirtshaus*	**seize sth**	*etwas ergreifen, packen*
Raj	*britische Herrschaft über*	selection	*Auswahl*
	Indien	**fail to do sth**	*es nicht schaffen, etwas*
admitted	*zugelassen*		*zu tun*
wireless	*drahtlos*	impact	*Bedeutung; Einschlag;*
access	*Zugang; Eintritt*	*Aufprall*	
function room	*Veranstaltungsraum*	**submit sth**	*etwas einreichen,*
honey	*Honig*		*zustellen*
speakeasy	*(scherzhaft) US „Flüster-*	required	*erforderlich, benötigt,*
	kneipe" mit illegalem		*vorgeschrieben*
	Alkoholausschank aus	at hand	*zu Hand, greifbar*
	der Zeit der Prohibition	work experience	*Berufserfahrung, Arbeits-*
atmosphere	*(hier) Stimmung*		*erfahrung; (BE) Prakti-*
booking	*Reservierung*		*kum*
advisable	*ratsam, empfehlenswert*	previous	*vorangehend; vorherig;*
conspicuous	*auffällig, auffallend*		*früher*
faithful	*getreu*	employment	*Beschäftigung;*
trailer	*Anhänger; (AE) Wohn-*		*Anstellung*
	wagen	slightly	*geringfügig; leicht*
remain	*verbleiben*	a tool for screening ...	*ein Werkzeug um ... zu*
laudably	*löblich, lobenswert*		*überprüfen*
tongue-in-cheek	*mit ironischem Unter-*	applicant	*Antragsteller(in);*
	ton, nicht ganz ernst-		*Stellenbewerber(in)*
	gemeint	eliminated	*ausgeschieden; beseitigt*
drown	*ertrinken*	on the basis of	*anhand von;*
hip	*schick*		*in Anlehnung an*
justify	*rechtfertigen;*	recruiter	*(hier) Personal-*
	legitimieren		*vermittler(in)*
etiquette	*Anstandsregel,*		
	Umgangsformen	**13**	
waiter service	*Bedienung* 🅣	extensive	*umfangreich*
bar	*(hier:) Tresen* 🅣	browse	*im Internet browsen /*
queue	*Menschenschlange* 🅣		*surfen, etwas durch-*
draught	*vom Fass* 🅣		*stöbern*
flavour Geschmack T			
hops	*Hopfen* 🅣	**14**	
malted barley	*Braugerste, Gerstenmalz*	timeless	*zeitlos*
	🅣	album	*(hier) Langspielplatte*
yeast	*Hefe* 🅣	quoted	*zitiert*
carpet	*Teppich* 🅣	**slip out**	*hinausschleichen*
armchair	*Armsessel, Polstersessel*	poignant	*ergreifend*
	🅣	sustained	*anhaltend, ausdauernd*
spirits	*Spirituosen* 🅣	**sketch**	*skizzieren, vorzeichnen*
		open audition	*öffentliches Vorsprechen,*
12			*freie Sprechprobe*
internship	*Praktikum*	trendy	*modisch schick*
focus on sth	*sich auf etwas*	**cut sth to ribbons**	*zerschneiden, in Streifen*
	konzentrieren		*schneiden*

pill	*(hier) Verhütungspille*	puberty	*Pubertät, Geschlechts-*
grab sb by the scruff	*jmdn am Kragen packen*		*reife*
of the neck		adolescence	*Jugend; Entwicklungs-*
flush	*durchspülen; ausspülen*		*jahre*
pregnant	*schwanger*		

15

croupier	*Kasinoangestellte(r)*
make out (that)	*(hier) vortäuschen;*
	so tun, als ob
kidnapped	*entführt*
abortion	*Abtreibung; Schwanger-*
	schaftsabbruch
inspired by sth	*durch / von etwas*
	angeregt
piece sth together	*etwas zusammensetzen;*
	einen Reim auf etwas
	machen

16

complain about	*sich über jmdn / etwas*
sb / sth	*beklagen, sich be-*
	schweren
clunk against sth	*mit einem dumpfen*
	Geräusch gegen etwas
	schlagen; gegen etwas
	klappern
give up	*aufgeben*
despair	*Verzweiflung*
nag sb about sth	*herumnörgeln; jmdm*
	mit etwas in den Ohren
	liegen
appendix	*Anhang*
(pl.) appendices	
phonetic	*Lautschrift*
transcription	
findings	*(Forschungs)Ergebnisse,*
	Resultate

17

meaningful	*bedeutungsvoll; sinnvoll*
grip	*greifen, klemmen*
attached	*angeschlossen;*
	angebaut; beigefügt
optician	*Optiker(in)*
resigned	*resigniert*
disappointed	*enttäuscht*
submissive	*unterwürfig*
misunderstood	*missverstanden*
thoughtful	*fürsorglich, rücksichtsvoll*

18

provide	*bereitstellen*
humorous	*humorvoll*
lifeguard	*Rettungsschwimmer(in);*
	Badewärter
security guard	*Sicherheitsbedienstete(r)*
supervise	*beaufsichtigen;*
	kontrollieren
gal	*(AE slang) Mädchen*
unrelated	*ohne Bezug*
promotion	*Werbung, Werbe-*
	veranstaltung
urban renewal	*Stadtsanierung*
pest control	*Schädlingsbekämpfung*
test tube	*Reagenzglas*
ensure	*sicherstellen, gewähr-*
	leisten

19

listening	*Hörverständnis*
comprehension	
identify	*erkennen; identifizieren*
revise	*korrigieren*

20

pun	*Wortspiel, Wortwitz*
brake fluid	*Bremsflüssigkeit*
bra	*Büstenhalter, BH*
reservation	*Voranmeldung, Reser-*
	vierung; Reservat,
	Schutzgebiet
bladder	*Blase*
infection	*Infizierung, Ansteckung*
pointless	*sinnlos; ohne Spitze*

UNIT 2

21

expectation	*Erwartung*
finalize	*etwas endgültig be-*
	schließen; fertig machen
assess	*bewerten, einschätzen*
tone	*(hier) allg. Stimmung*

22

end up	*(letztendlich) gelangen*

realistic	*realistisch*
tough	*zäh, hartnäckig, taff*
struggle	*sich anstrengen / abrackern; kämpfen*
rewarding	*lohnend*
go for sth	*anstreben; sich für etwas entscheiden*
athlete	*Athlet(in)*
give sth a try	*etwas ausprobieren; es auf ein Versuch ankommen lassen*
pessimistic	*pessimistisch*

23

management	*Unternehmensführung; Verwaltung*
baked	*gebacken*
bean	*Bohne*
tinned food	*Konserven*
search engine	*Suchmaschine*
enquiry, (AE) inquiry	*Anfrage, Erkundigung*
anxiety, anxieties	*Angst, Ängste*

24

depending on	*abhängig von*
sample	*Muster, Kostprobe*
handwriting	*Handschrift*
nowadays	*heutzutage*
handle sth	*etwas handhaben, mit etwas umgehen*
covering letter	*Begleitbrief, Bewerbungsschreiben*
expanding	*sich ausdehnend, stetig wachsend*
outstanding	*hervorragend*
intern	*(hier) Praktikant(in)*
security	*Sicherheits-*
human resources	*Personalabteilung*
recruitment	*Anwerbung von neuen Mitarbeitern*
manpower	*menschliche Arbeitsleistung*
vacancy	*freie, unbesetzte Stelle*
employment agency	*Zeitarbeitsvermittlung*
administration	*Verwaltung*
work permit	*Arbeitserlaubnis*
aware	*bewusst*
unpaid	*unbezahlt*
leisure	*Freizeit*
facility	*Einrichtung*

student grant	*Ausbildungsförderung, Stipendium*
available	*erhältlich, verfügbar; vorliegend*
for up to	*bis einschließlich*
testimonial	*Arbeitszeugnis; Empfehlungsschreiben*

25

bulletin board	*Anschlagtafel, schwarzes Brett*
halfway through studies (pl.)	*halb durch, mitten drin Studium*
applied science	*angewandte Naturwissenschaft*
satisfactory	*zufriedenstellend*
enclosed	*anbei, in der Anlage*
in due course	*zur gegebenen Zeit*
rundown	*Zusammenfassung*
proper, properly	*(hier) korrekt*
print-out	*Ausdruck*
event sales	*Veranstaltungsverkäufe, Demo-Verkäufe*
flexible	*(hier) anpassungsfähig*
global player	*eine Weltfirma, eine weltweit tätige Firma*
canned (soups)	*Konserven*
development	*Entwicklung*
boost	*ankurbeln; steigern*
word processing	*Textverarbeitung*
spreadsheet	*Kalkulationsblatt; Tabellenkalkulation*
team spirit	*Teamgeist*
sense of humour	*Sinn für Humor*

26

related to	*verwandt mit*
commentator	*Berichterstatter(in), Komment-ator(in)*
method	*Methode*
gain	*gewinnen; erzielen*
component	*Bestandteil*
operating system	*Betriebssystem*
I see.	*Ich verstehe.*
how come	*wie kam es, wieso*

27

diligent	*gewissenhaft*
quick-witted	*aufgeweckt*
persistent	*beharrlich*

nerve-racking	*nervenaufreibend*
weakness	*Schwäche*
disqualify sb	*jmdn. ausschließen, disqualifizieren*
significant	*wesentlich*
achievement	*Errungenschaft; Leistung*
sign language	*Zeichensprache*
B. A. (Bachelor of Arts)	*akademischer Grad*
appreciate sth	*etwas schätzen, für etwas dankbar sein*
conduct	*durchführen, ausführen, vornehmen*

28

track sb down	*jmn aufspüren*
treat sb	*mit jmdm umgehen*
vivid	*anschaulich, lebhaft*
memory	*Erinnerung*
fool around	*herumalbern; (hier) sich treiben lassen*
CEO (Chief Executive Officer)	*Generaldirektor(in)*
tremendously	*enorm, gewaltig*
in the course of	*im Verlauf (von)*
accept	*annehmen*
profession	*Beruf*
fulfilled	*erfüllt*
odd	*(hier) gelegentlich*
energetic	*dynamisch, energie-geladen, tatkräftig*
proud (of)	*stolz (auf)*
I think of you fondly.	*Ich denke gern an dich.*
conference	*Tagung, Konferenz*
thin	*dünn werden*

29

reply	*Erwiderung, Antwort*
giggle	*Gekicher*
laugh	*das Lachen*
zig-zag course	*Zickzackkurs*
map sth out	*etwas entwerfen / festlegen*
initial	*anfänglich, Anfangs-*
marriage	*Ehe*
break up (broke, broken)	*auseinanderbrechen; scheitern*
row	*Streit, Auseinander-setzung*
squabble	*Zankerei*
impressed	*beeindruckt*

turn out	*ausgehen, herausstellen*
account	*(hier) Bericht*
cheerful	*fröhlich, heiter*
enthusiastic	*begeistert, schwärmerisch*
depressing	*bedrückend, deprimierend*
cautious	*behutsam, zurück-haltend, vorsichtig*
witty	*geistreich, witzig*
caring	*fürsorglich, mitfühlend*
sentimental	*rührselig, sentimental*
letterhead	*Briefkopf*

30

as a matter of fact	*tatsächlich, in der Tat*
asap (as soon as possible)	*sobald als möglich*
hire sb	*jmdn einstellen, anheuern*
do a placement	*ein Praktikum durchführen*
eager	*eifrig, arbeitsfreudig*
vocational school	*berufsbildende Schule*
various	*verschieden, mannigfaltig*
in addition	*dazu, zusätzlich*
bookkeeping	*Buchführung*
general knowledge	*Allgemeinwissen*

31

temp (temporary worker)	*Aushilfskraft, Zeitarbeiter(in)*
urgent, urgently	*dringend*
increase	*anwachsen, (sich) erhöhen / vergrößern*
marketability	*Marktfähigkeit*
sector	*Fachgebiet; Bereich*
general office clerk	*Bürokauffrau, Bürokaufmann*
switchboard operator	*Telefonist(in)*
seasoned	*(hier) erfahren, bewährt*
vary	*ändern, sich ändern; verändern*
proficient	*kompetent, tüchtig*
willing	*bereit, willig*
salary	*Gehalt*
duration	*Zeitdauer; Laufzeit*
résumé (AE: *auch:* resumé, resume)	*Lebenslauf*

analyse	*kritisch untersuchen, auswerten*
criterion, (pl.) criteria	*Bewertungsgrundlage, Kriterium*
salutation	*Anrede, Begrüßung*
punctuation	*Interpunktion, Zeichensetzung*

32

exercise book	*Schreibheft, Übungsheft*
professional bike racer	*Rennrad Profi*
unpunctual	*unpünktlich*

33

grid	*Rastergitter*
iron (clothes)	*bügeln*
preposition	*Präposition*

34

trainee	*Auszubildende(r)* 🅣
trained	*ausgebildet* 🅣
baker	*Bäcker(in)* 🅣
bakery	*Bäckerei*
countryside	*die Landschaft; Natur* 🅣
spectacular	*eindrucksvoll* 🅣
bread roll	*Brötchen* 🅣
sourdough	*Sauerteig* 🅣
speciality	*Spezialität* 🅣
neighbouring town	*Nachbarort* 🅣

UNIT 3

35

demographic	*bevölkerungsstatistisch*
trend	*Entwicklung, Tendenz*
avoid	*vermeiden*

36

newcomer	*Neuankömmling*
Poland	*Polen*
Russia	*Russland*
Flemisch	*flämisch*
refugee	*Flüchtling*
Ireland	*Irland*
settlement	*Siedlung*
port	*Hafen; Hafenstadt*
settle	*besiedeln; sich niederlassen*
encourage	*ermuntern, ermutigen*
former	*ehemalig, früher*

India	*Indien*
descendant	*Nachkomme*
TV presenter	*Fernsehansager(in)*
shape	*formen, gestalten, bilden*
numerous	*zahlreich*
ethnic	*ethnisch*
radio station	*Radiosender, Rundfunkanstalt*
diverse	*unterschiedlich, verschieden*
distinct	*eindeutig, deutlich*
prominent	*hervorspringend, markant*
mosque	*Moschee*
escape	*entkommen, flüchten*
persecution	*Verfolgung*
rural	*ländlich*
post-war	*Nachkriegs-*
unrest	*Unruhen*

37

tap	*Wasserhahn* 🅣
busy	*(hier) vielbefahren* 🅣
plug in	*einstecken, einstöpseln* 🅣
hairdryer	*Fön, Haartrockner* 🅣
socket	*Anschlussdose* 🅣T
cloakroom	*Garderobe* 🅣
caller	*Anrufer(in)* 🅣
term	*Begriff*
misleading	*irreführend*
root	*Wurzel*
descent	*Abstammung*
characterize	*charakterisieren*
pluralism	*Pluralismus*
variety	*Vielfalt*
diversity	*Verschiedenheit; Mannigfaltigkeit*
undesirable	*unerwünscht*
segregation	*Rassentrennung; Segregation*
isolation	*Isolierung*
process	*Verfahren; Ablauf*
intermarry	*eine Mischehe eingehen*
conform to sth	*sich an etwas anpassen*
dominant	*beherrschend*
interpret	*deuten, auslegen, interpretieren*
originate	*herstammen; entspringen*

38

aging	alternd
warn sb (of sth)	jmdn (vor etwas) warnen
particularly	besonders, vor allem
within	innerhalb, binnen
shift	Verschiebung, Verlagerung
challenge	Herausforderung
welfare	Fürsorge; Wohlfahrt
healthcare	Gesundheitswesen
abuse	Missbrauch
neglect	Vernachlässigung, Verwahrlosung
celebration	Feier, Freudenfest
estimate	schätzen, abschätzen
elder, elderly	älterer; bejahrt
decade	Jahrzehnt, Dekade
rising	ansteigend, wachsend
consequence	Folge, Auswirkung
improved	verbessert, aufgebessert
nutrition	Ernährung
sanitation	Sanitäreinrichtungen; Hygiene
well-being	Wohlbefinden, Wohl-ergehen
contributing factor	entscheidender Faktor
contribute	beisteuern, mitwirken
mismanaged	schlecht verwaltet, schlecht geführt
policy	politische Linie
current	aktuell, gegenwärtig
preparation	Vorbereitung
joint	gemeinsam
cast out	verstoßen, austreiben, vertreiben
underemployed	unterbeschäftigt, nicht ausgelastet
vulnerable	verletzlich, verwundbar
reduce	verringern, drosseln, abbauen
legislation	Gesetzgebung
funded (by)	finanziert (von)
extended family	Großfamilie
nuclear family	Kernfamilie, Kleinfamilie
physical	körperlich
mental	geistig, seelisch
density	Dichte
distribution	Verteilung, Verbreitung
vital	lebenswichtig; grund-legend

square	Quadrat-
derive sth by	sich von etwas ableiten

39

remarkable	bemerkenswert
gain	Anstieg, Zuwachs
life expectancy	Lebenserwartung
according to	zufolge, gemäß; in Anlehnung an
imply	andeuten; unterstellen
citizen	Bürger(in)
growth	Wachstum, Zuwachs, Zunahme
forecast	Voraussage, Prognose
assumption	Annahme; Prämisse
branch	(hier) Verzweigung
overcome	bewältigen, überwinden
outcome	Ergebnis, Resultat

40

deliver	liefern, austragen
Alsatian	Deutscher Schäferhund
homesick	Heimweh haben
caretaker	Hausmeister(in)
primary school	Grundschule
Thank goodness!	Gott sei Dank!
earnest	ernst, ernsthaft
posh	vornehm
question tag	Bestätigungsfrage, Frageanhängsel

41

founder	Gründer(in)
accountancy	Buchführung, Buch-haltung
flick between	hin und her schalten
cater for sb	(hier) die besonderen Bedürfnisse einer Gruppe berücksichtigen; jmdn beliefern / versorgen
niche	Nische
plain sailing (Idiom)	unproblematisch
impartial	unvoreingenommen, vorurteilslos
work-related	die Arbeit betreffend
invaluable	außerordentlich wertvoll, unschätzbar
mentioned	erwähnt

42

strife	*Streit, Zank*
face	*begegnen*
stretch	*dehnen, strecken*
ridiculous	*lächerlich*
is supposed to be a …	*soll … sein*
upper-class lady	*Dame der Oberschicht*
cool down	*sich beruhigen*

43

heated	*erhitzt*
verbally abusive	*verbal ausfallend*
aggressive	*angriffslustig, streit-süchtig*
rejected	*abgelehnt, abgewiesen*
ignored	*missachtet, ignoriert*
constructive(ly)	*konstruktiv*
understanding	*Verständnis, Über-einkunft; Einsicht*
strategy	*Strategie*
resolve	*beheben, klären*
dispute	*Auseinandersetzung, Konflikt*
there's no point in (doing sth)	*es hat keinen Sinn (etwas zu tun)*
reason with sb	*mit jmdm vernünftig reden*
provoke	*heraufbeschwören, provozieren*
interrupt	*dazwischenreden, jmdm ins Wort fallen*
ramble	*schwafeln*
formulate	*entwerfen, formulieren*
patient	*geduldig*
break down	*auflösen, entgegen-wirken*
genuine(ly)	*echt, authentisch*
consider	*berücksichtigen*
point of view	*Ansicht, Standpunkt*
agreement	*Einigung, Zustimmung; Vereinbarung*
put a stop to sth	*etwas ein Ende machen*
admit	*zugeben, eingestehen*
it's my fault	*es ist meine Schuld*
benefit of the doubt	*günstige Auslegung zweifelhafter Umstände (in dubio pro reo)*
release tension	*sich entspannen*
defuse	*entschärfen*
visualization	*Veranschaulichung*

lovable	*liebenswert, liebenswürdig*
loving	*liebevoll*

44

nuclear reactor	*Kernreaktor*
stud-muffin (AE)	*Kerl, Mannsbild*
project (housing) (AE)	*Sozialbau*
ebony	*schwarz wie Ebenholz*
warrior	*Krieger(in)*
stolen	*gestohlen*
cure	*heilen*
cancer	*Krebs*
water fueled	*wasserbetrieben*
kick the snot out of sb	*jmdm sehr heftig treten*
henchman	*Handlanger, Scherge*

45

Commonwealth	*Gemeinschaft der Länder des ehemaligen Britischen Weltreichs*
contrast	*gegenüberstellen, kontrastieren*

UNIT 4

47

benefit	*Nutzen; Vorteil*
abbreviation	*Abkürzung*
pros and cons	*Für und Wider, Pro und Kontra*
dependence (on)	*Abhängigkeit (von), Anlehnung (an)*
evaluate	*beurteilen, abschätzen, auswerten*

48

indicate	*hinweisen, andeuten*
grouping	*Eingruppierung; Gliederung*
user	*Nutzer(in); Anwender(in)*
interest	*Interesse*
grant	*eine Erlaubnis erteilen; bewilligen, genehmigen*
socialize	*mit anderen Menschen Kontakte knüpfen*

49

involve	*beinhalten, einbeziehen*
membership	*Mitgliedschaft*

belief	Glaube, Überzeugung	**51**	
eliminate	beseitigen, ausmerzen	stuffy	bieder, steif
theft	Diebstahl	updated	aktualisiert
rise	Anstieg, Zunahme	character	Zeichen; Charakter
prevalent	geläufig, verbreitet	length	Länge
predator	Raubtier	**condense**	verdichten; kondensieren
claim	behaupten	whopping	kolossal
proceed	weitergehen, fortfahren	handy	handlich, griffig
caution	Vorsicht, Umsicht	pocket-sized	in Taschenformat
surroundings	Umgebung, Umfeld	read	(hier) Lektüre
judgement	Ermessen, Beurteilung	linguistic expert	Sprachwissen-
suitable	angemessen		schaftler(in)
return	(hier) ergeben	**grace**	schmücken, zieren
		envisage sth	sich etwas vorstellen
50		**spoil**	verderben
mighty	gewaltig, mächtig	pleasure	Freude
infect	anstecken, infizieren	**work sth out**	etwas ausrechnen
liberate	befreien, freisetzen	inspiring	anregend, begeisternd
judge	beurteilen, bewerten	hug	Umarmung
hand sth	in etwas abgeben	oral	mündlich
essay	Aufsatz, Abhandlung	acronym	Kürzel, Kurzwort
shorthand	Kurzschrift		
flabbergasted	verblüfft, entgeistert	**52**	
standard	normal, gewöhnlich	retrieval	Rückgewinnung,
riddled with	mit etwas durchsetzt		Wiederfindung
hieroglyphics	Hieroglyphen	increasing	zunehmend, steigend
blame sb (for)	jmdm die Schuld an	complexity	Komplexität
	etwas geben, jmdm	innovation	Neuheit; Neuerung
	etwas vorwerfen	acquaintance	Bekannte(r);
declining	rückläufig		Bekanntschaft
publisher	Verlag; Verleger	**flow**	fließen, strömen
despite	trotz; zum Trotz	trustworthiness	Zuverlässigkeit,
advent	Ankunft; Beginn		Vertrauenswürdigkeit
predictive	voraussagend	limitation	Einschränkung,
launch	Stapellauf, Start		Beschränkung
addict	Suchtkranke(r)	**cope (with sth)**	zurechtkommen,
liberation	Befreiung, Freisetzung		mit etwas fertigwerden
shortcut	Abkürzung	threshold	Schwelle; (tech.) Grenz-
adopt	annehmen, adoptieren		bereich
keen	eifrig	**access sth**	auf etwas zugreifen
get sth across to sb	jmdm etwas vermitteln /	**replace**	ersetzen, austauschen
	verständlich machen	**grasp**	begreifen; fassen,
advertising copy	Anzeigentext		auffassen
Biblical	Bibel-; biblisch	concept	Auffassung, Konzept
passage	Textstelle, Textauszug	tropical	Tropen-; tropisch
inconsistent	unbeständig,	**set aside (set, set)**	aufsparen, etwas beiseite
	uneinheitlich		legen
succumb	unterliegen	budget	Etat, Finanzplan
travesty	Travestie	destination	Zielort, Reiseziel
render	ausführen, wiedergeben	**narrow**	begrenzen, beschränken

parameter	*Bestimmungsgröße; Rahmen*	pseudonym	*Künstlername, Deckname*
gather	*ansammeln, gewinnen*	accountable	*verantwortlich , haftbar*
make sth a snap	*etwas sehr einfach machen*	client	*Auftraggeber(in); Mandant(in)*
contain	*enthalten, beinhalten*	compromising	*kompromittierend*
relevant	*entsprechend, maßgeblich*	**predict**	*voraussagen, vorhersagen*
manufacturer	*Hersteller*	**implement (sth)**	*etwas durchführen / umsetzen*
retailer	*Händler, Einzelhändler*	flighty	*unbeständig, flatterhaft*

53

massive	*gewaltig*	I reckon ... (AE)	*Ich meine ...*
query	*Anfrage*	psychic	*seelisch, psychisch*
retrieve	*abrufen, wieder auf-finden*	**affect sb / sth**	*sich auf jmn / etwas auswirken; jmdn / etwas beeinflussen*
knowledge	*Kenntnis; Erkenntnis; Wissensstand*	approach	*Ansatz, Vorgehen*
		paradigm	*Modell, Musterbeispiel, Paradigma*

54

Thanks to ...	*dank etwas; wegen*	**shift**	*schieben, verschieben; sich bewegen; schalten*
tap	*abklopfen*	implication	*Folgerung, Schluss-folgerung*
tweet	*twittern (eine Kurznach-richt auf einem sozialen Netzwerk absetzen)*		

55

respond	*auf etwas reagieren; erwidern*	**empower**	*befähigen, ermächtigen*
demand	*verlangen; beanspruchen*	**censor**	*zensieren*
integrate	*einbinden, eingliedern*	irrelevant	*bedeutungslos, unerheblich*
rely on	*sich auf jmdn / etwas verlassen*	**visualize**	*sich etwas bildlich vorstellen, etwas ver-anschaulichen*
privacy settings	*Sicherheitseinstellungen*		
nor	*auch nicht*	director	*(Schul-)direktor*
delete	*auslöschen, tilgen, ausstreichen,*	cognitive skill	*kognitive Fähigkeit*
modify	*abändern, verändern*	hitchhiker	*Anhalter*

56

assert	*behaupten (, dass ...); geltend machen*	high frequency	*Hochfrequenz* 🕚
sue	*(vor Gericht) klagen, prozessieren*	simplicity	*Einfachheit* 🕚
racy	*gewagt, pikant*	**broadcast**	*senden, etwas durch Rundfunk verbreiten* 🕚
go viral	*sich wie ein Virus ausbreiten*	conventional	*gebräuchlich, herkömmlich* 🕚
entire	*gesamt, komplett*	**announce (itself)**	*sich ankündigen* 🕚
presence	*Anwesenheit; Vorhandensein*	**establish**	*begründen; einrichten* 🕚
detrimental	*schädlich, abträglich*	approximately	*ungefähr* 🕚
evolve (into sth)	*sich (zu jmdm / etwas) entwickeln*	range	*Reichweite* 🕚
demise	*Untergang; Ableben*	**equip**	*ausstatten, ausrüsten* 🕚
		support	*fördern; unterstützen* 🕚

associate with	*mit etwas Umgang pflegen* 🅣	prestige	*Ansehen, Geltung*
flick between	*umschalten* 🅣	**61**	
spontaneously	*spontan* 🅣	geologist	*Geologe, Geologin*
recommend	*empfehlen, vorschlagen* 🅣	shipyard	*Schiffswerft*
		cargo	*Fracht, Ladung*
define	*definieren; genau bestimmen*	refinery	*Raffinerie*
at random	*zufällig, stichprobenartig, willkürlich*	**convert sth into sth**	*etwas in etwas umwandeln / verwandeln*
		crude oil	*Rohöl*
57		docks (pl.)	*Hafenanlage, Hafengebiet*
sheet of paper	*Blatt Papier*	estate agent	*Immobilienmakler*
trace back	*zurückverfolgen*	property market	*Immobilienmarkt*
date back	*(zeitlich) zurückliegen*	**rent (sth)**	*mieten*
		determine	*bestimmen*

UNIT 5

60		**62**	
structure	*Konstruktion, Gebilde*	depression	*Konjunkturtief*
primary	*Primär-*	slump	*Sturz, Absackung*
raw material	*Rohstoff*	trough	*Senke, Talsohle*
obtain	*erhalten, bekommen, erhalten*	severe	*schwerwiegend, stark*
grain	*Getreide*	consumption	*Verbrauch, Konsum*
forestry industry	*Holzwirtschaft*	decrease	*Abnahme, Verminderung*
ore	*Erz*	fall	*Fall, Rückgang*
mine	*abbauen, (durch Bergbau) fördern*	bankruptcy	*Bankrott, Konkurs, Insolvenz*
extract	*entnehmen, gewinnen*	unemployment	*Arbeitslosigkeit*
secondary	*Sekundär-*	recovery	*Erholung, Aufschwung*
finished goods	*Endprodukte, Erzeugnisse, Fertigwaren*	revival	*Konjunkturbelebung*
consumer	*Verbraucher, Konsument(in)*	expansion	*Erweiterung, Ausweitung, Wachsen*
tertiary	*Tertiär-*	order book	*Auftragsbuch*
mammoth	*Mammut*	fill up	*auffüllen*
importance	*Wichtigkeit, Bedeutung*	boom	*Aufschwung, Konjunktur*
utility	*Versorgungsunternehmen*	prosperity	*Hochkonjunktur; Wohlstand*
refuse collection	*Müllabfuhr*	peak	*Höhepunkt, Höchstwert*
loss	*Verlust*	intense	*heftig*
ultimately	*schlussendlich, letztmalig*	wage	*Lohn, Arbeitsentgelt*
close down	*aufgeben, (ein Geschäft) schließen*	downside	*Kehrseite, Nachteil*
split	*aufteilen, teilen, spalten*	shortage	*Mangel, Fehlbestand; Verknappung*
broadcasting	*Rundfunk*	recession	*Konjunkturrückgang, Rezession, Flaute*
issues (pl.)	*Belange, Angelegenheiten*	slowdown	*Verlangsamung*
		downswing	*Abwärtstrend*
postal service	*Postdienst*	**decline**	*fallen, abfallen, abnehmen*
		stagnation	*Wirtschaftsflaute*

standstill	*Stillstand*	for instance	*beispielsweise,*
expand	*aufgehen, ausweiten,*		*zum Beispiel*
	ausdehnen	**achieve sth**	*etwas erreichen / erzielen*
encouragement	*Aufmunterung,*	balance	*Ausgleich, Gleichgewicht*
	Ermunterung	**opt for**	*sich für etwas*
invest in	*anlegen*		*entscheiden*
machinery	*Mechanismus;*	core	*Kern*
	Maschinen; Maschinerie	compressed	*komprimiert,*
workforce	*Arbeitskräfte;*		*zusammengedrückt*
	Erwerbstätige	popularity	*Beliebtheit*
		have / take a day off	*sich einen Tag frei*
63			*nehmen*
plummet	*stürzen*	teleworking	*Telearbeit*
sight	*Sicht*	**accelerate**	*beschleunigen (sich)*
civil service	*öffentlicher Dienst /*	term-time	*Schulzeit*
	Verwaltung	**persuade**	*überreden, überzeugen*
mortgage	*Hypothek*		
foreclosure	*Kündigung einer Hypo-*	**66**	
	thek; gerichtliche Voll-	bookstore (AE)	*Buchhandlung*
	streckungserklärung	**launch sth**	*etwas auf den Markt*
optimism	*Optimismus*		*bringen*
conclusion	*Feststellung, Schluss-*	buzzword	*Modewort; abge-*
	folgerung		*droschene Phrase*
		financial year	*Bilanzjahr, Geschäftsjahr*
64		**generate**	*erwirtschaften,*
flexibility	*Biegsamkeit;*		*erbringen*
	Anpassungsfähigkeit	**go public**	*Börsengang*
researcher	*Forscher(in)*	home improvement	*Heimwerkerbedarf*
improvement	*Verbesserung,*	items	
	Aufbesserung	breakneck speed	*halsbrecherische*
in contrast	*zum Vergleich*		*Geschwindigkeit*
controversial	*umstritten, kontrovers*	observer	*Beobacher(in)*
schedule	*etwas zeitlich festlegen*	investor	*Anleger(in)*
job sharing	*Arbeitsplatzaufteilung*	convinced	*überzeugt*
average (out)	*den Durchschnitt*	express speed	*Eiltempo*
	ermitteln	annual sales	*Jahresumsatz*
commission sth	*in Auftrag geben*	stock	*Aktienkapital*
childcare	*Kinderbetreuung*	(stock) closed at	*Aktienpreis zum Schluss*
force sb to do sth	*jmdn nötigen, etwas zu*		*der Börse*
	tun	all-time	*beispiellos*
spokeswoman	*Pressesprecherin*	cybercommerce	*Internet-Handel*
routinely	*routinemäßig*	crown	*Krone*
prepared	*bereit*	**slip**	*rutschen*
taskforce	*Sonderkommando;*	reorganization plan	*Sanierungsplan*
	Sonderkommission	**make redundant**	*entlassen*
		quarter	*Quartal*
65		share price	*Aktienkurs*
creativity	*Einfallsreichtum,*	**venture (into)**	*sich (in ...) wagen*
	Kreativität	**file for bankruptcy**	*Insolvenzantrag stellen*
job satisfaction	*Arbeitszufriedenheit*		

buy out	*eine Mehrheit des Aktienkapitals aufkaufen*	straightforward	*geradeaus, überschaubar*
collapse	*Zusammenbruch; Kurssturz*	carefully-screened	*sorgfältig überprüft*
		mail-order catalogue	*Versandkatalog*
expenses	*Unkosten, Ausgaben, Spesen*	directory	*Adressenverzeichnis*
		enable	*ermächtigen, ermöglichen*
restructure	*sanieren; umordnen*	satisfied	*zufrieden*
lay off	*entlassen*		
unprofitable	*unrentabel, ertraglos*	**68**	
streamline	*rationalisieren, wettbewerbsfähiger gestalten*	failure	*Misserfolg, Scheitern*
		observe sth	*befolgen, beachten*
storage	*Lagerhaltung, Einlagerung*	occasion	*Anlass, Ereignis, Gelegenheit*
packaging	*Verpackung*	chairman,	*Vorsitzender, Vorstands-*
delivery	*Auslieferung*	chairperson	*vorsitzende(r)*
operation	*Arbeitsvorgang*	**call a meeting**	*eine Versammlung*
compete with sb	*jmdm Konkurrenz machen; sich mit jmdm messen*		*ansetzen/einberufen*
		agenda	*Tagesordnung*
		concerned	*betroffen*
auction	*Versteigerung*	purpose	*Absicht, Zweck*
earnings	*Einkommen, Einnehmen*	**last**	*dauern*
steadily	*stetig, beständig*	accordingly	*entsprechend*
continuously	*unaufhörlich*	punctuality	*Pünktlichkeit*
efficiency	*Produktivität, Effizienz*	absolute must	*absolutes Muss*
		effective	*wirksam*
67		**appoint sb**	*jmdn benennen/ berufen*
graduate student	*Student im Aufbaustudium*	**keep the minutes**	*Protokoll führen*
perfect	*vervollkommnen, perfektionieren*	proceedings	*Handlungsverlauf*
		distribute	*verteilen*
licence	*zulassen, eine Lizenz/ Konzession erteilen*	attendee	*Anwesende(r), Teilnehmer(in)*
limited	*eingeschränkt, begrenzt*	contribution	*Beitrag*
cheque	*Scheck*	appropriately	*geeignet, angemessen*
raise	*aufbringen, zusammen- stellen*	in good time	*rechtzeitig*
		allocate	*anweisen, zuweisen*
They'd made it!	*Sie hatten es geschafft!*	brief	*kurz*
enormously	*gewaltig, enorm*	confidential	*vertraulich*
debut	*erstes Auftreten, Debüt*	instructed	*beauftragt, angewiesen*
rocket	*wie eine Rakete hoch- schießen*		
		69	
worth	*wert*	corporation	*Unternehmen*
lion's share	*Löwenanteil*	confined	*eingeschlossen*
corporate client	*Firmenkunde*	co-worker	*Mitarbeiter(in), Kollege, Kollegin*
advertiser	*Anzeigenkunde, Werbeagentur*	partition	*Abtrennung, Trennwand*
cost-effective	*kostengünstig, wirtschaftlich*	cubicle	*Zelle, Nische*
		rather	*ziemlich*
in addition (to)	*zusätzlich (zu), darüber hinaus*	built-in	*eingebaut*
		overhead	*obenliegend*

cosy	*behaglich, gemütlich*	**air sth**	*belüften, auslüften,*
reflect	*spiegeln, widerspiegeln*		*durchlüften, entlüften*
dweller	*Bewohner(in)*	electrical appliance	*Elektrogerät*
supervisor	*Aufseher(in)*	washing machine	*Waschmaschine*
on the other hand	*andererseits*	long term	*Langzeit-, auf lange Sicht*
moveable	*beweglich, bewegbar*		
solid	*massiv, stabil*	**75**	
depressed	*deprimiert, nieder-*	drying	*Trocknung*
	geschlagen	ironing	*Bügeln*
white-collar worker	*Büroangestellte(r)*	laundry appliances	*Wäschereigeräte*
			(Waschmaschine,
70			*Trockner, Mangel, usw.)*
ashtray	*Aschenbecher* 🅣	HVAC (Heating,	*Heizung, Belüftung,*
a whole bunch of ...	*eine ganze Menge ...* 🅣	Ventilation,	*Klimatechnik*
water cooler	*Wasserkühler* 🅣	Air Conditioning)	
sunlight	*Sonnenlicht* 🅣	construction	*Bauingenieur(in)* 🅣
		engineer	
71		**fiddle about**	*tüfteln* 🅣
disorganized	*chaotisch*	**(with sth)**	
sociable	*gesellig, kontaktfreudig*	awning	*Markise* 🅣
manufacture	*anfertigen, erzeugen,*	**activate**	*betätigen, bedienen* 🅣
	herstellen	**pick up (wind)**	*zunehmen* 🅣
crop; crops	*Ernte; Gesamternte*	straw	*Stroh* 🅣
drill	*bohren*	supply	*Versorgung; Vorrat* 🅣
fishing	*Fischerei*	**depend on**	*abhängen von* 🅣
marketing	*Vertrieb, Marketing*	state-of-the-art	*hochmodern, auf*
			dem neuesten Stand der
72			*Technik* 🅣
equation	*Gleichung*		
postulate	*Voraussetzung, Postulat*	**76**	
approach (sth / sb)	*sich (jmdm / etwas)*	frequent	*häufig, regelmäßig*
	nähern, heranrücken	via	*durch, mittels*
infinity	*Endlosigkeit,*	command	*Befehl*
	Unendlichkeit	owner	*Besitzer(in)*
regardless (of)	*egal welcher, ungeachtet*	sensor	*Messfühler, Messsonde*
	der / des ...	**alert**	*alamieren, warnen*
		be short on / of	*an etwas knapp sein*
UNIT 6		estate	*Anwesen*
74		**install**	*einbauen, installieren*
Citizen's Advice	*Bürgerberatungsdienst*	**keep track of**	*den Überblick behalten,*
Bureau			*im Auge behalten*
except	*außer, ausgenommen,*	switch	*Schalter*
	mit Ausnahme von	knob	*Drehknopf*
power company	*Energieversorgungs-*	security panel	*Sicherheitskontrollfeld*
	unternehmen	hall	*Diele, Flur*
pressure sb	*bedrängen, unter Druck*	answerphone	*Anrufbeantworter*
	setzen	chores (pl.)	*Haushaltspflichten*
regulations (pl.)	*gesetzliche Vorschriften*	safety measures	*Sicherheitsvorkehrungen*
provider	*Anbieter, Lieferant*	**adjust**	*einstellen*
		motion detector	*Bewegungsmelder*

backyard (AE)	*Hinterhof, Garten hinter dem Haus*
leak	*Leck, undichte Stelle*
disconnect	*abkoppeln (vom Strom); eine Verbindung lösen*
accidentally	*versehentlich*
spark	*Funke*
fire brigade	*Feuerwehr*
exit	*Ausgang, Ausfahrt*
unlock	*aufschließen, entriegeln*
burglar	*Einbrecher(in)*
headquarters	*Zentrale, Hauptquartier*
glimpse	*flüchtiger Blick*
voice-controlled	*sprachgesteuert*
jukebox	*Musikautomat*
select	*(aus)wählen*
sliding	*ausziehbar*
wall panel	*Wandtafel*
underlying	*grundlegend*
packed with	*vollgestopft mit*
gadget	*Gerät, technischer Krimskrams*

77

comprehension	*Verständnis*

78

experimental model	*Versuchsmodell*
molecular valve	*Elektronenröhre*
accumulated	*angesammelt*
withdraw	*abziehen, sich zurückziehen*
IQ (Intelligence Quotient)	*Intelligenzquotient*
measurement	*Bemessung; Messwert*
living	*lebend*
characteristics (pl.)	*Eigenschaften, Besonderheiten*
color (AE)	*Farbe*
let go	*loslassen*
get in the way	*im Wege stehen*
intimate	*intim*
similarity	*Ähnlichkeit*
contest	*Wettbewerb*
requirement	*Voraussetzung*
assign	*anweisen; jmdm etwas auftragen*
one at a time	*einer nach dem anderen*
manipulation	*Beeinflussung*
touch	*Berührung*

much alike	*sehr ähnlich*
a great deal	*eine ganze Menge, sehr viel*
fist	*Faust*

79

All up to you.	*Alles hängt von dir ab.*
addition	*Ergänzung*
undergo	*durchmachen, sich etwas unterziehen*
correlation	*Wechselbeziehung, Übereinstimmung*
siblings (pl.)	*Geschwister*
schooling	*Schulausbildung*
admire	*bewundern, hoch schätzen*
broaden	*verbreiten; (sich) ausweiten*
deepen	*vertiefen*
word order	*Satzstellung*
matter	*Sache, Angelegenheit*
temperamental	*launisch, reizbar*
looks (pl.)	*Aussehen*
elsewhere	*anderswo, woanders*
make sth plain	*klarmachen*
blank spot	*Leerstelle*
unevenness	*Unebenheit*
keep close tabs on	*jmdn kontrollieren / beobachten*
self	*selbst, selber*
evaluator	*Gutachter(in)*
extended	*erweitert, verlängert*
discard	*Ausschuss*
astonishing	*erstaunlich*
resonance	*Resonanz*
coordinate	*koordinieren, abstimmen*
delicate(ly)	*feinfühlig*
morality	*Moralität, Sittlichkeit*

80

hybrid motor	*Hybridmotor*
dead end	*Sackgasse*
internal combustion engine	*Verbrennungsmotor*
durable	*haltbar, beständig*
efficient	*leistungsfähig*
fuel	*Treibstoff, Brennstoff*
fuel cell	*Brennstoffzelle*
charging station	*Ladestation*
charge (battery)	*aufladen*

forward	*vorwärts*
combine	*verbinden, zusammen-legen*
propulsion system	*Antrieb*
regenerative braking	*Rückarbeitsbremsung, Nutzbremsung*
aerodynamics (sing.)	*Aerodynamik*
lightweight material	*Leichtbauwerkstoff*
consist of	*aus etwas bestehen, sich aus etwas zusammen-setzen*
place	*legen, setzen, stellen*
chain	*Kette*
power	*Energie, Kraft*
generator	*Elektroaggregat, Drehstromgenerator*
transmission	*Übertragung*
load	*Ladung, Last*
gradient	*Gradient; Gefällstrecke*
emission	*Ausstoß, Abgas*
marketable	*verkaufsfähig, vermarktbar*
to date	*bis jetzt*
kick in	*(ugs) anlaufen, (sich) anschalten*
power split	*Leistungsverzweigung*
gearbox	*Getriebe*

81

shaft	*Übertragungswelle; Schaft*
differential	*Differenzialgetriebe; Hinterachsgetriebe*
high-capacity	*Hochleistungs-, leistungsstark*
illustration	*Bebilderung*

82

lawn	*Rasen*
mow	*mähen*
sit back	*sich zurücklehnen*
user-friendly	*benutzerfreundlich*
harmful	*schädlich*
exhaust emission	*Abgasausstoß*
random	*zufällig, willkürlich*
boundary	*Abgrenzung, Grund-stücksgrenze*
recharge	*(wieder) aufladen*
complaint	*Beschwerde*
obstacle	*Behinderung*

reverse	*wenden, herumdrehen; rückwärts fahren*
bury	*begraben, vergraben, eingraben*
wire	*Draht*
detect	*erfassen; aufspüren, aufdecken*
object	*Gegenstand*
blade	*Klinge*

83

raise	*anheben, erhöhen; höher stellen*
cutting height	*Schnitthöhe*
gradually	*allmählich*
preferred	*bevorzugt*
lawnmower	*Rasenmäher*
set running time	*angesetzte Betriebs-dauer*
timer	*Schaltuhr*
seemingly	*scheinbar*
throughout	*durchgehend, durchweg*
reliable	*verlässlich, zuverlässig*
regular	*(hier) normal*
grown over	*überwuchert*
disappear	*verschwinden*
screwdriver	*Schraubenzieher*
surface	*Oberfläche*
cover	*bedecken, zudecken*
pass over	*überfahren, übergehen*
simplify	*vereinfachen*
assist (with)	*helfen, behilflich sein*
tracker	*Aufspürer*
mower	*Mäher*

85

fuss	*Getue*

86

lie detector	*Lügendetektor*
slap sb	*jmdm abwatschen / ohrfeigen*
be ashamed of oneself	*sich schämen*
deserve	*verdienen*

UNIT 7

87

quit	*aufgeben*

88

risk	*Risiko, Wagnis*
heart attack	*Herzinfarkt*
condemn	*verurteilen; verdammen*
council	*Gemeinderat*
sunbed	*Sonnenbank*
leisure centre	*Freizeitzentrum*
outweigh	***aufwiegen, wettmachen***
spotlight	*Punktstrahler; Mittel-punkt des Interesses*
greed	*Gier*
monitor	*überwachen, kontrollieren*
withdrawn	*verschlossen, zurück-gezogen*
mood swings	*Stimmungs-schwankungen*
cardiac arrhythmia	*Herzrhythmusstörung*
chest	*Brust, Brustkorb*
liver	*Leber*
liver failure	*Leberversagen*
investigation	*Ermittlungen, Untersuchung*
spread	*Ausbreitung*
obesity	*Fettleibigkeit, Fettsucht*

89

dental assistant	*Zahnarzthelfer(in)*
calm	*beruhigen*
insurance	*Versicherung*
afford	*leisten können, erschwingen*
dental care	*Zahnpflege*
from all walks of life	*aus allen Gesellschafts-schichten*
orthodontic	*zahnmedizinisch(e)*
jaw	*Kiefer*
overbite	*Überbiss*
underbite	*Vorbiss, Vorstehen des Unterkiefers*
removable	*herausnehmbar*
appliance	*Gerät, Apparat*
brace	*Zahnspange*
progress	*Fortschritt*
expected	*erwartet*
maintain	*aufrechterhalten, einhalten*
inspire	*begeistern, anregen*
physician	*Mediziner(in)*

90

catastrophe	*Katastrophe, Unglück*
provision	*Versorgung*
regulation	*Regelung*
loosely-regulated	*(hier) nur minimal-geregelt*
limit	*begrenzen, einschränken*
federal government	*Bundesregierung*
insured	*versichert*
social security	*Sozialversicherung*
disability	*Arbeitsunfähigkeit, Behinderung*
unable	*unfähig*
military forces	*Militär, militärische Wehrdienste*
Census Bureau	*Behörde für Bevölkerungsstatistik*
i.e. (id est = that is)	*das heißt*
finance	*finanzieren*
income	*Einkommen*
amount	*Betrag; Menge*
pensioner	*Rentner(in)*
mandatory	*obligatorisch, vorgeschrieben*

92

junk food	*ungesunde Fertigkost*
commercial	*Werbesendung*
mayor	*Bürgermeister(in)*
sugary	*zuckerhaltig*
isolated	*vereinzelt*
broad	*breit; umfassend*
industrialized nations	*Industrieländer*
ability	*Fähigkeit*
labour-saving	*arbeitssparend*
consensus	*Konsens*
prevention	*Vorbeugung*
estimate	*Schätzung*
diabetes	*Zuckerkrankheit*
cardiovascular disease	*Herz-Kreislauf-Erkrankung*
disproportionately	*überproportional, unverhältnismäßig*
obese	*fettleibig, korpulent*
adolescent	*Jugendliche(r)*
sedentary	*sitzend*
packaged	*verpackt*
constant	*ständig, andauernd*
sweeten	*süßen; versüßen*
increase	*Anstieg, Steigerung*

cut	*Kürzung, Senkung*	rot	*verfaulen, verwesen*
multiple	*mehrfach, mannigfaltig*	ashes (pl.)	*Asche, Verbrennungs-*
strategy	*Strategie*		*rückstände*
scale	*Ausmaß, Größen-*	troops (pl.)	*Truppen*
	verhältnis		
challenging	*anspruchsvoll, heraus-*		
	fordernd		

97

ankle	*Fußknöchel*
appendix	*Blinddarm, Wurm-*
	fortsatz

93

Body Mass Index	*Körpermassenzahl*	elbow	*Ellbogen*
labelling	*Auszeichnung,*	kidney	*Niere*
	Etikettierung	lung	*Lunge*
		wrist	*Handgelenk*
		knuckle	*Fingerknöchel*

94

campaign	*Aktion, Kampagne*	spleen	*Milz*
despised	*verschmäht, verachtet*	avarice	*Gier, Habsucht*
underclass	*Unterschicht*	observation	*Überwachung;*
disgusting	*ekelhaft, widerlich*		*Beobachtung*
regarded	*betrachtet*	retiring	*zurückhaltend*
outcast	*Ausgestoßene(r), Paria*	corpulence	*Dickleibigkeit, Körperfülle*
migrant	*unstet, wandernd*		
addiction	*Sucht*		
substance	*Substanz, Stoff*		

UNIT 8

99

cartoon	*Karikatur*
letter of complaint	*Beschwerdebrief*

95

convey	*überbringen,*
	übermitteln

100

prestigious	*angesehen*
namely	*nämlich*
developing countries	*Entwicklungsländer*
filtration	*Filterung*
mechanical	*mechanisch*
attach to	*befestigen (an etwas),*
	anhängen; anlegen
above all	*vor allem*
contaminated	*verunreinigt, belastet*
drinkable	*trinkbar*
crucial	*entscheidend,*
	ausschlaggebend
water-borne	*durch Wasser übertragen*
diphtheria	*Diphtherie*
typhoid	*Typhus*
diarrhoea	*Durchfall*
innovative	*bahnbrechend, innovativ*
target sth	*abzielen (auf etwas)*
incredible	*unglaublich, wunderbar*
require	*benötigen, brauchen*
spare part	*Ersatzteil*
turquoise	*Türkis*
cylinder	*Zylinder*

96

stressful	*stressig, aufreibend* 🅣
gentle	*sanft* 🅣
accomplishment	*Errungenschaft* 🅣
enjoyment	*Vergnügen* 🅣
diagnose	*diagnostizieren, eine*
	Krankheit feststellen 🅣
supporter	*Unterstützer* 🅣
limitation	*Einschränkung,*
	Begrenzung 🅣
aging	*alternd* 🅣
cure	*Heilmittel, Heilung* 🅣
emphasize	*betonen* 🅣
honestly	*ehrlich, aufrichtig* 🅣
well-known	*gut bekannt*
advertising slogan	*Werbespruch*
obey	*gehorchen*
sobriety	*Nüchternheit*
good deed	*gute Tat, Wohltat*
weed	*Unkraut*
	(ugs. Marihuana)
mourning	*Trauer; Trauerkleidung*

resin	Harz, Kunstharz	hydrated	hydratisiert 🅣
high-impact proof	hochschlagfest	fancy	schick, apart 🅣
shell	Schale	harmless	harmlos 🅣
filter out	abfiltern	**brighten up**	aufhellen; aufmuntern 🅣
dip	eintauchen		
sip	nippen	sparkling water	Sprudel 🅣
mouthpiece	Mundstück	blend (of)	Gemisch, Verschnitt 🅣
wipe clean	abwischen	herb	Kraut, Heilkraut 🅣
demonstrate	beweisen, darstellen	invigorating	belebend, kräftigend 🅣
eradicate	ausmerzen, löschen	soothing	beruhigend, schmerz-linderd 🅣
contaminant	Schadstoff, Verunreinigung	convenience	Annehmlichkeit, Zweck-mäßigkeit 🅣
particle	Teilchen		
recommend	empfehlen, vorschlagen	urbane	weltgewandt, kultiviert 🅣
clog	verstopfen		
hydrologist	Gewässerkundige(r)	response	Antwort, Rückmeldung, Resonanz 🅣
phenomenon	Phänomen, Natur-erscheinung		
		feverish	fieberhaft 🅣
bottled water	Trinkwasser in Flaschen	boardroom	Sitzungssaal 🅣
commodity	Handelsware 🅣	lecture hall	Hörsaal, Auditorium 🅣
common good	Allgemeinwohl 🅣	**initiate**	einleiten, auslösen 🅣
source	Quelle, Herkunft 🅣		
transboundary	grenzüberschreitend 🅣	**101**	
take sth for granted	annehmen (als selbst-verständlich) 🅣	disinfection	Desinfektion, Desinfizierung
running water	fließendes Wasser 🅣	**disinfect**	desinfizieren
thought	Gedanke, Überlegung 🅣	**expose (to)**	aussetzen (jmdn./etwas)
upstream	flussaufwärts 🅣		
reroute	umleiten 🅣	UV radiation	Ultraviolettstrahlung
dump	abkippen, abladen 🅣	slide	Overheadfolie, Dia
pollutant	Umweltschadstoff 🅣	**overdo**	übertreiben
dam	Staudamm 🅣		
precious	kostbar, wertvoll 🅣	**102**	
resource	Produktionsmittel, Ressource 🅣	shrinking	schrumpfend
		roll	Röllchen
dry up	austrocknen, vertrocknen 🅣	soft	weich
		toffee	Karamell
luxury	Luxus 🅣	delicious	appetitlich, wohl-schmeckend
acquire	erwerben, anschaffen 🅣		
tangible	konkret, greifbar 🅣	exception	Ausnahme
intangible	immateriell, unbegreiflich 🅣	till	Kasse
		scoff	verschlingen
ample	ausreichend, üppig 🅣	ration	Zuteilung
climate change	Klimawandel 🅣	melting	schmelzend
sensational	aufsehenerregend 🅣	mouthful	Bissen, Happen; Schluck
jug	Krug 🅣	**charge (price)**	berechnen, (Preis) verlangen
wrap-around label	Rundumetikett 🅣		
convenient	zweckmäßig, praktisch 🅣	Come off it.	Ach was!, Jetzt mach mal halblang!
stylish	stilvoll, elegant 🅣	weekly	wöchentlich

fix	Schuss, Fix
devise	ersinnen, ausdenken
ingenious	genial
proof	Beweis
dishonest	unehrlich, verlogen
intention	Absicht, Vorsatz
fabric softener	Weichspüler
magically	magisch
diminished	vermindert
drained weight	Trockengewicht
revamped	umgestaltet
cleaning liquid	Reinigungsflüssigkeit
spray	Spraydose, Aerosol
suspect	verdächtigen, vermuten, ahnen
diluted	verdünnt
sneakily	heimtückisch, hinter- hältig
washing up liquid	Geschirrspülmittel
loo (slang)	Klo
kitchen towel	Papiertuch
over-the-counter	in Freihandel erhältlich, freiverkäuflich
prescription medicine	verschreibungspflichtiges Arzneimittel
tablet	Tablette
overall	insgesamt, allgemein
considerably	beträchtlich, erheblich
quantity	Anzahl, Menge
inflation	Abwertung, Teuerung
hidden	versteckt, verborgen
pose	darstellen
purchaser	Abnehmer, Erwerber
be fond of sb / sth	gernhaben (jmdn./ etwas)
disappointment	Enttäuschung
assume	vermuten, voraussetzen
occur	auftreten, sich ereignen, stattfinden
shed light on sth	über etwas Aufschluss geben
addressee	Adressat(in)
apology	Entschuldigung
restitution	Entschädigung, Rückerstattung

103

dairy	Milchprodukte
protein	Eiweiß

104

stroll	schlendern, bummeln
produce section	Obst und Gemüse Abteilung
grocery store (AE)	Lebensmittelladen
make up one's mind	(sich) entscheiden
trustworthy	zuverlässig, vertrauens- würdig
pesticide	Schädlingsbekämpfungs- mittel
harm	schaden, verletzen
health-conscious	gesundheitsbewusst
whereas	wohingegen; während
carbon footprint	CO2-Fußabdruck
familiar	gewohnt, vertraut
representation	Darstellung
greenhouse gases	Treibhausgase
measure	Maß; Maßnahme
measure	messen, abmessen
carbon dioxide (CO_2)	Kohlendioxid
pick	abpflücken
debate	Debatte
antibiotics	Antibiotika
irradiation	Bestrahlung
concern	Sorge, Besorgnis
adopter	Adoptierende(r)
shopper	Einkäufer(in)
outraged	empört, entrüstet
shipping	Versand
agribusiness	Agrarindustrie

105

retain	behalten, beibehalten
leguminous	hülsenfruchtartig
refrigerated container	Kühlcontainer
abundant	ergiebig, reichlich
eventually	endlich, letztendlich, schließlich
demand	Nachfrage; Forderung
topsoil	Humus, Mutterboden
groundwater	Grundwasser
offset	aufwiegen, ausgleichen
substitute	austauschen, auswechseln
viability	Durchführbarkeit, Viabilität
truck (AE)	Lastwagen
round-trip	hin und zurück
grape	Traube
appearance	Aussehen

calorific content	*Brennwert*

106

unripe	*unreif*
processing	*Verarbeitung*
wax	*Wachs*
dye	*Farbstoff, Färbemittel*
ripen	*heranreifen, reif werden*
ethylene gas	*Kohlenwasserstoffgas (C₂H₄), Ethylen*
handling	*Abwicklung, Handhabung*
purchase	*erwerben, ankaufen*
grower	*Anbauer, Erzeuger*
open-minded	*aufgeschlossen, vorurteilsfrei*
orchard	*Obstplantage*
seller	*Verkäufer(in)*
source	*Quelle, Entstehungsort*

107

distinguish (between)	*unterscheiden (zwischen)*
fertilizer	*Düngemittel*
examine	*untersuchen, prüfen*
balcony	*Balkon*
minimize	*herabsetzen, auf ein Mindestmaß verkleinern*
processed food	*industriell verarbeitetes Lebensmittel*
dried goods	*Kurzwaren*
ingredient	*Backzutat*
can	*konservieren*
dry	*trocknen, abtrocknen, ausdörren*
point	*Punkt, Spitze*

108

foodstuff	*Nahrungsmittel*
fortnight	*zwei Wochen*
rented	*gemietet*
exhausted	*erschöpft, todmüde*
pop into	*reinschauen, einen kurzen Besuch abstatten*
raspberry	*Himbeere*
on sale	*zum Verkauf*
package	*verpacken*
porridge	*Haferbrei*
pasteurize	*keimfrei machen*
bottle	*abfüllen*
cold-storage	*Kühlhauslagerung*

warehouse hub	*zentrales Warenhaus*
chilled	*abgekühlt*

109

harvest	*ernten, abernten*
seal	*hermetisch verschließen*
wholesale market	*Großhandelsmarkt*
overseas	*Übersee, Ausland*
branch	*Filiale*
pineapple	*Ananas*
ripening room	*Reifekammer*
freshness	*Frische*
repeatedly	*mehrmals, wiederholt*
inspector	*Qualitätsprüfer(in)*
declare	*feststellen, deklarieren*
ripe	*reif*
lorry driver	*Lastwagenfahrer(in)*
load	*laden, beladen*
critic	*Kritiker(in)*
plentiful	*reichlich*
smoothly-functioning	*reibungslos funtionierend*
overland	*Überland-, über Land*
executive	*Führungskraft*
strawberry	*Erdbeere*

110

myth	*Mythos* T
evidence	*Beweis; Indiz* T
air-freighted	*als Luftfracht transportiert* T
oversimplified	*zu stark vereinfacht* T
reject	*zurückweisen, ablehnen* T
out of season	*außerhalb der Saison* T
aviation fuel	*Flugbenzin* T
trap	*fangen, einfangen* T
manual labour	*Handarbeit* T
mechanized	*mechanisiert* T
cow muck	*Kuhmist* T
irrigation	*Bewässerung* T
consume	*verbrauchen; verzehren*
unhelpful	*nicht hilfreich*

111

cauliflower	*Blumenkohl*
maize (AE: corn)	*Mais*
pear	*Birne*
noodles (pl.)	*Nudeln*

112

creamy	*sahnig*
beloved	*innigst geliebt*
fission	*Kernspaltung*

UNIT 9

114

seat belt	*Sitzgurt*
get hold of sth	*auftreiben, in die Hände bekommen*

115

visual	*optisch, bildlich*
textual	*textlich, textbezogen*
objective	*sachlich, vorurteilslos*

116

advertising	*Werbung*
intend to	*beabsichtigen, vorhaben etwas zu tun*
controversy	*Meinungsverschieden-heit, Kontroverse*
publicize	*bekannt machen, publizieren*
offensive	*anstößig, beleidigend*
expressionless	*ausdruckslos*
bathing suit	*Badeanzug*
high heels	*Stöckelschuhe*
pin down	*niederhalten, festnageln*
shirtless	*ohne Hemd*
glorify	*verherrlichen*
gang rape	*Gruppenvergewaltigung*
sexual	*sexuell*
fantasy	*Einbildung; Fantasterei*
outrage	*Empörung*
spread	*ausbreiten, verbreiten*
take sth out of circulation	*aus dem Umlauf nehmen*
regret	*bedauern, bereuen*
perceive	*wahrnehmen*
insist on	*bestehen, beharren*
demean	*erniedrigen*
naked	*nackt*
emaciated	*abgemagert, ausgemergelt*
anorexia	*Magersucht, Anorexie*
sufferer	*Leidende(r)*
resemble	*ähneln, ähnlich sein*
concentration camp	*Konzentrationslager*

draw attention to sth	*Aufmerksamkeit auf etwas lenken*
eating disorder	*Essstörung*
code of conduct	*Verhaltenskodex*
exploit	*ausbeuten, ausnutzen*
deplore	*missbilligen; verurteilen*
dying	*sterbend*
praise	*Lob, Belobigung*
support	*Unterstützung*
health ministry	*Gesundheitsministerium*
disturbing	*beunruhigend, aufwühlend*
shoulder	*schultern, auf sich nehmen*
responsibility	*Verantwortung*
interestingly	*interessanterweise*
applaud	*Beifall spenden*
initiative	*Anstoß, Initiative*
culprit	*Täter(in); Schuldige(r)*
drive	*Drang, Aktion*

117

cause a stir	*Staub aufwirbeln, Aufsehen erregen*
acceptable	*annehmbar, passabel*

118

melt	*schmelzen, sich auflösen*
stout	*dunkles Starkbier*
sugar-coated	*überzuckert, dragiert*

119

transparent	*durchsichtig*
adhesive tape, sellotape	*Klebeband*
sticking plaster, elastoplast	*Heftpflaster*
wound	*Wunde*
scratch	*Kratzer*
tissue paper	*Seidenpapier*
handkerchief	*Taschentuch*
kleenex	*Papiertaschentuch*
corresponding	*zugehörig*
strip	*Streifen*
fastener	*Verschluss, Befestigung*
velcro	*Klettverschluss, Klettband*
ballpoint pen	*Kugelschreiber*
billboard	*Anschlagtafel, Reklame-fläche*

lick	*lecken, ablecken*
intently	*aufmerksam, bedacht*
wag	*wedeln*
tail	*Schwanz*

120

wristwatch	*Armbanduhr*
Satnav	*Navi*
shaving foam	*Rasierschaum*
air freshener	*Raumspray*
cleanser	*Reinigungsmittel*
towel	*Handtuch*
eye-catching	*auffällig*
sensitive	*empfindlich, feinfühlig*
laboratory-tested	*laborgeprüft*
space-saving	*platzsparend, raum-sparend*
luxurious	*luxuriös, opulent*
fashionable	*elegant, modisch*
durable	*dauerhaft, langlebig*
portable	*tragbar*
versatile	*vielseitig*
low-maintenance	*pflegeleicht, wartungs-arm*
sinful	*sündhaft*

121

target group	*Zielgruppe*
award	*prämieren*
understandable	*verständlich*

122

shower curtain	*Duschvorhang*
liquid soap	*Flüssigseife*
sanitary towel	*Damenbinde*
razor blade	*Rasierklinge*
mouthwash	*Mundwasser*
egg timer	*Eieruhr*
tablecloth	*Tischdecke*
vertical, vertically	*senkrecht*

123

aubergine (BE), eggplant (AE)	*Aubergine* **T**
quicksand	*Treibsand* **T**
guinea pig	*Meerschweinchen* **T**
grocer	*Lebensmittelhändler* **T**
make amends	*entschädigen, wieder-gutmachen* **T**
preacher	*Prediger(in)* **T**

humanitarian	*Philanthrop* **T**
recite	*vortragen, aufsagen* **T**
recital	*Vortrag, Liederabend* **T**
ship	*ausliefern, versenden* **T**
driveway	*Auffahrt* **T**
parkway (AE)	*Bundesstraße* **T**
slim	*knapp, schmal* **T**
wise guy	*Klugscheißer* **T**
lunacy	*Wahnsinn* **T**
minced meat	*Hackfleisch*
pine tree	*Pinie*
amend	*berichtigen, verbessern*
laughable	*lächerlich*

124

cuddly	*kuschelig*
juicy	*saftig*
long-lasting	*dauerhaft; lang-andauernd*
waterproof	*wasserdicht*
slipper	*Latsche*
kitten	*Kätzchen*

UNIT 10

125

indigenous	*einheimisch*
residence permit	*Aufenthalts-genehmigung*

126

medieval	*mittelalterlich*
blacksmith	*Hufschmied, Grob-schmied*
roofer	*Dachdecker(in)*
miller	*Müller(in)*
flint	*Feuerstein, Flint*
amber	*Bernstein*
peddler	*Hausierer(in)*
coloured	*bunt, farbig*
ribbon	*Band, Bändel*
thread	*Faden*
needle	*Nadel*
critical	*entscheidend*
prosper	*wachsen und gedeihen*
navigable	*schiffbar, befahrbar*
joint-stock company	*Aktiengesellschaft*
stock market	*Börse*
maximization	*Maximierung*
manufactured products	*industriegefertigte Güter*

porcelain	Porzellan		**130**	
wealth	Reichtum, Vermögen		globe	Weltkugel
relations	Beziehungen, Verhältnisse		goods	Waren, Güter
			commonplace	gewöhnlich
mutual	gegenseitig, gemeinsam		tidal wave	Flutwelle
home grown	im eigenen Land entstanden		**sweep**	fegen, rauschen
			competitive	konkurrenzfähig, wettbewerbsfähig
127			inherent, inherently	inhärent
customer base	Kundenstamm		despotic	despotisch, tyrannisch
few	wenige		**rule**	herrschen, beherrschen
restriction	Beschränkung, Einschränkung		**flourish**	gedeihen, aufblühen
			tax avoidance	Steuervermeidung
savage	grausam, brutal		closure	Betriebsstilllegung
dominate	beherrschen		opponent	Gegner(in)
deregulation	Entregulierung, Abschaffung von beschränkenden Bestimmungen		accountability	Verantwortlichkeit, Haftung
			deliberate, deliberately	absichtlich, bedacht
outsourcing	Ausgliederung von Betriebsfunktionen		**overpower**	überwältigen, bezwingen
			accuse	anklagen
128			**pass sth off as**	ausgeben (etwas als ... übergeben)
distant	fern		colonialist designs	Kolonialambitionen
faraway	fern		socialism	Sozialismus
desire	Sehnsucht		communism	Kommunismus
longing	Sehnsucht		destruction	Zerstörung; Vernichtung
urge	Drang, Antrieb		impediment	Behinderung, Hindernis
itchy feet	Wanderlust			
curious	neugierig		**131**	
satisfy	befriedigen		investment	Investition
			inequality	Ungleichheit
129			contagious	ansteckend
cocoa bean	Kakaobohne 🅣		HIV = Human Immuno- deficiency Virus disease	Humane Immun- schwächekrankheit
modernize	erneuern, modernisieren 🅣		AIDS = Acquired Immune Deficiency Syndrome	erworbenes Immun- mangelsyndrom
decent	anständig 🅣			
slave	Sklave, Sklavin 🅣			
guilt	Schuld 🅣			
two-edged	zweischneidig 🅣		remote	entfernt
sword	Schwert 🅣		minor	gering, unbedeutend
scruple	Skrupel, Bedenken 🅣		beneficial	förderlich, positiv
frighten	erschrecken, verängstigen 🅣		intermingling	Vermischung
			speedy	flott, schnell
perspective	Blickwinkel		exploitation	Ausbeutung, Ausbeuterei
participant	Beteiligte(r); Teil-nehmer(in)		inhumane	unmenschlich
clarify	aufklären, verdeutlichen			

mismanage	*misswirtschaften, schlecht verwalten*
regulate	*regeln, regulieren*
enforce	*durchsetzen*
on-going	*gegenwärtig*

132

document	*Urkunde, Dokument*
potential	*eventuell, möglich*
qualify	*qualifizieren*
citizenship	*Staatsbürgerschaft*
eligible	*geeignet, berechtigt*
skilled worker	*Facharbeiter(in)*
register	*anmelden, eintragen*
stated	*angegeben*
spouse	*Ehepartner(in)*
approve	*genehmigen, befürworten*
deny	*ablehnen, abschlagen*
notification	*Mitteilung, schriftliche Benachrichtigung*

133

admission	*Eintritt, Zulassung*
asylee (AE)	*Asylsuchende(r)*
retire	*zurückziehen (sich aus dem Berufsleben ...), in Rente gehen*
swearing-in	*Vereidigung*
oath	*Eid*
allegiance	*Treue*
official ceremony	*Festakt*

134

contractor	*Unternehmer(in)*
vendor	*Verkäufer(in); Zwischen-händler(in); Lieferant*
conduct	*Handlungsweise, Verhalten*
unprecedented	*beispiellos*
praise	*loben, anpreisen*
pioneer work	*Pionierarbeit*
ethics	*Ethik*
supplier	*Zulieferbetrieb*
fulfill	*erfüllen (eine Be-dingung), ableisten*
hazardous	*gefährlich*
victor	*Sieger(in)*
unheard of	*unerhört, gänzlich unbekannt*

comply with	*einhalten, befolgen*

135

filthy	*dreckig*
derelict	*verfallen, herunter-gekommen*
hand-stitched	*handgenäht*
unauthorized	*unberechtigt, unbefugt*
garment	*Kleidungsstück*
prohibit	*verbieten, untersagen*
violation	*Nichteinhaltung; Vertragsverletzung*

136

iron	*Eisen*
horseshoe	*Hufeisen*
organism	*Organismus*
vicious	*bösartig*

UNIT 11

137

misunderstanding	*Missverständnis*
stereotype	*Klischeevorstellung*

138

ambassador	*Botschafter(in)*
pancake	*Pfannkuchen*
curd	*Quark, Topfen*
dumpling	*Kloß, Knödel*
cinnamon	*Zimt*
bun	*Brötchen*
walnut	*Walnuss*

139

lecturer	*Dozent(in)*
mix	*Mischung, Gemisch*
tempt	*verlocken, verleiten*
cherry	*Kirsche*
scone	*brötchenartiges Gebäck*
sausage roll	*Würstchenrolle* 🅣
roast veal	*gebratenes Kalbsfleisch* 🅣
poultry	*Geflügel* 🅣
chop	*zerhacken* 🅣
mince	*durchdrehen, fein hacken* 🅣
teaspoonful	*Teelöffel ... (Maßeinheit)* 🅣
powdered	*gemahlen; gepulvert* 🅣
pepper	*Pfeffer* 🅣

stock	*Brühe* 🅣	chapatti	*dünner Fladen aus Weizenmehl*
pan	*Topf* 🅣	turnover	*Absatz*
thicken	*eindicken* 🅣	just reward	*gerechter Lohn*
flour	*Mehl* 🅣	**honour**	*ehren, beehren*
stir	*umrühren* 🅣	reluctant	*widerwillig, zurückhaltend*
coat	*bedecken, überzehen* 🅣		
breadcrumbs	*Paniermehl* 🅣	feature article	*Sonderbeitrag*
fry	*in der Pfanne braten* 🅣		
puff pastry	*Blätterteig* 🅣		

141

rags (pl.)	*Lumpen, Klamotten*
riches (pl.)	*Reichtümer*
rags-to-riches story	*Geschichte vom Tellerwäscher, der zum Millionär wurde*
arouse	*entfachen, hervorrufen*
colloquial (coll.)	*umgangssprachlich (ugs.)*
idiom	*Redensart, Spracheigentümlichkeit*

Continued from first column:

pinch together	*zusammenzwicken* 🅣
brush	*bepinseln* 🅣
bake	*backen* 🅣
oven	*Backofen* 🅣

140

fairy tale	*Märchen*
penniless	*mittellos*
generation	*Menschenalter*
colonial times	*Kolonialzeiten*
unwelcome	*unwillkommen, unlieb*
militant	*kämpferisch, streitbar*
nationalism	*Nationalismus*
Legend has it that ...	*Nach der Legende ...*
life insurance policy	*Lebensversicherungspolice*
street sweeper	*Straßenkehrer*
samosa	*frittierte Teigtasche gefüllt mit Gemüse oder Fleischbrät*
jalebi	*indische Süßspeise*
kulfi	*indische Eisspezialität*
tiny	*winzig*
subsequent	*später*
branch out	*verzweigen (sich)*
chutney	*Zubereitung aus Früchten und Gewürzen*
pickles	*eingelegtes Gemüse*
flood in	*einströmen*
racial	*Rassen-, rassisch*
harassment	*Bedrohung, Schikane*
turn sb out of	*hinauswerfen*
on the move	*in Bewegung*
site	*Standort*
food processing	*Lebensmittelverarbeitung*
scattered	*verstreut*
takeover	*Übernahme*
supply	*beliefern*
pappadum, papadam	*dünner frittierte Fladen aus Linsenmehl*

142

hotelier	*Hotelbesitzer(in)*
pub landlord	*Gastwirt(in)*
shopkeeper	*Geschäftsinhaber(in)*
wink at sb	*zublinzeln*
nod	*nicken, zunicken*
misinterpret	*missdeuten, falsch auffassen*
pat on the back	*Schulterklopfen, Klaps*
gesture	*Geste, Handbewegung*
condescension	*Herablassung*
contempt	*Geringschätzung, Verachtung*
maple leaf	*Ahornblatt*
badge	*Abzeichen*
tear off	*abreißen*
arrogant	*überheblich*
loudmouthed	*großmäulig*
opinionated	*rechthaberisch*
surname	*Nachname* 🅣
shorten	*abkürzen, verkürzen* 🅣
host country	*Gastgeberland, Aufnahmestaat* 🅣
mainland	*Festland* 🅣
assimilate	*anpassen (sich), angleichen (sich)* 🅣
patriotism	*Patriotismus* 🅣

143

come of age	*volljährig / mündig werden*
unsuitable	*ungeeignet*
conversion	*Bekehrung*
prime minister	*Premierminister(in)*
baptise	*taufen*
prejudice	*Vorurteil*
aristocratic	*adlig, aristokratisch*

144

coarse(ly)	*grob*
unsalted	*ungesalzen*
peeled	*geschält*
steamed	*gedämpft, gedünstet*
diced	*gewürfelt*
pinch of	*Prise*
parsley	*Petersilie*
shortcrust pastry	*Mürbeteig*
bracket	*Klammer*
crisp	*knusprig, kross*
leek	*Lauch, Porree*
seasoning	*Würze (meist Pfeffer und Salz)*
thorough(ly)	*gründlich*
heat	*erhitzen*
moisten	*anfeuchten, befeuchten*
tart tin	*Backblech mit Mulden*
line	*auslegen*
shallow	*flach*
greased	*gefettet*

145

librarian	*Bibliothekar(in)*
sweets	*Bonbons*

UNIT 12

148

work experience	*Praktikum*
tourism	*Tourismus*
accommodation	*Unterbringung, Unterkunft*
schedule	*einplanen, (zeitlich) festsetzen* Ⓣ
book	*buchen, reservieren* Ⓣ
soft drink	*alkoholfreies Getränk* Ⓣ
catering service	*Verpflegungsdienst* Ⓣ

149

greeting	*Begrüßung*
Best regards	*mit besten / freundlichen Grüßen*
additional	*zusätzlich*
confirmation	*Bestätigung*

150

restored	*wiederhergestellt, renoviert*
spacious	*geräumig*
en suite facilities	*Zimmer mit Bad*
split	*aufteilen*
fireplace	*Kamin, offene Feuerstelle*
dressing room	*Ankleideraum*
four-poster bed	*Himmelbett*

151

comfort	*Bequemlichkeit*
iron	*Bügeleisen*
ironing board	*Bügelbrett*
on the rocks	*mit Eis*
amenity	*Annehmlichkeit*
bathrobe	*Bademantel*
safe	*Tresor, Safe*
trouser press	*Hosenspanner*
work out	*trainieren*
gym (gymnasium)	*Turnhalle, Fitnessstudio*

152

cooperation	*Zusammenarbeit*
accessible	*erreichbar, zugänglich*
cuisine	*Kochkunst*
dish	*Gericht*
USP (Unique Selling Point)	*einmaliges Verkaufsargument*

153

dot	*Punkt*
booking service	*Reservierungsdienst*
fee	*Gebühr, Honorar*
The line is engaged.	*Die Leitung ist besetzt.*
speak up	*lauter sprechen*
I'm putting you through now.	*Ich verbinde Sie jetzt.*
Please hold the line.	*Bitte am Apparat bleiben.*
get back to sb (about sth)	*jmdm antworten*

reconstruct	*wiederherstellen, wieder aufbauen*

154
doubts (pl.) — *Zweifel*

155
appeal (to) — *ansprechen, Anklang finden*
upmarket — *gehoben, vornehm*
decorated — *verziert; mit Möbel ausgestattet, eingerichtet*

play it safe — *auf Nummer Sicher gehen*

157
texting — *eine SMS-Nachricht schreiben*
provisional — *provisorisch*
draft — *Entwurf*
be of assistance (to sb.) — *(jmdm.) helfen*

English A–Z word list

Diese Liste enthält alle Wörter in alphabetischer Reihenfolge. Die Wörter, die zum Grundwortschatz gehören (siehe Basic word list), sind hier nicht aufgeführt.
Die Zahl am rechten Rand gibt die Seitenzahl an.
Die englischen **Verben** sind fett markiert.
🅣 = Das Wort befindet sich im Transkript der Hörverständnistext.

a great deal *eine ganze Menge, sehr viel* 78

a whole bunch of ... *eine ganze Menge ...* 🅣 70

abbreviation *Abkürzung* 47

ability *Fähigkeit* 92

abortion *Abtreibung; Schwangerschaftsabbruch* 15

above all *vor allem* 100

absolute must *absolutes Muss* 68

abundant *ergiebig, reichlich* 105

abuse *Missbrauch* 38

accelerate *(sich) beschleunigen* 65

accept *annehmen* 28

acceptable *annehmbar, passabel* 117

access *Zugang; Eintritt* 11

access sth *auf etwas zugreifen* 52

accessible *erreichbar, zugänglich* 152

accidentally *versehentlich* 76

accommodation *Unterbringung, Unterkunft* 148

accomplishment *Errungenschaft* 🅣 96

according to *zufolge, gemäß; in Anlehnung an* 39

accordingly *entsprechend* 68

account *Bericht; Konto* 29

accountability *Verantwortlichkeit, Haftung* 130

accountable *haftbar, verantwortlich* 54

accountancy *Buchführung, Buchhaltung* 41

accumulated *angesammelt* 78

accuse *anklagen* 130

achieve sth *etwas erreichen / erzielen* 65

achievement *Errungenschaft; Leistung* 27

acquaintance *Bekannte(r); Bekanntschaft* 52

acquire *erwerben, anschaffen* 🅣 100

acronym *Kürzel, Kurzwort* 51

activate *betätigen, bedienen* 🅣 75

addict *Suchtkranke(r)* 50

addiction *Sucht* 94

addition *Ergänzung* 79

additional *zusätzlich* 149

addressee *Adressat(in)* 102

adhesive tape, sellotape *Klebeband* 119

adjust *einstellen* 76

administration *Verwaltung* 24

admire *bewundern, hochschätzen* 79

admission *Eintritt, Zulassung* 133

admit *zugeben, eingestehen* 43

admitted *zugelassen* 11

adolescence *Jugend; Entwicklungsjahre* 17

adolescent *Jugendliche(r)* 92

adopt *annehmen, adoptieren* 50

adopter *Adoptierende(r)* 104

adulterer *Ehebrecher* 10

advent *Ankunft; Beginn* 50

advertiser *Anzeigenkunde, Werbeagentur* 67

advertising *Werbung* 116

advertising copy *Anzeigentext* 50

advertising slogan *Werbespruch* 96

advisable *ratsam, empfehlenswert* 11

aerodynamics (sing.) *Aerodynamik* 80

affect sb / sth *sich auf jmn / etwas auswirken; jmdn / etwas beeinflussen* 54

afford *leisten können, erschwingen* 89

agenda *Tagesordnung* 68

aggressive *angriffslustig, streitsüchtig* 43

aging *alternd* 38

aging *alternd* 🅣 96

agreement *Einigung, Zustimmung; Vereinbarung* 43

agribusiness *Agrarindustrie* 104

AIDS (Acquired Immune Deficiency Syndrome) *erworbenes Immunmangelsyndrom* 131

air freshener *Raumspray* 120

air sth *belüften, auslüften, durchlüften, entlüften* 74

air-freighted *als Luftfracht transportiert* 🅣 110

album *Album; Langspielplatte* 14

alert *alarmieren, warnen* 76

allegiance *Treue* 133

allocate *anweisen, zuweisen* 68

Alsatian *Deutscher Schäferhund* 40

ambassador *Botschafter(in)* 138

amber *Bernstein* 126

amend *berichtigen, verbessern* 123

amenity *Annehmlichkeit* 151

amid *inmitten, mitten drin* 10

amount *Betrag; Menge* 90

ample *ausreichend, üppig* Ⓣ 100

analyse *kritisch untersuchen, auswerten* 31

ankle *Fußknöchel* 97

announce (itself) *sich ankündigen* Ⓣ 56

annual sales *Jahresumsatz* 66

anorexia *Anorexie, Magersucht* 116

answerphone *Anrufbeantworter* 76

antibiotics **Antibiotika** 104

anxiety, anxieties *Angst, Ängste* 23

apology *Entschuldigung* 102

appeal *ansprechen, Anklang finden* 155

appearance *Aussehen* 105

appendix *Blinddarm, Wurmfortsatz* 97

appendix (pl.) appendices *Anhang* 16

applaud *akklamieren, Beifall spenden* 116

appliance *Gerät, Apparat* 89

applicant *Antragsteller(in); Stellenbewerber(in)* 12

applied science *angewandte Naturwissenschaft* 25

appoint sb *jmdn benennen / berufen* 68

appreciate sth *etwas schätzen, für etwas dankbar sein* 27

approach *Ansatz, Vorgehen* 54

approach (sth / sb) *sich (jmdm / etwas) nähern, heranrücken* 72

appropriately *geeignet, angemessen* 68

approve *genehmigen, befürworten* 132

approximately *ungefähr* Ⓣ 56

aristocratic *adelig, aristokratisch* 143

armchair *Armsessel, Polstersessel* Ⓣ 11

arouse *entfachen, hervorrufen* 141

arrogant *überheblich* 142

as a matter of fact *tatsächlich, in der Tat* 30

asap (as soon as possible) *sobald als möglich* 30

ashes (pl.) *Asche, Verbrennungsrückstände* 96

ashtray *Aschenbecher* Ⓣ 70

assemble *(sich) versammeln* 10

assert *behaupten (, dass …); geltend machen* 54

assess *bewerten, einschätzen* 21

assign *anweisen; jmdm etwas auftragen* 78

assimilate *anpassen (sich), angleichen (sich)* Ⓣ 142

assist (with) *helfen, behilflich sein* 83

associate with *mit etwas Umgang pflegen* Ⓣ 56

assume *vermuten, voraussetzen* 102

assumption *Annahme; Prämisse* 39

astonishing *erstaunlich* 79

asylee (AE) *Asylsuchende(r)* 133

at hand *zu Hand, greifbar* 12

at random *zufällig, willkürlich, stichprobenartig* 56

athlete *Athlet(in)* 22

atmosphere *Stimmung* 11

attach to *befestigen (an etwas), anhängen; anlegen* 100

attached *angeschlossen; angebaut; beigefügt* 17

attend *besuchen, beiwohnen* 8

attendee *Anwesende(r), Teilnehmer(in)* 68

aubergine (BE), eggplant (AE) *Aubergine* Ⓣ 123

auction *Versteigerung* 66

available *erhältlich, verfügbar; vorliegend* 24

avarice *Gier, Habsucht* 97

avenger *Rächer(in)* 10

average (out) *den Durchschnitt ermitteln* 64

aviation fuel *Flugbenzin* Ⓣ 110

avoid *vermeiden* 35

award *prämieren* 121

aware *bewusst* 24

awning *Markise* Ⓣ 75

B.A. (Bachelor of Arts) *akademischer Grad* 27

backyard (AE) *Hinterhof, Garten hinter dem Haus* 76

badge *Abzeichen* 142

bake *backen* Ⓣ 139

baked *gebacken* 23

baker *Bäcker(in)* Ⓣ 34

bakery *Bäckerei* 34

balance *Ausgleich, Gleichgewicht* 65

balcony *Balkon* 107

ballpoint pen *Kugelschreiber* 119

bankruptcy *Bankrott, Konkurs, Insolvenz* 62

baptise *taufen* 143

bar *Tresen; Theke; Ausschank; Stange* Ⓣ 11

bathing suit *Badeanzug* 116

bathrobe *Bademantel* 151

be appointed *ernannt werden* 10

be ashamed of oneself *sich schämen* 86

be fond of sb / sth *gernhaben (jmdn. / etwas)* 102

be of assistance (to sb.) *(jmdm.) helfen* 157

be short on / of sth *knapp an etwas sein* 76

be willing to do sth. *bereit sein, etwas zu tun* 8

bean *Bohne* 23

belief *Glaube, Überzeugung* 49

beloved *innigst geliebt* 112

beneficial *förderlich, positiv* 131

benefit *Nutzen; Vorteil* 47

Best regards *mit besten / freundlichen Grüßen* 149

Biblical *Bibel-; biblisch* 50

billboard *Anschlagtafel, Reklamefläche* 119

birch *Birke* 8

blacksmith *Hufschmied, Grobschmied* 126

bladder *Blase* 20

blade *Klinge* 82

blame sb (for) *jmdm die Schuld an etwas geben, jmdm etwas vorwerfen* 50

blank spot *Leerstelle* 79

blend (of) *Gemisch, Verschnitt* 🅣 100

boardroom *Sitzungssaal* 🅣 100

Body Mass Index *Körpermassenzahl* 93

book *buchen, reservieren* 🅣 148

booking *Reservierung* 11

booking service *Reservierungsdienst* 153

bookkeeping *Buchführung* 30

bookstore (AE) *Buchhandlung* 66

boom *Aufschwung, Konjunktur* 62

boost *ankurbeln; steigern* 25

bottle *abfüllen* 108

bottled water *Trinkwasser in Flaschen* 100

boundary *Abgrenzung, Grundstücksgrenze* 82

bra *Büstenhalter, BH* 20

brace *Zahnspange* 89

bracket *Klammer* 144

brake fluid *Bremsflüssigkeit* 20

branch *Verzweigung* 39

branch *Filiale* 109

branch out *verzweigen (sich)* 140

bread roll *Brötchen* 🅣 34

breadcrumbs *Paniermehl* 🅣 139

break down *auflösen, entgegenwirken* 43

break up (broke, broken) *auseinanderbrechen; scheitern* 29

breakneck speed *halsbrecherische Geschwindigkeit* 66

breathless *atemlos* 10

brief *kurz* 68

brighten up *aufhellen; aufmuntern* 🅣 100

broad *breit; umfassend* 92

broadcast *senden, etwas durch Rundfunk verbreiten* 🅣 56

broadcasting *Rundfunk* 60

broaden *verbreiten; (sich) ausweiten* 79

browse *im Internet browsen / surfen, etwas durchstöbern* 13

brush *bepinseln* 🅣 139

budget *Etat, Finanzplan* 52

built-in *eingebaut* 69

bulletin board *Anschlagtafel, schwarzes Brett* 25

bun *Brötchen* 138

burglar *Einbrecher(in)* 76

bury *begraben, vergraben, eingraben* 82

busy *beschäftigt; vielbefahren* 🅣 37

buy out *eine Mehrheit des Aktienkapitals aufkaufen* 66

buzzword *Modewort; abgedroschene Phrase* 66

call a meeting *eine Versammlung ansetzen / einberufen* 68

caller *Anrufer(in)* 🅣 37

calm *beruhigen* 89

calorific content *Brennwert* 105

campaign *Aktion, Kampagne* 94

can *konservieren* 107

cancer *Krebs* 44

canned (soups) *Konserven* 25

carbon dioxide (CO$_2$) *Kohlendioxid* 104

carbon footprint *CO$_2$-Fußabdruck* 104

cardiac arrhythmia *Herzrhythmusstörung* 88

cardiovascular disease *Herz-Kreislauf Erkrankung* 92

carefully-screened *sorgfältig überprüft* 67

caretaker *Hausmeister(in)* 40

cargo *Fracht, Ladung* 61

caring *fürsorglich, mitfühlend* 29

carpet *Teppich* 🅣 11

cartoon *Karikatur* 99

cast out *verstoßen, austreiben, vertreiben* 38

catastrophe *Katastrophe, Unglück* 90

cater for sb *jmdn beliefern / versorgen; die besonderen Bedürfnisse einer Gruppe berücksichtigen* 41

catering service *Verpflegungsdienst* 🅣 148

cauliflower *Blumenkohl* 111

cause a stir *Staub aufwirbeln, Aufsehen erregen* 117

caution *Vorsicht, Umsicht* 49

cautious *behutsam, zurückhaltend, vorsichtig* 29

ceiling fan *Deckenventilator* 11

celebration *Feier, Freudenfest* 38

censor *zensieren* 55

Census Bureau *Behörde für Bevölkerungsstatistik* 90

CEO (Chief Executive Officer) *Generaldirektor(in)* 28

chain *Kette* 80

chairman, chairperson *Vorsitzender, Vorstandsvorsitzende(r)* 68

challenge *Herausforderung* 38

challenging *anspruchsvoll, herausfordernd* 92

chapatti *dünner Fladen aus Weizenmehl* 140

character *Zeichen; Charakter* 51

characteristics (pl.) *Besonder-heiten, Eigenschaften* 78

characterize *charakterisieren* 37

charge (battery) *aufladen* 80

charge (price) *berechnen, (Preis) verlangen* 102

charging station *Ladestation* 80

cheerful *fröhlich, heiter* 29

cheque *Scheck* 67

cherry *Kirsche* 139

chest *Brust, Brustkorb* 88

childcare *Kinderbetreuung* 64

chilled *abgekühlt* 108

chop *zerhacken* 🔊 139

chores (pl.) *Haushaltspflichten* 76

church service *Gottesdienst* 8

chutney *Zubereitung aus Früchten und Gewürzen* 140

cinnamon *Zimt* 138

citizen *Bürger(in)* 39

Citizen's Advice Bureau *Bürgerberatungsdienst* 74

citizenship *Staatsbürgerschaft* 132

civil service *öffentlicher Dienst / Verwaltung* 63

claim *behaupten, beteuern* 49

clarify *aufklären, verdeutlichen* 129

cleaning liquid *Reinigungs-flüssigkeit* 102

cleanser *Reinigungsmittel* 120

client *Auftraggeber(in); Mandant(in)* 54

climate change *Klimawandel* 🔊 100

cloakroom *Garderobe* 🔊 37

clog *verstopfen* 100

close down *aufgeben, (ein Geschäft) schließen* 60

closure *Betriebsstilllegung* 130

clunk against sth *mit einem dumpfen Geräusch gegen etwas schlagen; gegen etwas klappern* 16

co-worker *Mitarbeiter(in), Kollege, Kollegin* 69

coarse(ly) *grob* 144

coat *bedecken, überziehen* 🔊 139

cocoa bean *Kakaobohne* 🔊 129

code of conduct *Verhaltens-kodex* 116

cognitive skill *kognitive Fähigkeit* 55

cold-storage *Kühlhaus-lagerung* 108

collapse *Zusammenbruch; Kurssturz* 66

colloquial (coll.) *umgangs-sprachlich (ugs.)* 141

colonial times *Kolonialzeiten* 140

colonialist designs *Kolonial-ambitionen* 130

color (AE) *Farbe* 78

coloured *bunt, farbig* 126

combine *verbinden, zusammenlegen* 80

come of age *volljährig / mündig werden* 143

Come off it. *Ach was!, Jetzt mach mal halblang!* 102

comfort *Bequemlichkeit* 151

command *Befehl* 76

commentator *Bericht-erstatter(in), Kommen-tator(in)* 26

commercial *Werbesendung* 92

commission sth *in Auftrag geben* 64

commodity *Handelsware* 🔊 100

common good *Allgemeinwohl* 🔊 100

commonplace *gewöhnlich* 130

Commonwealth *Gemeinschaft der Länder des ehemaligen Britischen Weltreichs* 45

communism *Kommunismus* 130

compete with sb *jmdm Konkurrenz machen; sich mit jmdm messen* 66

competence *Befähigung, Können; Sachkunde* 12

competitive *konkurrenzfähig, wettbewerbsfähig* 130

complain about sb / sth *sich über jmdn / etwas beklagen, sich beschweren* 16

complaint *Beschwerde* 82

complexity *Komplexität* 52

comply with *einhalten, befolgen* 134

component *Bestandteil* 26

comprehension *Verständnis* 77

compressed *komprimiert, zusammengedrückt* 65

compromising *kompro-mittierend* 54

concentration camp *KZ (Konzentrationslager)* 116

concept *Auffassung, Konzept* 52

concern *Sorge, Besorgnis* 104

concerned *betroffen* 68

conclusion *Feststellung, Schlussfolgerung, Fazit* 63

condemn *verurteilen; verdammen* 88

condense *verdichten; kondensieren* 51

condescension *Herablassung* 142

conduct *durchführen, aus-führen, vornehmen* 27

conduct *Handlungsweise, Verhalten* 134

conference *Tagung, Konferenz* 28

confidential *vertraulich* 68

confined *eingeschlossen* 69

confirmation *Bestätigung* 149

conform to sth *sich an etwas anpassen* 37

consensus *Konsens* 92

consequence *Folge, Auswirkung* 38

consider *berücksichtigen* 43

considerably *beträchtlich, erheblich* 102

consist of *aus etwas bestehen, sich aus etwas zusammensetzen* 80

conspicuous *auffällig, auffallend* 11

constant *ständig, andauernd* 92

construction engineer *Bauingenieur(in)* 🔊 75

constructive(ly) *konstruktiv* 43

consume *verbrauchen; verzehren* 110

consumer *Verbraucher, Konsument(in)* 60

consumption *Verbrauch, Konsum* 62

contagious *ansteckend* 131

contain *enthalten, beinhalten* 52

contaminant *Schadstoff, Verunreinigung* 100

contaminated *verunreinigt, belastet* 100

contempt *Geringschätzung, Verachtung* 142

contest *Wettbewerb* 78

continuously *unaufhörlich* 66

contractor *Unternehmer(in)* 134

contrast *gegenüberstellen, kontrastieren* 45

contribute *beisteuern, mitwirken* 38

contributing factor *entscheidender Faktor* 38

contribution *Beitrag* 68

controversial *umstritten, kontrovers* 64

controversy *Meinungsverschiedenheit, Kontroverse* 116

convenience *Annehmlichkeit, Zweckmäßigkeit* 🔊 100

convenient *zweckmäßig, praktisch* 🔊 100

conventional *gebräuchlich, herkömmlich* 🔊 56

conversion *Bekehrung* 143

convert sth into sth *etwas in etwas umwandeln / verwandeln* 61

convey *überbringen, übermitteln* 95

convinced *überzeugt* 66

cool down *sich beruhigen* 42

cooperation *Zusammenarbeit* 152

coordinate *koordinieren, abstimmen* 79

cope (with sth) *zurechtkommen, mit etwas fertigwerden* 52

core *Kern* 65

corporate client *Firmenkunde* 67

corporation *Unternehmen* 69

corpulence *Dickleibigkeit, Körperfülle* 97

correlation *Wechselbeziehung, Übereinstimmung* 79

corresponding *zugehörig* 119

cost-effective *kostengünstig, wirtschaftlich* 67

cosy *behaglich, gemütlich* 69

council *Gemeinderat* 88

countryside *die Landschaft, Natur* 🔊 34

cover *bedecken, zudecken* 83

covering letter *Begleitbrief, Bewerbungsschreiben* 24

cow muck *Kuhmist* 🔊 110

creamy *sahnig* 112

creativity *Einfallsreichtum, Kreativität* 65

crisp *knusprig, kross* 144

criterion, (pl.) criteria *Bewertungsgrundlage, Kriterium* 31

critic *Kritiker(in)* 109

critical *entscheidend* 126

crop; crops *Ernte; Gesamternte* 71

croupier *Kasinoangestellte(r)* 15

crown *Krone* 66

crucial *entscheidend, ausschlaggebend* 100

crude oil *Rohöl* 61

cubicle *Zelle, Nische* 69

cuddly *kuschelig* 124

cuisine *Kochkunst* 152

culprit *Täter(in); Schuldige(r)* 116

cumulative *kumulativ, sich anhäufend* 10

curd *Quark* 138

cure *heilen* 44

cure *Heilmittel, Heilung* 🔊 96

curious *neugierig* 128

current *aktuell, gegenwärtig* 38

curriculum vitae (CV) *Lebenslauf* 7

customer base *Kundenstamm* 127

cut *Kürzung, Senkung* 92

cut sth to ribbons *in Streifen schneiden, zerschneiden* 14

cutting height *Schnitthöhe* 83

cybercommerce *Internet-Handel* 66

cylinder *Zylinder* 100

dairy *Milchprodukte* 103

dam *Staudamm* 🔊 100

date back *(zeitlich) zurückliegen* 57

dead *die Toten* 10

dead end *Sackgasse* 80

debate *Debatte* 104

debut *erstes Auftreten, Debüt* 67

decade *Jahrzehnt, Dekade* 38

decent *anständig* 🔊 129

declare *feststellen, deklarieren* 109

decline *fallen, abfallen, abnehmen* 62

declining *rückläufig* 50

decorated *(hier) eingerichtet, mit Möbel ausgestattet* 155

decrease *Abnahme, Verminderung* 62

deepen *vertiefen* 79

define *definieren; genau bestimmen* 56

definite *bestimmt* 10

defuse *entschärfen* 43

delete *auslöschen, tilgen, ausstreichen* 54

deliberate, deliberately *bedacht, absichtlich* 130

delicate(ly) *feinfühlig* 79

delicious *appetitlich, wohl-schmeckend* 102

deliver *liefern, austragen* 40

delivery *Auslieferung* 66

demand *verlangen; beanspruchen* 54

demand *Nachfrage; Forderung* 105

demean *erniedrigen* 116

demise *Untergang; Ableben* 54

demographic *bevölkerungs-statistisch* 35

demonstrate *beweisen, darstellen* 100

density *Dichte* 38

dental assistant *Zahnarzthelfer(in)* 89

dental care *Zahnpflege* 89

deny *ablehnen, abschlagen* 132

depend on (sb./sth) *abhängen (von jmdm/etwas)* 🔵 75

dependence (on) *Abhängigkeit (von), Anlehnung (an)* 47

depending on *abhängig von* 24

deplore *missbilligen; verurteilen* 116

depressed *deprimiert, nieder-geschlagen* 69

depressing *bedrückend, deprimierend* 29

depression *Konjunkturtief* 62

deregulation *Entregulierung, Abschaffung von beschrän-kenden Bestimmungen* 127

derelict *verfallen, herunter-gekommen* 135

derive sth by *sich von etwas ableiten* 38

descendant *Nachkomme* 36

descent *Abstammung* 37

deserve *verdienen* 86

desire *Sehnsucht* 128

despair *Verzweiflung* 16

despised *verschmäht, verachtet* 94

despite *trotz; zum Trotz* 50

despotic *despotisch, tyrannisch* 130

destination *Zielort, Reiseziel* 52

destruction *Zerstörung; Vernichtung* 130

detect *erfassen; aufspüren, aufdecken* 82

determine *bestimmen* 61

detrimental *schädlich, abträglich* 54

devastating *verheerend* 10

developing countries *Entwicklungsländer* 100

development *Entwicklung* 25

devise *ersinnen, ausdenken* 102

diabetes *Zuckerkrankheit* 92

diagnose *diagnostizieren, eine Krankheit feststellen* 🔵 96

diarrhoea *Durchfall* 100

diced *gewürfelt* 144

differential *Differenzial-getriebe; Hinterachsgetriebe* 81

diligent *gewissenhaft* 27

diluted *verdünnt* 102

diminished *vermindert* 102

dip *eintauchen* 100

diphtheria *Diphtherie* 100

director *Direktor* 55

directory *Adressenverzeichnis* 67

disability *Arbeitsunfähigkeit, Behinderung* 90

disappear *verschwinden* 83

disappointed *enttäuscht* 17

disappointment *Enttäuschung* 102

discard *Ausschuss* 79

disconnect *abkoppeln (vom Strom); eine Verbindung lösen* 76

disgusting *ekelhaft, widerlich* 94

dish *Gericht* 152

dishonest *unehrlich, verlogen* 102

disinfect *desinfizieren* 101

disinfection *Desinfektion, Desinfizierung* 101

disorganized *chaotisch* 71

disproportionately *über-proportional, unverhält-nismäßig* 92

dispute *Auseinandersetzung, Konflikt* 43

disqualify sb *jmdn. aus-schließen, disqualifizieren* 27

distant *fern* 128

distinct *eindeutig, deutlich* 36

distinguish (between) *unter-scheiden (zwischen)* 107

distribute *verteilen* 68

distribution *Verteilung, Verbreitung* 38

disturbing *beunruhigend, aufwühlend* 116

diverse *unterschiedlich, verschieden* 36

diversity *Verschiedenheit; Mannigfaltigkeit* 37

do a placement *ein Praktikum durchführen* 30

docks (pl.) *Hafenanlage, Hafengebiet* 61

document *Urkunde, Dokument* 132

dominant *beherrschend* 37

dominate *beherrschen* 127

dot *Punkt* 153

doubts (pl.) *Zweifel* 154

downside *Kehrseite, Nachteil* 62

downswing *Abwärtstrend* 62

draft *Entwurf* 157

drained weight *Trocken-gewicht* 102

draught *vom Fass* 🔵 11

draw attention to sth *Aufmerksamkeit auf etwas lenken* 116 dressing room *Ankleideraum* 150

dried goods *Kurzwaren* 107

drill *bohren* 71

drinkable *trinkbar* 100

drive *Drang, Aktion* 116

driveway *Auffahrt* 🅣 123

drown *ertrinken* 11

dry *trocknen, abtrocknen, ausdörren* 107

dry up *austrocknen, vertrocknen* 🅣 100

drying *Trocknung* 75

dump *abkippen, abladen* 🅣 100

dumpling *Kloß, Knödel* 138

durable *haltbar, beständig* 80

durable *dauerhaft, langlebig* 120

duration *Zeitdauer; Laufzeit* 31

duty *Dienst* 10

dweller *Bewohner(in)* 69

dye *Farbstoff, Färbemittel* 106

dying *sterbend* 116

eager *eifrig, arbeitsfreudig* 30

earnest *ernst, ernsthaft* 40

earnings *Einkommen, Einnehmen* 66

eating disorder *Essstörung* 116

ebony *schwarz wie Ebenholz* 44

effect *Wirkung, Auswirkung* 10

effective *wirksam* 68

efficiency *Produktivität, Effizienz* 66

efficient *leistungsfähig* 80

egg timer *Eieruhr* 122

elbow *Ellbogen* 97

elder, elderly *älterer; bejahrt* 38

electrical appliance *Elektrogerät* 74

eligible *geeignet, berechtigt* 132

eliminate *beseitigen, ausmerzen* 49

eliminated *ausgeschieden; beseitigt* 12

elsewhere *anderswo, woanders* 79

emaciated *abgemagert, ausgemergelt* 116

emission *Ausstoß, Abgas* 80

emphasize *betonen* 🅣 96

employment *Beschäftigung; Anstellung* 12

employment agency *Zeitarbeitsvermittlung* 24

empower *befähigen, ermächtigen* 55

en suite facilities *Zimmer mit Bad* 150

enable *ermächtigen, ermöglichen* 67

enclosed *anbei, in der Anlage* 25

encourage *ermuntern, ermutigen* 36

encouragement *Aufmunterung, Ermunterung* 62

end up *(letztendlich) gelangen* 22

energetic *dynamisch, energiegeladen, tatkräftig* 28

enforce *durchsetzen* 131

enjoyment *Vergnügen* 🅣 96

enormously *gewaltig, enorm* 67

enquiry, (AE) inquiry *Anfrage, Erkundigung* 23

ensure *sicherstellen, gewährleisten* 18

enthusiastic *begeistert, schwärmerisch* 29

entire *gesamt, komplett* 54

envisage sth *sich etwas vorstellen* 51

equation *Gleichung* 72

equip *ausstatten, ausrüsten* 🅣 56

eradicate *ausmerzen, löschen* 100

escape *entkommen, flüchten* 36

essay *Aufsatz, Abhandlung* 50

establish *begründen; einrichten* 🅣 56

estate *Anwesen* 76

estate agent *Immobilienmakler* 61

estimate *schätzen, abschätzen* 38

estimate *Schätzung* 92

ethics *Ethik* 134

ethnic *ethnisch* 36

ethylene gas *Kohlenwasserstoffgas (C_2H_4), Ethylen* 106

etiquette *Anstandsregel, Umgangsformen* 11

evaluate *beurteilen, abschätzen, auswerten* 47

evaluator *Gutachter(in)* 79

event sales *Veranstaltungsverkäufe, Demo-Verkäufe* 25

eventually *endlich, letztendlich, schließlich* 105

evidence *Beweis; Indiz* 🅣 110

evil *böse, übel* 10

evolve (into sth) *sich (zu jmdm / etwas) entwickeln* 54

examine *untersuchen, prüfen* 107

except *außer, ausgenommen, mit Ausnahme von* 74

exception *Ausnahme* 102

exchange programme *Austauschprogramm* 8

executive *Führungskraft* 109

exercise book *Schreibheft, Übungsheft* 32

exhaust emission *Abgasausstoß* 82

exhausted *erschöpft, todmüde* 108

exhilarating *berauschend* 10

exit *Ausgang, Ausfahrt* 76

expand *aufgehen, ausweiten, ausdehnen* 62

expanding *sich ausdehnend, stetig wachsend* 24

expansion *Erweiterung, Ausweitung, Wachsen* 62

expectation *Erwartung* 21

expected *erwartet* 89

expenses *Unkosten, Ausgaben, Spesen* 66

experimental model *Versuchs-modell* 78

exploit *ausbeuten, ausnutzen* 116

exploitation *Ausbeutung, Ausbeuterei* 131

expose (to) *aussetzen (jmdn./ etwas)* 101

express speed *Eiltempo* 66

expressionless *ausdruckslos* 116

extended *erweitet, verlängert* 79

extended family *Großfamilie* 38

extensive *umfangreich* 13

extract *entnehmen, gewinnen* 60

eye-catching *auffällig* 120

fabric softener *Weichspüler* 102

face *begegnen* 42

facility *Einrichtung* 24

fail to do sth *es nicht schaffen, etwas zu tun* 12

failure *Misserfolg, Scheitern* 68

fairground ride *Rummelplatz-fahrgeschäft* 10

fairy tale *Märchen* 140

faithful *getreu* 11

fall *Fall, Rückgang* 62

fallout *Konsequenzen, Nach-wirkungen; radioaktiver Niederschlag* 10

familiar *gewohnt, vertraut* 104

fancy *schick, apart* ⓣ 100

fantasy *Einbildung; Fantasterei* 116

faraway *fern* 128

fashionable *elegant, modisch* 120

fastener *Verschluss, Befestigung* 119

father *zeugen* 10

feature article *Sonderbeitrag* 141

federal government *Bundes-regierung* 90

fee *Gebühr, Honorar* 153

fertilizer *Düngemittel* 107

feverish *fieberhaft* ⓣ 100

few *wenige* 127

fiddle about (with sth) *tüfteln* ⓣ 75

file for bankruptcy *Insolvenz-antrag stellen* 66

fill up *auffüllen* 62

filter out *abfiltern* 100

filthy *dreckig* 135

filtration *Filterung* 100

finalize *etwas endgültig be-schließen; fertig machen* 21

finance *finanzieren* 90

financial year *Bilanzjahr, Geschäftsjahr* 66

findings *(Forschungs) Ergebnisse, Resultate* 16

finished goods *Endprodukte, Erzeugnisse, Fertigwaren* 60

fire brigade *Feuerwehr* 76

fireplace *Kamin, offene Feuer-stelle* 150

fishing *Fischerei* 71

fission *Kernspaltung* 112

fist *Faust* 78

fix *Schuss, Fix* 102

flabbergasted *verblüfft, ent-geistert* 50

flavour *Geschmack* ⓣ 11

Flemisch *flämisch* 36

flexibility *Biegsamkeit; Anpassungsfähigkeit* 64

flexible *anpassungsfähig; elastisch, biegsam* 25

flick between *hin und her schalten* 41

flick between *umschalten* ⓣ 56

flighty *unbeständig, flatterhaft* 54

flint *Feuerstein, Flint* 126

flood in *einströmen* 140

flour *Mehl* ⓣ 139

flourish *gedeihen, aufblühen* 130

flow *fließen, strömen* 52

flush *durchspülen; ausspülen* 14

focus on sth *sich auf etwas konzentrieren* 12

food processing *Lebensmittel-verarbeitung* 140

foodstuff *Nahrungsmittel* 108

fool around *herumalbern; sich treiben lassen* 28

for instance *beispielsweise, zum Beispiel* 65

for up to *bis einschließlich* 24

force sb to do sth *jmdn nö-tigen, etwas zu tun* 64, 131

forecast *Voraussage, Prognose* 39

foreclosure *Kündigung einer Hypothek (Bank); gericht-liche Vollstreckungs-erklärung* 63

forestry industry *Holz-wirtschaft* 60

former *ehemalig, früher* 36

formulate *entwerfen, formulieren* 43

fortnight *zwei Wochen* 108

forward *vorwärts* 80

founder *Gründer(in)* 41

four-poster bed *Himmelbett* 150

frequent *häufig, regelmäßig* 76

freshness *Frische* 109

frighten *erschrecken, verängstigen* ⓣ 129

from all walks of life *aus allen Gesellschaftsschichten* 89

fry *in der Pfanne braten* ⓣ 139

fuel *Treibstoff, Brennstoff* 80

fuel cell *Brennstoffzelle* 80

fulfill *erfüllen (eine Beding-ung), ableisten* 134

fulfilled *erfüllt* 28

function room *Veranstaltungs-raum* 11

funded (by) *finanziert (von)* 38

fuss *Getue* 85

gadget *Gerät, technischer Krimskrams* 76

gain *gewinnen; erzielen* 26

gain *Anstieg, Zuwachs* 39

gal *(AE slang) Mädchen* 18

gang rape *Gruppenvergewaltigung* 116

garment *Kleidungsstück* 135

gather *ansammeln, gewinnen* 52

gearbox *Getriebe* 80

gender *Geschlecht* 8

general knowledge *Allgemeinwissen* 30

general office clerk *Bürokauffrau, Bürokaufmann* 31

generate *erwirtschaften, erbringen* 66

generation *Menschenalter* 140

generator *Elektroaggregat, Drehstromgenerator* 80

genre *Kunstgattung* 10

gentle *sanft* ⓣ 96

genuine(ly) *echt, authentisch* 43

geologist *Geologe, Geologin* 61

gesture *Geste, Handbewegung* 142

get back to sb (about sth) *jmdm antworten* 153

get hold of sth *auftreiben, in die Hände bekommen* 114

get in the way *im Wege stehen* 78

get sth across to sb *jmdm etwas vermitteln / verständlich machen* 50

getting started *erste Shritte* 7

giggle *Gekicher* 29

give sth a try *etwas ausprobieren; es auf einen Versuch ankommen lassen* 22

give up *aufgeben* 16

glimpse *flüchtiger Blick* 76

global player *eine Weltfirma, eine weltweit tätige Firma* 25

globe *Weltkugel* 130

glorify *verherrlichen* 116

go for sth *anstreben; sich für etwas entscheiden* 22

go public *Börsengang* 66

go viral *sich wie ein Virus ausbreiten* 54

good deed *gute Tat, Wohltat* 96

goods *Waren, Güter* 130

grab sb by the scruff of the neck *jmdn am Kragen packen* 14

grace *schmücken, zieren* 51

gradient *Gradient; Gefällstrecke* 80

gradually *allmählich* 83

graduate student *Student im Aufbaustudium* 67

grain *Getreide* 60

grant *eine Erlaubnis erteilen; bewilligen, genehmigen* 48

grape *Traube* 105

grasp *begreifen; fassen, auffassen* 52

greased *gefettet* 144

greed *Gier* 88

greenhouse gases *Treibhausgase* 104

greeting *Begrüßung* 149

grid *Rastergitter* 33

grip *greifen, klemmen* 17

grocer *Lebensmittelhändler* ⓣ 123

grocery store (AE) *Lebensmittelladen* 104

groundwater *Grundwasser* 105

grouping *Eingruppierung; Gliederung* 48

grower *Anbauer, Erzeuger* 106

grown over *überwuchert* 83

growth *Wachstum, Zuwachs, Zunahme* 39

guilt *Schuld* ⓣ 129

guinea pig *Meerschweinchen* ⓣ 123

gym (gymnasium) *Turnhalle, Fitnessstudio* 151

hairdryer *Fön, Haartrockner* ⓣ 37

halfway through *halb durch, mitten drin* 25

hall *Diele, Flur* 76

hand sth in *etwas abgeben* 50

hand-stitched *handgenäht* 135

handkerchief *Taschentuch* 119

handle sth *etwas handhaben, mit etwas umgehen* 24

handling *Abwicklung, Handhabung* 106

handwriting *Handschrift* 24

handy *handlich, griffig* 51

hang (hanged, hanged) oneself *sich erhängen* 10

harassment *Bedrohung, Schikane* 140

harm *schaden, verletzen* 104

harmful *schädlich* 82

harmless *harmlos* ⓣ 100

harvest *ernten, abernten* 109

have / take a day off *sich einen Tag frei nehmen* 65

hazardous *gefährlich* 134

hazelnut *Haselnuss* 8

headquarters *Zentrale, Hauptquartier* 76

headteacher *Schulleiter(in)* 10

health ministry *Gesundheitsministerium* 116

health-conscious *gesundheitsbewusst* 104

healthcare *Gesundheitswesen* 38

heart attack *Herzinfarkt* 88

heat *erhitzen* 144

heated *erhitzt* 43

henchman *Handlanger, Scherge* 44

herb *Kraut, Heilkraut* ⓣ 100

hidden *versteckt, verborgen* 102

hieroglyphics *Hieroglyphen* 50

high frequency *Hochfrequenz* ⓣ 56

high heels *Stöckelschuhe* 116

high-capacity *Hochleistungs-, leistungsstark* 81

high-impact proof *hochschlag-fest* 100

hiking *Wandern* 8

hip *schick* 11

hire sb *jmdn einstellen, anheuern* 30

hitchhiker *Anhalter* 55

HIV = Human Immuno-deficiency Virus disease *Humane Immunschwäche-krankheit* 131

home grown *im eigenen Land entstanden* 126

home improvement items *Heimwerkerbedarf* 66

homesick *Heimweh haben* 40

honestly *ehrlich, aufrichtig* Ⓣ 96

honey *Honig* 11

honour *ehren, beehren* 140

hops *Hopfen* Ⓣ 11

horseshoe *Hufeisen* 136

host country *Gastgeberland, Aufnahmestaat* Ⓣ 142

hotelier *Hotelbesitzer(in)* 142

how come *wie kam es, wieso* 26

hug *Umarmung* 51

human resources *Personal-abteilung* 24

humanitarian *Philanthrop* Ⓣ 123

humorous *humorvoll* 18

HVAC (Heating, Ventilation, Air Conditioning) *Heizung, Belüftung, Klimatechnik* 75

hybrid motor *Hybridmotor* 80

hydrated *hydratisiert* Ⓣ 100

hydrologist *Gewässer-kundige(r)* 100

i.e. (id est = that is) *das heißt* 90

I'm putting you through now. *Ich verbinde Sie jetzt.* 153

identify *erkennen; identifizieren* 19

idiom *Redensart, Spracheigen-tümlichkeit* 141

ignored *missachtet, ignoriert* 43

illustration *Bebilderung* 81

impact *Bedeutung; Einschlag; Aufprall* 12

impartial *unvoreingenommen, vorurteilslos* 41

impediment *Behinderung, Hindernis* 130

implement (sth) *etwas umsetzen / durchführen* 54

implication *Folgerung, Schluss-folgerung* 54

imply *andeuten; unterstellen* 39

importance *Wichtigkeit, Bedeutung* 60

impressed *beeindruckt* 29

improved *verbessert, aufgebessert* 38

improvement *Verbesserung, Aufbesserung* 64

in addition *dazu, zusätzlich* 30

in addition (to) *zusätzlich (zu), darüber hinaus* 67

in contrast *zum Vergleich* 64

in due course *zur gegebenen Zeit* 25

in good time *rechtzeitig* 68

in the course of *im Verlauf (von)* 28

income *Einkommen* 90

inconsistent *unbeständig, uneinheitlich* 50

increase *anwachsen, (sich) erhöhen / vergrößern* 31

increase *Anstieg, Steigerung* 92

increasing *zunehmend, steigend* 52

incredible *unglaublich, wunderbar* 100

India *Indien* 36

indicate *hinweisen, andeuten* 48

indigenous *einheimisch* 125

industrialized nations *Industrieländer* 92

inequality *Ungleichheit* 131

infect *anstecken, infizieren* 50

infection *Infizierung, Ansteckung* 20

infinity *Endlosigkeit, Unend-lichkeit* 72

inflation *Abwertung, Teuerung* 102

ingenious *genial* 102

ingredient *Backzutat* 107

inherent(ly) *inhärent* 130

inhumane *unmenschlich* 131

initial *anfänglich, Anfangs-* 29

initiate *einleiten, auslösen* Ⓣ 100

initiative *Anstoß, Initiative* 116

innovation *Neuheit; Neuerung* 52

innovative *bahnbrechend, innovativ* 100

insist on *bestehen, beharren* 116

inspector *Qualitätsprüfer(in)* 109

inspire *begeistern, anregen* 89

inspired by sth *durch / von etwas angeregt* 15

inspiring *anregend, begeisternd* 51

install *einbauen, installieren* 76

instructed *beauftragt, angewiesen* 68

insult *Beleidigung, Kränkung* 10

insurance *Versicherung* 89

insured **versichert** 90

intangible *immateriell, unbegreiflich* Ⓣ 100

integrate *einbinden, eingliedern* 54

intend to *beabsichtigen, vorhaben etwas zu tun* 116

intense *heftig* 62

intention *Absicht, Vorsatz* 102

intently *aufmerksam, bedacht* 119

interest *Interesse* 48

interestingly *interessanter-weise* 116

intermarry *eine Mischehe eingehen* 37

intermingling *Vermischung* 131

intern *Praktikant(in); Voluntär(in); Assistenzarzt, Assistenzärztin* 24

internal combustion engine *Verbrennungsmotor* 80

internship *Praktikum* 12

interpret *deuten, auslegen, interpretieren* 37

interrupt *dazwischenreden, jmdm ins Wort fallen* 43

intimate *intim* 78

invaluable *außerordentlich wertvoll, unschätzbar* 41

invest in *anlegen* 62

investigation *Ermittlungen, Untersuchung* 88

investment *Investition* 131

investor *Anleger(in)* 66

invigorating *belebend, kräftigend* 🕔 100

involve *beinhalten, einbeziehen* 49

involved *beteiligt* 43

IQ (Intelligence Quotient) *Intelligenzquotient* 78

Ireland *Irland* 36

iron *Eisen* 136

iron *Bügeleisen* 151

iron (clothes) *bügeln* 33

ironing *Bügeln* 75

ironing board *Bügelbrett* 151

irradiation *Bestrahlung* 104

irrelevant *bedeutungslos, unerheblich* 55

irrigation *Bewässerung* 🕔 110

is supposed to be a ... *soll ... sein* 42

isolated *vereinzelt* 92

isolation *Isolierung* 37

issues (pl.) *Belange, Angelegenheiten* 60

itchy feet *Wanderlust* 128

jalebi *indische Süßspeise* 140

jaw *Kiefer* 89

job satisfaction *Arbeitszufriedenheit* 65

job sharing *Arbeitsplatzaufteilung* 64

joint *gemeinsam* 38

joint-stock company *Aktiengesellschaft* 126

judge *beurteilen, bewerten* 50

judgement *Ermessen, Beurteilung* 49

jug *Krug* 🕔 100

juicy *saftig* 124

jukebox *Musikautomat* 76

junk food *ungesunde Fertigkost* 92

just reward *gerechter Lohn* 140

justify *rechtfertigen; legitimieren* 11

keen *eifrig* 50

keep close tabs on *jmdn kontrollieren/beobachten* 79

keep the minutes (of a meeting) *Protokoll führen* 68

keep track of *Überblick behalten, im Auge behalten* 76

kick in (ugs) *anlaufen, (sich) anschalten* 80

kidnapped *entführt* 15

kidney *Niere* 97

kitchen towel *Papiertuch* 102

kitten *Kätzchen* 124

kleenex *Papiertaschentuch* 119

knob *Drehknopf* 76

knowledge *Kenntnis; Wissensstand, Erkenntnis* 53

knuckle *Fingerknöchel* 97

kulfi *indische Eisspezialität* 140

labelling *Auszeichnung, Etikettierung* 93

laboratory-tested *laborgeprüft* 120

labour-saving *arbeitssparend* 92

lack of *mangels, an etwas mangeln* 11

last *dauern* 68

laudably *löblich, lobenswert* 11

laugh *das Lachen* 29

laughable *lächerlich* 123

launch *Stapellauf, Start* 50

launch sth *etwas auf den Markt bringen* 66

laundry appliances *Wäschereigeräte (Waschmaschine, Trockner, Mangel, usw.)* 75

lawn *Rasen* 82

lawnmower *Rasenmäher* 83

lay off *entlassen* 66

leak *Leck, undichte Stelle* 76

lecture hall *Hörsaal, Auditorium* 🕔 100

lecturer *Dozent(in)* 139

leek *Lauch, Porree* 144

Legend has it that ... *Nach der Legende ...* 140

legislation *Gesetzgebung* 38

leguminous *hülsenfruchtartig* 105

leisure *Freizeit* 24

leisure centre *Freizeitzentrum* 88

length *Länge* 51

let go *loslassen* 78

Let the storm run its course. *Lassen Sie dem Sturm seinen Lauf.* 43

letter of complaint *Beschwerdebrief* 99

letterhead *Briefkopf* 29

liberate *befreien, freisetzen* 50

liberation *Befreiung, Freisetzung* 50

librarian *Bibliothekar(in)* 145

licence *zulassen, eine Lizenz/Konzession erteilen* 67

lick *lecken, ablecken* 119

lie detector *Lügendetektor* 86

life expectancy *Lebenserwartung* 39

life insurance policy *Lebensversicherungspolice* 140

lifeguard *Rettungsschwimmer(in); Bademärter* 18

lightweight material *Leichtbauwerkstoff* 80

limit *begrenzen, einschränken* 90

limitation *Einschränkung, Beschränkung* 52

limited *eingeschränkt, begrenzt* 67

line *auslegen* 144

linguistic expert *Sprach-wissenschaftler(in)* 51

lion's share *Löwenanteil* 67

liquid soap *Flüssigseife* 122

listening comprehension *Hörverständnis* 19

listening text *Hörtext* 7

liver *Leber* 88

liver failure *Leberversagen* 88

living *lebend* 78

load *Ladung, Last* 80

load *laden, beladen* 109

long term *Langzeit-, auf lange Sicht* 74

long-lasting *dauerhaft; lang-andauernd* 124

longing *Sehnsucht* 128

loo (slang) *Klo* 102

looks (pl.) *Aussehen* 79

loosely-regulated *minimal-geregelt* 90

lorry driver *Lastwagen-fahrer(in)* 109

loss *Verlust* 60

loudmouthed *großmäulig* 142

lovable *liebenswert, liebens-würdig* 43

loving *liebevoll* 43

low-maintenance *pflegeleicht, wartungsarm* 120

lunacy *Wahnsinn* ⓣ 123

lung *Lunge* 97

luxurious *luxuriös, opulent* 120

luxury *Luxus* ⓣ 100

machinery *Mechanismus; Maschinen; Maschinerie* 62

magically *magisch* 102

mail-order catalogue *Versand-katalog* 67

mainland *Festland* ⓣ 142

maintain *aufrechterhalten, einhalten* 89

maize (AE: corn) *Mais* 111

make amends *entschädigen, wiedergutmachen* ⓣ 123

make out (that) *vortäuschen; so tun, als ob* 15

make redundant *entlassen* 66

make sth a snap *etwas sehr einfach machen* 52

make sth plain *klarmachen* 79

make up one's mind *entscheiden (sich)* 104

malted barley *Braugerste, Gerstenmalz* ⓣ 11

mammoth *Mammut* 60

management *Unternehmens-führung; Verwaltung* 23

mandatory *obligatorisch, vorgeschrieben* 90

manipulation *Beeinflussung* 78

manpower *menschliche Arbeitsleistung* 24

manual labour *Handarbeit* ⓣ 110

manufacture *anfertigen, erzeugen, herstellen* 71

manufactured products *industriegefertigte Güter* 126

manufacturer *Hersteller* 52

map sth out *etwas entwerfen / festlegen* 29

maple leaf *Ahornblatt* 142

marketability *Marktfähigkeit* 31

marketable *verkaufsfähig, vermarktbar* 80

marketing *Vertrieb, Marketing* 71

marriage *Ehe* 29

massive *gewaltig* 53

matter *Sache, Angelegenheit* 79

maximization *Maximierung* 126

mayor *Bürgermeister* 92

meaningful *bedeutungsvoll; sinnvoll* 17

measure *Maß; Maßnahme* 104

measure *messen, abmessen* 104

measurement *Bemessung; Messwert* 78

mechanical *mechanisch* 100

mechanized *mechanisiert* ⓣ 110

medieval *mittelalterlich* 126

melt *schmelzen, sich auflösen* 118

melting *schmelzend* 102

membership *Mitgliedschaft* 49

memorably *denkwürdig, unvergesslich* 10

memory *Erinnerung* 28

mental *geistig, seelisch* 38

mentioned *erwähnt* 41

method *Methode* 26

mighty *gewaltig, mächtig* 50

migrant *unstet, wandernd* 94

militant *kämpferisch, streitbar* 140

military forces *Militär, mili-tärische Wehrdienste* 90

miller *Müller(in)* 126

mince *durchdrehen, fein hacken* ⓣ 139

minced meat *Hackfleisch* 123

mine *abbauen, (durch Berg-bau) födern* 60

minimize *herabsetzen, auf ein Mindestmaß ver-kleinern* 107

minor *gering, unbedeutend* 131

misinterpret *missdeuten, falsch auffassen* 142

misleading *irreführend* 37

mismanage *misswirtschaften, schlecht verwalten* 131

mismanaged *schlecht ver-waltet, schlecht geführt* 38

misunderstanding *Miss-verständnis* 137

misunderstood *miss-verstanden* 17

mix *Mischung, Gemisch* 139

modernize *erneuern, modernisieren* ⓣ 129

modify *abändern, verändern* 54

moisten *anfeuchten, befeuchten* 144

molecular valve *Elektronenröhre* 78

monitor *überwachen, kontrollieren* 88

mood swings *Stimmungsschwankungen* 88

morality *Moralität, Sittlichkeit* 79

mortgage *Hypothek* 63

mosque *Moschee* 36

motion detector *Bewegungsmelder* 76

mourning *Trauer; Trauerkleidung* 96

mouthful *Bissen, Happen; Schluck* 102

mouthpiece *Mundstück* 100

mouthwash *Mundwasser* 122

moveable *beweglich, bewegbar* 69

mow *mähen* 82

mower *Mäher* 83

much alike *sehr ähnlich* 78

multiple *mehrfach, mannigfaltig* 92

mutual *gegenseitig, gemeinsam* 126

myth *Mythos* 🅣 110

nag sb about sth *herumnörgeln; jmdm mit etwas in den Ohren liegen* 16

naked *nackt* 116

namely *nämlich* 100

narrow *begrenzen, beschränken* 52

nationalism *Nationalismus* 140

navigable *schiffbar, befahrbar* 126

needle *Nadel* 126

neglect *Vernachlässigung, Verwahrlosung* 38

neighbouring town *Nachbarort* 🅣 34

nerve-racking *nervenaufreibend* 27

newcomer *Neuankömmling* 36

niche *Nische* 41

nod *nicken, zunicken* 142

noodles (pl.) *Nudeln* 111

nor *auch nicht* 54

notification *Mitteilung, schriftliche Benachrichtigung* 132

nowadays *heutzutage* 24

nuclear family *Kernfamilie, Kleinfamilie* 38

nuclear reactor *Kernreaktor* 44

numerous *zahlreich* 36

nutrition *Ernährung* 38

oath *Eid* 133

obese *fettleibig, korpulent* 92

obesity *Fettleibigkeit, Fettsucht* 88

obey *gehorchen* 96

object *Gegenstand* 82

objective *sachlich, vorurteilslos* 115

observation *Überwachung; Beobachtung* 97

observe sth *befolgen, beachten* 68

observer *Beobachter(in)* 66

obstacle *Behinderung* 82

obtain *erhalten, bekommen, erhalten* 60

occasion *Anlass, Ereignis, Gelegenheit* 68

occasional(ly) *gelegentlich* 8

occur *auftreten, sich ereignen, stattfinden* 102

odd *gelegentlich; eigenartig, seltsam* 28

offensive *anstößig, beleidigend* 116

official ceremony *Festakt* 133

offset *aufwiegen, ausgleichen* 105

on sale *zum Verkauf* 108

on the basis of *anhand von; in Anlehnung an* 12

on the move *in Bewegung* 140

on the other hand *andererseits* 69

on the rocks *mit Eis* 151

on-going *gegenwärtig* 131

one at a time *einer nach dem anderen* 78

open audition *öffentliches Vorsprechen, freie Sprechprobe* 14

open-minded *aufgeschlossen, vorurteilsfrei* 106

operating system *Betriebssystem* 26

operation *Arbeitsvorgang* 66

opinionated *rechthaberisch* 142

opponent *Gegner(in)* 130

opt for *sich für etwas entscheiden* 65

optician *Optiker(in)* 17

optimism *Optimismus* 63

oral *mündlich* 51

orchard *Obstplantage* 106

order book *Auftragsbuch* 62

ore *Erz* 60

organism *Organismus* 136

originate *herstammen; entspringen* 37

orthodontic *zahnmedizinisch(e)* 89

out of season *außerhalb der Saison* 🅣 110

outcast *Ausgestoßene(r), Paria* 94

outcome *Ergebnis, Resultat* 39

outrage *Empörung* 116

outraged *empört, entrüstet* 104

outsourcing *Ausgliederung von Betriebsfunktionen* 127

outstanding *hervorragend* 24

outweigh *aufwiegen, wettmachen* 88

oven *Backofen* 🅣 139

over-the-counter *in Freihandel erhältlich, freiverkäuflich* 102

overall *insgesamt, allgemein* 102

overbite *Überbiss* 89

overcome *bewältigen, überwinden* 39

overdo *übertreiben* 101

overhead *obenliegend* 69

overland *Überland-, über Land* 109

overlook *übersehen, nicht bemerken* 10

overpower *überwältigen, bezwingen* 130

overseas *Übersee, Ausland* 109

oversimplified *zu stark vereinfacht* Ⓣ 110

owner *Besitzer(in)* 76

package *verpacken* 108

packaged *verpackt* 92

packaging *Verpackung* 66

packed with *vollgestopft mit* 76

pan *Topf* Ⓣ 139

pancake *Pfannkuchen* 138

pappadum, papadam *dünner frittierte Fladen aus Linsenmehl* 140

paradigm *Modell, Musterbeispiel, Paradigma* 54

parameter *Bestimmungsgröße; Rahmen* 52

parkway (AE) *Bundesstraße* Ⓣ 123

parsley *Petersilie* 144

participant *Beteiligte(r); Teilnehmer(in)* 129

particle *Teilchen* 100

particularly *besonders, vor allem* 38

partition *Abtrennung, Trennwand* 69

pass over *überfahren, übergehen* 83

pass sth off as *ausgeben (etwas als etwas …)* 130

passage *Textstelle, Textauszug* 50

pasteurize *keimfrei machen* 108

pat on the back *Klaps, Schulterklopfen* 142

patient *geduldig; Patient(in)* 43

patriotism *Patriotismus* Ⓣ 142

peak *Höhepunkt, Höchstwert* 62

pear *Birne* 111

peddler *Hausierer(in)* 126

peeled *geschält* 144

peer *spähen* 10

penniless *mittellos* 140

pensioner *Rentner(in)* 90

pepper *Pfeffer* Ⓣ 139

perceive *wahrnehmen* 116

perfect *vervollkommnen, perfektionieren* 67

persecution *Verfolgen* 36

persistent *beharrlich* 27

perspective *Blickwinkel* 129

persuade *überreden, überzeugen* 65

pessimistic *pessimistisch* 22

pest control *Schädlingsbekämpfung* 18

pesticide *Schädlingsbekämpfungsmittel* 104

phenomenon *Phänomen, Naturerscheinung* 100

phonetic transcription *Lautschrift* 16

physical *körperlich* 38

physician *Mediziner(in)* 89

pick *abpflücken* 104

pick sth *etwas auswählen* 11

pick up (wind) *zunehmen* Ⓣ 75

pickles *eingelegtes Gemüse* 140

piece sth together *etwas zusammensetzen; einen Reim auf etwas machen* 15

piled *aufgestapelt* 10

pill *Tablette, Pille, Verhütungspille* 14

pin down *niederhalten, festnageln* 116

pinch of *Prise* 144

pinch together *zusammen zwicken* Ⓣ 139

pine tree *Pinie* 123

pineapple *Ananas* 109

pioneer work *Pionierarbeit* 134

place *legen, setzen, stellen* 80

plain sailing *(Idiom) unproblematisch* 41

play it safe *auf Nummer Sicher gehen* 155

pleasant *angenehm, freundlich* 10

Please hold the line. *Bitte am Apparat bleiben.* 153

pleasure *Freude* 51

plentiful *reichlich* 109

plug in *einstecken, einstöpseln* Ⓣ 37

plummet *stürzen* 63

pluralism *Pluralismus* 37

pocket-sized *in Taschenformat* 51

poignant *ergreifend* 14

point *Punkt, Spitze* 107

point of view *Ansicht, Standpunkt* 43

pointless *sinnlos; ohne Spitze* 20

Poland *Polen* 36

policy *politische Linie* 38

pollutant *Umweltschadstoff* Ⓣ 100

pop into *reinschauen, einen kurzen Besuch abstatten* 108

popularity *Beliebtheit* 65

porcelain *Porzellan* 126

porridge *Haferbrei* 108

port *Hafen; Hafenstadt* 36

portable *tragbar* 120

pose *darstellen* 102

posh *vornehm* 40

post-war *Nachkriegs-* 36

postal service *Postdienst* 60

postulate *Voraussetzung, Postulat* 72

potential *eventuell, möglich* 132

poultry *Geflügel* Ⓣ 139

powdered *gemahlen; gepulvert* Ⓣ 139

power *Energie, Kraft* 80

power company *Energieversorgungsunternehmen* 74

power split *Leistungsverzweigung* 80

praise *Lob, Belobigung* 116
praise *loben, anpreisen* 134
preacher *Prediger* ⓣ 123
precious *kostbar, wertvoll* ⓣ 100
predator *Raubtier* 49
predict *voraussagen, vorhersagen* 54
predictive *voraussagend* 50
preference *Vorliebe* 7
preferred *bevorzugt* 83
pregnant *schwanger* 14
prejudice *Vorurteil* 143
preparation *Vorbereitung* 38
prepared *bereit* 64
preposition *Präposition* 33
prescription medicine *verschreibungspflichtiges Arzneimittel* 102
presence *Anwesenheit; Vorhandensein* 54
pressure sb *bedrängen, unter Druck setzen* 74
prestige *Ansehen, Geltung* 60
prestigious *angesehen* 100
prevalent *geläufig, verbreitet* 49
prevention *Vorbeugung* 92
previous *vorangehend; vorherig; früher* 12
primary *Primär-* 60
primary school *Grundschule* 40
prime minister *Premierminister(in)* 143
print-out *Ausdruck* 25
privacy settings *Sicherheitseinstellungen* 54
proceed *weitergehen, fortfahren* 49
proceedings *Handlungsverlauf* 68
process *Verfahren; Ablauf* 37
processed food *industriell verarbeitetes Lebensmittel* 107
processing *Verarbeitung* 106
produce section *Obst und Gemüse Abteilung* 104
productive *produktiv, aktiv* 7
profession *Beruf* 28

professional bike racer *Rennrad Profi* 32
proficient *kompetent, tüchtig* 31
profile *Stechbrief, Kurzbiografie* 8
progress *Fortschritt* 89
progressive *fortschrittlich* 10
prohibit *verbieten, untersagen* 135
project housing (AE) *Sozialbau* 44
prominent *hervorspringend, markant* 36
promotion *Werbung, Werbeveranstaltung* 18
proof *Beweis* 102
proper, properly *korrekt, angemessen* 25
property market *Immobilienmarkt* 61
propulsion system *Antrieb* 80
pros and cons *Für und Wider, Pro und Kontra* 47
prosper *wachsen und gedeihen* 126
prosperity *Hochkonjunktur; Wohlstand* 62
protein *Eiweiß* 103
proud (of) *stolz (auf)* 28
provide *bereitstellen* 18
provider *Anbieter, Lieferant* 74
provision *Versorgung* 90
provisional *provisorisch* 157
provoke *heraufbeschwören, provozieren* 43
pseudonym *Deckname, Künstlername* 54
psychic *seelisch, psychisch* 54
pub (public house) *Wirtshaus, Gaststätte* 10
pub landlord *Gastwirt(in)* 142
puberty *Pubertät, Geschlechtsreife* 17
publicize *bekannt machen, publizieren* 116
publisher *Verlag; Verleger* 50
puff pastry *Blätterteig* ⓣ 139
pun *Wortspiel, Wortwitz* 20
punctuality *Pünktlichkeit* 68

punctuation *Interpunktion, Zeichensetzung* 31
purchase *erwerben, ankaufen* 106
purchaser *Abnehmer, Erwerber* 102
purpose *Absicht, Zweck* 68
put a stop to sth *etwas ein Ende machen* 43
qualify *qualifizieren* 132
quantity *Anzahl, Menge* 102
quarter *Quartal* 66
query *Anfrage* 53
question tag *Bestätigungsfrage, Frageanhängsel* 40
queue *Menschenschlange* ⓣ 11
quick-witted *aufgeweckt* 27
quicksand *Treibsand* ⓣ 123
quit *aufgeben* 87
quoted *zitiert* 14
racial *Rassen-, rassisch* 140
racy *gewagt, pikant* 54
radio station *Radiosender, Rundfunkanstalt* 36
rags (pl.) *Lumpen, Klamotten* 141
rags-to-riches story *Geschichte vom Tellerwäscher, der zum Millionär wurde* 141
raise *aufbringen, zusammenstellen* 67
raise *anheben, erhöhen; höher stellen* 83
Raj *britische Herrschaft über Indien* 11
ramble *schwafeln* 43
random *zufällig, willkürlich* 82
range *Reichweite* ⓣ 56
raspberry *Himbeere* 108
rather *ziemlich* 69
ration *Zuteilung* 102
raw material *Rohstoff* 60
razor blade *Rasierklinge* 122
read *Lektüre, das Lesen* 51
realistic *realistisch* 22
reason with sb *mit jmdm vernünftig reden* 43
receptive *rezeptiv* 7

recession *Konjunkturrückgang, Rezession, Flaute* 62

recharge *(wieder) aufladen* 82

recital *Vortrag, Liederabend* 🅣 123

recite *vortragen, aufsagen* 🅣 123

recommend *empfehlen, vorschlagen* 🅣 56, 100

reconstruct *wiederherstellen, wieder aufbauen* 153

recovery *Erholung, Aufschwung* 62

recruiter *Anwerber(in); Personalvermittler(in)* 12

recruitment *Anwerbung von neuen Mitarbeitern* 24

reduce *verringern, drosseln, abbauen* 38

refinery *Raffinerie* 61

reflect *spiegeln, widerspiegeln* 69

refrigerated container (reefer) *Kühlcontainer* 105

refugee *Flüchtling* 36

refuse collection *Müllabfuhr* 60

regarded *betrachtet* 94

regardless (of) *egal welcher, ungeachtet der / des ...* 72

regenerative braking *Rückarbeitsbremsung, Nutzbremsung* 80

register *anmelden, eintragen* 132

regret *bedauern, bereuen* 116

regular *normal; regelmäßig* 83

regulate *regeln, regulieren* 131

regulation *Regelung* 90

regulations (pl.) *gesetzliche Vorschriften* 74

reject *zurückweisen, ablehnen* 🅣 110

rejected *abgelehnt, abgewiesen* 43

related to *verwandt mit* 26

relations *Beziehungen, Verhältnisse* 126

release tension *sich entspannen* 43

relevant *entsprechend, maßgeblich* 52

reliable *verlässlich, zuverlässig* 83

reluctant *widerwillig, zurückhaltend* 140

rely on *sich auf jmdn / etwas verlassen* 54

remain *verbleiben* 11

remarkable *bemerkenswert* 39

remote *entfernt* 131

removable *herausnehmbar* 89

render *ausführen, wiedergeben* 50

renowned *renommiert* 11

rent (sth) *mieten* 61

rented *gemietet* 108

reorganization plan *Sanierungsplan* 66

repeatedly *mehrmals, wiederholt* 109

replace *ersetzen, austauschen* 52

reply *Erwiderung, Antwort* 29

reported speech *indirekte Rede* 35

representation *Darstellung* 104

request *Bitte; Anfrage* 8

require *benötigen, brauchen* 100

required *erforderlich, benötigt, vorgeschrieben* 12

requirement *Voraussetzung* 78

reroute *umleiten* 🅣 100

researcher *Forscher(in)* 64

resemble *ähneln, ähnlich sein* 116

reservation *Voranmeldung, Reservierung; Reservat, Schutzgebiet* 20

residence permit *Aufenthaltsgenehmigung* 125

resigned *resigniert* 17

resin *Harz, Kunstharz* 100

resolve *beheben, klären* 43

resonance *Resonanz* 79

resource *Produktionsmittel, Ressource* 🅣 100

respond *auf etwas reagieren; erwidern* 54

response *Antwort, Rückmeldung, Resonanz* 🅣 100

responsibility *Verantwortung* 116

restitution *Entschädigung, Rückerstattung* 102

restored *wiederhergestellt, renoviert* 150

restriction *Beschränkung, Einschränkung* 127

restructure *sanieren; umordnen* 66

résumé (AE: *auch:* resumé, resume) *Lebenslauf* 31

retailer *Händler, Einzelhändler* 52

retain *behalten, beibehalten* 105

retire *zurückziehen (sich aus dem Berufsleben ...), in Rente gehen* 133

retiring *zurückhaltend* 97

retrieval *Rückgewinnung, Wiederfindung* 52

retrieve *abrufen, wieder auffinden* 53

revamped *umgestaltet* 102

reverse *wenden, herumdrehen; rückwärts fahren* 82

revise *korrigieren* 19

revitalise *neu beleben, wiederbeleben* 10

revival *Konjunkturbelebung* 62

rewarding *lohnend* 22

ribbon *Band, Bändel* 126

riches (pl.) *Reichtümer* 141

riddled with *mit etwas durchsetzt* 50

ridiculous *lächerlich* 42

ripe *reif* 109

ripen *heranreifen, reif werden* 106

ripening room *Reifekammer* 109

rise *Anstieg, Zunahme* 49

rising *ansteigend, wachsend* 38

risk *Risiko, Wagnis* 88

roast veal *gebratenes Kalbsfleisch* 🅣 139

rocket *wie eine Rakete hochschießen* 67

roll *Röllchen* 102

roofer *Dachdecker(in)* 126

root *Wurzel* 37

rot *verfaulen, verwesen* 96

round-trip *hin und zurück* 105

routinely *routinemäßig* 64

row *Streit, Auseinandersetzung* 29

rule *herrschen, beherrschen* 130

rundown *(ugs) Zusammenfassung* 25

running water *fließendes Wasser* 🅣 100

rural *ländlich* 36

Russia *Russland* 36

safe *Tresor, Safe* 151

safety measures *Sicherheitsvorkehrungen* 76

salary *Gehalt* 31

salutation *Anrede, Begrüßung* 31

samosa *frittierte Teigtasche gefüllt mit Gemüse oder Fleischbrät* 140

sample *Muster, Kostprobe* 24

sanitary towel *Damenbinde* 122

sanitation *Sanitäreinrichtungen; Hygiene* 38

satisfactory *zufriedenstellend* 25

satisfied *zufrieden* 67

satisfy *befriedigen* 128

Satnav *Navi* 120

sausage roll *Würstchenrolle* 🅣 139

savage *grausam, brutal* 127

scale *Ausmaß, Größenverhältnis* 92

scattered *verstreut* 140

schedule *einplanen, (zeitlich) festsetzen* 64, 🅣 148

schooling *Schulausbildung* 79

scoff *verschlingen* 102

scone *brötchenartiges Gebäck* 139

scratch *Kratzer* 119

screwdriver *Schraubenzieher* 83

scruple *Skrupel, Bedenken* 🅣 129

seal *hermetisch verschließen* 109

search engine *Suchmaschine* 23

seasoned *erfahren, bewährt; gewürzt* 31

seasoning *Würze (meist Pfeffer und Salz)* 144

seat belt *Sitzgurt* 114

secondary *Sekundär-* 60

sector *Fachgebiet; Bereich* 31

security *Sicherheits-* 24

security guard *Sicherheitsbedienstete(r)* 18

security panel *Sicherheitskontrollfeld* 76

sedentary *sitzend* 92

seemingly *scheinbar* 83

segregation *Rassentrennung; Segregation* 37

seize sth *etwas ergreifen, packen* 12

select *(aus)wählen* 76

selection *Auswahl* 12

self *selbst, selber* 79

seller *Verkäufer(in)* 106

sensational *aufsehenerregend* 🅣 100

sense of humour *Sinn für Humor* 25

sensitive *empfindlich, feinfühlig* 120

sensor *Messfühler, Messsonde* 76

sentimental *rührselig, sentimental* 29

set aside (set, set) *aufsparen, etwas beiseite legen* 52

set running time *angesetzte Betriebsdauer* 83

settle *besiedeln; sich niederlassen* 36

settlement *Siedlung* 36

severe *schwerwiegend, stark* 62

sexual *sexuell* 116

shaft *Übertragungswelle; Schaft* 81

shallow *flach* 144

shape *formen, gestalten, bilden* 36

share price *Aktienkurs* 66

shaving foam *Rasierschaum* 120

shed light on sth *über etwas Aufschluss geben* 102

sheet of paper *Blatt Papier* 57

shell *Schale* 100

shift *Verschiebung, Verlagerung* 38

shift *schieben, verschieben; sich bewegen; schalten* 54

ship *ausliefern, versenden* 🅣 123

shipping *Versand* 104

shipyard *Schiffswerft* 61

shirtless *ohne Hemd* 116

shopkeeper *Geschäftsinhaber(in)* 142

shopper *Einkäufer(in)* 104

shortage *Mangel, Fehlbestand; Verknappung* 62

shortcrust pastry *Mürbeteig* 144

shortcut *Abkürzung* 50

shorten *abkürzen, verkürzen* 🅣 142

shorthand *Kurzschrift* 50

shoulder *schultern, auf sich nehmen* 116

shower curtain *Duschvorhang* 122

shrinking *schrumpfend* 102

siblings (pl.) *Geschwister* 79

sight *Sicht* 63

sign language *Zeichensprache* 27

significant *wesentlich* 27

similarity *Ähnlichkeit* 78

simple *einfach* 9

simplicity *Einfachheit* Ⓣ 56
simplify *vereinfachen* 83
sinful *sündhaft* 120
sip *nippen* 100
sit back *sich zurücklehnen* 82
site *Standort* 140
sketch *skizzieren, vorzeichnen* 14
skilled worker *Facharbeiter(in)* 132
slap sb *jmdm abwatschen/ohrfeigen* 86
slave *Sklave, Sklavin* Ⓣ 129
slide *Overheadfolie, Dia* 101
sliding *ausziehbar* 76
slightly *geringfügig; leicht* 12
slim *knapp, schmal* Ⓣ 123
slip *rutschen* 66
slip out *hinausschleichen* 14
slipper *Hausschuh, Latsche* 124
slowdown *Verlangsamung* 62
slump *Sturz, Absackung* 62
smart *gewieft, gerissen, gewitzt* 10
smoothly-functioning *reibungslos funtionierend* 109
sneakily *heimtückisch, hinterhältig* 102
sobriety *Nüchternheit* 96
sociable *gesellig, kontaktfreudig* 71
social security *Sozialversicherung* 90
socialism *Sozialismus* 130
socialize *mit anderen Menschen Kontakte knüpfen* 48
socket *Anschlussdose* Ⓣ 37
soft *weich* 102
soft drink *alkoholfreies Getränk* Ⓣ 148
solid *massiv, stabil* 69
soothing *beruhigend, schmerzlindernd* Ⓣ 100
source *Quelle, Herkunft* Ⓣ 100, 106
sourdough bread *Sauerteig* Ⓣ 34

space-saving *platzsparend, raumsparend* 120
spacious *geräumig* 150
spare part *Ersatzteil* 100
spark *Funke* 76
sparkling water *Sprudel* Ⓣ 100
speak up *lauter sprechen* 153
speciality *Spezialität* Ⓣ 34
spectacular *eindrucksvoll* Ⓣ 34
speedy *flott, schnell* 131
spirits *Spirituosen* Ⓣ 11
spleen *Milz* 97
split *aufteilen, teilen, spalten* 60, 150
spoil *verderben* 51
spokeswoman *Pressesprecherin* 64
spontaneously *spontan* Ⓣ 56
spotlight *Punktstrahler; Mittelpunkt des Interesses* 88
spouse *Ehepartner(in)* 132
spray *Spraydose, Aerosol* 102
spread *Ausbreitung* 88
spread *ausbreiten, verbreiten* 116
spreadsheet *Kalkulationsblatt; Tabellenkalkulation* 25
squabble *Zankerei* 29
square *Quadrat-* 38
staff *Personal, Mitarbeiterstab* 10
stagnation *Wirtschaftsflaute* 62
standard *normal, gewöhnlich* 50
standstill *Stillstand* 62
state-of-the-art *hochmodern, auf dem neuesten Stand der Technik* Ⓣ 75
stated *angegeben* 132
steadily *stetig, beständig* 66
steamed *gedämpft, gedünstet* 144
stereotype *Klischeevorstellung* 137
sticking plaster, elastoplast *Heftpflaster* 119
stir *umrühren* Ⓣ 139

stock *Aktienkapital* 66
stock *Brühe* Ⓣ 139
stock market *Börse* 126
stolen *gestohlen* 44
storage *Lagerhaltung, Einlagerung* 66
stout *dunkles Starkbier* 118
straightforward *geradeaus, überschaubar* 67
strategy *Strategie* 92
straw *Stroh* Ⓣ 75
strawberry *Erdbeere* 109
streamline *rationalisieren, wettbewerbsfähiger gestalten* 66
street sweeper *Straßenkehrer* 140
stressful *stressig, aufreibend* Ⓣ 96
stretch *dehnen, strecken* 42
strife *Streit, Zank* 42
strip *Streifen* 119
stroll *schlendern, bummeln* 104
structure *Konstruktion, Gebilde* 60
struggle *sich anstrengen/abrackern; kämpfen* 22
stud-muffin (AE) *Kerl, Mannsbild* 44
student grant *Ausbildungsförderung, Stipendium* 24
studies (pl.) *Studium* 25
stuffy *bieder, steif* 51
stylish *stilvoll, elegant* Ⓣ 100
submissive *unterwürfig* 17
submit sth *etwas einreichen, zustellen* 12
subsequent *später* 140
substance *Substanz, Stoff* 94
substitute *austauschen, auswechseln* 105
substitute teacher *Aushilfslehrer(in)* 10
succumb *unterliegen* 50
sue *(vor Gericht) klagen, prozessieren* 54
sufferer *Leidende(r)* 116
sugar-coated *überzuckert, dragiert* 118

sugary *zuckerhaltig* 92

suitable *angemessen* 49

summary *Zusammenfassung* 7

sunbed *Sonnenbank* 88

sunlight *Sonnenlicht* Ⓣ 70

supervise *beaufsichtigen; kontrollieren* 18

supervisor *Aufseher(in)* 69

supplier *Zulieferbetrieb* 134

supply *Versorgung; Vorrat* Ⓣ 75

supply *beliefern* 140

support *fördern; unterstützen* Ⓣ 56

support *Unterstützung* 116

supporter *Unterstützer* Ⓣ 96

surface *Oberfläche* 83

surname *Nachname* Ⓣ 142

surroundings *Umgebung, Umfeld* 49

suspect *verdächtigen, vermuten, ahnen* 102

sustained *anhaltend, ausdauernd* 14

swearing-in *Vereidigung* 133

sweep *fegen, rauschen* 130

sweeten *süßen; versüßen* 92

sweets *Bonbons* 145

switch *Schalter* 76

switchboard operator *Telefonist(in)* 31

sword *Schwert* Ⓣ 129

tablecloth *Tischdecke* 122

tablet *Tablette* 102

tail *Schwanz* 119

take sth for granted *annehmen (als selbstverständlich)* Ⓣ 100

take sth out of circulation *aus dem Umlauf nehmen* 116

takeover *Übernahme* 140

tangible *konkret, greifbar* Ⓣ 100

tap *Wasserhahn* Ⓣ 37

tap *abklopfen* 54

target group *Zielgruppe* 121

target sth *abzielen (auf etwas)* 100

tart tin *Backblech mit Mulden* 144

taskforce *Sonderkommando; Sonderkommission* 64

tax avoidance *Steuervermeidung* 130

team spirit *Teamgeist* 25

tear off *abreißen* 142

teaspoonful *Teelöffel ... (Maßeinheit)* Ⓣ 139

teleworking *Telearbeit* 65

temp (temporary worker) *Aushilfskraft, Zeitarbeiter(in)* 31

temperamental *launisch, reizbar* 79

tempt *verlocken, verleiten* 139

tend to *zu etwas neigen* 10

term *Begriff* 37

term-time *Schulzeit* 65

tertiary *Tertiär-* 60

test tube *Reagenzglas* 18

testimonial *Arbeitszeugnis; Empfehlungsschreiben* 24

texting *eine SMS-Nachricht schreiben* 157

textual *textlich, textbezogen* 115

Thank goodness! *Gott sei Dank!* 40

Thanks to ... *dank etwas; wegen* 54

The line is engaged. *Die Leitung ist besetzt.* 153

theft *Diebstahl* 49

They'd made it! *Sie hatten es geschafft!* 67

thicken *eindicken* Ⓣ 139

thin *dünn werden* 28

thorough(ly) *gründlich* 144

thought *Gedanke, Überlegung* Ⓣ 100

thoughtful *fürsorglich, rücksichtsvoll* 17

thread *Faden* 126

threshold *Schwelle; (tech.) Grenzbereich* 52

thriller *Krimi; Reißer* 10

thrilling *spannend* 10

throughout *durchgehend, durchweg* 83

tidal wave *Flutwelle* 130

till *Kasse* 102

timeless *zeitlos* 14

timer *Schaltuhr* 83

tinned food *Konserven* 23

tiny *winzig* 140

tissue paper *Seidenpapier* 119

to date *bis jetzt* 80

toffee *Karamell* 102

tone *Tönung; Laut, Ton* 21

tongue-in-cheek *mit ironischem Unterton, nicht ganz ernstgemeint* 11

topsoil *Humus, Mutterboden* 105

touch *Berührung* 78

tough *zäh, hartnäckig, (ugs.) taff* 22

tourism *Tourismus* 148

towel *Handtuch* 120

trace back *zurückverfolgen* 57

track sb down *jmn aufspüren* 28

tracker *Aufspürer* 83

trailer *Anhänger; (AE) Wohnwagen* 11

trained *ausgebildet* Ⓣ 34

trainee *Auszubildende(r)* Ⓣ 34

transboundary *grenzüberschreitend* Ⓣ 100

transmission *Übertragung* 80

transparent *durchsichtig* 119

trap *fangen, einfangen* Ⓣ 110

travesty *Travestie* 50

treat sb *mit jmdm umgehen* 28

treatment *Behandlung* 10

tremendously *enorm, gewaltig* 28

trend *Entwicklung, Tendenz* 35

trendy *modisch schick* 14

troops (pl.) *Truppen* 96

tropical *Tropen-; tropisch* 52

trough *Senke, Talsohle* 62

trouser press *Hosenspanner* 151

truck (AE) *Lastwagen* 105

trustworthiness *Zuverlässig-keit, Vertrauenswürdigkeit* 52

trustworthy *zuverlässig, vertrauenswürdig* 104

turn out *ausgehen, heraus-stellen* 29

turn sb out of *hinauswerfen* 140

turnover *Absatz* 140

turquoise *Türkis* 100

TV presenter *Fernseh-ansager(in)* 36

tweet *twittern (eine Kurz-nachricht auf einem sozialen Netzwerk absetzen)* 54

two-edged *zweischneidig* ⓣ 129

typhoid *Typhus* 100

ultimately *schlussendlich, letztmalig* 60

unable *unfähig* 90

unauthorized *unberechtigt, unbefugt* 135

underbite *Vorbiss, Vorstehen des Unterkiefers* 89

underclass *Unterschicht* 94

underemployed *unter-beschäftigt, nicht ausge-lastet* 38

undergo *durchmachen, sich etwas unterziehen* 79

underlying *grundlegend* 76

understandable *verständlich* 121

understanding *Verständnis, Übereinkunft; Einsicht* 43

undesirable *unerwünscht* 37

unemployment *Arbeitslosig-keit* 62

unevenness *Unebenheit* 79

unheard of *unerhört, gänzlich unbekannt* 134

unhelpful *nicht hilfreich* 110

unlock *aufschließen, entriegeln* 76

unpaid *unbezahlt* 24

unprecedented *beispiellos* 134

unprofitable *unrentabel, ertraglos* 66

unpunctual *unpünktlich* 32

unrelated *ohne Bezug* 18

unrest *Unruhen* 36

unripe *unreif* 106

unsalted *ungesalzen* 144

unsuitable *ungeeignet* 143

unwelcome *unwillkommen, unlieb* 140

updated *aktualisiert* 51

upmarket *gehoben, vornehm* 155

upper-class lady *Dame der Oberschicht* 42

upstream *flussaufwärts* ⓣ 100

urban renewal *Stadtsanierung* 18

urbane *weltgewandt, kultiviert* ⓣ 100

urge *Drang, Antrieb* 128

urgent, urgently *dringend* 31

user *Nutzer(in); Anwender(in)* 48

user-friendly *benutzerfreund-lich* 82

USP (Unique Selling Point) *einmaliges Verkaufs-argument* 152

utility *Verorgungsunter-nehmen* 60

UV radiation *Ultraviolett-strahlung* 101

vacancy *freie, unbesetzte Stelle* 24

variety *Vielfalt* 37

various *verschieden, mannig-faltig* 30

vary *ändern, sich ändern; verändern* 31

velcro *Klettverschluss, Klettband* 119

vendor *Verkäufer(in); Zwischenhändler(in); Lieferant* 134

venture (into) *sich (in …) wagen* 66

verbally abusive *verbal ausfallend* 43

versatile *vielseitig* 120

vertical, vertically *senkrecht* 122

via *durch, mittels* 76

viability *Durchführbarkeit, Viabilität* 105

vicious *bösartig* 136

victor *Sieger(in)* 134

violation *Nichteinhaltung; Vertragsverletzung* 135

visual *optisch, bildlich* 115

visualization *Veranschau-lichung* 43

visualize *sich etwas bildlich vorstellen, etwas veran-schaulichen* 55

vital *lebenswichtig; grundlegend* 38

vivid *anschaulich, lebhaft* 28

vocational qualifications *Berufsabschlüsse* 7

vocational school *berufs-bildende Schule* 30

voice-controlled *sprach-gesteuert* 76

vulnerable *verletzlich, verwundbar* 38

wag *wedeln* 119

wage *Lohn, Arbeitsentgelt* 62

waiter service *Bedienung* ⓣ 11

wall panel *Wandtafel* 76

walnut *Walnuss* 138

warehouse hub *zentrales Warenhaus* 108

warn sb (of sth) *jmdn (vor etwas) warnen* 38

warrior *Krieger(in)* 44

washing machine *Wasch-maschine* 74

washing up liquid *Geschirr-spülmittel* 102

water cooler *Wasserkühler* ⓣ 70

water fueled *wasserbetrieben* 44

water-borne *durch Wasser übertragen* 100

waterproof *wasserdicht* 124

wax *Wachs* 106

weakness *Schwäche* 27

wealth *Reichtum, Vermögen* 126

weed *Unkraut (ugs. Marihuana)* 96

weekly *wöchentlich* 102

welfare *Fürsorge; Wohlfahrt* 38

well-being *Wohlbefinden, Wohlergehen* 38

well-known *gut bekannt* 96

whereas *wohingegen; während* 104

white-collar worker *Büroangestellte(r)* 69

wholesale market *Großhandelsmarkt* 109

whopping *kolossal* 51

willing *bereit, willig* 31

wink at sb *zublinzeln* 142

wipe clean *abwischen* 100

wire *Draht* 82

wireless *drahtlos* 11

wise guy *Klugscheißer* 🅣 123

withdraw *abziehen, sich zurückziehen* 78

withdrawn *verschlossen, zurückgezogen* 88

within *innerhalb, binnen* 38

witty *geistreich, witzig* 29

word order *Satzstellung* 79

word processing *Textverarbeitung* 25

work experience *Berufserfahrung, Arbeitserfahrung; (BE) Praktikum* 12

work experience *Praktikum* 148

work out *trainieren* 151

work permit *Arbeitserlaubnis* 24

work sth out *etwas ausrechnen* 51

work-related *die Arbeit betreffend* 41

workforce *Arbeitskräfte; Erwerbstätige* 62

worship sb *jmdn anbeten* 10

worth *wert* 67

wound *Wunde* 119

wrap-around label *Rundumetikett* 🅣 100

wrist *Handgelenk* 97

wristwatch *Armbanduhr* 120

yeast *Hefe* 🅣 11

zig-zag course *Zickzackkurs* 29

Deutsch A–Z Wortliste

Die Zahl am rechten Rand gibt den Einführungsort des englischen Wortes als Seitenzahl an.
Die englischen **Verben** sind fett markiert.
🅣 = Das englische Wort wurde zuerst in einem Hörverständnistext eingeführt.

abändern **modify** 54
abbauen (durch Bergbau)
   mine 60
abfiltern **filter out** 100
abfüllen **bottle** 108
Abgas *emission* 80
Abgasausstoß *exhaust*
   emission 82
abgeben **hand sth in** 50
abgekühlt *chilled* 108
abgelehnt *rejected* 43
abgemagert *emaciated* 116
Abgrenzung *boundary* 82
Abhandlung *essay* 50
abhängen (von jmdm / etwas)
   depend on (sb. / sth) 🅣 75
abhängig von *depending on*
   24
Abhängigkeit (von)
   dependence (on) 47
abklopfen **tap** 54
abkoppeln (vom Strom)
   disconnect 76
abkürzen **shorten** 🅣 146
Abkürzung *abbreviation;*
   short-cut 47
ablehnen **deny** 132
ablehnen **reject** 🅣 110
ableiten (sich von etwas)
   derive sth by 38
Abnahme *decrease* 62
Abnehmer, Erwerber
   purchaser 102
abpflücken **pick** 104
abrackern **struggle** 22
abreißen **tear off** 142
abrufen **retrieve** 53
Absatz *turnover* 140
Absicht, Vorsatz *intention* 102
Absicht, Zweck *purpose* 68
absichtlich *deliberate, deliber-*
   ately 130

absolutes Muss *absolute must*
   68
Abstammung *descent* 37
abträglich *detrimental* 54
Abtreibung *abortion* 15
Abtrennung *partition* 69
Abwärtstrend *downswing* 62
Abwertung, Teuerung
   inflation 102
Abwicklung, Handhabung
   handling 106
abwischen **wipe clean** 100
Abzeichen *badge* 142
abziehen, sich zurückziehen
   withdraw 78
abzielen (auf etwas) **target sth**
   100
Ach was!, Jetzt mach mal halb-
   lang! *Come off it.* 102
adelig *aristocratic* 143
Adoptierende(r) *adopter* 104
Adressat(in) *addressee* 102
Adressenverzeichnis *directory*
   67
Aerodynamik *aerodynamics*
   (sing.) 80
Agrarindustrie *agribusiness*
   104
ähneln **resemble** 116
Ähnlichkeit *similarity* 78
Ahornblatt *maple leaf* 142
Aktiengesellschaft *joint-stock*
   company 126
Aktienkapital *stock* 66
Aktienkurs *share price* 66
Aktienmehrheit in einer Firma
   kaufen **buy out** 66
Aktienpreis zum Schluss der
   Börse *(stock) closed at* 66
Aktion *drive* 116
Aktion, Kampagne *campaign*
   94
aktualisiert *updated* 51

aktuell *current* 38
alarmieren, warnen **alert** 76
alkoholfreies Getränk
   soft drink 🅣 148
Alles hängt von dir ab. *All up*
   to you. 79
Allgemeinwissen *general*
   knowledge 30
Allgemeinwohl *common good*
   🅣 100
allmählich *gradually* 83
als Luftfracht transportiert *air*
   freight, air-freighted 🅣 110
älterer; bejahrt *elder, elderly*
   38
alternd *aging* 38 🅣 96
Ananas *pineapple* 109
Anbauer *grower* 106
anbei, in der Anlage *enclosed*
   25
anbeten **worship sb** 10
Anbieter, Lieferant *provider* 74
andererseits *on the other hand*
   69
ändern, sich ändern *vary* 31
anderswo *elsewhere* 79
andeuten **imply** 39
anfänglich, Anfangs- *initial* 29
anfertigen, erzeugen **manu-**
   facture, produce 71
anfeuchten **moisten** 144
Anfrage, Erkundigung *query,*
   enquiry, (AE) inquiry 23
angegeben *stated* 132
Angelegenheit *matter* 79
Angelegenheiten *issues*
   (pl.) 60
angemessen *suitable* 49
angenehm, freundlich
   pleasant 10
angeregt (durch / von etwas)
   inspired by sth 15

angesammelt *accumulated* 78

angeschlossen; beigefügt *attached* 17

angesehen *prestigious* 100

angesetzte Betriebsdauer *set running time* 83

angewandte Naturwissenschaft *applied science* 25

angriffslustig *aggressive* 43

Angst, Ängste *anxiety, anxieties* 23

anhaltend, ausdauernd *sustained* 14

Anhalter *hitchhiker* 55

anhand von *on the basis of* 12

Anhang *appendix (pl.) appendices* 16

Anhänger; (AE) Wohnwagen *trailer* 11

anheben, erhöhen **raise** 83

anklagen **accuse** 130

Ankleideraum *dressing room* 150

ankündigen **announce (itself)** ⓣ 56

Ankunft, Beginn *advent* 50

ankurbeln; steigern **boost** 25

Anlass, Gelegenheit *occasion* 68

anlaufen, (sich) anschalten **kick in** *(ugs)* 80

anlegen **invest in** 62

Anleger(in) *investor* 66

anmelden, eintragen **register** 132

Annahme *assumption* 39

annehmbar *acceptable* 117

annehmen **accept** 28

annehmen **adopt** 50

annehmen (als selbstverständlich) **take sth for granted** ⓣ 100

Annehmlichkeit *amenity* 151

anpassen **conform to sth** 37

anpassen (sich) **assimilate** ⓣ 142

anpassungsfähig *flexible* 25

Anpassungsfähigkeit *flexibility* 64

anregen **inspire** 89

anregend *inspiring* 51

Anrufbeantworter *answerphone* 76

Anrufer(in) *caller* ⓣ 37

ansammeln **gather** 52

Ansatz, Vorgehen *approach* 54

anschaffen **acquire** ⓣ 100

anschaulich, lebhaft *vivid* 28

Anschlussdose *socket* ⓣ 37

Ansehen *prestige* 60

Ansicht, Standpunkt *point of view* 43

ansprechen, Anklang finden **appeal** 155

anspruchsvoll *challenging* 92

anständig *decent* ⓣ 129

Anstandsregel *etiquette* 11

anstecken **infect** 50

ansteckend *contagious* 131

ansteigend *rising* 38

Anstellung *employment* 12

anstreben **go for sth** 22

Antibiotika *antibiotics* 104

Antragsteller(in); Stellenbewerber(in) **applicant** 12

Antrieb *propulsion system* 80

Antwort **response** ⓣ 100

antworten (jmdm) **get back to sb (about sth)** 153

anwachsen **increase** 31

anweisen **assign** 78

Anwerbung von neuen Mitarbeitern *recruitment* 24

Anwesen *estate* 76

Anwesenheit *presence* 54

Anzeigenkunde *advertiser* 67

Anzeigentext *advertising copy* 50

apart *fancy* ⓣ 100

Arbeitserfahrung *work experience* 12

Arbeitserlaubnis *work permit* 24

Arbeitskräfte *workforce* 62

Arbeitsleistung (menschliche) *manpower* 24

Arbeitslosigkeit *unemployment* 62

Arbeitsplatzaufteilung *job sharing* 64

arbeitssparend *labour-saving* 92

Arbeitsvorgang *operation* 66

Arbeitszufriedenheit *job satisfaction* 65

Armbanduhr *wristwatch* 120

Armsessel *armchair* ⓣ 11

Asche *ashes (pl.)* 96

Aschenbecher *ashtray* ⓣ 70

Asylsuchende(r) *asylee (AE)* 133

atemlos *breathless* 10

Athlet(in) *athlete* 22

Aubergine *aubergine (BE), eggplant (AE)* ⓣ 123

auch nicht *nor* 54

auf dem neuesten Stand der Technik *state-of-the-art* ⓣ 75

auf sich nehmen **shoulder** 116

aufbringen, zusammenstellen **raise** 67

aufdecken; erfassen **detect** 82

Aufenthaltsgenehmigung *residence permit* 125

Auffahrt *driveway* ⓣ 123

auffallend *conspicuous* 11

auffällig *eye-catching* 120

auffüllen **fill up** 62

aufgeben **give up** 16

aufgeben **quit** 87

aufgeben (ein Geschäft) **close down** 60

aufgeschlossen *open-minded* 106

aufgestapelt *piled* 10

aufgeweckt *quick-witted* 27

aufladen (z.B. Akku) **charge (battery)** 80

auflösen **break down** 43

aufmerksam *intent(ly)* 119

Aufmerksamkeit auf etwas lenken **draw attention to sth** 116

aufmuntern **brighten up** ⓣ 100

aufrechterhalten **maintain** 89

Aufschluss geben (über etwas) **shed light on sth** 102

Aufschwung *boom* 62

Aufsehen erregen **cause a stir** 117

aufsehenerregend *sensational* 🅣 100

Aufseher(in) *supervisor* 69

aufspüren **track sb down** 28

Aufspürer *tracker* 83

aufteilen **split** 150

Auftrag erteilen **commission sth** 64

Auftraggeber(in) *client* 54

Auftragsbuch *order book* 62

Auftreten (erstes) *debut* 67

aus allen Gesellschaftschichten *from all walks of life* 89

aus dem Umlauf nehmen **take sth out of circulation** 116

ausbeuten *exploit* 116

Ausbeutung *exploitation* 131

ausbreiten **spread** 116

ausbreiten (wie ein Virus) **go viral** 54

Ausbreitung *spread* 88

ausdehnen **expand** 62

Ausdruck *print-out* 25

ausdruckslos *expressionless* 116

auseinanderbrechen **break up (broke, broken)** 29

Auseinandersetzung *dispute* 43

ausführen, wiedergeben **render** 50

Ausgang *exit* 76

ausgeben (etwas als etwas …) **pass sth off as** 130

ausgebildet *trained* 🅣 34

Ausgestoßene(r) *outcast* 94

ausgleichen **offset** 105

Ausgliederung von Betriebs- funktionen *outsourcing* 127

Aushilfskraft *temp (temporary worker)* 31

Aushilfslehrer(in) *substitute teacher* 10

auslegen **line** 144

ausliefern **ship** 🅣 123

Auslieferung *delivery* 66

auslöschen **delete** 54

auslöschen **eradicate** 100

Ausnahme *exception* 102

ausprobieren **try** es auf einen Versuch ankommen lassen **give sth a try** 22

ausrechnen **work sth out** 51

ausschlaggebend *crucial* 100

Ausschuss *discard* 79

Aussehen *looks (pl.), appearance* 79

außer *except* 74

außerhalb der Saison *out of season* 🅣 110

außerordentlich wertvoll *invaluable* 41

aussetzen (jmdn. / etwas) **expose (to)** 101

ausstatten **equip** 🅣 56

austauschen **substitute** 105

Austauschprogramm *exchange programme* 8

austrocknen **dry up** 🅣 100

Auswahl *selection* 12

auswählen **pick sth** 11

auswählen **select** 76

auswerten **analyse** 31

Auswirkung *effect* 10

ausziehbar *sliding* 76

Auszubildende(r) *trainee* 🅣 34

backen **bake** 🅣 139

Bäcker(in) *baker* 🅣 34

Bäckerei *bakery* 34

Backofen *oven* 🅣 139

Backzutat *ingredient* 107

Badeanzug *bathing suit* 116

Bademantel *bathrobe* 151

bahnbrechend *innovative* 100

Balkon *balcony* 107

Band *ribbon* 126

Bankrott *bankruptcy* 62

Bauingenieur(in) *construction engineer* 🅣 75

beabsichtigen **intend to** 116

beachten **observe sth** 68

beaufsichtigen **supervise** 18

beauftragt *instructed* 68

Bebilderung *illustration* 81

bedauern **regret** 116

bedecken, überziehen **coat** 🅣 139

bedecken, zudecken **cover** 83

Bedeutung *impact* 12

bedeutungslos *irrelevant* 55

bedeutungsvoll *meaningful* 17

Bedienung *waiter service* 🅣 11

Bedrohung *harassment* 140

bedrückend *depressing* 29

beeindruckt *impressed* 29

beeinflussen **affect** 54

Beeinflussung *manipulation* 78

beenden **stop** etwas ein Ende machen **end sth, put a stop to sth** 43

befähigen, ermächtigen **empower** 55

Befähigung *competence* 12

Befehl *command* 76

befestigen (an etwas) **attach to** 100

befreien **liberate** 50

befriedigen **satisfy** 128

begegnen **face** 42

begehrt (als Partner) *eligible* 132

begeistert *enthusiastic* 29

begraben **bury** 82

begreifen **grasp** 52

begrenzen, beschränken **narrow** 52

begrenzen, einschränken **limit** 90

begrenzt *limited* 67

Begriff *term* 37

Begrüßung *greeting* 149

Begrüßung *salutation* 31

Behandlung *treatment* 10

beharrlich *persistent* 27

behaupten **claim** 49

beherrschen **dominate** 127

beherrschend *dominant* 37

Behinderung *disability* 90

Behinderung *obstacle* 82

Behörde für Bevölkerungs-
    statistik *Census Bureau* 90
beibehalten **retain** 105
Beifall spenden **applaud** 116
beispiellos *unprecedented* 134
beispielsweise *for instance* 65
beisteuern **contribute** 38
Beitrag *contribution* 68
beiwohnen **attend** 8
bekannt machen **publicize**
    116
Bekannte(r) *acquaintance* 52
Bekehrung *conversion* 143
belebend *invigorating* ⓣ 100
beleidigend *offensive* 116
Beleidigung *insult* 10
Beliebtheit *popularity* 65
beliefern **supply** 140
belüften **air sth** 74
bemerkenswert *remarkable*
    39
benötigen **require** 100
benutzerfreundlich *user-
    friendly* 82
Beobacher(in) *observer* 66
bepinseln **brush** ⓣ 139
Bequemlichkeit *comfort* 151
Bequemlichkeit *convenience*
    ⓣ 100
berauschend *exhilarating* 10
berechnen, (Preis) verlangen
    charge (price) 102
bereit *prepared* 64
bereit sein, etwas zu tun
    be willing to do sth. 8
bereitstellen **provide** 18
Bericht *account* 29
Berichterstatter(in)
    commentator 26
berichtigen **amend** 123
Bernstein *amber* 126
berücksichtigen **consider** 43
Beruf *profession* 28
berufen **appoint sb** 68
Berufsabschlüsse *vocational
    qualifications* 7
berufsbildende Schule
    vocational school 30
beruhigen **cool down, calm
    (down)** 42

beruhigend **soothing** ⓣ 100
Berührung *touch* 78
beschleunigen **accelerate** 65
beschuldigen **blame sb (for)**
    50
Beschwerde *complaint* 82
Beschwerdebrief *letter of
    complaint* 99
beschweren **complain about
    sb/sth** 16
beseitigen *eliminate* 49
beseitigt *eliminated* 12
besiedeln *settle* 36
Besitzer(in) *owner* 76
besonders *particularly* 38
Bestandteil *component* 26
Bestätigung *confirmation* 149
Bestätigungsfrage *question
    tag* 40
bestehen (auf) **insist on** 116
bestehen (aus) **consist of** 80
bestimmen **determine** 61
bestimmt *definite* 10
Bestimmungsgröße *parameter*
    52
Bestrahlung *irradiation,
    radiation* 104
betätigen **activate** ⓣ 76
beteiligt *involved* 43
Beteiligte(r) *participant* 129
betonen **emphasize** ⓣ 96
betrachtet *regarded* 94
Betriebsstilllegung *closure*
    130
Betriebssystem *operating
    system* 26
betroffen *concerned* 68
beunruhigend *disturbing* 116
beurteilen **judge** 50
Beurteilung *judgement* 49
bevölkerungsstatistisch
    demographic 35
bevorzugt *preferred* 83
Bewässerung *irrigation* ⓣ
    110
bewegbar *moveable* 69
Bewegungsmelder *motion
    detector* 76
Beweis *proof, evidence* 102

beweisen, darstellen
    demonstrate 100
Bewerbungsschreiben
    covering letter 24
bewerten, auswerten **evaluate**
    47
bewerten, einschätzen **assess**
    21
Bewohner(in) **dweller**
    (scherzhaft) 69
bewundern **admire** 79
bewusst *aware* 24
Beziehungen *relations* 126
Bibel-; biblisch *Biblical* 50
Bibliothekar(in) *librarian* 145
bieder *stuffy* 51
Bilanzjahr *financial year* 66
bildlich *visual* 115
Birke *birch* 8
Birne *pear* 111
bis einschließlich *for up to* 24
bis jetzt *to date* 80
Bissen; Schluck *mouthful* 102
Bitte am Apparat bleiben.
    Please hold the line. 153
Bitte; Anfrage *request* 8
Blase *bladder* 20
Blatt Papier *sheet of paper* 57
Blätterteig *puff pastry* ⓣ 139
Blickwinkel *perspective* 129
Blinddarm *appendix* 97
Blumenkohl *cauliflower* 111
Bohne *bean* 23
bohren **drill** 71
Bonbons *sweets* 145
Börse *stock market* 126
Börsengang *go public* 66
bösartig *vicious* 136
böse, übel *evil* 10
Botschafter(in) *ambassador*
    138
braten **fry** ⓣ 139
Braugerste *malted barley* ⓣ
    11
breit; umfassend *broad* 92
Bremsflüssigkeit *brake fluid*
    20
Brennstoffzelle *fuel cell* 80
Brennwert *calorific content*
    105

Briefkopf *letterhead* 29

Brötchen *bread roll, bun* Ⓣ 34

Brühe *stock* Ⓣ 139

Brustkorb, Brust *chest* 88

brutal *savage* 127

buchen, reservieren *book* Ⓣ 148

Buchhaltung *bookkeeping, accountancy* 30

Buchhandlung *bookstore (AE), bookshop (BE)* 66

Bügelbrett *ironing board* 151

Bügeleisen *iron* 151

bügeln *iron (clothes)* 33

Bügeln *ironing* 75

Bundesregierung *federal government* 90

Bundesstraße *parkway (AE)* Ⓣ 123

bunt *coloured* 126

Bürger(in) *citizen* 39

Bürgerberatungsdienst *Citizen's Advice Bureau* 74

Bürgermeister(in) *mayor* 92

Büroangestellte(r) *white-collar worker* 69

Bürokauffrau, Bürokaufmann *general office clerk* 31

Büstenhalter, BH *bra* 20

chaotisch *disorganized* 71

charakterisieren *characterize* 37

CO_2-Fußabdruck *carbon footprint* 104

Dachdecker(in) *roofer* 126

Dame der Oberschicht *upper-class lady* 42

Damenbinde *sanitary towel* 122

darstellen *pose* 102

Darstellung *representation* 104

das heißt (d. h.) *i.e. (id est = that is)* 90

dauerhaft *durable* 120

dauern *last* 68

Debatte *debate* 104

Deckenventilator *ceiling fan* 11

definieren *define* 56

deprimiert *depressed* 69

Desinfektion *disinfection* 101

desinfizieren *disinfect* 101

Deutscher Schäferhund *Alsatian* 40

diagnostizieren *diagnose* Ⓣ 96

Dichte *density* 38

Dickleibigkeit *corpulence* 97

die Arbeit betreffend *work-related* 41

Die Leitung ist besetzt. *The line is engaged.* 153

Diebstahl *theft* 49

Dienst *duty* 10

Differenzialgetriebe; Hinterachsgetriebe *differential* 81

Dingsbums *(ugs.) gadget* 76

Diphtherie *diphtheria* 100

Direktor *director* 55

disqualifizieren *disqualify sb* 27

Dozent(in) *lecturer* 139

Draht *wire* 82

drahtlos *wireless* 11

Drang *urge* 128

dreckig *filthy* 135

Drehknopf *knob* 76

dringend *urgent, urgently* 31

Düngemittel *fertilizer* 107

dünn werden *thin* 28

durch, mittels *via* 76

Durchfall *diarrhoea* 100

Durchführbarkeit *viability* 105

durchführen, ausführen *conduct* 27

Durchschnitt ermitteln *average (out)* 64

durchsetzen *enforce* 131

durchsetzt *riddled with* 50

durchsichtig *transparent* 119

durchspülen *flush* 14

durchstöbern; surfen *browse* 13

durchweg *throughout* 83

Duschvorhang *shower curtain* 122

dynamisch, tatkräftig *energetic* 28

Ebenholz (schwarz wie ~) *ebony* 44

echt, authentisch *genuine(ly)* 43

Ehe *marriage* 29

Ehebrecher *adulterer* 10

ehemalig *former* 36

Ehepartner(in) *spouse* 132

ehren *honour* 140

ehrlich, aufrichtig *honestly* Ⓣ 96

Eid *oath* 133

Eieruhr *egg timer* 122

eifrig *eager* 30

eifrig *keen* 50

Eigenschaften *characteristics (pl.)* 78

Eiltempo *express speed* 66

ein Praktikum durchführen *do a placement* 30

einbeziehen *involve* 49

Einbildung *fantasy* 116

einbinden *integrate* 54

Einbrecher(in) *burglar* 76

eindeutig, deutlich *distinct* 36

eindicken *thicken* Ⓣ 139

eindrucksvoll *spectacular* Ⓣ 34

einer nach dem anderen *one at a time* 78

einfach *simple* 9

Einfachheit *simplicity* Ⓣ 56

Einfallsreichtum *creativity* 65

eingebaut *built-in* 69

eingelegtes Gemüse *pickles* 140

eingerichtet, mit Möbeln ausgestattet *decorated* 155

eingeschlossen *confined* 69

Eingruppierung *grouping* 48

einhalten, befolgen *comply with* 134

einheimisch *indigenous* 125

Einigung, Vereinbarung *agreement* 43

Einkäufer(in) *shopper* 104

Einkommen *earnings* 66

Einkommen *income* 90

einleiten, auslösen *initiate* (T) 100

einmaliges Verkaufsargument *USP (Unique Selling Point)* 152

einplanen, (zeitlich) festsetzen *schedule* (T) 148

einreichen, zustellen *submit sth* 12

Einrichtung *facility* 24

Einschränkung *limitation* 52

Einschränkung *restriction* 127

Einsicht, Übereinkunft *understanding* 43

einstecken, einstöpseln *plug in* (T) 37

einstellen *adjust* 76

einstellen, anheuern *hire sb* 30

einströmen *flood in* 140

eintauchen *dip* 100

Eisen *iron* 136

Eiweiß *protein* 103

ekelhaft *disgusting* 94

Elektroaggregat, Drehstromgenerator *generator* 80

Elektrogerät *electrical appliance* 74

Elektronenröhre *molecular valve* 78

Ellbogen *elbow* 97

empfehlen *recommend* 100

Empfehlungsschreiben *testimonial* 24

empfindlich *sensitive* 120

empört *outraged* 104

Empörung *outrage* 116

Endprodukte *finished goods* 60

Energie, Kraft *power* 80

Energieversorgungsunternehmen *power company* 74

enorm *tremendously* 28

entfernt *remote* 131

entführt *kidnapped* 15

enthalten *contain* 52

entlassen *lay off, make redundant* 66

entnehmen, gewinnen *extract* 60

Entregulierung, Abschaffung von beschränkenden Bestimmungen *deregulation* 127

entriegeln *unlock* 76

Entschädigung *restitution* 102

entschärfen *defuse* 43

entscheiden (sich für etwas) *opt for* 65

entscheiden (sich) *make up one's mind* 104

entscheidend *critical* 126

entscheidender Faktor *contributing factor* 38

Entschuldigung *apology* 102

entspannen *release tension* 43

entsprechend *accordingly* 68

enttäuscht *disappointed* 17

Enttäuschung *disappointment* 102

entwerfen *map sth out* 29

entwickeln (sich) *evolve (into sth)* 54

Entwicklung *development* 25

Entwicklungsländer *developing countries* 100

Entwurf *draft* 157

Erdbeere *strawberry* 109

erfahren, bewährt *seasoned* 31

erforderlich *required* 12

erfüllen (eine Bedingung), ableisten *fulfill* 134

erfüllt *fulfilled* 28

Ergänzung *addition* 79

ergeben *return* 49

Ergebnis, Resultat *outcome* 39

Ergebnisse, Resultate *findings* 16

ergiebig *abundant* 105

ergreifen *seize sth* 12

ergreifend *poignant* 14

erhalten, bekommen *obtain* 60

erhältlich, verfügbar *available* 24

erheblich *considerably* 102

erhitzen *heat* 144

erhitzt *heated* 43

Erholung, Aufschwung *recovery* 62

Erinnerung *memory* 28

Ermittlungen *investigation* 88

ermöglichen *enable* 67

ermuntern *encourage* 36

Ermunterung *encouragement* 62

Ernährung *nutrition* 38

ernannt werden *be appointed* 10

erneuern *modernize* (T) 129

erniedrigen *demean* 116

ernsthaft *earnest* 40

Ernte *crop; crops* 71

ernten *harvest* 109

Errungenschaft *accomplishment* (T) 96

Errungenschaft; Leistung *achievement* 27

Ersatzteil *spare part* 100

erschöpft *exhausted* 108

erschrecken *frighten* (T) 129

ersetzen *replace* 52

ersinnen *devise* 102

erstaunlich *astonishing* 79

erste Schritte *getting started* 7

ertrinken *drown* 11

erwähnt *mentioned* 41

erwartet *expected* 89

Erwartung *expectation* 21

Erweiterung *expansion* 62

erweitert, verlängert *extended* 79

erwerben *purchase* 106

erwidern; auf etwas reagieren *respond* 54

Erwiderung, Antwort *reply* 29

erwirtschaften, erbringen *generate* 66

erworbenes Immunmangelsyndrom *AIDS = Acquired Immune Deficiency Syndrome* 131

Erz *ore* 60

erzielen *achieve sth* 65

Essstörung *eating disorder* 116

Etat *budget* 52

Ethik *ethics* 134

ethnisch *ethnic* 36

Etikettierung *labelling* 93

etwas beiseite legen **set aside (set, set)** 52

etwas schätzen **appreciate sth** 27

eventuell, möglich *potential* 132

Facharbeiter(in) *skilled worker* 132

Fachgebiet; Bereich *sector* 31

Faden *thread* 126

Fähigkeit *ability, skill* 92

Fall, Rückgang *fall* 62

fallen, abnehmen **decline** 62

fangen **trap** 🔵 110

Farbe *color (AE)* 78

Färbemittel *dye* 106

Faust *fist* 78

fegen, rauschen **sweep** 130

Feier *celebration* 38

fein hacken **mince** 🔵 139

feinfühlig *delicate(ly)* 79

fern *distant, faraway* 128

Fernsehansager(in) *TV presenter* 36

fertig machen **finalize** 21

Festakt *official ceremony* 133

Festland *mainland* 🔵 142

festlegen (zeitlich) **schedule** 64

festnageln **pin down** 116

feststellen, deklarieren **declare** 109

Feststellung, Schlussfolgerung, *conclusion* 63

fettleibig *obese* 92

Fettleibigkeit *obesity* 88

Feuerstein, Flint *flint* 126

Feuerwehr *fire brigade* 76

fieberhaft *feverish* 🔵 100

Filiale *branch* 109

Filterung *filtration* 100

finanzieren **finance** 90

finanziert (von) *funded (by)* 38

Fingerknöchel *knuckle* 97

Firmenkunde *corporate client* 67

Fischerei *fishing* 71

Fitnessstudio *gym* 151

flach *shallow* 144

flämisch *Flemisch* 36

fließen **flow** 52

fließendes Wasser *running water* 🔵 100

flott, schnell *speedy* 131

flüchten **escape** 36

flüchtiger Blick *glimpse* 76

Flüchtling *refugee* 36

Flugbenzin *aviation fuel* 🔵 110

Flur *hall* 76

flussaufwärts *upstream* 🔵 100

Flüssigseife *liquid soap* 122

Flutwelle *tidal wave* 130

Folge, Auswirkung *consequence* 38

Folgerung *implication* 54

Fön *hairdryer* 🔵 37

förderlich, positiv *beneficial* 131

formen, gestalten **shape** 36

formulieren **formulate** 43

Forscher(in) *researcher* 64

Fortschritt *progress* 89

fortschrittlich *progressive* 10

Fracht *cargo* 61

frei nehmen **have / take a day off** 65

freie, unbesetzte Stelle *vacancy* 24

freiverkäuflich *over-the-counter* 102

Freizeit *leisure* 24

Freizeitzentrum *leisure centre* 88

Freude *pleasure* 51

Frische *freshness* 109

fröhlich *cheerful* 29

Führungskraft *executive* 109

Funke *spark* 76

Für und Wider, Pro und Kontra *for and against, pros and cons* 47

Fürsorge; Wohlfahrt *welfare* 38

fürsorglich *caring* 29

Fußknöchel *ankle* 97

Garderobe *cloakroom* 🔵 37

Gastgeberland, Aufnahme-staat *host country* 🔵 142

Gastwirt(in) *pub landlord* 142

gebacken *baked* 23

gebratenes Kalbsfleisch *roast veal* 🔵 139

gebräuchlich, herkömmlich *conventional* 🔵 56

Gebühr, Honorar *fee* 153

Gedanke, Überlegung *thought* 🔵 100

gedeihen **flourish** 130

geduldig *patient* 43

gedünstet *steamed* 144

geeignet, angemessen *appropriate(ly)* 68

gefährlich *hazardous* 134

gefettet *greased* 144

Geflügel *poultry* 🔵 139

gegenseitig *mutual* 126

Gegenstand *object* 82

gegenüberstellen **contrast** 45

gegenwärtig *on-going* 131

Gegner(in) *opponent* 130

Gehalt *salary* 31

gehoben, vornehm *upmarket* 155

gehorchen **obey** 96

geistig, seelisch *mental* 38

geistreich, witzig *witty* 29

Gekicher *giggle* 29

geläufig, verbreitet *prevalent* 49

gelegentlich *occasionally* 8

geltend machen **assert** 54

gemahlen; gepulvert *powdered* 🔵 139

gemäß; in Anlehnung an *according to* 39

Gemeinderat *council* 88

gemeinsam *joint* 38

Gemeinschaft der Länder des ehemaligen Britischen Weltreichs *Commonwealth* 45 gemietet *rented* 108

Gemisch, Verschnitt *blend (of)* Ⓣ 100

gemütlich *cosy* 69

genehmigen **grant** 48

genehmigen, befürworten **approve** 132

Generaldirektor(in) *CEO (Chief Executive Officer)* 28

genial *ingenious* 102

Geologe, Geologin *geologist* 61

geradeaus, überschaubar *straightforward* 67

Gerät *appliance* 89

geräumig *spacious* 150

gerechter Lohn *just reward* 140

Gericht *dish* 152

gering, unbedeutend *minor* 131

geringfügig; leicht *slight(ly)* 12

gern *like, be fond of* 28

gernhaben (jmdn./etwas) **be fond of sb/sth** 102

gesamt, komplett *entire* 54

Geschäftsinhaber(in) *shopkeeper* 142

geschält *peeled* 144

Geschirrspülmittel *washing up liquid* 102

Geschlecht *gender* 8

Geschmack *flavour* Ⓣ 11

Geschwister *siblings (pl.)* 79

Gesetzgebung *legislation* 38

gesetzliche Vorschriften *regulations (pl.)* 74

Geste, Handbewegung *gesture* 142

gestohlen *stolen* 44

gesundheitsbewusst *health-conscious* 104

Gesundheitsministerium *health ministry* 116

Gesundheitswesen *healthcare* 38

Getreide *grain* 60

getreu *faithful* 11

Getriebe *gearbox* 80

Getue *fuss* 85

gewagt, pikant *racy* 54

gewaltig *massive, enormous* 53

Gewässerkundige(r) *hydrologist* 100

gewieft, gerissen *smart* 10

gewinnen; erzielen **gain** 26

gewissenhaft *diligent* 27

gewöhnlich *commonplace* 130

gewürfelt *diced* 144

Gier *greed* 88

Gleichgewicht *balance* 65

Gleichung *equation* 72

Gott sei Dank! *Thank goodness!* 40

Gottesdienst *church service* 8

Gradient; Gefällstrecke *gradient* 80

greifbar, zu Hand *at hand* 12

greifen, klemmen **grip** 17

grenzüberschreitend *transboundary* Ⓣ 100

grob *coarse(ly)* 144

Größenverhältnis *scale* 92

Großfamilie *extended family* 38

Großhandelsmarkt *wholesale market* 109

großmäulig *loudmouthed* 142

Gründer(in) *founder* 41

grundlegend *underlying* 76

gründlich *thorough(ly)* 144

Grundschule *primary school* 40

Grundwasser *groundwater* 105

Gruppenvergewaltigung *gang rape* 116

gut bekannt *well-known* 96

Gutachter(in) *evaluator* 79

gute Tat *good deed* 96

Habsucht, Gier *avarice* 97

Hackfleisch *minced meat* 123

Hafen; Hafenstadt *port* 36

Hafenanlage *docks (pl.)* 61

Haferbrei *porridge* 108

haftbar, verantwortlich *accountable* 54

halb durch, mitten drin *halfway through* 25

halsbrecherische Geschwindigkeit *breakneck speed* 66

haltbar, beständig *durable* 80

Handarbeit *manual labour* Ⓣ 110

Handelsware *commodity* Ⓣ 100

Handgelenk *wrist* 97

handgenäht *hand-stitched* 135

handhaben, mit etwas umgehen **handle sth** 24

Handlanger, Scherge *henchman* 44

Händler *retailer* 52

handlich, griffig *handy* 51

Handlungsverlauf *proceedings* 68

Handlungsweise, Verhalten *conduct* 134

Handschrift *handwriting* 24

Handtuch *towel* 120

hängen, erhängen **hang (hanged, hanged) oneself** 10

harmlos *harmless* Ⓣ 100

Harz, Kunstharz *resin* 100

Haselnuss *hazelnut* 8

Haushaltspflichten *chores (pl.)* 76

Hausierer(in) *peddler* 126

Hausmeister(in) *caretaker* 40

Hefe *yeast* Ⓣ 11

heftig *intense* 62

Heftpflaster *sticking plaster, elastoplast* 119

heilen **cure** 44

Heilmittel, Heilung *cure* Ⓣ 96

heimtückisch *sneakily* 102

Heimweh haben *homesick* 40

Heimwerkerbedarf *home improvement items* 66

Heizung, Belüftung, Klimatechnik *HVAC (Heating, Ventilation, Air Conditioning)* 75

helfen **assist (with)** 83

helfen (jmdm.) **be of assis-tance (to sb.)** 157

Herablassung *condescension* 142

herabsetzen, auf ein Mindest-maß verkleinern **minimize** 107

heranreifen **ripen** 106

heraufbeschwören, provo-zieren **provoke** 43

Herausforderung *challenge* 38

herausnehmbar *removable* 89

herausstellen **turn out** 29

Herkunft, Quelle *source* 🅣 100

hermetisch verschließen **seal** 109

herrschen **rule** 130

herstammen; entspringen **originate** 37

Hersteller *manufacturer* 52

herumalbern **fool around** 28

herumnörgeln; jmdm mit etwas in den Ohren liegen **nag sb about sth** 16

hervorragend *outstanding* 24

hervorrufen **arouse** 141

hervorspringend, markant *prominent* 36

Herzinfarkt *heart attack* 88

Herz-Kreislauf Erkrankung *cardiovascular disease* 92

Herzrhythmusstörung *cardiac arrhythmia* 88

heutzutage *nowadays* 24

Hieroglyphen *hieroglyphics* 50

Himbeere *raspberry* 108

Himmelbett *four-poster bed* 150

hin und her schalten **flick between** 41

hin und zurück *round-trip* 105

hinausschleichen **slip out** 14

hinauswerfen **turn sb out of** 140

Hindernis *impediment* 130

Hinterhof, Garten hinter dem Haus *backyard (AE)* 76

hinweisen, andeuten **indicate** 48

Hochfrequenz *high frequency* 🅣 56

Hochkonjunktur; Wohlstand *prosperity* 62

Hochleistungs-, leistungsstark *high-capacity* 81

hochschlagfest *high-impact proof* 100

Höhepunkt *peak* 62

Holzwirtschaft *forestry industry* 60

Honig *honey* 11

Hopfen *hops* 🅣 11

Hörsaal *lecture hall* 🅣 100

Hörtext *listening text* 7

Hörverständnis *listening comprehension* 19

Hosenspanner *trouser press* 151

Hotelbesitzer(in) *hotelier* 142

Hufeisen *horseshoe* 136

Hufschmied, Grobschmied *blacksmith* 126

hülsenfruchtartig *leguminous* 105

Humane Immunschwäche-krankheit *HIV = Human Immunodeficiency Virus disease* 131

humorvoll *humorous* 18

Humus, Mutterboden *topsoil* 105

Hybridmotor *hybrid motor* 80

hydratisiert *hydrated* 🅣 100

Hypothek *mortgage* 63

Ich verbinde Sie jetzt. *I'm put-ting you through now.* 153

identifizieren **identify** 19

im eigenen Land entstanden; selbstgezogen *homegrown* 126

im Verlauf (von) *in the course of* 28

im Wege stehen **get in the way** 78

immateriell, unbegreiflich *intangible* 🅣 100

Immobilienmakler *estate agent* 61

Immobilienmarkt *property market* 61

in Bewegung *on the move* 140

in Rente gehen **retire** 133

in Streifen schneiden **cut sth to ribbons** 14

Indien *India* 36

Indiz *clue, evidence* 🅣 110

industriegefertigte Güter *manufactured products* 126

Industrieländer *industrialized nations* 92

industriell verarbeitete Lebens-mittel *processed food* 107

Infizierung, Ansteckung *infection* 20

inhärent *inherent, inherently* 130

Initiative *initiative* 116

inmitten *amid* 10

innerhalb *within* 38

innigst geliebt *beloved* 112

insgesamt *overall* 102

Insolvenzantrag stellen **file for bankruptcy** 66

installieren **install** 76

Intelligenzquotient *IQ (Intelli-gence Quotient)* 78

interessanterweise *interestingly* 116

Interesse *interest* 48

Internet-Handel *cyber-commerce* 66

interpretieren **interpret** 37

Interpunktion *punctuation* 31

intim *intimate* 78

Investition *investment* 131

Irland *Ireland* 36

irreführend *misleading* 37

Isolierung *isolation* 37

Jahresumsatz *annual sales* 66

Jahrzehnt *decade* 38

Jugend; Entwicklungsjahre *adolescence* 17

Jugendliche(r) *adolescent* 92

Kakaobohne *cocoa bean* 🅣 129

Kamin, offene Feuerstelle *fireplace* 150

kämpferisch *militant* 140

Karamell *toffee* 102

Karikatur *cartoon* 99

Kasinoangestellte(r) *croupier* 15

Kasse *till* 102

Katastrophe *catastrophe* 90

Kätzchen *kitten* 124

Kehrseite, Nachteil *downside* 62

keimfrei machen **pasteurize** 108

Kenntnis; Wissensstand *knowledge* 53

Kerl, Mannsbild *stud-muffin (AE)* 44

Kern *core* 65

Kernreaktor *nuclear reactor* 44

Kernspaltung *fission* 112

Kette *chain* 80

Kiefer *jaw* 89

Kinderbetreuung *childcare* 64

Kirsche *cherry* 139

klagen, prozessieren (vor Gericht) **sue** 54

Klammer *bracket* 144

klappern (gegen etwas) **clunk against sth** 16

klären **resolve** 43

klarmachen **make sth plain** 79

Klebeband *adhesive tape, sellotape* 119

Kleidungsstück *garment* 135

Kleinfamilie *nuclear family* 38

Klettverschluss *velcro* 119

Klimawandel *climate change* 🅣 100

Klinge *blade* 82

Klischeevorstellung *stereotype* 137

Klo *loo (slang)* 102

Kloß *dumpling* 138

Klugscheißer *wise guy* 🅣 123

knapp an etwas sein **be short on / of sth** 76

knusprig *crisp* 144

Kochkunst *cuisine* 152

kognitive Fähigkeit *cognitive skill* 55

Kohlendioxid *carbon dioxide (CO_2)* 104

Kohlenwasserstoffgas (C_2H_4), Ethylen *ethylene gas* 106

Kolonialambitionen *colonialist designs* 130

Kolonialzeiten *colonial times* 140

kolossal *whopping* 51

Kommunismus *communism* 130

kompetent, tüchtig *proficient* 31

Komplexität *complexity* 52

komprimiert, zusammen-gedrückt *compressed* 65

kompromittierend *compromising* 54

Konjunkturbelebung *revival* 62

Konjunkturrückgang, Rezession *recession* 62

Konjunkturtief *depression* 62

konkret, greifbar *tangible* 🅣 100

Konkurrenz machen; sich mit jmdm messen **compete with sb** 66

konkurrenzfähig *competitive* 130

Konsens *consensus* 92

Konsequenzen, Nach-wirkungen *fallout* 10

Konserven *tinned food, canned ...* 23

konservieren **can** 107

Konstruktion *structure* 60

konstruktiv *constructive(ly)* 43

Kontakte mit Menschen knüpfen **socialize** 48

kontaktfreudig *sociable* 71

kontrollieren; beobachten **keep close tabs on** 79

Konzentrationslager (KZ) *concentration camp* 116

konzentrieren **focus on sth** 12

Konzept *concept* 52

koordinieren, abstimmen **coordinate** 79

körperlich *physical* 38

Körpermassenzahl *Body Mass Index* 93

korrekt, anständig *proper(ly)* 25

kostbar *precious* 🅣 100

kostengünstig, wirtschaftlich *cost-effective* 67

Kratzer *scratch* 119

Kraut, Heilkraut *herb* 🅣 100

Krebs *cancer* 44

Krieger(in) *warrior* 44

Krimi *thriller* 10

Kriterium *criterion, (pl.) criteria* 31

Kritiker(in) *critic* 109

Krone *crown* 66

Krug *jug* 🅣 100

Kugelschreiber *ballpoint pen* 119

Kühlcontainer *refrigerated container (reefer)* 105

Kühlhauslagerung *cold-storage* 108

Kuhmist *cow muck* 🅣 110

kumulativ, sich anhäufend *cumulative* 10

Kundenstamm *customer base* 127

Kündigung einer Hypothek (Bank); Vollstreckungs-erklärung (Gericht) *foreclosure* 63

Kunstgattung *genre* 10

Künstlername *pseudonym* 54

kurz *brief* 68

Kürzel, Kurzwort *acronym* 51

Kurzschrift *shorthand* 50

Kürzung, Senkung *cut* 92

Kurzwaren *dried goods* 107

kuschelig *cuddly* 124

laborgeprüft *laboratory-tested* 120

Lachen *laugh* 29

lächerlich *ridiculous, laughable* 42

laden, beladen **load** 109

Ladestation *charging station* 80

Ladung, Last *load* 80

Lagerhaltung *storage* 66

ländlich *rural* 36

Landschaft; Natur *countryside* 🔵 34

langandauernd *long-lasting* 124

Länge *length* 51

Langspielplatte *album* 14

Langzeit-, auf lange Sicht *long term* 74

Lastwagen *truck (AE)* 105

Lastwagenfahrer(in) *lorry driver* 109

Latsche *slipper* 124

Lauch *leek* 144

lauter sprechen s*peak up* 153

Lautschrift *phonetic transcription* 16

lebend *living* 78

Lebenserwartung *life expectancy* 39

Lebenslauf (BE) *curriculum vitae / CV, (AE) résumé* (auch: *resumé, resume*) 7

Lebensmittelhändler *grocer* 🔵 123

Lebensmittelladen *grocery store (AE)* 104

Lebensmittelverarbeitung *food processing* 140

Lebensversicherungspolice *life insurance policy* 140

lebenswichtig; grundlegend *vital* 38

Leber *liver* 88

Leberversagen *liver failure* 88

Leck *leak* 76

lecken **lick** 119

Leerstelle *blank spot* 79

legen, stellen **place** 80

Leichtbauwerkstoff *lightweight material* 80

Leidende(r) *sufferer* 116

leisten können **afford** 89

leistungsfähig *efficient* 80

Leistungsverzweigung *power split* 80

Lektüre *read* 51

letztendlich *eventually* 105

letztendlich gelangen **end up** 22

liebenswert *lovable* 43

liebevoll *loving* 43

liefern **deliver** 40

Lob *praise* 116

loben **praise** 134

löblich *laudable, laudably* 11

Lohn *wage* 62

lohnend *rewarding* 22

loslassen **let go** 78

Löwenanteil *lion's share* 67

Lügendetektor *lie detector* 86

Lumpen, Klamotten *rags (pl.)* 141

Lunge *lung* 97

luxuriös *luxurious* 120

Luxus *luxury* 🔵 100

mächtig *mighty* 50

Mädchen *(AE slang) gal* 18

Magersucht *anorexia* 116

magisch *magically* 102

mähen **mow** 82

Mäher *mower* 83

Mais *maize (AE: corn)* 111

Mammut *mammoth* 60

Mangel *shortage* 62

mangels, an etwas mangeln *lack of* 11

Märchen *fairy tale* 140

Marketing *marketing* 71

Markise *awning* 🔵 75

Marktfähigkeit *marketability* 31

Maß; Maßnahme *measure* 104

maßgeblich, relevant *relevant* 52

massiv, stabil *solid* 69

Maximierung *maximization* 126

mechanisch *mechanical* 100

mechanisiert *mechanized* 🔵 110

Mechanismus; Maschinen *machinery* 62

Mediziner(in) *physician* 89

Meerschweinchen *guinea pig* 🔵 123

Mehl *flour* 🔵 139

mehrfach, mannigfaltig *multiple* 92

mehrmals, wiederholt *repeatedly* 109

Meinungsverschiedenheit *controversy* 116

Menge *amount* 90

Menge *quantity* 102

Menge: eine ganze ~, sehr viel *a whole bunch of ~, a great deal* 🔵 70

Menschenalter *generation* 140

Menschenschlange *queue* 🔵 11

messen **measure** 104

Messfühler *sensor* 76

Messwert *measurement* 78

Methode *method* 26

mieten **rent (sth)** 61

Milchprodukte *dairy* 103

Militär *military forces* 90

Milz *spleen* 97

minimalgeregelt *loosely-regulated* 90

Mischehe eingehen **intermarry** 37

Mischung *mix* 139

missachtet *ignored* 43

missbilligen; verurteilen **deplore** 116

Missbrauch *abuse* 38

missdeuten, falsch auffassen **misinterpret** 142

Misserfolg, Scheitern *failure* 68

missverstanden *misunderstood* 17

Missverständnis *misunderstanding* 137

misswirtschaften **mismanage** 131

mit besten / freundlichen Grüßen *Best regards* 149

mit Eis *on the rocks* 151

Mitarbeiter(in) *co-worker* 69

Mitgliedschaft *membership* 49

Mitteilung *notification* 132

mittelalterlich *medieval* 126

mittelos *penniless* 140

Modell, Musterbeispiel *paradigm* 54

Modewort; abgedroschene Phrase *buzzword* 66

modisch *fashionable* 120

modisch schick *trendy* 14

Moralität, Sittlichkeit *morality* 79

Moschee *mosque* 36

Müllabfuhr *refuse collection* 60

Müller(in) *miller* 126

mündlich *oral* 51

Mundstück *mouthpiece* 100

Mundwasser *mouthwash* 122

Mürbeteig *shortcrust pastry* 144

Musikautomat *jukebox* 76

Muster, Kostprobe *sample* 24

Mythos *myth* 🔊 110

Nach der Legende ... *Legend has it that ...* 140

Nachbarort *neighbouring town* 🔊 34

Nachfrage; Forderung *demand* 105

Nachkomme *descendant* 36

Nachkriegs- *post-war* 36

Nachname *surname* 🔊 142

nackt *naked* 116

Nadel *needle* 126

nähern **approach (sth/sb)** 72

Nahrungsmittel *foodstuff* 108

nämlich *namely* 100

Nationalismus *nationalism* 140

Navi *Satnav* 120

neigen (zu etwas) **tend to** 10

nervenaufreibend *nerve-racking* 27

Neuankömmling *newcomer* 36

neugierig *curious* 128

Neuheit; Neuerung *innovation* 52

nicht hilfreich *unhelpful* 110

nicht schaffen, etwas zu tun **fail to do sth** 12

Nichteinhaltung; Vertragsverletzung *violation* 135

nicken **nod** 142

Niere *kidney* 97

nippen **sip** 100

Nische *niche* 41

normal, gewöhnlich *standard* 50

Nüchternheit *sobriety* 96

Nudeln *noodles (pl.)* 111

Nutzen; Vorteil *benefit* 47

Nutzer(in) *user* 48

obenliegend *overhead* 69

Oberfläche *surface* 83

obligatorisch, vorgeschrieben *mandatory* 90

Obst und Gemüse Abteilung *produce section* 104

Obstplantage *orchard* 106

öffentlicher Dienst / Verwaltung *civil service* 63

ohne Bezug *unrelated* 18

ohne Hemd *shirtless* 116

ohrfeigen **slap sb** 86

Optiker(in) *optician* 17

Optimismus *optimism* 63

Organismus *organism* 136

Overheadfolie, Dia *slide* 101

packen **grab, clutch**

am Kragen packen **grab sb by the scruff of the neck** 14

Paniermehl *breadcrumbs* 🔊 139

Papiertaschentuch *kleenex* 119

Papiertuch *kitchen towel* 102

Patriotismus *patriotism* 🔊 142

Personal *staff* 10

Personalabteilung *human resources* 24

Personalvermittler(in) *recruiter* 12

pessimistisch *pessimistic* 22

Petersilie *parsley* 144

Pfannkuchen *pancake* 138

Pfeffer *pepper* 🔊 139

Phänomen, Naturerscheinung *phenomenon* 100

Philanthrop *humanitarian* 🔊 123

Pinie *pine tree* 123

Pionierarbeit *pioneer work* 134

platzsparend *space-saving* 120

Pluralismus *pluralism* 37

Polen *Poland* 36

politische Linie *policy* 38

Porzellan *porcelain* 126

Postdienst *postal service* 60

Praktikant(in) *intern* 24

Praktikum *internship, (BE) work experience* 12

prämieren **award** 121

Präposition *preposition* 33

Prediger *preacher* 🔊 123

Premierminister(in) *prime minister* 143

Pressesprecherin *spokeswoman* 64

Primär- *primary* 60

Prise *pinch of* 144

Produktionsmittel, Ressource *resource* 🔊 100

produktiv, aktiv *productive* 7

Produktivität, Effizienz *efficiency* 66

Protokoll führen **keep the minutes (of a meeting)** 68

provisorisch *provisional* 157

Pubertät *puberty* 17

Punkt (rund) *dot* 153

Pünktlichkeit *punctuality* 68

Punktstrahler; Mittelpunkt des Interesses *spotlight* 88

Quadrat- *square* 38

qualifizieren **qualify** 132

Qualitätsprüfer(in) *inspector* 109

Quark *curd* 138

Quartal *quarter* 66

Quelle, Entstehungsort *source* 106

Rächer(in) *avenger* 10

Radiosender *radio station* 36

Raffinerie *refinery* 61

Rasen *lawn* 82

Rasenmäher *lawnmower* 83

Rasierklinge *razor blade* 122

Rasierschaum *shaving foam* 120

Rassen-, rassisch *racial* 140

Rassentrennung *segregation* 37

Rastergitter *grid* 33

rationalisieren, wettbewerbs-fähiger gestalten **stream-line** 66

ratsam *advisable* 11

Raubtier *predator* 49

Raumspray *air freshener* 120

Reagenzglas *test tube* 18

realistisch *realistic* 22

rechtfertigen **justify** 11

rechthaberisch *opinionated* 142

rechtzeitig *in good time* 68

Redensart *idiom* 141

regelmäßig *frequent* 76

regeln, regulieren **regulate** 131

Regelung *regulation* 90

reibungslos funtionierend *smoothly-functioning* 109

reichlich *plentiful* 109

Reichtümer *riches (pl.)* 141

Reichweite *range* ⓣ 56

reif *ripe* 109

Reifekammer *ripening room* 109

Reinigungsflüssigkeit *cleaning liquid* 102

Reinigungsmittel *cleanser* 120

reinschauen, einen kurzen Besuch abstatten **pop into** 108

Reklamefläche *billboard* 119

Rennrad Profi *professional bike racer* 32

renommiert *renowned* 11

Rentner(in) *pensioner* 90

Reservierung *booking* 11

Reservierungsdienst *booking service* 153

resigniert *resigned* 17

Resonanz *resonance* 79

Rettungsschwimmer(in); Badewärter *lifeguard* 18

rezeptiv *receptive* 7

Risiko, Wagnis *risk* 88

Rohöl *crude oil* 61

Rohstoff *raw material* 60

Röllchen *roll* 102

routinemäßig *routinely* 64

Rückarbeitsbremsung, Nutzbremsung *regenerative braking* 80

Rückgewinnung, Wieder-findung *retrieval* 52

rückläufig *declining* 50

rücksichtsvoll *thoughtful* 17

rührselig *sentimental* 29

Rummelplatzfahrgeschäft *fair-ground ride* 10

Rundfunk *broadcasting* 60

Rundumetikett *wrap-around label* ⓣ 100

Russland *Russia* 36

rutschen **slip** 66

sachlich *objective* 115

Sackgasse *dead end* 80

saftig *juicy* 124

sahnig *creamy* 112

sanft *gentle* ⓣ 96

sanieren; umordnen **restructure** 66

Sanierungsplan *reorganization plan* 66

Sanitäreinrichtungen; Hygiene *sanitation* 38

Satzstellung *word order* 79

Sauerteig *sourdough* ⓣ 34

schaden, verletzen **harm** 104

schädlich *harmful* 82

Schädlingsbekämpfung *pest control* 18

Schädlingsbekämpfungsmittel *pesticide* 104

Schadstoff, Verunreinigung *contaminant* 100

Schale *shell* 100

Schalter *switch* 76

Schaltuhr *timer* 83

schämen (sich) **be ashamed of oneself** 86

schätzen **estimate** 38

Schätzung *estimate* 92

Scheck *(BE) cheque, (AE) check* 67

scheinbar *seemingly* 83

schick *hip* 11

schieben; schalten **shift** 54

schiffbar, befahrbar *navigable* 126

Schiffswerft *shipyard* 61

schlecht geführt *mismanaged* 38

schlendern **stroll** 104

schlussendlich, letztmalig *ultimately* 60

schmal *slim* ⓣ 123

schmelzen **melt** 118

schmelzend *melting* 102

schmücken **grace** 51

Schnitthöhe *cutting height* 83

Schraubenzieher *screwdriver* 83

Schreibheft, Übungsheft *exercise book* 32

schrumpfend *shrinking* 102

Schulausbildung *schooling* 79

Schuld *fault, guilt* 43

Schuldige(r) *culprit* 116

Schulleiter(in) *headteacher* 10

Schulterklopfen *pat on the back* 142

Schulzeit *term-time* 65

Schuss, Fix *fix* 102

Schwäche *weakness* 27

schwafeln **ramble** 43

schwanger *pregnant* 14

Schwanz *tail* 119

schwarzes Brett *bulletin board* 25

Schwelle; (tech.) Grenzbereich *threshold* 52

Schwert *sword* ⓣ 129

schwerwiegend, stark *severe* 62

seelisch, psychisch *psychic* 54

Sehnsucht *desire, longing* 128

sehr ähnlich *much alike* 78

Seidenpapier *tissue paper* 119

Sekundär- *secondary* 60

selbst, selber *self* 79

senden, etwas durch Rundfunk verbreiten **broadcast** ⓣ 56

Senke, Talsohle *trough* 62

senkrecht *vertical, vertically* 122

sexuell *sexual* 116

sich etwas unterziehen
   undergo 79

sicher gehen ***play it safe*** 155

Sicherheits- *security* 24

Sicherheitsbedienstete(r)
   security guard 18

Sicherheitseinstellungen
   privacy settings 54

Sicherheitskontrollfeld
   security panel 76

Sicherheitsvorkehrungen
   safety measures 76

sicherstellen, gewährleisten
   ensure 18

Sicht *sight* 63

Siedlung *settlement* 36

Sieger(in) *victor* 134

Sinn für Humor *sense of
   humour* 25

sinnlos *pointless*
   es hat keinen Sinn (etwas
   zu tun); *there's no point in
   (doing sth)* 20

sitzend *sedentary* 92

Sitzgurt *seat belt* 114

Sitzungssaal *boardroom* ⊤
   100

skizzieren ***sketch*** 14

Sklave, Sklavin *slave* ⊤ 129

Skrupel, Bedenken *scruple* ⊤
   129

SMS-Nachricht schreiben
   texting 157

sobald als möglich *asap
   (as soon as possible)* 30

soll ... sein ***is supposed to be ...***
   42

Sonderbeitrag *feature article*
   141

Sonderkommission *taskforce*
   64

Sonnenbank *sunbed* 88

Sonnenlicht *sunlight* ⊤ 70

Sorge, Besorgnis *concern* 104

sorgfältig überprüft *carefully-
   screened* 67

Sozialbaugebiet *project
   (housing) (AE)* 44

Sozialismus *socialism* 130

Sozialversicherung
   social security 90

spähen ***peer*** 10

spannend *thrilling* 10

später *subsequent* 140

Speisen und Getränke liefern
   cater (for) 41

Spezialität *speciality* ⊤ 34

Spirituosen *spirits* ⊤ 11

Spitze, Punkt *point* 107

spontan *spontaneously* ⊤ 56

sprachgesteuert *voice-
   controlled* 76

Sprachwissenschaftler(in)
   linguistic expert 51

Spraydose *spray* 102

Sprudel *sparkling water* ⊤
   100

Staatsbürgerschaft *citizenship*
   132

Stadtsanierung *urban renewal*
   18

ständig, andauernd *constant*
   92

Standort *site* 140

Starkbier (dunkles) *stout* 118

Start *launch* 50

stattfinden, sich ereignen
   occur 102

Staudamm *dam* ⊤ 100

Steckbrief, Kurzbiografie
   profile 8

Steigerung *increase* 92

sterbend *dying* 116

stetig, beständig *steadily* 66

Steuervermeidung
   tax avoidance 130

Stillstand *standstill* 62

stilvoll, elegant *stylish* ⊤ 100

Stimmung *atmosphere, tone*
   11

Stimmungsschwankungen
   mood swings 88

Stipendium *student grant* 24

Stöckelschuhe *high heels* 116

stolz (auf) *proud (of)* 28

Straßenkehrer *street sweeper*
   140

Strategie *strategy* 92

strecken ***stretch*** 42

Streifen *strip* 119

Streit *row* 29

stressig *stressful* ⊤ 96

Stroh *straw* ⊤ 75

Student im Aufbaustudium
   graduate student 67

Studium *studies (pl.)* 25

Sturz, Absackung *slump* 62

stürzen ***plummet*** 63

Substanz, Stoff *substance* 94

Suchmaschine *search engine*
   23

Sucht *addiction* 94

Suchtkranke(r) *addict* 50

sündhaft *sinful* 120

süßen; versüßen ***sweeten*** 92

Tabellenkalkulation *spreadsheet* 25

Tablette *tablet* 102

Tagesordnung *agenda* 68

Tagung *conference* 28

Taschenformat *pocket-sized*
   51

Taschentuch *handkerchief* 119

tatsächlich, in der Tat
   as a matter of fact 30

taufen ***baptise*** 143

Teamgeist *team spirit* 25

Teelöffel ... (Maßeinheit)
   teaspoonful ⊤ 139

Teilchen *particle* 100

teilen ***split*** 60

Teilnehmer(in) *attendee* 68

Telearbeit *teleworking* 65

Telefonist(in) *switchboard
   operator* 31

Tellerwäscher-zum-Millionär
   Geschichte *rags-to-riches
   story* 141

Tendenz *trend* 35

Teppich *carpet* ⊤ 11

Tertiär- *tertiary* 60

textlich, textbezogen *textual*
   115

Textstelle *passage* 50

Textverarbeitung
   word processing 25

Tischdecke *tablecloth* 122

Topf *pan* ⊤ 139

Toten *the dead* 10

Tourismus *tourism* 148

tragbar *portable* 120

trainieren **work out** 151

Traube *grape* 105

Trauer; Trauerkleidung
mourning 96

Travestie *travesty* 50

Treibhausgase *greenhouse
gases* 104

Treibsand *quicksand* (T) 123

Treibstoff *fuel* 80

Tresen *bar* (T) 11

Tresor *safe* 151

treten **kick**
jmdn sehr heftig treten
kick the snot out of sb 44

Treue *allegiance* 133

trinkbar *drinkable* 100

Trinkwasser in Flaschen
bottled water 100

Trockengewicht
drained weight 102

trocknen, abtrocknen **dry** 107

Trocknung *drying* 75

Tropen-; tropisch *tropical* 52

trotz *despite* 50

Truppen *troops (pl.)* 96

tüfteln **fiddle about (with sth)**
(T) 75

Türkis *turquoise* 100

twittern **tweet** 54

Typhus *typhoid* 100

tyrannisch *despotic* 130

überarbeiten **revise** 19

Überbiss *overbite* 89

Überblick behalten **keep
track of** 76

überbringen, übermitteln
convey 95

überfahren, übergehen
pass over 83

überheblich *arrogant* 142

Überland-, über Land *overland*
109

Übernahme *takeover* 140

überproportional,
unverhältnismäßig
disproportionately 92

überreden **persuade** 65

Übersee, Ausland *overseas*
109

übersehen, nicht bemerken
overlook 10

übertragen durch Wasser
water-borne 100

Übertragung *transmission* 80

Übertragungswelle; Schaft
shaft 81

übertreiben **overdo** 101

überwachen, kontrollieren
monitor 88

Überwachung; Beobachtung
observation 97

überwältigen, bezwingen
overpower 130

überwinden **overcome** 39

überwuchert *grown over* 83

überzeugt *convinced* 66

Überzeugung *belief* 49

überzuckert, dragiert
sugar-coated 118

Ultraviolettstrahlung
UV radiation 101

Umarmung *hug* 51

umfangreich *extensive* 13

Umgang pflegen **associate
with** (T) 56

umgangssprachlich (ugs.)
colloquial (coll.) 141

Umgebung *surroundings* 49

umgehen (mit jmdm) **treat sb**
28

umgestaltet *revamped* 102

umleiten **reroute** (T) 100

umrühren **stir** (T) 139

umschalten **flick between** (T)
56

umsetzen, durchführen
implement (sth) 54

umstritten *controversial* 64

umwandeln **convert sth
into sth** 61

Umweltschadstoff *pollutant*
(T) 100

unaufhörlich *continuously* 66

unbefugt *unauthorized* 135

unbeständig, flatterhaft
flighty 54

unbeständig, uneinheitlich
inconsistent 50

unbezahlt *unpaid* 24

Unebenheit *unevenness* 79

unehrlich *dishonest* 102

Unendlichkeit *infinity* 72

unerhört, gänzlich unbekannt
unheard of 134

unerwünscht *undesirable* 37

unfähig *unable* 90

ungeachtet der /des …
regardless (of) 72

ungeeignet *unsuitable* 143

ungefähr *approximately* (T)
56

ungesalzen *unsalted* 144

ungesunde Fertigkost
junk food 92

unglaublich, wunderbar
incredible 100

Ungleichheit *inequality* 131

Unkosten, Ausgaben *expenses*
66

Unkraut (ugs. Marihuana)
weed 96

unmenschlich *inhumane* 131

unproblematisch *plain sailing*
41

unpünktlich *unpunctual* 32

unreif *unripe* 106

unrentabel, ertraglos
unprofitable 66

Unruhen *unrest* 36

unter Druck setzen **pressure sb**
74

unterbeschäftigt, nicht ausge-
lastet *underemployed* 38

unterbrechen **interrupt** 43

Untergang; Ableben *demise*
54

Unterkunft *accommodation*
148

unterliegen **succumb** 50

Unternehmen *corporation* 69

Unternehmensführung;
Verwaltung *management*
23

Unternehmer(in) *contractor*
134

unterscheiden (zwischen) **distinguish (between)** 107

Unterschicht *underclass* 94

unterschiedlich, verschieden *diverse* 36

unterstützen **support** Ⓣ 56

Unterstützer *supporter* Ⓣ 96

Unterstützung *support* 116

untersuchen **examine** 107

unterwürfig *submissive* 17

unvergesslich *memorably* 10

unvoreingenommen *impartial* 41

unwillkommen *unwelcome* 140

üppig *ample* Ⓣ 100

Urkunde, Dokument *document* 132

Verachtung *contempt* 142

veranlagungsgemäß *temperamental* 79

Veranschaulichung *visualization* 43

Veranstaltungsraum *function room* 11

Veranstaltungsverkäufe *event sales* 25

Verantwortlichkeit, Haftung *accountability* 130

Verantwortung *responsibility* 116

Verarbeitung *processing* 106

verbal ausfallend *verbally abusive* 43

verbessert *improved* 38

Verbesserung *improvement* 64

verbieten **prohibit** 135

verbinden, zusammenlegen **combine** 80

verbleiben **remain** 11

verblüfft, entgeistert *flabbergasted* 50

Verbrauch, Konsum *consumption* 62

verbrauchen; verzehren **consume** 110

Verbraucher(in) *consumer* 60

verbreiten; (sich) ausweiten **broaden** 79

Verbrennungsmotor *internal combustion engine* 80

verdächtigen, vermuten **suspect** 102

verdammen **condemn** 88

verderben **spoil** 51

verdeutlichen **clarify** 129

verdichten; kondensieren **condense** 51

verdienen **deserve** 86

verdünnt *diluted* 102

Vereidigung *swearing-in* 133

vereinfachen **make sth a snap** 52

vereinfachen **simplify** 83

vereinfacht *simplified* zu stark vereinfacht *over-simplified* Ⓣ 110

vereinzelt *isolated* 92

Verfahren; Ablauf *process* 37

verfallen, heruntergekommen *derelict* 135

verfaulen, verwesen *rot* 96

Verfolgen *persecution* 36

Vergnügen *enjoyment* Ⓣ 96

Verhaltenskodex *code of conduct* 116

verheerend *devastating* 10

verherrlichen **glorify** 116

Verhütungspille *pill* 14

Verkäufer(in), Lieferant *seller, vendor* 106

verkaufsfähig, vermarktbar *marketable* 80

Verlag; Verleger *publisher* 50

verlangen; beanspruchen **demand** 54

Verlangsamung *slowdown* 62

verlassen (sich auf) **rely on** 54

verletzlich, verwundbar *vulnerable* 38

verlocken, verleiten **tempt** 139

Verlust *loss* 60

vermarkten, auf den Markt bringen **launch sth** 66

vermeiden **avoid** 35

vermindert *diminished* 102

Vermischung *intermingling* 131

Vermögen *wealth* 126

vermuten, voraussetzen **assume** 102

Vernachlässigung *neglect* 38

vernünftig (mit jmdm) reden **reason with sb** 43

Verorgungsunternehmen *utility* 60

verpacken **package** 108

verpackt *packaged* 92

Verpackung *packaging* 66

Verpflegungsdienst *catering service* Ⓣ 148

verringern, abbauen **reduce** 38

versammeln **assemble** 10

Versammlung einberufen **call a meeting** 68

Versand *shipping* 104

Versandkatalog *mail-order catalogue* 67

Verschiebung, Verlagerung *shift* 38

verschieden, mannigfaltig *various* 30

Verschiedenheit; Mannigfaltigkeit *diversity* 37

verschlingen **scoff** 102

verschlossen, zurückgezogen *withdrawn* 88

Verschluss, Befestigung *fastener* 119

verschmäht, verachtet *despised* 94

verschreibungspflichtiges Arzneimittel *prescription medicine* 102

verschwinden **disappear** 83

versehentlich *accidentally* 76

versichert *insured* 90

Versicherung *insurance* 89

Versorgung *provision* 90

verständlich *understandable* 121

verständlich machen, jmdm etwas vermitteln **get sth across to sb** 50

Verständnis *comprehension* 77

versteckt *hidden* 102

verstehen **understand**
Ich verstehe. *I see.* 26
Versteigerung *auction* 66
verstopfen **clog** 100
verstoßen, vertreiben **cast out** 38
verstreut *scattered* 140
Versuchsmodell *experimental model* 78
verteilen **distribute** 68
Verteilung, Verbreitung *distribution* 38
vertiefen **deepen** 79
vertraulich *confidential* 68
vertraut, gewohnt *familiar* 104
verunreinigt, belastet *contaminated* 100
vervollkommnen, perfektionieren **perfect** 67
Verwaltung *administration* 24
verwandt mit *related to* 26
Verzweiflung *despair* 16
verzweigen (sich) **branch out** 140
Verzweigung *branch* 39
vielbefahren *busy* 🔵 37
Vielfalt *variety* 37
vielseitig *versatile* 120
vollgestopft mit *packed with* 76
volljährig / mündig werden **come of age** 143
vom Fass *draught* 🔵 11
vor allem *above all* 100
Voranmeldung, Reservierung; Reservat, Schutzgebiet *reservation* 19
Voraussage, Prognose *forecast* 39
voraussagen **predict** 54
voraussagend *predictive* 50
Voraussetzung, Postulat *requirement, postulate* 72
Vorbereitung *preparation* 38
Vorbeugung *prevention* 92
vorherig; früher *previous* 12
Vorliebe *preference* 7
vornehm *posh* 40
Vorrat *supply* 🔵 75

Vorsicht *caution* 49
vorsichtig *cautious* 29
Vorsitzender, Vorstands-vorsitzende(r) *chairman, chairperson* 68
Vorsprechen *audition* 14
Vorstehen des Unterkiefers *underbite* 89
vorstellen, etwas veran-schaulichen **visualize, envisage sth** 51
vortäuschen; so tun, als ob **make out (that)** 15
Vortrag, Liederabend *recital* 🔵 123
vortragen, aufsagen **recite** 🔵 123
Vorurteil *prejudice* 143
vorwärts *forward* 80
Wachs *wax* 106
wachsen und gedeihen **prosper** 126
wachsend, sich ausdehnend *expanding* 24
Wachstum, Zunahme *growth* 39
wagen (sich) **venture (into)** 66
Wahnsinn *lunacy* 🔵 123
wahrnehmen **perceive** 116
Walnuss *walnut* 138
Wanderlust *itchy feet* 128
Wandern *hiking* 8
wandernd, unstet *migrant* 94
Wandtafel *wall panel* 76
Waren, Güter *goods* 130
Warenhauszentrum, Güterverteilzentrum *warehouse hub* 108
warnen (vor etwas) **warn sb (of sth)** 38
wartungsarm *low-main-tenance* 120
Wäschereigeräte (Wasch-maschine, Trockner, Mangel, usw.) *laundry appliances* 75
Waschmaschine *washing machine* 74
wasserbetrieben *water fueled* 44

wasserdicht *waterproof* 124
Wasserhahn *tap* 🔵 37
Wasserkühler *water cooler* 🔵 70
Wechselbeziehung, Überein-stimmung *correlation* 79
wedeln **wag** 119
wegen; dank etwas *Thanks to ...* 54
weich *soft* 102
Weichspüler *fabric softener* 102
weitergehen, fortfahren **proceed** 49
weltgewandt, kultiviert *urbane* 🔵 100
Weltkugel *globe* 130
weltweit tätige Firma *global player* 25
wenden, rückwärts fahren **reverse** 82
wenige *few* 127
Werbesendung *commercial* 92
Werbespruch *advertising slogan* 96
Werbeveranstaltung *promotion* 18
Werbung *advertising* 116
Werkzeug um ... zu überprüfen *tool for screening ...* 12
wert *worth* 67
wesentlich *significant* 27
Wettbewerb *contest* 78
wettmachen **outweigh** 88
Wichtigkeit *importance* 60
widerspiegeln **reflect** 69
widerwillig *reluctant* 140
wie eine Rakete hochschießen **rocket** 67
wie kam es, wieso *how come* 26
wieder aufladen **recharge** 82
wiederbeleben, neu beleben **revitalise** 10
wiedergutmachen **make amends** 🔵 123
wiederhergestellt, renoviert *restored* 150

wiederherstellen, wieder aufbauen *reconstruct* 153

willig, bereit *willing* 31

willkürlich, zufällig *random* 82

winzig *tiny* 140

wirksam *effective* 68

Wirtschaftsflaute *stagnation* 62

Wirtshaus, Gaststätte *pub (public house)* 10

wöchentlich *weekly* 102

wohingegen; während *whereas* 104

Wohlbefinden, Wohlergehen *well-being* 38

wohlschmeckend *delicious* 102

Wortspiel, Wortwitz *pun* 20

Wunde *wound* 119

Würstchenrolle, „Würstchen im Schlafrock" *sausage roll* Ⓣ 139

Würze (meist Pfeffer und Salz) *seasoning* 144

Wurzel *root* 37

zäh, hartnäckig, (ugs.) taff *tough* 22

zahlreich *numerous* 36

Zahnarzthelfer(in) *dental assistant* 89

zahnmedizinisch *orthodontic* 89

Zahnpflege *dental care* 89

Zahnspange *brace* 89

Zank, Streit *strife* 42

Zankerei *squabble* 29

Zeichen *character* 51

Zeichensprache *sign language* 27

Zeitarbeitsvermittlung *employment agency* 24

Zeitdauer *duration* 31

zeitlos *timeless* 14

Zelle, Nische *cubicle* 69

zensieren *censor* 55

Zentrale, Hauptquartier *headquarters* 76

zerhacken *chop* Ⓣ 139

Zerstörung *destruction* 130

zeugen *father* 10

Zickzackkurs *zig-zag course* 29

Zielgruppe *target group* 121

Zielort *destination* 52

ziemlich *rather* 69

Zimmer mit Bad *en suite facilities* 150

Zimt *cinnamon* 138

zitiert *quoted* 14

zublinzeln *wink at sb* 142

zuckerhaltig *sugary* 92

Zuckerkrankheit *diabetes* 92

zufällig, stichprobenartig *at random* 56

zufrieden *satisfied* 67

zufriedenstellend *satisfactory* 25

Zugang; Eintritt *access* 11

zugänglich *accessible* 152

zugeben, eingestehen *admit* 43

zugehörig *corresponding* 119

zugelassen *admitted* 11

zugreifen (auf etwas) *access sth* 52

zulassen, eine Lizenz / Konzession erteilen *licence* 67

Zulieferbetrieb *supplier* 134

zum Vergleich *in contrast* 64

zum Verkauf *on sale* 108

Zunahme *rise* 49

zunehmen *pick up (wind)* Ⓣ 75

zunehmend, steigend *increasing* 52

zur gegebenen Zeit *in due course* 25

zurechtkommen, mit etwas fertigwerden *cope (with sth)* 52

zurückhaltend *retiring* 97

zurücklehnen (sich) *sit back* 82

zurückliegen (zeitlich) *date back* 57

zurückverfolgen *trace back* 57

Zusammenarbeit *cooperation* 152

Zusammenbruch; Kurssturz *collapse* 66

Zusammenfassung *summary, (AE) rundown* 7

zusammensetzen; einen Reim auf etwas machen *piece sth together* 15

zusammenzwicken *pinch together* Ⓣ 139

zusätzlich *additional* 149

zusätzlich (zu) *in addition (to)* 67

zusätzlich, dazu *in addition* 30

Zuteilung *ration* 102

zuverlässig *reliable* 83

zuverlässig, vertrauenswürdig *trustworthy* 104

Zuverlässigkeit, Vertrauenswürdigkeit *trustworthiness* 52

Zuwachs *gain* 39

zuweisen *allocate* 68

zweckmäßig, praktisch *convenient* Ⓣ 100

zwei Wochen *fortnight* 108

Zweifel *doubts (pl.)* 154

Zweifel *doubt* günstige Auslegung zweifelhafter Umstände (in dubio pro reo) *(give sb.) the benefit of the doubt* 43

zweischneidig *two-edged* Ⓣ 129

zwingen, jmdn nötigen, etwas zu tun *force sb to do sth* gezwungen sein, etwas zu tun *forced (by sb) to do sth* 64

Zylinder *cylinder* 100